Wissenschaftliche Untersuchungen
zum Neuen Testament · 2. Reihe

Herausgeber / Editor
Jörg Frey (Zürich)

Mitherausgeber / Associate Editors
Friedrich Avemarie (Marburg)
Markus Bockmuehl (Oxford)
Hans-Josef Klauck (Chicago, IL)

282

Rodrigo J. Morales

The Spirit and the Restoration of Israel

New Exodus and New Creation Motifs in Galatians

Mohr Siebeck

RODRIGO J. MORALES, born 1976; 2002 Master of Theological Studies degree in biblical studies from the University of Notre Dame; 2007 Ph. D. in New Testament from Duke University; assistant professor of theology at Marquette University in Milwaukee, Wisconsin.

BS
2685.52
.M67
2010

ISBN 978-3-16-150435-8
ISSN 0340-9570 (Wissenschaftliche Untersuchungen zum Neuen Testament, 2. Reihe)

Die Deutsche Nationalbibliothek lists this publication in the Deutsche Nationalbibliographie; detailed bibliographic data are available on the Internet at *http://dnb.d-nb.de*.

© 2010 by Mohr Siebeck, Tübingen, Germany.

This book may not be reproduced, in whole or in part, in any form (beyond that permitted by copyright law) without the publisher's written permission. This applies particularly to reproductions, translations, microfilms and storage and processing in electronic systems.

The book was printed by Laupp & Göbel in Nehren on non-aging paper and bound by Buchbinderei Nädele in Nehren.

Printed in Germany.

For my parents

Acknowledgements

The present study is a lightly revised and expanded version of the doctoral thesis I submitted to the Graduate Program in Religion at Duke University in April 2007. I would like to thank Prof. Jörg Frey for accepting this work as part of the *WUNT II* Series. I would also like to thank Dr. Henning Ziebritzki, Ms. Anna Krüger, and the editorial staff of Mohr Siebeck for their invaluable help in seeing the project to completion.

It is not until one works on a project of this length that one realizes that the lengthy acknowledgements typically found at the beginning of such works are anything but lip service. The present study would be far worse were it not for the support, guidance, and good humor of my professors, friends, and family.

The first word of thanks goes to the members of my committee. From the first time I interacted with him as an undergraduate in his Introduction to the New Testament course, Richard Hays has shown himself to be a model Christian scholar. He directed this work with characteristic wisdom and generosity of spirit. For his sound advice, perceptive criticism, and genuine excitement for my thesis, as well as his continued help and support in the publication process, I am deeply grateful. Ellen Davis kindly read each chapter in draft form and offered wise and incisive comments, as well as constant encouragement throughout the process. Joel Marcus's insightful questions and keen critical eye helped me to clarify my thinking, as well as my prose and argumentation. Additionally, he helped make it possible for me to spend a research semester at the University of Durham, which proved crucial to the development of the project. Warren Smith asked stimulating theological questions that pushed me to think more carefully about the theological implications of my exegesis and was a source of encouragement during the final stages of writing.

Thanks are due also to members of the Department of Theology and Religious Studies at the University of Durham. I wrote the first draft of the central chapter of the thesis there in the spring of 2006 while participating in the Duke-Durham Exchange Program. I am grateful to Duke's Graduate Program in Religion and the Department of Theology and Religious Studies at the University of Durham, as well as to both universities, for this opportunity. During my time there John Barclay was the epitome of graciousness, both as a host and as a reader. My indebtedness to his work is evident in chapter five of the present study, but most of all it was the conversations we had that spring that refined my thinking on Galatians 3-4. Loren Stuckenbruck also gave generously of his time to work through the spirit references in the Dead Sea Scrolls, which helped to shape the direction of chapters three and four. I am also grateful for the feedback I received on a portion of my research that I presented at the departmental New Testament Seminar.

Third, I would like to thank the many friends who helped me through this process. In various ways Kavin Rowe, Daniel Kirk, Steve Turnbull, Leroy Huizenga, Brad Trick, Tim Wardle, Sarah Johnson, Matt Thiessen, Colin Miller, T.J. Lang, Nathan Eubank, Brant Pitre and Bill Wright contributed to my work, whether by reading and commenting on it or by offering advice and outlets for venting. Hans Arneson offered helpful feedback and much needed encouragement during the finishing stages of the initial project. A special word of thanks goes to Dave Moffitt. It was conversations with him that helped me find a topic, and he graciously read and commented on much of the work-in-progress.

Thanks also go to my graduate assistant for the 2009-2010 academic year, Geoff Holsclaw, who helped me with proofreading and with double-checking the indices.

Finally, I would like to thank my parents, Tarsicio and Milagros Morales. They have been a constant source of support throughout my studies and my life in general, and it is with sincere and profound gratitude that I dedicate this work to them.

Solemnity of St. Joseph, 2010   Rodrigo J. Morales

Table of Contents

Acknowledgments... VII

Chapter 1. Introduction.. 1

Status Quaestionis... 1
Thesis.. 4
Significance.. 5
Outline of the Argument... 6
Methodology... 7
A Note on Terminology: "Restoration Eschatology" and "Restoration of Israel".. 10

Chapter 2. New Exodus, New Creation I: The Spirit and the Restoration of Israel in the OT Prophetic Literature........................ 13

Introduction... 13
Methodology... 14
The Spirit and Restoration Eschatology in Isaiah................................... 15
    Isaiah 11:1-16: Messiah, Spirit, Creation, Exodus.......................... 15
    Isaiah 32:15-20: Righteousness, Peace, and the Spirit..................... 18
    Isaiah 42:1-9: The Servant and the Spirit... 19
    Isaiah 43:14-44:8: Seed, Blessing, King, Israel................................ 20
    Isaiah 48:16: The Lord GOD has sent me and his spirit................... 23
    Isaiah 57:14-21 (LXX): The Spirit and Peace................................... 23
    Isaiah 59:15b-21: Spirit and Covenant.. 24
    Isaiah 61:1-11: The Spirit and the Praise of the Nations.................. 25
    Isaiah 63:7-64:12: Spirit, Exodus, and Fatherhood......................... 26
    The Spirit and the Restoration of Israel in Isaiah: Summary........... 28
The Spirit and Restoration Eschatology in Ezekiel................................ 29
    Ezekiel 11:14-21: New Spirit and Restoration................................. 29
    Ezekiel 18:30-32: New Heart and New Spirit.................................. 31
    Ezekiel 36:16-38: The Restoration of Israel..................................... 32
    Ezekiel 37:1-14: The Valley of Dry Bones...................................... 33

Ezekiel 39:21-29: The Restoration of Jacob..34
    The Spirit and the Restoration of Israel in Ezekiel: Summary.............35
Excursus: Exile and the Heart in Deuteronomy 35
The Spirit and Restoration Eschatology in Joel 38
The Spirit and Restoration Eschatology in the Prophets: Summary.............39

Chapter 3. New Exodus, New Creation II: The Spirit and the Restoration of Israel in the Second Temple Period............................41

Introduction..41
Methodology...42
Jubilees: Restoration, Adoption, and Spirit..43
The Treatise on the Two Spirits: The Spirits of Truth and Injustice............48
The Words of the Luminaries: Holy Spirit, Blessing, and Restoration.........52
4Q521: The Messiah, the Spirit, and the Eternal Kingdom 55
The *Psalms of Solomon*: The Messiah's Spirit and the Restoration 57
The *Similitudes of Enoch*: The Lord of the Spirits and the Spirit of the Elect One..60
The *Testament of Judah*: The Spirit of Sonship and Resurrection...............64
The *Testament of Levi*: Spirit of Holiness and New Creation......................68
Excursus: The Testaments of Judah and Levi: Christian, Jewish, or Admixture?...69
Hellenistic Judaism: The Spirit and no Restoration.....................................73
Spirit and Restoration Eschatology in the Second Temple Period: Summary..75

Chapter 4. New Exodus and the Spirit in Galatians 3-4: From Death to Life, From Slavery to Sonship......................................78

Introduction 78
Methodology 80
Galatians 3:1-5: "Who has believed our message?"......................................81
Galatians 3:10-14: Life and Death, The Blessing and The Curse................86
    The pattern of argumentation in Galatians 3 87
    Galatians 3:10 and Deuteronomy 27:26.. 88
    Galatians 3:11 and Habakkuk 2:4..96
    Galatians 3:12 and Leviticus 18:5..100
    Leviticus 18:5 in Ezekiel 20..101
    Leviticus 18:5 in Nehemiah 9...103
    Again, Galatians 3:12 and Leviticus 18:5..104
    Galatians 3:13 and the "Curse of the Law"... 105

Galatians 3:14 and the promise of the Spirit 109
Galatians 4:1-7: From Slavery to Sonship 114
    The inheritance analogy in Galatians 4:1-2 115
    Galatians 4:1-7 and Galatians 3:23-29 117
    Galatians 4:1-2: the heir under guardians and stewards 118
    Excursus: Israel as νήπιος, idolatry, and the knowledge of God 119
    Galatians 4:3-7: New Exodus and the Spirit 121
    The fullness of (the) time 123
    The sending of the Son 123
    The outpouring of the Spirit 126
    No longer a slave but a son 129
    Galatians 4:1-7: Summary 129
The Outpouring of the Spirit and the Galatian Situation 130
Conclusion 130

Chapter 5. New Creation and the Spirit in Galatians 5-6: Bearing Fruit unto Eternal Life 132

Introduction 132
Methodology 134
Galatians 5:2-6: Awaiting the Hope of Righteousness by the Spirit 135
Galatians 5:13-26: The Spirit and the Flesh 140
    Excursus: The "Flesh" as a power? 141
    Galatians 5:13-15: Fulfilling the Law 143
    Galatians 5:16-18: The Spirit and the flesh 146
    Galatians 5:19-21: The works of the flesh 151
    Galatians 5:22-23: The fruit of the Spirit 155
    Galatians 5:24-26: Crucifying the flesh, living by the Spirit 159
Galatians 6:1-2: Correction in the Spirit of Gentleness 160
Galatians 6:7-8: Reaping Eternal Life 161
Conclusion 163

Chapter 6. Conclusion: The Spirit and the Restoration of Israel 164

Summary 164
Major Contributions 168
    Paul, the Spirit, and Second Temple Judaism 168
    The Words of the Luminaries, the Curse of the Law, and the
    Outpouring of the Spirit 169
    The Outpouring of the Spirit and the Blessing of Abraham 169
    The Curse of the Law and Life and Death 170

    Life and Death, the Spirit, and the Coherence of Galatians................ 171
Areas for Further Research.. 172
    Galatians and Romans.. 172
    The Commandments of God..172
    Reconciliation and the Spirit..172

Bibliography.. 175
Index of Ancient Sources..185
Index of Modern Authors... 197
Index of Subjects... 199

Chapter 1

Introduction

At the outset of the central argument in the Letter to the Galatians, Paul asks his readers the question: "This alone I want to know from you: was it from works of the Law that you received the Spirit, or from the proclamation of faith?" (Gal 3:2).[1] From this point forward, the Spirit plays a crucial role in Paul's argument, appearing at climactic moments in his case (3:13-14; 4:4-6; 4:29-31), as well as undergirding the final hortatory section of the epistle (5:5; 5:16-25; 6:8). The tone of the question, in addition to the rest of the argument, makes quite clear the answer that Paul expects to hear – the Galatians received the Spirit from the proclamation of faith. Although the answer to the question is obvious, the presupposition of that answer remains elusive: what significance does Paul attach to the reception of the Spirit? Perhaps equally puzzling, why does Paul connect the gift of the Spirit with the blessing of Abraham (Gal 3:13-14)? The present work seeks to answer these questions by exploring various OT prophetic themes that connect the outpouring of the Spirit with the restoration of Israel, and by tracing the development of these themes in the Second Temple period. The premise of the study is that these traditional Jewish expectations about the Spirit shed light on Paul's argument in Galatians 3-6.

Status Quaestionis

Although studies of Galatians since the time of the Reformation have focused primarily on the contentious issue of justification by faith, scholars have more recently begun to recognize the centrality of the Spirit in Paul's argument. In a volume that presents a tradition-historical approach to Paul's pneumatology, Johannes Vos devotes a chapter to the relationship between the Spirit and the inheritance of Abraham in Galatians.[2] In addition, Vos includes a chapter on salvation and the Spirit in the OT and in early Judaism.[3] Vos rightly acknowledges the connection between the gift of the Spirit and the inclusion of

---

[1] Unless otherwise noted, translations of the NT are my own.
[2] Johannes Sijko Vos, *Traditionsgeschichtliche Untersuchungen zur paulinischen Pneumatologie* (Assen: Van Gorcum, 1973), 85-106.
[3] Ibid., 34-73.

the Gentiles within Paul's understanding of the covenant with Abraham. Moreover, he rightly notes that for Paul the gift of the Spirit comes about solely on the basis of the proclamation of the gospel. The main weakness in Vos's study is that with rare exception he fails to relate his treatment of the Spirit in the OT and Judaism to his interpretation of Galatians. Even when he does relate the two, he does so only by referring the reader back to the previous chapter without giving a detailed analysis of the points of overlap between Galatians and the OT.[4]

David Lull's *The Spirit in Galatia* explores the experience of the Spirit among the Galatians in two major sections.[5] In the first part, he argues that the initial reception of the Spirit took place in the context of preaching rather than baptism. The second part of the study then considers the significance of the Spirit for Paul under the headings of soteriology, Christology, and eschatology. Lull makes important connections in this second part, explaining the soteriological role of the Spirit in terms of the eschatological new creation to which Paul refers at the end of Galatians and connecting this latter term with Paul's reference to the kingdom of God and the Israel of God. Nevertheless, the study remains preliminary and largely underdeveloped. While Lull does well to redress the neglect of the Spirit in so many studies of Galatians and to highlight the significance of the Spirit on a global level, his discussion does not offer as much as one would hope for by way of probing exegetical analysis. Most noteworthy is the paucity of OT and Second Temple Jewish texts examined in the study.[6]

In *The Cross and the Spirit*, Charles Cosgrove also addresses the centrality of the Spirit in Paul's argument and makes a strong case that Gal 3:1-5 deserves more prominence in the discussion of Galatians than the history of interpretation has afforded it.[7] The central point of Cosgrove's study is that these verses open up a window into the problem Paul was addressing in Galatia: "[W]hether believers can promote their ongoing experience of the Spirit by doing the Law."[8] Cosgrove makes a compelling case that for Paul life in the Spirit and participation in the cross are inseparable. It is only through the cross, Paul argues, that the Galatians received the Spirit and can continue in

---

[4] For example, Vos (*Paulinische Pneumatologie*, 92-93) asserts that the primary background to Paul's understanding of the Spirit in Gal 3:6-14 is to be found in Deutero-Isaiah. Rather than giving a detailed comparison of texts, however, he simply refers the reader to the previous chapter on the Spirit in the OT.

[5] David J. Lull, *The Spirit in Galatia: Paul's Interpretation of Pneuma as Divine Power* (SBLDS 49; Ann Arbor: Scholars Press, 1980).

[6] Only three OT texts (Gen 21:10-12; Isa 54:1; Hosea 2:1) appear in the scripture index of the book, in addition to the apocryphal 2 Esdras 3:21-22; see ibid., 225.

[7] Charles H. Cosgrove, *The Cross and the Spirit: A Study in the Argument and Theology of Galatians* (Macon: Mercer University, 1988).

[8] Ibid., 2.

the Spirit. Although in the course of his argument Cosgrove notes some of the Second Temple Jewish expectations about the Spirit, he does not fully explore the significance of these expectations for Paul's argument, nor does he sufficiently address the importance of restoration eschatology in Paul's reasoning. In effect, Cosgrove's work asks different questions than the present study. Whereas Cosgrove argues *that* the Spirit is a central issue in Galatians and that it is closely connected with the cross, he does not ask *why* the Spirit plays such a crucial role in Paul's argument.

Gordon Fee's study *God's Empowering Presence* devotes approximately one hundred pages to discussing the role of the Spirit in Galatians.[9] Fee reaches four conclusions with regard to the Spirit.[10] First, the Spirit has replaced the Torah as an "identity marker" for the Christian community. Second, the Spirit serves as the means of coming to completion in the Christian life. Third, the Spirit functions for Paul as "the main eschatological reality, the certain evidence that the future has begun and the guarantee of its consummation."[11] Finally, the Spirit serves as God's personal presence among Christians. In the course of his exegesis, Fee makes note of the various prophetic texts that connect the Spirit with new exodus imagery, but he does not explore the significance of these texts for Paul's argument. Moreover, Fee downplays the significance of developments in the intertestamental period for Paul's understanding of the Spirit, devoting a mere five and a half pages to discussion of the writings of that era.[12] One unfortunate result of this neglect is Fee's assertion that the "curse of the Law" in Gal 3:13-14 refers to Torah observance.[13]

Each of these four major studies acknowledges the eschatological significance of the Spirit for Paul, but none adequately develops the most pertinent background of the Spirit as an eschatological sign. Despite the many references to the "last age," the "new creation," "the new aeon," and other equivalent terms, none explores the prophetic texts that connect the Spirit with the restoration of Israel and the importance of the motifs associated with the Spirit for Paul's argument. Moreover, none of these works traces the development of these themes in the Second Temple period in order to establish the cultural and religious context in which Paul's argument most makes sense. A closer examination of the various expectations about the Spirit in both the OT and the Second Temple period will help to show how Paul's emphasis on the Spirit both corresponds to and deviates from his contemporary setting.

---

[9] Gordon D. Fee, *God's Empowering Presence: The Holy Spirit in the Letters of Paul* (Peabody: Hendrickson, 1994), 367-471.
[10] Ibid., 469-71.
[11] Ibid., 470.
[12] Ibid., 910-15.
[13] Ibid., 392.

Thesis

The present study will demonstrate that the key to understanding the role of the Spirit in Galatians can be found in some of the OT Prophets and Jewish traditions stemming from those texts that associate the outpouring of the Spirit with the restoration of Israel. There is good *prima facie* evidence that prophecies of restoration, especially (though not limited to) those found in Isaiah, play a significant role in Paul's thought, particularly in Galatians. The term he uses to describe his message, "gospel," most likely has its roots in the good news proclaimed in the second half of Isaiah.[14] Furthermore, Paul describes his call and ministry in language drawn from that very section of Isaiah: "But when the one who set me apart from my mother's womb and called me through his grace was pleased to reveal his Son in me, in order that I might preach him among the Gentiles..." (Gal 1:15-16; cf. Isa 49:5-6; the description of Paul's being "set apart from his mother's womb" also resembles Jer 1:4, perhaps even more closely than Isa 49:5-6). Both the manner of Paul's call and his mission to the Gentiles dovetail with some of the central themes of Deutero-Isaiah.[15] It should not be surprising, therefore, to see restoration themes from both Isaiah and later appropriations of Isaiah undergirding the argument of the epistle.

This collocation of themes relating the Spirit, the heart, sonship, and the curses of Deuteronomy will help to shed light on how Paul understands the curse of the Law in Gal 3:10-14. *Pace* Fee, the curse Paul has in mind is not Torah observance in general, but rather the curse that the Law pronounces on the nation for failure to obey the covenant, as N. T. Wright and James M. Scott have independently argued.[16] The manifestation of the Spirit, I will argue, demonstrates Israel's redemption from the curse, and further illuminates Paul's references to the "kingdom of God" in Gal 5:21 and to the Christian community as the "Israel of God" in 6:16.[17] Indeed, eschatological expectations about the Spirit also undergird the hortatory argument in Galatians 5-6,

---

[14] See the discussion on pp. 81-86 below.

[15] For a persuasively argued reading of Romans along these lines, see J. Ross Wagner, Jr., *Heralds of the Good News: Isaiah and Paul in Concert in the Letter to the Romans* (Leiden: Brill, 2002).

[16] N. T. Wright, *The Climax of the Covenant: Christ and the Law in Pauline Theology* (Minneapolis: Fortress, 1992), 137-56; see also *idem*, *The New Testament and the People of God* (Christian Origins and the Question of God 1; Minneapolis: Fortress, 1992); James M. Scott, "'For as Many as are of Works of the Law are Under a Curse' (Galatians 3.10)," in *Paul and the Scriptures of Israel* (ed. Craig A. Evans and James A. Sanders; JSNTSup 83; Sheffield: Sheffield Academic, 1993), 187-221. Scott's essay adumbrates some of the key themes to be explored in the present study.

[17] On the latter text see G. K. Beale, "Peace and Mercy Upon the Israel of God: The Old Testament Background of Galatians 6,16b," *Bib* 80 (1999): 204-23.

though in a way that stands traditional Jewish understandings of the Law on their head. This revisionary re-reading of Israel's history, though, is one of many threads that hold the hortatory section of the epistle together with the exegetical argument in Galatians 3-4.

Significance

The present study makes several contributions to biblical scholarship. First, it provides a more detailed treatment of the connection between the Spirit and restoration eschatology in Second Temple Judaism than has been offered to date. Although some studies have appeared with brief overviews of the role of the Spirit in many texts of this period, for the most part these works tend not to provide detailed exegesis of some of the key texts. Rather, they offer summaries with a number of citations but little in-depth discussion.[18] Other works focus on different aspects of Spirit-endowment such as prophecy and inspired exegesis that have less bearing than restoration eschatology on Galatians.[19] The present study provides a fuller picture of the variety of eschatological expectations surrounding the Spirit in Second Temple Judaism. One important aspect of these expectations is the connection between the outpouring of the Spirit and redemption from the curses of the Law. This connection leads to a second contribution of the study.

The close association between the giving of the Spirit and the redemption of Israel, both in the Prophets and in the Second Temple period, helps to clarify Paul's understanding of the "curse of the Law" in Gal 3:13. The way that texts such as the *Words of the Luminaries* and the *Testament of Judah* describe the outpouring of the Spirit as the solution to Israel's status under the curses of Leviticus and/or Deuteronomy suggests that Paul's appeal to the Spirit functions in an analogous manner. In Galatians as in these other texts, the reception of the Spirit signals the redemption of Israel from the curse and the empowerment of believers to order their lives rightly before God.

---

[18] See, e.g., Robert P. Menzies, *The Development of Early Christian Pneumatology with special reference to Luke-Acts* (JSNTSup 54; Sheffield: Sheffield Academic, 1991), 53-76, and more recently Finny Philip, *The Origins of Pauline Pneumatology* (WUNT 2.194; Tübingen: Mohr/Siebeck, 2005), 77-88. Earlier exceptions to this deficiency are Max-Alain Chevallier, *L'Esprit et le Messie dans le bas-judaïsme et le Nouveau Testament* (Paris: Presses Universitaires de France, 1958) and *idem, Souffle de Dieu: le Saint-Esprit dans le Nouveau Testament* (Point Théologique 26; Paris: Éditions Beauchesne, 1978); the wider availability of texts, especially from Qumran, since the publication of Chevallier's works justifies a new study.

[19] See, e.g., John R. Levison, *The Spirit in First Century Judaism* (AGJU 29; Leiden; New York: Brill, 1997).

With respect to this understanding of the curse as that pronounced by Deuteronomy, the present study also advances the discussion about the substance of the curse. By paying close attention to the significance of life and death in the epistle, I offer an interpretation of the curse in Gal 3:10-14 that makes better sense of Paul and at the same time fits with Deuteronomy's own description of the curse. One feature of Paul's argument that distinguishes him from some of his contemporaries is his lack of clear reference to exile and return. In contrast to the emphasis on exile in both Deuteronomy and some texts from the Second Temple period, the category of exile is conspicuously absent in Paul's writings. Rather, the key categories for his understanding of the curse and of the Spirit are death and life, respectively, suggesting that Paul fundamentally interpreted the curse of Deuteronomy as consisting of death.[20]

The significance of this association between the Spirit and life in Galatians remains underdeveloped to date. The exploration of this association is a third major contribution of the present study. The contrast between life and death runs like a leitmotif throughout the epistle, beginning with Gal 2:15-21. Moreover, Paul fundamentally understands the contrast between the Spirit and the Law in terms of life and death. Whereas the Law is unable to make alive (Gal 3:21), the one who sows to the Spirit will reap eternal life (Gal 6:8). As will become evident through a careful exegesis of several of these passages, this contrast between life and death is a crucial one to make sense of how Galatians fits together as a whole.

Outline of the Argument

Chapter two, "New Exodus, New Creation I: The Spirit and the Restoration of Israel in the OT Prophetic Literature," traces the connection between the outpouring of the Spirit and the restoration of Israel in the OT prophetic corpus. By examining these themes in a number of passages from Isaiah, Ezekiel and Joel, the present work demonstrates that the gift of the Spirit was one important aspect of OT eschatological expectations. Moreover, I show that this hope can be expressed with a variety of images. Rather than depicting a monolithic eschatological program, the prophets variously associate the Spirit with fruitfulness, the renewal of the heart, sonship and several other motifs. In addition, these themes most often appear in the context of descriptions of a new exodus and/or a new creation – a significant point for understanding Paul's emphasis at the end of Galatians on "new creation" (Gal 6:16).

Equally important for our understanding of Paul's argument is the development of these eschatological motifs in the so-called intertestamental period,

---

[20] As we will see, Deuteronomy itself often describes the curse in terms of death.

which is the focus of the third chapter, "New Exodus, New Creation II: The Spirit and the Restoration of Israel in the Second Temple Period." Paul did not write in a vacuum, but in the world of first-century Judaism. An exploration of the themes of the Spirit and restoration in such literature as the *Psalms of Solomon*, the *Testaments of the Twelve Patriarchs*, *Jubilees*, the Dead Sea Scrolls, and other pseudepigraphical literature will help to demonstrate that such expectations continued to influence first century Jewish beliefs in a variety of texts and genres.

The fourth chapter, "New Exodus and the Spirit in Galatians 3-4: From Death to Life, From Slavery to Sonship," provides exegetical probes of three key texts with respect to the Spirit in Galatians 3-4 (Gal 3:1-5; 3:10-14; 4:1-7). In particular, it focuses on the role of the Spirit with regard to questions of the curse of the Law and sonship . Moreover, it addresses the question of the inheritance of Abraham referred to in Galatians 3, demonstrating that Paul reads the promises to Abraham through the Galatians' experience of the Spirit in light of the eschatological expectations of the time. For Paul, in other words, the gift of the Spirit fulfills the promise to Abraham, albeit in a transposed key in terms of the worldwide restoration of Israel via the mission to the Gentiles and the heavenly Jerusalem.

The eschatological outpouring of the Spirit also undergirds Paul's ethical arguments in Galatians 5-6, the subject of the fifth chapter, "New Creation and the Spirit in Galatians 5-6: Bearing Fruit Unto Eternal Life." Much of Paul's argument regarding so-called ethical issues relies heavily on the gift of the Spirit. Although the textual connections with the OT and Second Temple literature are not as strong in Galatians 5-6, this chapter shows that thematically Paul's argument continues to presuppose the inauguration of the eschatological age as described in the Prophets and the Second Temple period.

Methodology

It is important to note at the outset that, with a few exceptions, the present study does not argue that Paul consciously alludes to the specific OT and Second Temple texts considered in chapters two and three. Rather, the purpose of exploring these texts is to establish the kinds of expectations that were available to Paul and his contemporaries.[21] There are different reasons for

---

[21] The present study thus differs methodologically from Richard B. Hays, *Echoes of Scripture in the Letters of Paul* (New Haven: Yale University, 1989). Whereas Hays sought to understand Paul as a reader of Scripture, my goal is to demonstrate how Second Temple Jewish expectations about the Spirit shape Paul's argument. Although this will necessarily involve some discussion of how Paul interprets texts, the focus is not so much on Paul's hermeneutical approach or on detecting conscious allusions as it is on themes that appear in a

examining the OT and the Second Temple literature. Since they were available to Paul, the OT texts present a reliable source for the themes and images that he uses. The Second Temple literature shows which of these texts still influenced eschatological expectations among Jews of the period, as well as which themes tended to appear together, and so provide a helpful body of literature to compare with Paul's use of OT imagery.

Because the focus of the study is on Second Temple Jewish understandings of the outpouring of the Spirit as they reflect earlier prophetic expectations, the reader will note that chapter two on the Spirit in the OT Prophets makes little note of modern distinctions between redactional layers in the texts. The reason for this approach can be stated quite simply: neither Paul nor his Second Temple Jewish contemporaries and near contemporaries would have read OT texts in this way, and so the results of source, form and redaction criticism have little to no bearing on the appropriation of themes from the OT in the Second Temple period. On the other hand, one must take care not to assume that Jews of this period read their sacred books in a manner analogous to contemporary canonical criticism.[22] The goal of the second chapter, then, is to set forth all of the images that were available both to Paul and to his contemporaries relating the outpouring of the Spirit to the restoration of Israel. In some ways my approach shares a number of similarities with Francis Watson's recent contribution to Pauline studies.[23] The present work investigates the relationship between Israel's Scriptures on the one hand and Second Temple Jewish and Pauline reception of those Scriptures on the other. The main difference between my approach and Watson's is that whereas Watson focuses on explicit citation and interpretation of OT texts, the present work considers how broader OT and Second Temple themes shape Paul's understanding of the Spirit, for the most part without asserting whether or how Paul was consciously interpreting the scriptural texts about the Spirit.

This articulation serves as a helpful transition to what I intend to achieve with respect to Galatians in the present work. As has already been noted, the goal of the study is not to suggest that Paul alludes to all or any of the texts discussed in chapters two and three. Rather, the analysis of these texts serves to describe one "encyclopedia" of late Second Temple Jewish expectations regarding the Spirit and the restoration of Israel in order to show how Paul's argument fits within his cultural context.[24] Any such approach, however, runs

---

variety of texts and as a result influence the language and imagery that Paul highlights in his own argument.

[22] See, e.g., John Barton, *Oracles of God: Perceptions of Ancient Prophecy in Israel after the Exile* (New York: Oxford University, 1986), 149-51.

[23] Francis Watson, *Paul and the Hermeneutics of Faith* (New York: T&T Clark, 2004).

[24] I borrow the term "encyclopedia" from Umberto Eco (*A Theory of Semiotics* [Bloomington: Indiana University, 1979]). Eco uses the word to describe the various possibilities of conveying meaning with concrete "*contextual* and *circumstantial selections*" (p. 105). The

the risk of appearing arbitrary – how does one legitimately choose which texts shed light on Galatians? One helpful way to address the question is to think in terms of multiply attested collocations of themes.[25] In other words, each text considered in chapters two and three does not stand on its own, but rather gains significance for Paul's thought when it shares a number of themes with other texts and with Galatians. So, for example, Isa 44:3, 4Q504, and the *Testament of Judah* all in some way connect the outpouring of the Spirit with the blessing, and the latter two texts do so in contexts that speak of Israel's suffering under the curses of Deuteronomy and/or Leviticus. When these themes appear together in Galatians 3 in the context of Paul's discussion of the curse of the Law, it seems probable that he is tapping into and addressing an expectation available in various circles of Second Temple Judaism. As we will see, Paul's argument often reflects certain patterns found in a number of the texts we consider below, but perhaps equally as often he modifies or challenges those patterns. Even if Paul did not know any of the texts discussed in chapter three of the present study, many of the themes that they employ are present in the OT prophetic texts available to Paul. Like many of his contemporaries, Paul most likely often used these motifs without consciously alluding to the OT texts in which the themes feature prominently.[26]

---

meaning a speaker or listener associates with a given word or set of words depends on the speaker's historical and cultural context. Eco uses the example of the word "whale," which connotes different things in ancient and modern contexts, and within modern contexts in scientific as opposed to literary settings (pp. 112-14). In the present study, we will seek to describe an "encyclopedia" of images and ideas associated with the outpouring of the Spirit for Paul as a first-century Jew familiar with the Scriptures of Israel living in a time of expectation about the Spirit and the restoration of Israel. I should also note that the primary goal of this study is to make sense of Paul's argument irrespective of how his audience would have received it. This is not to deny that Galatians is a contingent text addressing specific historical circumstances in the Galatian churches. Rather, it is to affirm that the primary object of study is Paul's argument, not a reconstruction of the make-up of the Galatian churches. On the problematic nature of the biblical literacy of Paul's congregations, see Christopher D. Stanley, "'Pearls Before Swine': Did Paul's Audiences Understand his Biblical Quotations?" *NovT* 41 (1999): 124-44; idem, *Arguing with Scripture: The Rhetoric of Quotations in the Letters of Paul* (New York/London: T&T Clark, 2004), 38-61.

[25] I owe this formulation to a private conversation with James Scott. For a similar approach articulated in terms of tradition and its interpretations, see Sylvia C. Keesmaat, *Paul and his Story: (Re)interpreting the Exodus Tradition* (JSNTSup 181; Sheffield: Sheffield Academic, 1999), 15-53.

[26] For a recent articulation of a similar approach to the relationship between Israel's Scriptures and Paul's writings, see Roy E. Ciampa, "Scriptural Language and Ideas," in *As it is Written: Studying Paul's Use of Scripture* (ed. Stanley E. Porter and Christopher D. Stanley; SBLSymS 50; Atlanta: Society of Biblical Literature, 2008), 41-57.

A Note on Terminology: "Restoration Eschatology" and "Restoration of Israel"

Before proceeding, it is necessary to clarify how I understand and use the terms "restoration eschatology" and "restoration of Israel," since they play a significant part in this study. My understanding of these terms is indebted to the work of E. P. Sanders, who famously suggested that "in general terms it may be said that [in the first-century] 'Jewish eschatology' and 'the restoration of Israel' are almost synonymous."[27] Despite their different emphases, many of the writings of the early Christian movement saw God's act in Jesus as fulfilling the promises to Israel. It is primarily these promises that shape my understanding of the "restoration of Israel."

The terms "restoration eschatology" and "restoration of Israel," however, function in multiple ways in the present work. With regard to the OT Prophets and later Second Temple Jewish literature, the terms refer to the expectation that God would finally act to bring the tribes of Israel back to the land, sometimes under a Davidic ruler – in other words, he would *restore* Israel to its former glory. With respect to Paul, the terms describe the apostle's conviction that God had begun to fulfill his promises to redeem Israel through the death and resurrection of Jesus. In a sense it might be misleading to label Paul's thought as "restoration eschatology" since his understanding of God's acts differs in significant ways from that of some of his contemporaries. Indeed, one could argue that Paul thinks more in terms of "redemption" than "restoration." To be sure, Paul deviates from more common Jewish expectations in that he places no emphasis on the physical land of Israel, but his understanding of the outpouring of the Spirit is nevertheless rooted in the prophetic hopes of the OT.[28] What holds together the various uses of the terms

---

[27] E. P. Sanders, *Jesus and Judaism* (Philadelphia: Fortress, 1985), 97; cf. Wright, *The New Testament and the People of God*, 268-72 and 299-301.

[28] John P. Meier (*A Marginal Jew. Rethinking the Historical Jesus. Volume Two: Mentor, Message, and Miracles* [ABRL; New York: Doubleday, 1994], 31) provides a helpful definition of the term "eschatological" that acknowledges a broad range of meaning and nuance while maintaining a basic definition that applies to practically all the texts commonly categorized under the term: "[I]n general [the word 'eschatological'] may be used to refer to the definitive end of the history of God's people as they have experienced it from the time of their election. It is an end–but also a new beginning–brought about by God's wrathful judgment and extermination of sinners within his holy people and by the salvation of those who have proved faithful or who sincerely repent in the last hour–in some cases, by accepting the just rule of a new, ideal king, in other cases by obeying the preaching of a final prophet sent to them. All these themes, in various combinations, can be encompassed under the rubric of the 'prophetic eschatology' found in the OT and in some works of intertestamental literature. The extent to which the state of Israel after the end-and-new-beginning is in continuity with ordinary, earthly realities and the extent to which Israel is transferred into an idealized, magical, or heavenly world vary from author to author."

"restoration eschatology" and "restoration of Israel" is their rootedness in the prophetic promises of hope for Israel. Both Paul and his contemporaries appeal to these hopes and thus in different ways reflect "restoration eschatology."

Again, to say this is not to deny the radical nature of the cross for Paul's thought, and indeed for early Christianity in general. There was not a one-to-one correspondence between the prophecies of restoration and the Christ event. Unlike the authors of texts such as the *Psalms of Solomon*, Paul did not expect a nationalistic return of the tribes of Israel to the land under an earthly Davidic ruler. Nevertheless, he did believe that through the cross and the outpouring of the Spirit God had begun to fulfill the promises spoken through the prophets. Indeed, though Paul's message of the cross was not at all clear from the writings of the OT (as though Jesus' death on the cross were the obvious solution that all first-century Jews would have expected), Paul's emphasis on the phenomenon of the Spirit makes the most sense in light of eschatological expectations that frequently appear in the context of a hope for the restoration of Israel. Nevertheless, it is crucial, especially with respect to a polemical text like Galatians, not to overemphasize the continuity of Paul's thought with the OT to the exclusion of the discontinuities also present in the epistle. Bearing in mind these qualifications, let us turn now to consider the relationship between the outpouring of the Spirit and restoration eschatology in the OT Prophets.

Chapter 2

New Exodus, New Creation I: The Spirit and the Restoration of Israel in the OT Prophetic Literature

Introduction

Although the Spirit of God plays various roles in the prophetic literature of the OT, perhaps the most dominant theme taken up by the early Christian movement is the eschatological outpouring of the Spirit.[1] This theme, though by no means the only or even the most pervasive one in the prophetic corpus, nevertheless appears in a number of significant texts. The goal of the present chapter is to demonstrate the connection between the Spirit and the restoration of Israel in some of the prophetic texts that play a prominent role in the NT, particularly in the writings of Paul. More specifically, I will seek to show that the prophets often describe this restoration with images of a new creation and/or a new exodus, and that they often associate it with an outpouring of the Spirit. At the end of the chapter, I will briefly note some of the themes that will reappear later in the discussion of both Second Temple Jewish literature and Galatians 3-6. Perhaps the most significant contribution of this treatment concerns the debate over the curse to which Paul refers in Gal 3:10-14. If Paul thinks of the Spirit in terms of restoration eschatology, then the curse of Gal 3:10 most likely refers to Israel's punishment as described in Deuteronomy 27-30, a curse taken up and addressed by some of the prophets. In what follows, then, I will demonstrate the significance of the Spirit in the oracles of restoration in three books of the prophetic corpus, beginning with Isaiah, which has the most references to the Spirit and the restoration of Israel, continuing with Ezekiel, and ending with Joel, which has only one such oracle and plays little if any role in Galatians.

---

[1] Whenever I refer to the "Spirit" (with a capital "s") throughout this study, I am referring to the Spirit of God, not some general concept of "spirit." I will use "Spirit" with a capital "s" throughout the study as shorthand for the Spirit of God and will state explicitly if and when I mean "spirit" in some other sense. A number of texts that we will consider in this and the following chapter are ambiguous as to whether they refer to the divine Spirit or the human spirit. Therefore, many of the capitalizations in the pages to follow should be taken not as dogmatic assertions, but rather as interpretative suggestions.

Methodology

Before turning to the OT texts, three methodological points should be addressed. As noted in the introduction, for the purposes of the present discussion, the various redactional layers postulated by modern commentators will play no role in this study for one simple reason: neither Paul nor his Second Temple Jewish contemporaries and near contemporaries would have thought in these categories. Whether or not they read Isaiah, for example, as a unified whole, they had no notion of a first, a second, and a third Isaiah.[2]

On the other hand, it is by no means clear whether or not Second Temple Jews, including Paul, read the Prophets as narrative wholes, such that they would have discerned a clear program, such as "Isaiah's New Exodus," in the pages of Scripture.[3] For these reasons, in the sections that follow we will consider a variety of oracles from the prophetic books without suggesting that any of them contains a clear concept such as *the* new exodus or *the* new creation. Rather, I will seek to demonstrate that the various prophetic texts often connect the outpouring of the Spirit with motifs drawing on creation typology, exodus typology, or both, and almost always in the context of restoration eschatology. As we will see in chapter three, a number of texts from the Second Temple period draw on different parts of the prophetic corpus without distinguishing between different layers in the books, but also without betraying knowledge of a clear "new exodus" program.

Finally, it is important to acknowledge that the texts chosen for discussion in this chapter do not by any means exhaust the theme of restoration eschatology in the prophets. Indeed, a number of texts in the OT, most prominently

---

[2] Cf. the judgment of John Barton, *Oracles of God: Perceptions of Ancient Prophecy in Israel after the Exile* (New York: Oxford University, 1986), 146-47 (emphasis original): "[The NT writers] had no particular theory about how a prophetic book *ought* to be compiled: they simply had a number of such books, all of which contained – just like the Torah – a variety of types of material. It is hopelessly anachronistic to think that they had any sort of idea that the different genres within the books of the prophets should be read in different ways, or even that the different prophetic books differed in the kinds of material they contained." A few pages later (*Oracles of God*, 149) Barton makes the helpful observation: "Thus the normal methods of biblical criticism, which have been so successful in penetrating to the heart of the message of the prophets through the accumulated accretions of the centuries, are powerless to show us how these books looked to a reader in the time of Philo or Josephus."

[3] The difficulty of assessing whether the NT writers would have read such a program right off the pages of Isaiah, for example, calls into question some of the methodological assumptions of Rikki E. Watts, *Isaiah's New Exodus and Mark* (WUNT 2.88; Tübingen: J.C.B. Mohr [Paul Siebeck], 1997) and David W. Pao, *Acts and the Isaianic New Exodus* (WUNT 2.130; Tübingen: J.C.B. Mohr [Paul Siebeck], 2000). I am grateful to Ross Wagner for drawing my attention to this issue in a conversation on March 17, 2005. For a perceptive discussion of whether or not Second Temple Jews would have read any books in the OT as literary wholes, see again Barton, *Oracles of God*, 149-51.

Jeremiah, speak of the restoration of Israel with no reference to the Spirit. The current chapter does not seek to provide an exhaustive account of restoration eschatology in the prophetic corpus, but rather to describe the narrower phenomenon of the outpouring of the Spirit and its connection with the restoration of Israel.

The Spirit and Restoration Eschatology in Isaiah

Isaiah 11:1-16: Messiah, Spirit, Creation, Exodus[4]

Although Isaiah 11 does not play any discernible role in Galatians, it nevertheless merits our attention for two reasons. As the first passage in Isaiah to connect the Spirit with the themes of new creation and new exodus it deserves careful consideration, since it sets the tone for the use of these themes in other parts of Isaiah. In addition, the passage had a considerable impact on Second Temple Judaism as a whole, and especially some of the texts to be considered in the next chapter.[5] As we will see, several of those texts connect the outpouring of the Spirit with the coming of a messianic figure and the restoration of Israel, images that have their roots in this passage from Isaiah.

Although vv. 1-9 and vv. 10-16 clearly constitute two distinct units, I will consider them together for two reasons.[6] First, the two oracles share the

---

[4] At the outset of this chapter the problem of which text to consider, the Hebrew or the Greek, presents itself. Unless otherwise noted, quotations are taken from the NRSV, which itself relies primarily on the MT. Nevertheless, throughout I will consult both the Greek and the Hebrew. In addition, certain passages (Isaiah 57, Joel) manifest important themes only in the Greek; in these cases, I will focus on the LXX and provide my own translations. The reason for consulting both Greek and Hebrew is that the different texts we consider later in the study would have relied on different traditions. So, even if Paul may have relied primarily on the Greek traditions of Isaiah (cf. J. Ross Wagner, Jr., *Heralds of the Good News: Isaiah and Paul in Concert in the Letter to the Romans* [Leiden: Brill, 2002], 344-46), other texts from the Second Temple period (e.g., the Hebrew writings of the Dead Sea Scrolls) would have relied on Hebrew traditions. The purpose of consulting both texts is not to trace a development in concepts as the Hebrew texts were translated into Greek.

[5] The passage plays a prominent role in some of the *Psalms of Solomon*, for example. For a more detailed study of the significance of Isa 11:1-9 in the apocrypha and pseudepigrapha, see Michael A. Knibb, "Isaianic Traditions in the Apocrypha and Pseudepigrapha," in *Writing and Reading the Scroll of Isaiah: Studies of an Interpretive Tradition* (ed. Craig C. Broyles and Craig A. Evans; VTSup 70.2; Leiden: Brill, 1997).

[6] Several commentators treat the oracles as separate but related. See Joseph Blenkinsopp, *Isaiah 1-39: A New Translation with Introduction and Commentary* (AB 19; New York: Doubleday, 2000), 266: "Isaiah 11:10-16 consists formally of two appendices to the preceding poem." See also Christopher R. Seitz, *Isaiah 1-39* (IBC; Louisville: John Knox, 1993), 95-96; R. E. Clements, *Isaiah 1-39* (NCB; Grand Rapids: Eerdmans, 1980), 125; John D. W. Watts (*Isaiah 1-33* [WBC 24; Waco: Word Books, 1985], 167-80) divides the poem at v. 11,

theme of restoration.[7] The first signals this restoration in that it looks to a righteous ruler from the stump of Jesse who will mete out right judgment. The second section describes the restoration in terms of an ingathering of Israel and Judah, using language and themes reminiscent of the exodus from Egypt. Second, both passages refer to Jesse and to his family tree.[8] Moreover, the oracle of the return beginning at v. 10 speaks of "that day" twice (11:10, 11), the day when the shoot from the stump of Jesse comes out to rule the nations, thus suggesting that the latter oracle is an extended description of the things to come about during the reign of the leader described in 11:1-9.

Most importantly for the present project, Isaiah characterizes this reign as one marked by a bestowal of the Spirit of the Lord upon the ruler.[9] Describing the ruler as a branch from the stump of Jesse, the oracle declares that "the spirit of the LORD shall rest on him" and proceeds to enumerate the gifts of this Spirit. Following the elaboration of the attributes of the Spirit, the oracle goes on to describe how this ruler will govern the people: he will judge "with righteousness," judging not by appearances but with integrity and justice. Indeed, this ruler wears two belts, one of "righteousness" (צדק, δικιαοσύνη) and one of "faithfulness" (אמונה, ἀληθεία).

Once the prophet recounts the attributes of the king, he then portrays the conditions of the kingdom over which he will reign, and he uses imagery that evokes the situation in paradise before the expulsion of Adam and Eve. Creatures normally considered mortal enemies lie down together in the blissful conditions of the Garden of Eden: wolves with lambs, leopards with kids, children with asps. Just as before the punishment of humanity predation did not exist, so this king will enjoy a reign of peace. There will be neither pain nor destruction on God's holy mountain (11:9). In other words, when the ruler from the stump of Jesse, whom God anoints with his own Spirit, comes, God's holy mountain will become a new creation, and knowledge of the Lord will fill the earth "as the waters cover the sea" (11:9).[10]

---

taking 11:1-10 to be one "episode" and 11:11-16 to be a subsequent one. Brevard S. Childs (*Isaiah* [OTL; Louisville: Westminster/John Knox, 2001], 99) suggests that the chapter consists of two main units, with v. 10 serving as a transition between the two.

[7] Cf. Seitz, *Isaiah 1-39*, 95: "The material in Isaiah 11 is organized around the theme of Israel's restoration." See also Childs, *Isaiah*, 106.

[8] Blenkinsopp, *Isaiah 1-39*, 267; Clements, *Isaiah 1-39*, 125.

[9] In a suggestive but underdeveloped article, William Dumbrell proposes that the descent of the Spirit upon the rulers of Israel demonstrates a connection between the Spirit and the kingdom of God in the OT. The oracle of Isaiah 11, Dumbrell suggests, taps into and confirms this tradition. See William J. Dumbrell, "Spirit and Kingdom of God in the Old Testament," *RTR* 33 (1974): 1-10, esp. 5-6.

[10] Blenkinsopp (*Isaiah 1-39*, 263-65) notes that various ancient texts commonly connected a new, peaceful political order with a restoration of the creation. Moreover, he notes that the shift is not as striking as some have suggested: "The transition to peaceful coexistence in the animal world is not so abrupt; indeed those commentators who insist on making the following

The subsequent oracle, beginning at v. 10, adds to the creation theme of vv. 1-9 imagery reminiscent of the exodus account.[11] As noted above, the use of the phrase "root of Jesse" (שרש ישי, ἡ ῥίζα Ιεσσαι) and of the time indication "on that day" demonstrates that the two oracles are closely connected and are intended to describe the same reign.[12] Not only, then, is the reign of this root of Jesse to establish a new creation – it will also bring about the restoration of the tribes of Israel from their exile in a manner analogous to the exodus from Egypt. Indeed, the prophet describes this action to be accomplished as a second act of God on behalf of the people Israel: "On that day the Lord will extend his hand yet a second time to recover the remnant that is left of his people, from Assyria, from Egypt, from Pathros, from Ethiopia, from Elam, from Shinar, from Hamath, and from the coastlands of the sea" (11:11). In this act, the prophet notes, God will perform deeds akin to those he first accomplished for Israel when he brought them out of Egypt: "And the LORD will utterly destroy the tongue of the sea of Egypt; and will wave his hand over the River with his scorching wind; and will split it into seven channels and make a way to cross on foot" (11:15).[13] These references to the taming of the sea and the creation of a pathway recall the escape of the Israelites through the Red Sea, and the prophet explicitly draws a connection between God's new act and the exodus: "so there shall be a highway from Assyria for the remnant that is left of his people, as there was for Israel *when they came up from the land of Egypt*" (11:16, emphasis added).[14]

In these two related oracles of Isaiah 11, then, we see a number of the key themes that will play a prominent role in the present study: the bestowal of the Spirit, a new creation, and an ingathering of the dispersed tribes of Israel in a new exodus.

---

verses into a separate poem may be missing a subtle parallel between 3-5 and 6-8 consisting in the contrast between the strong and the weak in both the human and zoological realms." Seitz (*Isaiah 1-39*, 106-07) suggests that the imagery of predatory animals may refer to the nations troubling Israel. Childs (*Isaiah*, 104) takes vv. 6-9 to describe an eschatological goal: "The prophetic picture is not a return to an ideal past, but the restoration of creation by a new act of God through the vehicle of a righteous ruler. The description in vv. 6-9 is a massive extension of the promise in chapter 9 that focuses on the eschatological deliverance of God's people." See also Robert Murray, *The Cosmic Covenant: Biblical Themes of Justice, Peace and the Integrity of Creation* (London: Sheed & Ward, 1992), 103-10.

[11] So Childs, *Isaiah*, 104.

[12] Cf. ibid., 106: "By picking up key words from vv. 1 and 12, v. 10 joins the two oracles together in a larger unit. The two oracles are thus construed mutually to interpret each other." See also Clements, *Isaiah 1-39*, 125.

[13] On the exodus imagery of this verse, see Clements, *Isaiah 1-39*, 127; Blenkinsopp, *Isaiah 1-39*, 268; Childs, *Isaiah*, 104.

[14] This reference to the first exodus tells against Clements's (*Isaiah 1-39*, 126) suggestion that the word translated "a second time" in v. 11 is secondary.

Isaiah 32:15-20: Righteousness, Peace, and the Spirit

Isaiah 32 evokes some of the themes already seen in Isa 11:1-16. The beginning of the chapter once again describes the rule of the righteous king, a reign characterized by righteousness and justice (Isa 32:1). This description of the setting aright of the government of the people is followed by a warning addressed to the complacent women of Israel, a warning that speaks of impending doom in terms that reflect the cursing of the ground in Genesis 3, as well as the exile. The prophet warns the women to weep for the soil of the people, which will "grow up in thorns and briers" (32:13; cf. Gen 3:18).[15] Further, the city will become abandoned and desolate: "For the palace will be forsaken, the populous city deserted; the hill and the watchtower will become dens forever, the joy of wild asses, a pasture for flocks" (32:14). In this context of cursing and exile, the prophet holds out hope for restoration, and once again the sign of that restoration is the outpouring of God's Spirit.

The desolation described in 32:9-14 is to last "until a Spirit from on high is poured out on us" (32:15, NRSV modified).[16] The outpouring of this Spirit, which is to be equated with God's own Spirit,[17] reverses the punishment of the preceding verses. Insofar as the thorns and thistles of v. 13 signify the cursing of the first creation, the turning of the wilderness into a fruitful field in v. 15 may be seen as an act of new creation.[18] The outpouring of the Spirit, then, once again goes hand in hand with a restoration motif, one described in terms of a new creation.

In addition to this new creation motif, the conditions that will accompany this restoration merit further consideration. The outpouring of the Spirit results in justice (משפט, κρίμα) and righteousness (צדקה, δικαιοσύνη) abiding in

---

[15] The reference to thorns and briers also points to Isa 5:6; 7:23-25. See Seitz, *Isaiah 1-39*, 229; Childs, *Isaiah*, 241; Clements, *Isaiah 1-39*, 262.

[16] On the reversal of Isa 32:9-14 in Isa 32:15-20, see Wonsuk Ma, *Until the Spirit Comes: The Spirit of God in the Book of Isaiah* (JSOTSup 271; Sheffield: Sheffield Academic, 1999), 78-80.

[17] So Blenkinsopp, *Isaiah 1-39*, 434; Childs, *Isaiah*, 241; Clements (*Isaiah 1-39*, 263) seems undecided on the matter. The description of God's throne in Isa 6:1 as "high and lofty" (ונשא רם; ὑψηλοῦ καὶ ἐπηρμένου), as well as his dwelling in Isa 33:5, "The LORD is exalted, he dwells on high" (נשגב יהוה כי שכן מרום; ἅγιος ὁ θεὸς ὁ κατοικῶν ἐν ὑψηλοῖς), suggests that the "Spirit from on high" refers to God's own Spirit.

[18] Blenkinsopp (*Isaiah 1-39*, 434) contrasts the reversal in Isaiah, in which wilderness becomes fruitful field, with the reversal in Jeremiah 4:26, which proceeds in the opposite direction. The Jeremiah oracle describes punishment in terms of the reversal of creation, thus suggesting that this Isaianic oracle envisions a new creation, or at least a restoration of the first creation. See also Childs, *Isaiah*, 241: "The divine change is characterized by justice and equity, a term familiar throughout the book of Isaiah for the messianic age. Stress is laid particularly on the peace, security, and freedom of the new age (cf. 30:23ff.). The radical change in both nature and society is also a hallmark of Isaiah's vision of the new age of God's rule (2:1ff.)."

the wilderness and the field. It is worth noting that twice now the term δι-καιοσύνη has appeared in conjunction with the outpouring of the Spirit, a theme that we will see reappear in writings from the Second Temple period and in Galatians. Furthermore, this righteousness results in another significant eschatological condition: "the effect of righteousness will be peace (שלום; εἰρήνη)" (32:17). This peace goes hand in hand with an expectation of a renewal or transformation of the created order, an act brought about by the Spirit of God. As Blenkinsopp notes, this theme develops into a cosmic context in the latter parts of Isaiah.[19]

Isaiah 42:1-9: The Servant and the Spirit

The first of the so-called servant songs, Isa 42:1-9, is important for the present study, not because it talks about a general outpouring of the Spirit (which it does not, at least not explicitly), but because of the important themes tied to the servant's reception of the Spirit. In addition, if, as some commentators suggest, the servant represents all of Israel (cf. Isa 49:3), then the passage presents yet another example of the outpouring of the Spirit on Israel being connected with the restoration of Israel.[20]

The song begins by drawing attention to the Lord's servant, who pleases the Lord. The Lord puts his own Spirit upon the servant (Isa 42:1), empowering him to "bring forth justice (משפט; κρίσιν) to the nations (לגוים; τοῖς ἔθνεσιν)," a task similar to the one ascribed to the righteous king in Isaiah 11.[21] Also like Isaiah 11, Isa 42:5 once again evokes God's act of creation as the basis of the liberation that he is about to accomplish: "Thus says God, the LORD, who created the heavens and stretched them out, who spread out the earth and what comes from it, who gives breath to the people upon it and

---

[19] Blenkinsopp, *Isaiah 1-39*, 434, pointing to Isa 65:17; 66:22.

[20] The identity of the servant has been the subject of much scholarly debate. Joseph Blenkinsopp (*Isaiah 40-55: A New Translation with Introduction and Commentary* [AB 19A; New York: Doubleday, 2002], 210-11) suggests that the original referent of the "servant" language most likely was Cyrus, but acknowledges that the ambiguity of the language allows for various applications. In particular, he notes that "much of what is said in these verses could also be said of Israel either projecting an ideal Israel or an Israel in the guise of one of the great figures from its past." On early interpretation of the servant as "Israel" and "Jacob," see Klaus Baltzer, *Deutero-Isaiah* (Hermeneia; Minneapolis: Fortress, 2001), 125. For a forceful argument that the servant is in some way Israel, see Childs, *Isaiah*, 325: "For anyone who takes the larger literary context seriously, there can be no avoiding the obvious implication that *in some way* Israel is the servant who is named in 42:1." Claus Westermann (*Isaiah 40-66* [trans. David M. G. Stalker; OTL; Philadelphia: Westminster, 1969], 97) suggests a connection with Moses.

[21] John N. Oswalt (*The Book of Isaiah: Chapters 40-66* [NICOT; Grand Rapids: Eerdmans, 1998], 109-10) notes this connection and suggests a messianic interpretation of the servant based upon it.

spirit to those who walk in it." Baltzer suggests that the reference to giving "breath" to the people may recall Gen 2:7, thus helping to explain the broader, universal character of the passage: "The creation of humanity is the reason for the sending of the Servant, and the reason too for the universality of his Torah – its validity for all human beings."²² It is noteworthy that the oracle asserts that God calls the servant "in righteousness" (בצדק; ἐν δικαιοσύνῃ) and as a "light of the nations" (לאור גוים; εἰς φῶς ἐθνῶν), given that these two themes feature prominently in Galatians. Following this description, the prophet announces the task set out for the servant, one of liberation and release of the oppressed. Although the language is not as explicit as some of the other passages we have considered and will consider, the emphasis on the "new things" (42:9) that God is bringing about suggests that this oracle, too, envisions the restoration of Israel.²³ Once again, this restoration is accompanied by an outpouring of the Spirit, and once again the Spirit is closely associated with the theme of righteousness.

Isaiah 43:14-44:8: Seed, Blessing, King, Israel

One of the most intriguing and suggestive Isaianic passages with regard to the outpouring of the Spirit is Isa 44:1-5. Although the most significant motifs appear in 44:1-5, it is worth considering the broader context of the passage, which, I suggest, extends at least from 43:14 to 44:8.²⁴ This section contains four units connected by the theme of God's election of Israel and, like much of the second half of Isaiah, promises Israel restoration after the punishment she receives for her sins.

Not surprisingly, the first unit (43:14-21) describes God's rescue of Israel from Babylon in terms of a new exodus.²⁵ The prophet announces the Lord as Israel's "Redeemer" (גאל, ὁ λυτρούμενος), the same root used to describe

---

²² Baltzer, *Deutero-Isaiah*, 131; see also Westermann, *Isaiah 40-66*, 99; Paul D. Hanson, *Isaiah 40-66* (*IBC*; Louisville: John Knox, 1995), 46-47. Childs (*Isaiah*, 326) also suggests that the oracle has a universal scope based on the parallel between "people" and "nation." Moreover, he notes that much of the terminology in 42:5-9 ("righteousness," "covenant," "people") evokes Israel's exodus traditions, as does the formula "I am Yahweh."

²³ Cf. the similar phrase in Isa 48:6 (חדשות; τὰ καινά) in the context of another oracle of restoration, as well as the broad restoration themes throughout Isaiah 40-48.

²⁴ Blenkinsopp (*Isaiah 40-55*, 234-38) discusses 44:6-8 together with 44:21-23, but the latter verses add little of importance to the present study.

²⁵ There is disagreement about the precise delineation of this oracle. Here I side with Blenkinsopp, *Isaiah 40-55*, 225-26 in reading 43:14-21 as a unit. Oswalt (*Isaiah 40-66*, 150-56) and Childs (*Isaiah*, 336-37) also take 43:14-21 to be a discrete unit within the larger context. Others have suggested a division at v. 16, taking the unit to be 43:16-21 (Westermann, *Isaiah 40-66*, 126-29; Hanson, *Isaiah 40-66*, 71-76; Baltzer, *Deutero-Isaiah*, 171-75).

God's action at key points in the exodus narrative (cf. Ex 6:6 and 15:13).[26] The series of epithets used in this section ("YHWH," "Holy One," "Creator") emphasize Israel's covenantal relationship with the Lord.[27] After the Lord announces his plans to rescue Israel from Babylon, in 43:15 he refers to himself as the creator (בורא, καταδείξας) of Israel and its king (מלך, βασιλεύς), two more words that emphasize the unique claim that the God of Israel has on his people.[28] The oracle then proceeds to recount the acts of the Lord in the exodus, how he makes a way in the sea for his people and causes chariot and horse alike to drown in the sea (43:16-17). All of this leads up to a declaration of the new thing that the Lord is about to do for Israel, a deliverance that is to be even greater than the first exodus. Once again the Lord will redeem his "chosen people" (43:20), the people whom he formed (43:21). Moreover, the deference of the wild beasts to the Lord evokes the new creation imagery commonly found throughout Deutero-Isaiah, reflecting the peaceful conditions known in Eden (cf. Isa 11:6-9). This creation motif, combined with the ingathering of Israel from various points of the globe throughout Deutero-Isaiah, suggests that the prophet has in mind something more than simply a return of a portion of Israel from Mesopotamia.[29]

A number of key words connect this first unit with Isa 44:6-8, which functions as the second bookend around the two central oracles of 43:22-28 and 44:1-5.[30] Once again, in 44:6 the prophet refers to the Lord as the king (מלך, ὁ βασιλεύς) and redeemer (גאל, ῥυσάμενος) of Israel, again emphasizing the unique relationship the Lord has with Israel.[31] He then asks who has declared the "things to come" (אתה, τὰ ἐπερχόμενα), reflecting the "former things" (ראשנות, τὰ πρῶτα) and the "new thing" (חדשה, καινά) of 43:18-19. In 44:8, reprising the word of encouragement of 44:2, the Lord refers again to his ability to declare things from of old (מאז, ἀπ' ἀρχῆς), thus forging another connection with 43:14-21 (cf. τὰ ἀρχαῖα at 43:18). Further, the self-designation "rock" (צור) reaffirms God's status as protector of Israel, a status that also re-

---

[26] Childs, *Isaiah*, 336; on other exodus language throughout the passage, see Blenkinsopp, *Isaiah 40-55*, 227.

[27] Cf. Oswalt, *Isaiah 40-66*, 153.

[28] Westermann, *Isaiah 40-66*, 125-26; Oswalt, *Isaiah 40-66*, 153-54; Baltzer, *Deutero-Isaiah*, 169-70.

[29] So Blenkinsopp, *Isaiah 40-55*, 228; Childs, *Isaiah*, 337; Hanson, *Isaiah 40-66*, 75-76; Baltzer, *Deutero-Isaiah*, 174.

[30] On some of the similarities between 44:6-8 and 43:16-21, cf. Baltzer, *Deutero-Isaiah*, 188-89; Blenkinsopp, *Isaiah 40-55*, 236.

[31] It is worth noting that the Greek translates the same root (גאל) with two different words in 43:14 and 44:6. This may suggest two different translators for the different oracles.

flects the earlier description of God's deliverance of Israel first from Egypt and later from Babylon.[32]

Sandwiched in between these two oracles of God's foreknowledge and protection are two related oracles, one of judgment and one of redemption.[33] The first unit, 43:22-28, accuses Israel of its sins and explains Israel's punishment, though at the same time sounding a note of hope in God's forgiveness (43:25). More significant for the present study, though, is 44:1-5, in which the prophet describes the restoration that will follow Israel's punishment. The oracle not only shares the common theme of the outpouring of the Spirit at the restoration first sounded in Isaiah 32; it also contains a number of keywords and themes to which we will return when we discuss Galatians 3-4.

Continuing the theme that we have seen throughout Isa 43:14-44:8, the prophet refers to Israel's status as God's elect people. Because of this status God then promises to redress the punishment described in 43:22-28.[34] In language that reflects the earlier announcement of an exodus-like deliverance (43:14-21), the Lord promises to pour out "water on the thirsty land" (אֶצָק־מַיִם עַל־צָמֵא; ἐγὼ δώσω ὕδωρ ἐν δίψει).[35] The oracle then goes on to interpret this water as referring to God's own Spirit: "I will pour my Spirit upon your descendants, and my blessing on your offspring" (44:3b, NRSV modified). Note the parallelism between 44:3b and 43:20b. In the latter verse, God promises to give water in the wilderness in order "to give drink to my chosen people"; similarly, Isa 44:3b makes reference to Israel's chosen status by promising the outpouring of the Spirit on Israel's descendants and associating this outpouring with the blessing. Isa 44:1-5, then, serves as an expansion and description of the restoration promised in 43:14-21, making more explicit the blessing to be poured out on Israel's offspring. Finally, the result of this outpouring is a closer relationship between Israel and God. Those who receive the Spirit will call themselves by the name of the Lord (44:5) and will take up the name Israel (וּבְשֵׁם יִשְׂרָאֵל יְכַנֶּה; εἰμι ἐπὶ τῷ ὀνόματι Ισραηλ).[36]

---

[32] Curiously, the word "rock" appears only in the Hebrew text. The Greek drops this metaphor and speaks only of God's uniqueness.

[33] Blenkinsopp (*Isaiah 40-55*, 230) notes the importance of reading 43:22-28 in the context both of what precedes and of what follows the oracle.

[34] Cf. Childs, *Isaiah*, 341: "The connection between this promise of salvation is so close to the preceding disputation that many commentators have seen fit to fuse the two into one literary unit, regardless of the signs of once independent genres."

[35] Cf. "water in the wilderness, rivers in the desert" (ἐν τῇ ἐρήμῳ ὕδωρ καὶ ποταμοὺς ἐν τῇ ἀνύδρῳ) in 43:20. Although the Greek of 44:3 only includes the phrase "water on the thirsty land," the parallels between 44:3 and 43:20 are clearer in the Hebrew, which in 44:3 includes the phrase "and streams on the dry ground" after "water on the thirsty land" (וְנֹזְלִים עַל־יַבָּשָׁה; cf. נְהָרוֹת בִּישִׁימֹן at 43:20).

[36] It is possible that this passage may play a part in Paul's designation of "all those who walk by this rule of faith" as "the Israel of God" (Gal 6:16).

Isaiah 48:16: The Lord GOD has sent me and his spirit

Embedded within yet another oracle that promises restoration to Israel (Isa 48:12-22), Isa 48:16, though not describing a general outpouring of the Spirit, nevertheless associates the coming of the Spirit with the restoration of Israel.[37] The oracle begins with a familiar expression in Isaiah, "I am the first, and I am the last" (48:12; cf. 41:4; 44:6) and declares God's power in creating the heavens and the earth as the basis for his action on behalf of Israel, as well as to distinguish the God of Israel from false idols. The text continues to affirm Israel's election ("I, even I, have spoken and called him, I have brought him, and he will prosper in his way"), after which the prophet declares, "And now the Lord GOD has sent me *and his spirit*" (48:16b, emphasis mine).[38] The abruptness of this first-person address has led to much speculation about the identity of the speaker. Despite the continued debate on the matter, the important point for the present study is that once again we see a sending of the Spirit appear in the context of an oracle promising Israel's restoration. Immediately following this announcement, the prophet reasserts the Lord's status as Israel's redeemer and upbraids the Israelites for their transgressions, which prevented them from receiving the blessing promised to the patriarchs (48:17-19). Once again, though, God promises to bring Israel out in a new exodus (48:20-21), ending the oracle with a declaration that reappears in Isaiah 57:21: "There is no peace for the wicked."[39]

Isaiah 57:14-21 (LXX): The Spirit and Peace

Isaiah 57:14-21 (LXX), though lacking some of the new creation/exodus themes seen in many of the passages considered thus far, nevertheless remains an important text for our study in that the Greek textual tradition joins two important motifs that have appeared a number of times in Isaiah, the Spirit and peace. The oracle appears in a context similar to that of Isaiah 43:14-44:8. After a brief reflection on the "righteous one," who perishes and yet is buried in peace (57:1-2), the prophet upbraids Israel for its idolatrous prac-

---

[37] Isa 48:16, though a bit jarring due to the sudden shift in person, nevertheless has good textual support. See Blenkinsopp, *Isaiah 40-55*, 292. The abruptness of the verse has posed problems to commentators for some time. For a brief but helpful summary of some of the interpretative options and an argument that the speaker of 48:16b should be understood as the servant of Isaiah 49, see Childs, *Isaiah*, 377-78.

[38] Blenkinsopp (*Isaiah 40-55*, 292) suggests that the oracle has been cut off here, since there is no indication that the Spirit would be the object of God's sending.

[39] Blenkinsopp (*Isaiah*, 295-96) notes the following features in the text that point to an exodus background for the passage: the command to "go out" (48:20; cf. Exod 11:8; 12:41; 13:3-4); the verb "to take flight" (48:20; cf. Exod 12:11); the provision of water in the wilderness (48:21; cf. Exod 17:1-7). Interestingly, rather than εἰρήνη, as one would expect, both 48:22 (LXX) and 57:21 (LXX) state that there is no rejoicing (χαίρειν) for the wicked.

tices. The passage then sets up a contrasting picture of two mountains. The wicked of Israel offer up sacrifice to pagan idols on a "high and lofty mountain" (ἐπ' ὄρος ὑψηλὸν καὶ μετέωρον; 57:7). By contrast, "the ones who take their refuge in [the Lord] will possess the land and inherit my holy mountain" (οἱ δὲ ἀντεχόμενοί μου κτήσονται γῆν καὶ κληρονομήσουσιν τὸ ὄρος τὸ ἅγιόν μου; 57:13).[40]

Following this contrast between the righteous and the wicked, the Greek text presents a word of consolation to the humble including an outpouring of the Spirit. To the broken-hearted (τοῖς συντετριμμένοις τὴν καρδίαν; 57:15) God promises to give life and patience (μακροθυμία). Moreover, he reassures the humble that his vengeance does not last forever (οὐκ εἰς τὸν αἰῶνα) nor will he remain wrathful forever (57:16). The sign of the end of this wrath and vengeance is once again the outpouring of God's own Spirit: "For the Spirit will go out from me, and I make every breath" (πνεῦμα γὰρ παρ' ἐμοῦ ἐξελεύσεται καὶ πνοὴν πᾶσαν ἐγὼ ἐποίησα; 57:16).[41] Just as we saw in Isaiah 32:15-20, the result of this going-forth of God's Spirit is peace, indeed "peace upon peace to those who are far and to those who are near" (εἰρήνην ἐπ' εἰρήνην τοῖς μακρὰν καὶ τοῖς ἐγγὺς οὖσιν) and healing from the Lord (57:19). Also as we saw in 32:15-20, the gift of the Spirit and of peace is connected to righteousness. The healing promised by God through the Spirit is to extend only to the righteous. The unrighteous (οἱ ἄδικοι) will continually be tossed about and will be unable to find rest (57:20), because once again, "there is no peace/rejoicing for the wicked" (57:21).[42]

Isaiah 59:15b-21: Spirit and Covenant

Isaiah 59 follows a by now familiar pattern of pointing out Israel's transgressions and then promising that God will rescue Israel from those transgressions. The first segment of the chapter acknowledges God's power to save and then proceeds to explain that it is because of her transgressions that the Lord does not listen to Israel (59:1-8). The second section (59:9-15a) asserts that the Israelites' sins have caused them to stumble about and suffer oppression. The passage is marked by an inclusio that comments on the lack of righteousness and justice among Israel: "Therefore justice (מִשְׁפָּט; ἡ κρίσις) is far from us, and righteousness (צְדָקָה; δικαιοσύνη) does not reach us" (59:9); "Justice (מִשְׁפָּט; τὴν κρίσιν) is turned back, and righteousness (צְדָקָה; ἡ δικαιοσύνη) stands at a distance" (59:14). In between these two bookends the prophet paints a discouraging picture of Israel's suffering because of its sins,

---

[40] The language of "holy mountain" and "inheritance" may also echo Exod 15:17, which speaks of the "mountain of your inheritance" (הַר נַחֲלָתְךָ; ὄρος κληρονομίας σου).

[41] It is important to note that this emphasis on God's Spirit is a change in the Greek from the Hebrew, which speaks of the (human) spirit growing faint.

[42] The Hebrew refers to "peace" (שָׁלוֹם), whereas the Greek speaks of "rejoicing" (χαίρειν).

and he uses heart imagery to describe their transgression: the Israelites "conceiv[ed] lying words and utter[ed] from the heart" (Isa 59:13, NRSV).[43] These "lying words" contrast with the words of God that the Lord promises to put on the mouths of the Israelites in 59:21.

Beginning in 59:15b, the Lord announces his plans to rescue Israel.[44] Appalled at the lack of justice in Israel (59:15b), the Lord takes it upon himself to restore justice and righteousness. Using imagery that is taken up by later Jewish and Christian writings (cf. Eph 6:13-17), he dons righteousness as a breastplate and the helmet of salvation to restore Israel (59:17). Wearing this armor God promises to come to Zion as its redeemer (Isa 59:20: גּוֹאֵל; ὁ ῥυόμενος), and then expresses the covenant that he plans for Israel, which involves the gift of the Spirit: "And this is my covenant with them, says the Lord: my Spirit, which is upon you, and the words which I put into your mouth will certainly not leave your mouth and the mouth of your seed, says the Lord, from now until eternity" (Isaiah 59:21 [LXX], my translation).[45] These "words" in the mouth of the prophet and of his children serve as a contrast to the "lying words" that the Israelites utter in 59:13, a connection seen more easily in the Hebrew, which in both instances uses דבר, than in the Greek, which uses λόγους in the first instance and ῥήματα in the second. In both cases, nevertheless, the themes are clearly present, and 59:21 serves as a fitting reversal of the problem depicted in the first half of the chapter, thus bringing the unit to a logical conclusion.[46]

Isaiah 61:1-11: The Spirit and the Praise of the Nations

The description of the prophet's anointing and his task in Isaiah 61 resembles both the description of the ideal king in Isaiah 11 and the commissioning of

---

[43] Hebrew: הֹרוֹ וְהֹגוֹ מִלֵּב דִּבְרֵי־שָׁקֶר; The Greek speaks literally of "unrighteous words": ἐκύομεν καὶ ἐμελετήσαμεν ἀπὸ καρδίας ἡμῶν λόγους ἀδίκους.

[44] Several commentators recognize Isa 59:15b as the beginning of a new unit. See Joseph Blenkinsopp, *Isaiah 56-66: A New Translation with Introduction and Commentary* (AB 19B; New York: Doubleday, 2003), 194-99; Oswalt, *Isaiah 40-66*, 525-32; Westermann, *Isaiah 40-66*, 349-50.

[45] καὶ αὕτη αὐτοῖς ἡ παρ' ἐμοῦ διαθήκη εἶπεν κύριος τὸ πνεῦμα τὸ ἐμόν ὅ ἐστιν ἐπὶ σοί καὶ τὰ ῥήματα ἃ ἔδωκα εἰς τὸ στόμα σου οὐ μὴ ἐκλίπῃ ἐκ τοῦ στόματός σου καὶ ἐκ τοῦ στόματος τοῦ σπέρματός σου εἶπεν γὰρ κύριος ἀπὸ τοῦ νῦν καὶ εἰς τὸν αἰῶνα.

[46] Blenkinsopp (*Isaiah 56-66*, 200-01) suggests that 59:21 belongs not with the immediately preceding oracle, but rather ties together the larger unit beginning at 56:1. While I would not deny this function of the verse, it seems to me that v. 21 also serves well to round out the smaller unit of Isaiah 59, especially given the emphasis on the rebellious words of Israel in 59:13 and the words of God in 59:21. See Oswalt, *Isaiah 40-66*, 530-32. Childs (*Isaiah*, 490) suggests that, despite its redactional nature, 59:21 serves canonically to summarize all of chapter 59.

the servant in Isaiah 42.[47] As in both of these passages, the prophet in Isaiah 61 announces that the Spirit of God anoints him for a special task (Isa 61:1). Like the servant of Isaiah 42, the prophet is called to proclaim liberty to captives and release to prisoners (61:1; cf. 42:7), and significantly the term used to describe his proclamation is the verb "to preach good news" (לבשׂר; εὐαγγελίσασθαι). His message is one of comfort for those who mourn, especially in Zion. Like some of the passages we have already examined, Isaiah 61 also connects the Spirit with righteousness, a term that occurs three times in the passage (61:3, 8, 11). Those whom the prophet comforts will be called "oaks of righteousness" (אילי הצדק; δικαιοσύνης φύτευμα; Isa 61:3) and they are to rebuild Jerusalem, an image pointing to restoration. Furthermore, this restoration has implications not only for Israel, but also for the nations: "Their descendants shall be known among the nations, and their offspring among the peoples; all who see them shall acknowledge that they are a people whom the LORD has blessed" (61:9). The final verse of the passage draws upon creation imagery to describe God's action in restoring Israel: "For as the earth brings forth its shoots, and as a garden causes what is sown in it to spring up, so the Lord GOD will cause righteousness and praise to spring up before all the nations" (61:11). Here again, then, we see a connection between the outpouring of the Spirit, the restoration of Israel, the bringing about of righteousness, and a witness to the Gentiles.

Isaiah 63:7-64:12: Spirit, Exodus, and Fatherhood

One final passage in Isaiah contains a number of important themes and keywords related to the Spirit. In Isa 63:7-64:12, a communal psalm of lament over Israel's misfortune, the prophet looks back explicitly to the exodus and begs that God would do a similar deed for Israel now suffering for her sins.[48] Most importantly for the present study, the lament emphasizes the role of the Spirit both as the cause of God's punishment of Israel and as the means God uses to bless Israel. In Isa 63:7-14, the prophet retells the story of the exodus, both as a form of praise and as the basis on which he later makes his plea to God to restore Israel, and the retelling emphasizes the role played by the Spirit throughout the first exodus in such a manner that suggests the expectation of a new outpouring of the Spirit. The first mention of the Spirit comes in v. 10, in which the prophet states that Israel's rebellion grieved the holy

---

[47] On the similarities with Isaiah 42, see Blenkinsopp, *Isaiah 56-66*, 221; Westermann, *Isaiah 40-66*, 365; Hanson, *Isaiah 40-66*, 223-24; on connections with both Isaiah 42 and Isaiah 11, see Oswalt, *Isaiah 40-66*, 562-63.

[48] The division of this section is standard. See Blenkinsopp, *Isaiah 56-66*, 251-55; Hanson, *Isaiah 40-66*, 235-41; Childs, *Isaiah*, 519-21; Westermann, *Isaiah 40-66*, 385-87; Oswalt, *Isaiah 40-66*, 600.

Spirit and caused God to turn against them.[49] Following this reversal, the people hearken to the days of Moses and ask, "Where is the one who put his holy Spirit in them?" The prophet connects the giving of the Spirit to the Israelites with the events of the exodus. Following the question about putting the Spirit within them, he recounts the most vivid event of the exodus, the parting of the waters of the sea (63:12), and asserts that the Spirit of the Lord gave Israel rest (63:14).[50]

On the basis of this deed, the prophet then makes an appeal to God to have mercy on Israel once again. Given the emphasis on the Spirit in the preceding passage and the significance of the Spirit in Ezekiel, to which we will turn shortly, the language that the prophet uses to express his desire is particularly interesting, focusing on God's status as Israel's Father (another motif that hearkens back to the exodus) and on the state of Israel's hearts, a theme that plays prominently in three passages from Ezekiel, as well as in Deuteronomy.[51] The prophet prays, "For you are our father, *though Abraham does not know us and Israel does not acknowledge us*, you, O LORD, are our father" (63:16a, emphasis mine). The passage goes on to describe God as Israel's "Redeemer from of old" (63:16b) and then diagnoses the problem that led to Israel's troubles as one of the heart: "Why, O Lord, do you make us stray from your ways and *harden our heart*, so that we do not fear you?"(63:17, emphasis mine). As we will see when we turn to Ezekiel and Deuteronomy, the fundamental problem that leads Israel to curse and exile and the problem which demands healing is the hardness of Israel's heart.[52] The prophet's anguished cry over the hardness of Israel's heart gives way to a plea for the res-

---

[49] Although it is a bit awkward, I have chosen to speak of the "holy Spirit" with a lowercase "h" in order to avoid using later Trinitarian terminology anachronistically with reference to the book of Isaiah. Childs (*Isaiah*, 524) perceptively describes the picture of the Spirit in this passage: "The spirit here is the holy presence of Yahweh, which is a form of his outward manifestation to Israel theologically retrojected to the period of the nation's inception. Although the holy spirit [*sic*] is here still far removed from its later New Testament understanding, there is nevertheless an adumbration in the Old Testament of the identity of the God of Israel both as the transcendent and immanent presence in creation and redemption." Cf. Blenkinsopp, *Isaiah 56-66*, 261, who sees in this text the beginnings of a development that would lead to the Christian doctrine of the Holy Spirit and the rabbinic concept of the spirit of prophecy.

[50] See Blenkinsopp, *Isaiah 56-66*, 261-62; Childs, *Isaiah*, 524; Westermann, *Isaiah 40-66*, 388-90.

[51] It is worth noting that this is the first instance in the book of Isaiah in which the prophet addresses God as "Father." On the exodus connotations of the language of fatherhood, cf. Exod 4:22; Hos 11:1. On the significance of the heart in Deuteronomy, see the excursus on pp. 35-38 below. The heart also plays a prominent role in Jeremiah (see esp. Jer 31:33), but we will not discuss this book since it nowhere mentions the outpouring of the Spirit.

[52] One might see in this tradition an ironic attribution of Pharaoh's hardness of heart in the exodus story (cf. Exod 8:32 *et passim*) to Israel.

toration of the tribes of Israel (63:17b-18). Intriguingly, in v. 19 the prophet describes Israel's state with the following words: "We have long been like those whom you do not rule, like those not called by your name." Although the language is not as clear or explicit as that of Isaiah 43 and 44, this passage nevertheless also seems to connect the presence or absence of the Spirit to the kingship of God.[53]

The rest of the passage, Isa 64:1-12, concludes the plea, asking the Lord to act again as he once did at the exodus. The prophet recalls how the mountains quaked at God's presence in the first exodus, and he declares that he is expectantly awaiting another such event (64:1-3). The prophet confesses the sins of the people, acknowledging that it is because of these that Israel has been punished. He then resumes the plea for God's action, once again based on the fatherhood of God (64:8). The oracle ends in a lament over the desolation of Zion/Jerusalem and a plea to God not to keep silent, but to act on Israel's behalf (64:10-12).

The Spirit and the Restoration of Israel in Isaiah: Summary

Having surveyed the various Isaianic texts that connect the Spirit with the restoration of Israel, it would be worthwhile to take stock of what we have seen thus far. On the one hand, there does not seem to be a clear, monolithic program concerning the role and function of the Spirit throughout the book. On the other hand, there is a set of patterns that provide a plausible background for later developments with regard to the Spirit, both in Second Temple Judaism more broadly and in Paul specifically. As we have seen, in many of the texts the Spirit functions as a sign (48:16) and even a means (32:15-20; 44:1-5) of the redemption/restoration of Israel. Moreover, the Spirit appears in passages that promise peace (57:14-21 [LXX]) as well as a new covenant (59:21 [LXX]), and the absence of the Spirit is at least one cause of Israel's state of desolation (63:7-64:12). In addition, as noted at the outset, most of these passages describe the restoration of Israel in images drawn from creation and/or the exodus, often together. Indeed, in some ways the Spirit might be said to be the agent of the new creation.

---

[53] Dumbrell ("Spirit and Kingdom of God") begins his treatment of the connection between the Spirit of the Lord and the kingdom of God with Isa 63:7-14, though curiously he does not make anything of Isa 63:19. A closer consideration of this verse with its implication that the absence of the Spirit results in the people living without God as king would strengthen his argument.

The Spirit and Restoration Eschatology in Ezekiel

Like Isaiah, the book of Ezekiel contains several passages that link the Spirit or a "new spirit" with the restoration of Israel from exile. At the same time, Ezekiel adds and deepens a further dimension of this restoration. Specifically, the oracles of Ezekiel substantially develop a theme to which Isa 63:17 alludes all too briefly: the renewal of the heart of the Israelites.

Ezekiel 11:14-21: New Spirit and Restoration

Ezekiel 11:14-21 is the first of three main oracles that promise Israel a new heart and a new spirit when they return to the land.[54] Like several of the oracles of Isaiah considered above, this passage occurs after a word of judgment by God, which the prophet follows with a plea for mercy (Ezek 11:1-13). Perhaps in answer to this entreaty, Ezekiel receives another word from the Lord, one that promises restoration to the scattered tribes. In answer to those Jews who live in the land and see the exile of their kinspeople as punishment, the Lord promises to bring back the exiles, "the whole house of Israel, all of them" (Ezek 11:15) to the land.[55] Particularly noteworthy is the language the prophet uses to describe the return from exile, inasmuch as it reflects important keywords and themes found in Deuteronomy 28 and 30.[56]

Deuteronomy 28, the well-known passage that announces the unleashing of both the blessings and the curses upon Israel on account of its unfaithfulness to the covenant, climaxes in the scattering of Israel among the nations. The description of this exile is significant in light of the way that Ezekiel and

---

[54] See the discussion of Ezek 18:30-32; 36:26-27 below. Scholars debate whether Ezek 11:14-21 comprises a discrete unit or whether it extends to v. 25. Joseph Blenkinsopp (*Ezekiel* [IBC; Louisville: John Knox, 1990], 62) treats 11:14-25 as a single unit independent of the preceding temple vision; Moshe Greenberg (*Ezekiel 1-20: A New Translation with Introduction and Commentary* [AB 22; Garden City: Doubleday, 1983], 193) divides 11:1-21 into two units consisting of vv. 1-13 and vv. 14-21, with 11:22-25 forming a bookend together with 8:1-3 around the central oracle; Daniel I. Block (*The Book of Ezekiel: Chapters 1-24* [NICOT; Grand Rapids: Eerdmans, 1997], 357) considers 11:22-25 to be an epilogue to the temple vision.

[55] On the significance of the corporate nature of this passage for understanding the renewal of the heart, see Paul Joyce, *Divine Initiative and Human Response in Ezekiel* (JSOTSup 51; Sheffield: Sheffield Academic, 1989), 112-13. Based on the context of the passage, Joyce argues that one should not overemphasize the individual nature of the heart/spirit imagery.

[56] Joyce (*Divine Initiative and Human Response*, 119) also notes some of the lexical connections between Ezekiel 11 and Deuteronomy. For a survey of the use of "gathering" and "scattering" language in Deuteronomy and the OT Prophets, see Geo Widengren, "Yahweh's Gathering of the Dispersed," in *In the Shelter of Elyon: Essays on Ancient Palestinian Life and Literature in Honor of G. W. Ahlström* (ed. W. Boyd Barrick and John R. Spencer; JSOTSup 31; Sheffield: Sheffield Academic, 1984), 227-45.

other prophetic texts take up the language of scattering. First, in Deut 28:64 Moses tells the people, "The LORD will scatter you among all peoples (והפיצך יהוה בכל־העמים, καὶ διασπερεῖ σε κύριος ὁ θεός σου εἰς πάντα τὰ ἔθνη), from one end of earth to the other." The passage then proceeds to describe Israel's affliction among the nations: "There the LORD will give you a trembling heart (לב רגז, καρδίαν ἀθυμοῦσαν), failing eyes, and a languishing spirit (ודאבון נפש; τηκομένην ψυχήν)" (Deut 28:65b). Finally, the passage stresses once more the poor state of the heart of the Israelites, describing the woes that they will pronounce on themselves "because of the dread that your heart (מפחד לבבך; ἀπὸ τοῦ φόβου τῆς καρδίας σου) shall feel and the sights that your eyes shall see" (Deut 28:67). The climax of the curses of Deuteronomy 28, then, combines the scattering of the tribes of Israel with a weak and fearful heart. The beginning of Deuteronomy 30, following the listing of the blessings and the curses, promises restoration to Israel:

When all these things have happened to you, the blessings and the curses that I have set before you, if you call them to mind among all the nations where the Lord your God has driven you (οὗ ἐάν σε διασκορπίσῃ κύριος),[57] and return to the Lord your God, and you and your children obey him with all your heart and with all your soul, just as I am commanding you today, then the Lord your God will restore your fortunes and have compassion on you, gathering you again from all the peoples (וקבצך מכל־העמים; συνάξει σε ἐκ πάντων τῶν ἐθνῶν) among whom the Lord your God has scattered you (אשר הפיצך יהוה אלהיך; εἰς οὓς διεσκόρπισέν σε κύριος). (Deut 30:1-3)

The promises announced in Ezekiel 11:16-17 use the same language found in Deuteronomy 28 and 30 to describe the return of the people from the nations:

Therefore say: Thus says the Lord GOD: Though I removed them far away among the nations (בגוים; εἰς τὰ ἔθνη), and though I scattered them among the countries (הפיצותים בארצות; διασκορπιῶ αὐτοὺς εἰς πᾶσαν τὴν γῆν), yet I have been a sanctuary to them for a little while in the countries where they have gone. Therefore say: Thus says the Lord GOD: I will gather you (וקבצתי אתכם; συνάξω αὐτούς) from the peoples, and assemble you out of the countries where you have been scattered (אשר נפצותם; οὗ διέσπειρα αὐτούς), and I will give you the land of Israel. (Ezek 11:16-17)

The oracle, thus, announces to the exiles that God is about to bring about the restoration promised in Deuteronomy 30 that follows the curses of Deuteronomy 28.

In light of these connections, it is significant that the passage goes on to offer Israel "one heart" and a "new spirit" (Ezek 11:19).[58] This renewal of the heart, too, most likely reflects Deuteronomy 30, which in v. 6 states, "Moreover, the LORD your God will circumcise your heart and the heart of your de-

---

[57] The Hebrew of Deut 30:1 uses a different root (נדח) than Deut 28:64 and Ezek 11:16, but the LXX uses the same Greek word.

[58] Some MSS read "a new heart" rather than "one heart," but the former is most likely the result of assimilation to the more common phrase found later in Ezek 18:31; 36:26.

scendants (אֶת־לְבָבְךָ וְאֶת־לְבַב זַרְעֶךָ; τὴν καρδίαν σου καὶ τὴν καρδίαν τοῦ σπέρματός σου), so that you will love the LORD your God with all your heart and with all your soul, in order that you may live."[59] The emphasis on the "one heart" in the Ezekiel passage may be influenced by the singular form found in Deuteronomy.[60] This image of a new heart, connected with the return of the exiles, occurs twice more in Ezekiel.

Ezekiel 18:30-32: New Heart and New Spirit

Though brief, Ezek 18:30-32 merits attention because it continues the theme begun in Ezekiel 11 concerning the renewal of heart and spirit. Following a lengthy discussion of the reward of the righteous and the punishment of the wicked, in which the Lord justifies his ways, the prophet announces the judgment of God in order to call Israel to repentance. This oracle describes the repentance in a way similar to what we saw in Ezekiel 11: "Get yourselves a new heart and a new spirit" (Ezek 18:31). At first glance this command might seem to be addressed to individual Israelites since the majority of Ezekiel 18 focuses on individual reward and punishment, and the exhortation addresses a plural "you" ("yourselves"). More careful consideration, however, suggests that this passage concerns the punishment and restoration of Israel as a whole.[61] The exhortation is couched between two vocatives addressing the house of Israel as a whole (Ezek 18:30a; 31b).[62] In addition, as one can see from the way the imagery appears in other parts of the book, "death" and "life" play an important part in the prophet's announcement of the restoration of Israel. Moreover, the language may point to Deut 30:15, in which Moses presents the people with the choice between life and death, a choice that hangs on the people's obedience to the commandments. This theme also appears frequently in Ezekiel. If this analysis is correct and Ezekiel 18 speaks to the restoration of Israel as a whole, then once again we see an instance in which this corporate restoration is accompanied by a "new spirit." In both the Ezekiel passages that we have considered thus far, the language about the "spirit" does not seem to refer to the Spirit of God. Rather, the spirit in these

---

[59] See again Joyce, *Divine Initiative and Human Response*, 120-21: "The moral renewal of Israel promised in Ezekiel is so similar to this material that the probability that Ezekiel 11 and 36 reflect deuteronomistic influence must be regarded as strong."

[60] It is possible, though less likely, that the promise of a new spirit may function as the remedy for the "languishing soul" described in Deut 28:65.

[61] Cf. the similar conclusion in Jon D. Levenson, *Resurrection and the Restoration of Israel: The Ultimate Victory of the God of Life* (New Haven/London: Yale, 2006), 177: "The prophet's focus, however, is not on contemporary individuals at all but on *generations*, and his principal point is that the guilt of ancestors which caused the destruction of the Judahite kingdom and the ensuing exile does not condemn their current descendants to unending misery."

[62] Cf. the reference to the "whole house of Israel" in Ezek 11:15.

two passages is an anthropological term, and these texts refer to a renewal or purification of the human spirit.[63] In the last three passages that we will consider, the prophet speaks more explicitly of God's own Spirit. It is difficult to delineate the relationship between the renewal of the human spirit and the giving of God's own Spirit in Ezekiel; this difficulty helps explain the ambiguity in the texts from the Second Temple period we will consider in the following chapter.

Ezekiel 36:16-38: The Restoration of Israel

The latter half of Ezekiel 36 plays an important role in the present study insofar as it brings together a number of the themes seen in Isaiah and in Ezekiel 11 and 18. Ezek 36:16-38 follows a pattern seen in several of the passages considered above.[64] The first section describes the punishment that God meted out to Israel on account of her sins. As in Ezekiel 11, the language the prophet uses to describe Israel's punishment once again reflects that of Deuteronomy. Describing the wrath that God poured out on Israel, the prophet, in the voice of God, states, "I scattered them among the nations (ואפיץ אתם בגוים; καὶ διέσπειρα αὐτοὺς εἰς τὰ ἔθνη), and they were dispersed through the countries" (Ezek 36:19a).[65] The result of this scattering, though, is that God's holy name is profaned among the nations. Out of concern for his holy name, the Lord announces that he is about to accomplish restoration for Israel.

The promise of restoration develops and clarifies themes seen in Ezekiel 11 and 18. Once again, most likely drawing on deuteronomistic themes and language, the prophet speaks of Israel receiving a new heart and a new spirit: "A new heart (לב חדש; καρδίαν καινήν) I will give you, and a new spirit I will put within you; and I will remove from your body the heart of stone and give you a heart of flesh" (Ezek 36:26).[66] This oracle, however, adds a new di-

---

[63] See Block, *Ezekiel 1-24*, 353. For a fuller discussion of the various uses of רוח in Ezekiel, see James Robson, *Word and Spirit in Ezekiel*, (Library of Hebrew Bible/Old Testament Studies 447; New York/London: T&T Clark, 2006), 79-94.

[64] This division is standard. See Daniel I. Block, *The Book of Ezekiel: Chapters 25-48* (NICOT; Grand Rapids: Eerdmans, 1997), 337-43; Blenkinsopp, *Ezekiel*, 164-70; Moshe Greenberg, *Ezekiel 21-37: A New Translation with Introduction and Commentary* (AB 22A; New York: Doubleday, 1997), 733-34; Walther Zimmerli, *Ezekiel 2* (trans. James D. Martin; Hermeneia; Philadelphia: Fortress, 1983), 244-45.

[65] Again, cf. Deut 28:64: "The LORD will scatter you among all peoples (והפיצך יהוה בכל־העמים, καὶ διασπερεῖ σε κύριος ὁ θεός σου εἰς πάντα τὰ ἔθνη), from one end of earth to the other." See also Widengren, "Yahweh's Gathering of the Dispersed," 233.

[66] The language of the heart also evokes the promises of Jer 31:31-34. See Zimmerli, *Ezekiel 2*, 249; Block, *Ezekiel 25-48*, 356 n. 97; Blenkinsopp, *Ezekiel*, 169, who also compares the idea of a new covenant to Deuteronomy. On the similarities between Ezekiel and Deuteronomy with respect to the heart, see again Joyce, *Divine Initiative and Human Response*, 120-21.

mension, one that does not appear in Ezekiel 11 or 18.[67] In this oracle, God promises to put his own Spirit within the hearts of the Israelites, thus enabling them to keep his statutes and commandments: "I will put my Spirit (רוּחִי; τὸ πνεῦμά μου) within you, and make you follow my statutes and be careful to observe my ordinances" (Ezek 36:27, NRSV modified). As suggested above, later readers may have interpreted the sending of God's own Spirit into the hearts of the Israelites as a remedy for the trembling heart and languishing spirit described in the curses of Deuteronomy 28.[68] This possibility becomes more likely when one notices that the empowerment of the Israelites to follow the commandments of the Lord leads to the restoration of Israel to the land and renewal of the covenant (Ezek 36:28), precisely the reversal of the climax of the curses of Deuteronomy.

Perhaps equally important for the present study is the language with which the prophet describes the restoration, language that evokes images of the creation account and suggests that this restoration will in fact be like a new creation. In Ezek 36:29-30, God promises that the land will bring forth fruit for the people of Israel so that they will no longer be a disgrace among the nations. The prophet then tells Israel that they will remember their ways, how they were evil and not good. The combination of language describing the fruitfulness of the land and the categories of good and evil for Israel's deeds alludes to the creation story. The allusion becomes much more explicit later in the passage: "And they will say, 'This land that was desolate has become like the garden of Eden'" (Ezek 36:35).[69] Once again, the restoration of Israel is portrayed as a new creation brought about by the bestowal of God's own Spirit in the hearts of the Israelites.

Ezekiel 37:1-14: The Valley of Dry Bones

The famous valley of dry bones oracle, one of the earliest OT texts to use resurrection imagery, describes the restoration of Israel from Babylon as a resurrection, the knitting together of bone and sinew. Following as it does upon Ezekiel 36 and sharing the theme of restoration, it is possible that this prophecy expands upon the new creation language touched upon in the preceding chapter, describing in different terms how this act of new creation is to come

---

[67] On the relationship with Ezekiel 11 and 18, see Greenberg, *Ezekiel 21-37*, 730; Block, *Ezekiel 25-48*, 355.

[68] Cf. Deut 28:65, 67.

[69] וְאָמְרוּ הָאָרֶץ הַלֵּזוּ הַנְּשַׁמָּה הָיְתָה כְּגַן־עֵדֶן; καὶ ἐροῦσιν ἡ γῆ ἐκείνη ἡ ἠφανισμένη ἐγενήθη ὡς κῆπος τρυφῆς. Although the Greek does not use the name Εδεμ, the imagery of a lush garden most likely evokes the primordial habitation of Adam and Eve.

about. Again, most significant for the present study is the role the Spirit plays in the resurrection of the bones.[70]

In this instance, the Greek translation of the text makes some modifications to the Hebrew, expanding some of the themes already present there. Beginning at Ezek 37:5, the Lord states, "I will cause breath to enter you, and you shall live."[71] The LXX modifies the Hebrew, stating, "I will put into you the Spirit of life."[72] Ezek 37:6, continuing the description of the reconstitution of bone and sinew, states that God will "put breath in you, and you shall live."[73] Once again the Greek translation, perhaps picking up on the concluding verse of the Hebrew or on the oracles of Ezekiel 36, specifies whose Spirit it is: "I will put *my* Spirit within you and you shall live" (Ezek 37:6 [LXX]).[74]

Following the description of what God plans to do, Ezekiel prophesies as he has been told and the bones come to life, after which the Lord gives Ezekiel the interpretation of the prophecy. The resurrection of the dry bones symbolizes Israel's return to the land from exile, the undoing of the curse (37:11-14). The final verse, recapitulating what has been said before, restates the promise: "I will put my Spirit (רוּחִי; τὸ πνεῦμά μου) within you, and you shall live, and I will place you on your own soil; then you shall know that I, the LORD, have spoken and will act, says the LORD" (37:14, NRSV modified). Once again, the Spirit serves as the means and the sign of the restoration of Israel that God promises to bring about.

Ezekiel 39:21-29: The Restoration of Jacob

The last oracle in Ezekiel to mention the outpouring of the spirit also occurs in the context of a restoration of Israel to the land. Like Ezekiel 36, this oracle emphasizes that God's punishment of Israel had the purpose of leading the nation to acknowledge the Lord as their God (Ezek 39:21-22; cf. Ezek 36:23, 38). Moreover, the oracle describes Israel's exile as the result of her sins and transgressions (Ezek 39:23-24). After the nation's punishment, however, God will act once again for the sake of his name (Ezek 39:25; cf. Ezek 36:22-23).[75] God will bring the exiles back to their own land, and they will acknowledge him because of their punishment and rescue. Like several of the oracles we have considered thus far in Ezekiel, this last one once again describes the return as an event accompanied by the outpouring of a spirit, in this case God's

---

[70] Blenkinsopp (*Ezekiel*, 173) describes "spirit" as the key term that holds the passage together.

[71] אני מביא בכם רוח וחייתם.

[72] ἐγὼ φέρω εἰς ὑμᾶς πνεῦμα ζωῆς. Alternately, the last phrase could be translated "a spirit of life," though the following verse seems to favor the translation given here.

[73] ונתתי בכם רוח וחייתם.

[74] δώσω πνεῦμά μου εἰς ὑμᾶς καὶ ζήσεσθε.

[75] So also Blenkinsopp, *Ezekiel*, 190.

own Spirit: "And I will never again hide my face from them, when I pour out my Spirit upon the house of Israel, says the Lord GOD" (Ezek 39:29, NRSV modified).[76]

The Spirit and the Restoration of Israel in Ezekiel: Summary

The texts we have considered in Ezekiel, though fewer in number than the Isaianic texts concerning the Spirit, nevertheless share a number of characteristics with the latter, while at the same time developing certain aspects only marginally present in Isaiah. In addition, the texts of Ezekiel have a more tightly focused theme. The most distinctive motif in these texts is the emphasis on the "new heart." As we saw above, these promises seem to correspond to the curses of Deuteronomy 28 and the word of promise of Deuteronomy 30, which point to both the terror that will seize Israel's heart in their exile and the need for a purification of the heart in order to obey the commands of the Lord. Another thread tying together four of the five passages is the promise of a return to the land, another promise that seems to point to the reversal of the curses of Deuteronomy 28.

Excursus: Exile and the Heart in Deuteronomy

As just noted, one aspect of the restoration that distinguishes Ezekiel from Isaiah is the stronger emphasis in the former on the renewal of the heart. Although I have already made reference to some of the passages in Deuteronomy that stress the importance of renewal of the heart, it would be worthwhile to take a moment to trace this theme more explicitly throughout the book of Deuteronomy in order to establish the connection between the exile and Israel's failure of heart, as well as between restoration and the renewal of the heart.[77]

The motif of the heart, and particularly of loving the Lord with all one's heart, appears several times in the book of Deuteronomy. Indeed, the connection between return from exile and renewal of the heart appears in Deuteron-

---

[76] It is worth noting that the LXX has "wrath (θυμός)" in place of the MT's "spirit (רוח)" in 39:29. Two explanations have been given for this change. Block, *Ezekiel 25-48*, 478 n. 89 argues that the LXX harmonizes the expression to Ezekiel's more typical phrase "to pour out wrath." The other possibility is that the MT changed חמה to רוח in order to conform to Ezekiel 37. See Finny Philip, *The Origins of Pauline Pneumatology* (WUNT 2.194; Tübingen: Mohr/Siebeck, 2005), 47 n. 66, citing Johan Lust, *Ezekiel and His Book: Textual and Literary Criticism and their Interrelation* (Leuven: Leuven University, 1986), 52-53.

[77] For a very brief discussion of some of these texts from Deuteronomy vis-à-vis Ezekiel, see again Joyce, *Divine Initiative and Human Response*, 120-21.

omy 4 and Deuteronomy 30, which frame the central section of the book.[78] Deuteronomy 4 recounts Moses' warning and exhortation to the people of Israel to follow the commandments the Lord has given them. As part of this exhortation, Moses warns the Israelites that if they perform evil and go after other gods, the Lord will punish them (Deut 4:25-28).[79] Specifically, Israel will be scattered among the nations (4:27), but afterward the Israelites will seek the Lord, and "you will find him if you search after him *with all your heart* and soul" (4:29, emphasis mine).[80] The result of this turning is a renewal and restoration of the covenant that God made with Israel (4:30-31).

In like manner, Deut 30:1-10 also envisions Israel's sin and eventual restoration, and once again focuses on the image of the heart. Following the listing of the blessings and the curses, and the announcement of their eventual fulfillment, the text describes a return of Israel to the Lord. The dominant keyword, occurring five times in a span of ten verses, is once again "heart" (לב; καρδία).[81] The text exhorts the Israelites to "return to the heart" (אל־ והשבת לבבך; καὶ δέξῃ εἰς τὴν καρδίαν σου) the things that are to come upon them, and then to return to YHWH "with all your heart and with all your soul" (Deut 30:1-2).[82] In response to this return, God promises to restore the fortunes of the Israelites and bring them back from the Gentiles among whom they have been scattered (Deut 30:3-5).[83] Deuteronomy 30:6 promises the Israelites a divine renewal of the heart, which will lead to new blessing: "Moreover, the LORD your God will circumcise your heart and the heart of your descendants, so that you will love the LORD your God with all your heart and with all your soul, in order that you may live." Again, this promise is connected with the restoration of Israel, as the curses which Israel received will then be put on her enemies and she will once again receive the blessings. All of this, again, will be the result of Israel turning to the Lord "with all your heart and with all your soul" (30:10).[84]

---

[78] Cf. Richard D. Nelson, *Deuteronomy: A Commentary* (OTL; Louisville: Westminster/John Knox, 2002), 69: "Along with the similar passage 30:1-10, this section [4:29-31] sets the whole book of Deuteronomy into a restoration framework." Jeffrey H. Tigay (*Deuteronomy* [The JPS Torah Commentary; Philadelphia: The Jewish Publication Society, 1996], 53) also notes a connection between Deut 4:29-31 and 30:1-5.

[79] Nelson (*Deuteronomy*, 68) connects this description of Israel's punishment with Deut 28:32, 62-64.

[80] את־יהוה אלהיך ומצאת כי תדרשנו בכל־לבבך ובכל־נפשך; καὶ εὑρήσετε ὅταν ἐκζητήσητε αὐτὸν ἐξ ὅλης τῆς καρδίας σου καὶ ἐξ ὅλης τῆς ψυχῆς σου ἐν τῇ θλίψει σου.

[81] The word appears at Deut 30:2, 6 (3x), 10.

[82] בכל־לבבך ובכל־נפשך; ἐξ ὅλης τῆς καρδίας σου καὶ ἐξ ὅλης τῆς ψυχῆς σου.

[83] Nelson (*Deuteronomy*, 348) helpfully lays out some of the correspondences between Deut 30:1-10 and the curses described in Deuteronomy 28.

[84] בכל־לבבך ובכל־נפשך; ἐξ ὅλης τῆς καρδίας σου καὶ ἐξ ὅλης τῆς ψυχῆς σου.

In between the two bookends of Deut 4:29-31 and 30:1-10, the heart motif appears a number of times. Most famously, the Shema (Deut 6:4-5) exhorts the Israelites to love the Lord with all their heart and with all their soul. The command is embedded in a context that describes Israel's entry into the land promised to Abraham, Isaac, and Jacob (Deut 6:10-12), and further evokes the exodus, urging the Israelites not to forget the Lord who brought them out of Egypt (Deut 6:12). Deuteronomy 10 reiterates the call to love the Lord "with all your heart and with all your soul" (10:12) and issues the command to "circumcise, then, the foreskin of your heart" (10:16).[85] This command, too, appears in conjunction with a reminder of what God did for Israel in liberating her from Egypt (10:22). Again in Deut 11:13 and 18, Moses exhorts the Israelites to love the Lord with all their heart and soul. Finally, in Deuteronomy 26, the familiar refrain to serve the Lord with all the heart and soul reappears (Deut 26:16), this time in the ratification of the covenant.

In addition to the positive calls for serving the Lord, we saw above a number of verses in which the heart also appears in a negative light, as part of the curses for disobedience to the covenant. Deuteronomy 28:1-68 describes the blessings for obeying and the curses for disobeying the covenant. Beginning at 28:47, the text proceeds to foretell the accomplishment of these curses on Israel, giving the reason for the curse: "Because you did not serve the LORD your God joyfully and *with gladness of heart* for the abundance of everything" (Deut 28:47, emphasis mine).[86] Given the repeated emphasis on the heart that we have seen throughout the book of Deuteronomy, it can hardly be a coincidence that the outbreak of the curse results from an unfaithful heart, and furthermore, that part of the curse afflicts the heart of the Israelites. As we saw above, Deut 28:65 warns that "The LORD will give you a *trembling heart* (רגז לב; καρδίαν ἀθυμοῦσαν), failing eyes, and a languishing spirit" (emphasis mine). A few verses later, the text describes the despair that will capture the Israelites "*because of the dread that your heart shall feel* (אשר תפחד לבבך; ἀπὸ τοῦ φόβου τῆς καρδίας σου ἃ φοβηθήσῃ) and the sights that your eyes shall see" (Deut 28:67, emphasis mine). Both positively and negatively, then, the heart is closely associated with the blessings and the curses of Deuteronomy.

We saw above how Ezekiel takes up this theme of the heart in the context of promises of restoration. Jeremiah, too, elaborates on the motif, most fa-

---

[85] The LXX refers to "hardness of heart" (τὴν σκληροκαρδίαν), but the basic idea remains the same. Nelson (*Deuteronomy*, 137) notes the contrast between the imperative to circumcise the heart in 10:16 and the promise that God will do so in Deut 30:6. Significantly, this twofold description shares some parallels with Ezekiel, which at one point orders Israel to get a new heart (Ezek 18:31), but later promises that God will give Israel a new heart (Ezek 36:26).

[86]: תחת אשר לא־עבדת את־יהוה אלהיך בשמחה ובטוב לבב מרב כל; ἀνθ' ὧν οὐκ ἐλάτρευσας κυρίῳ τῷ θεῷ σου ἐν εὐφροσύνῃ καὶ ἀγαθῇ καρδίᾳ διὰ τὸ πλῆθος πάντων.

mously in the new covenant prophecy of Jeremiah 31. This oracle, which promises a new covenant with the house of Judah and the house of Israel, once again looks back to the exodus, though as a point of contrast. Whereas Israel broke the covenant that the Lord made with them when he brought them out of Egypt, this new covenant will not be broken because God "will write [the Law] *on their hearts* (על-לבם; ἐπὶ καρδίας αὐτῶν)" (Jer 31:33 [=38:33 LXX], emphasis mine).[87] This implanting of the Law on the hearts of the Israelites, particularly because the prophet contrasts it with the Law that Israel broke when the Lord led them out of Egypt, serves to remedy the problem with the original covenant by giving the Israelites a heart that can obey the commandments of the Lord.

The Spirit and Restoration Eschatology in Joel

The final OT prophetic text to be considered in this chapter is also perhaps the most famous with regard to the outpouring of the Spirit due to its prominence in Peter's speech in Acts 2. Although the outpouring of the Spirit appears in both the MT and the LXX, the Greek text makes some significant modifications, and so we will focus on that version.

Joel 3:1-5 is the culmination of a larger section (2:18-3:5) announcing deliverance to Israel.[88] The first part of this oracle (2:18-20) describes the deliverance of the land from desolation and of the people from invaders.[89] The second section (2:21-27) then offers a poetic depiction of the restoration of the land and of the people, culminating in the acknowledgement of the Lord as Israel's God (2:27). The third and final section (3:1-5) is the one of central concern for the present study. Like several of the passages from Isaiah and Ezekiel that we considered above, Joel promises an outpouring of God's own Spirit on all of the people when he brings about the restoration of Israel: "And it shall come to pass after these things that I will pour out from my Spirit upon all flesh, and your sons and your daughters shall prophesy, your old men shall dream dreams and your young men shall see visions" (Joel 3:1 [LXX]).[90]

---

[87] For an insightful discussion of the "heart" in Jeremiah, see Timothy Polk, *The Prophetic Persona: Jeremiah and the Language of Self* (JSOTSupp 32; Sheffield: Sheffield Academic, 1984).

[88] So Hans Walter Wolff, *Joel and Amos* (trans. Waldemar Janzen, et al.; Hermeneia; Philadelphia: Fortress, 1977), 54-57; Douglas Stuart, *Hosea-Jonah* (WBC 31; Waco: Word Books, 1987), 254-58.

[89] I have slightly modified the division offered in Stuart, *Hosea-Jonah*, 257-58.

[90] καὶ ἔσται μετὰ ταῦτα καὶ ἐκχεῶ ἀπὸ τοῦ πνεύματός μου ἐπὶ πᾶσαν σάρκα καὶ προφητεύσουσιν οἱ υἱοὶ ὑμῶν καὶ αἱ θυγατέρες ὑμῶν καὶ οἱ πρεσβύτεροι ὑμῶν ἐνύπνια ἐνυπνιασθήσονται καὶ οἱ νεανίσκοι ὑμῶν ὁράσεις ὄψονται. In its original context, the reference to "all flesh" most likely was limited to Israel, as one can see by the discussion of the Gentiles

Following a description of fiery apocalyptic signs Joel 3:5 then describes the eschatological salvation promised by the Lord: "And it will be that everyone who calls upon the name of the Lord will be saved; for on Mount Zion and in Jerusalem there will be the one who is saved, as the Lord said, and those who have good news preached to them (εὐαγγελιζόμενοι), whom the Lord called beforehand" (Joel 3:5 [LXX]).[91] This salvation, as the text later explains, will come to pass "when [the Lord] restores the fortunes of Judah and Jerusalem" (Joel 4:1 [LXX]). Three significant themes, then, appear in this brief text: (1) the outpouring of the Spirit; (2) the restoration of Israel; and (3) the preaching of the good news. Like Isaiah and Ezekiel, Joel contributes to a broader prophetic vision of the outpouring of the Spirit as a sign and instrument of the eschatological restoration of Israel.[92]

The Spirit and Restoration Eschatology in the Prophets: Summary

Having surveyed the various texts that connect the Spirit with the restoration of Israel in Isaiah, Ezekiel and Joel, we can now draw some preliminary conclusions regarding the significance of the theme for the present study. The texts we have considered offer a variety of images and interpretations of the role of the Spirit in the restoration of Israel. Indeed, perhaps the most striking thing about these texts, particularly those from Isaiah, is the sheer diversity of images used to describe the restoration of Israel. Isaiah alone uses creation imagery, exodus imagery, the language of peace and righteousness, the fatherhood of God, and the establishment of a covenant. The motif of the heart, which appears briefly in Isaiah 63, plays a major part in Ezekiel's visions of the restoration of Israel, as do new creation and resurrection. Significantly for the chapter to come, Ezekiel offers two differing descriptions of the spirit that the people are to receive. On the one hand, Ezek 11:19-20 and 18:31 refer to a "new spirit" with no indication of how this spirit relates to God. On the other hand, the oracles in the latter parts of the book (Ezek 36:26-27; 37:6 [LXX], 14; 39:29) speak more explicitly of God putting his own Spirit in the Israelites. The one brief passage in Joel that we considered does not explicitly

---

in Joel 4:1-5 (LXX). See Wolff, *Joel and Amos*, 67; James L. Crenshaw, *Joel: A New Translation with Introduction and Commentary* (AB 24C; New York: Doubleday, 1995), 165.

[91] καὶ ἔσται πᾶς ὃς ἂν ἐπικαλέσηται τὸ ὄνομα κυρίου σωθήσεται ὅτι ἐν τῷ ὄρει Σιων καὶ ἐν Ιερουσαλημ ἔσται ἀνασῳζόμενος καθότι εἶπεν κύριος καὶ εὐαγγελιζόμενοι οὓς κύριος προσκέκληται.

[92] For a brief discussion of points of similarity between Joel 3:1-5 and Isa 44:1-5, see Philip, *The Origins of Pauline Pneumatology*, 67-68. Wolff (*Joel and Amos*, 60, 66) connects Joel's description of the outpouring of the Spirit to Ezek 39:29. Crenshaw (*Joel*, 164) suggests a possible connection with Isa 32:15.

use creation or exodus imagery, but in the LXX it does connect the Spirit with the preaching of good news.

Despite all of these differences, however, each of these texts connects the outpouring of the Spirit on all of God's people with the restoration of Israel. Perhaps most importantly, the regathering of Israel envisioned by many of these texts seems to respond to the curses of Deuteronomy 28, according to which Israel is scattered among the Gentiles. It is not only the imagery of return to the land, but the emphasis, especially in Ezekiel, on the heart that suggests this connection between the outpouring of the Spirit and redemption from the curses. The important question when considering Paul's thoughts on the significance of the Spirit is whether he (and to a lesser extent his readers) would have thought in these terms. Did at least some Jews in the Second Temple period see the curses of Deuteronomy still in effect and await the outpouring of the Spirit that would signal the undoing of those curses? To this question we now turn.

Chapter 3

New Exodus, New Creation II: The Spirit and the Restoration of Israel in the Second Temple Period

Introduction

In chapter two we saw that a number of themes tend to appear in the OT Prophets in conjunction with the outpouring of the Spirit and the restoration of Israel. Several of the texts considered connect this outpouring of the Spirit or a "new spirit" with a healing of the heart, a filial relationship with God, and the reversal of Israel's plight through a restoration of the people to the land. Furthermore, we saw that these prophets often describe the restoration using imagery of new exodus and new creation, sometimes together. Although by no means pervasive in the Second Temple period, these ideas nevertheless do surface in a number of texts in a way that sheds light on the cultural and religious context in which Paul wrote. In this chapter we will survey a number of late Second Temple Jewish texts that connect the outpouring of the Spirit or a spirit with the restoration of Israel.[1] As we will see, many of these texts draw together themes found in the OT prophetic corpus in a manner that suggests that these expectations remained important for Paul's contemporaries and near contemporaries. Because of these expectations, it would make sense for Paul to appeal to these categories to interpret the lived experience of the Spirit in the churches he founded. In addition to the texts that reflect eschatological expectations regarding the Spirit, we will also take a brief look at some aspects of the pneumatologies of Josephus and Philo, neither of whom connects the Spirit with eschatological hope. The purpose of including these two fig-

---

[1] There are various terms used to describe literature from this period: "intertestamental," "pseudepigraphal," "apocryphal," and "Second Temple," among others. I have chosen the last term because it accurately describes the historical period during which most of these texts were most likely written without prejudice as to whether or not canonical (i.e. deuterocanonical) texts arose during this time. With respect to my spelling of the term "spirit," as in chapter two I will spell the word with an upper-case 's' when describing God's Spirit, with a lower-case 's' when referring to any non-divine spirit, and the phrase 'holy Spirit' with lower-case 'h' and upper-case 's' to distinguish it from later Trinitarian theology. Due to the ambiguity in a number of the texts, as was the case in chapter two, in many cases the capitalization or lack thereof should not be taken as a dogmatic pronouncement, but as a tentative interpretation.

ures in the survey is twofold. First, this part of the study further underscores the diversity of Second Temple Jewish conceptions of the Spirit. Second, comparing these two figures with the other texts in the chapter will show that with regard to eschatology and the Spirit, Paul bears a closer affinity to apocalyptic or sectarian Judaism than to the strands of Hellenistic Judaism represented by Josephus and Philo.

Methodology

Before turning to the texts themselves, we must address two questions. First, what exactly are we seeking in these texts? Second, how should we organize this part of the study?

We may answer the first question briefly. The goal of this part of the study is to demonstrate the ways in which the various Second Temple texts appropriated and reinterpreted some of the themes we saw in chapter two connecting the Spirit or a spirit with the restoration of Israel. Specifically, we will look at texts that make this connection in order to explore how and to what extent significant related themes (the renewal of the heart, a filial relationship to God, the undoing of the curse) appear. An important part of this task will be to determine which, if any, of the prophetic texts we considered in chapter two shape the eschatological expectations of the later documents. This chapter in turn will help to establish an encyclopedia of certain Jewish hopes about the Spirit and restoration eschatology that helps to clarify the significance of the Spirit in Galatians.

The question of how to organize the texts to be studied is a little more difficult to answer. Whereas the OT prophetic corpus lent itself to easy organization, the Second Temple literature we will survey presents a host of problems. Because these texts do not belong to one clear collection of works, the question arises of the order in which we should examine each, as well as how to group the writings more generally. In addition, the possibility of Christian redaction or even authorship (e.g. the *Testaments of the Twelve Patriarchs*) complicates matters further.

The question of Christian influence is a difficult one that we will have to address in greater detail when we treat specific texts. For the moment, suffice it to say that it would be methodologically unwise to rule out any text that is suspected of containing Christian interpolations or influence since it is possible that such texts may also contain earlier traditions.[2] In addition, even documents that betray Christian influence are valuable in that they witness to other Christian interpretations that may shed light on how early believers in-

---

[2] It should also go without saying that the presence of interpolations ought not simply to be assumed, but rather must be the outcome of argument rather than its presupposition.

terpreted the activity of the Spirit and perhaps Paul's own statements about the topic.

As for the order in which we will survey the texts, since there is no one obvious choice, we will proceed simply by grouping the texts according to the way in which they describe the outpouring of the Spirit, treating those that see the outpouring as (primarily) collective together, followed by those that describe this outpouring as focused on a messianic or salvific figure. Within these categories, I will attempt to examine the texts in relative chronological order. So, for example, the *Psalms of Solomon*, which most likely date to the first century B.C., will be treated before the *Testaments of the Twelve Patriarchs*, which most scholars consider to be later, at least in their present form. Josephus and Philo, neither of whom presents an eschatological conception of the Spirit, will be discussed last and only briefly as a counterexample to the other texts.

Jubilees: Restoration, Adoption, and Spirit

Most likely written around the middle of the second century B.C., the book of *Jubilees* presents a retelling of the biblical story from creation in Genesis 1 to the institution of the Passover in Exodus 12.[3] *Jubilees* portrays the account as something revealed to Moses by the angel of the presence during his forty days on Mount Sinai (Exod 24:18) and offers a number of intriguing expansions and abbreviations of the different stories in Genesis and Exodus, about which much could be said. Most important for the present study is the theme of exile or curse and the way in which the text describes the solution to the problem of the curse by means of the creation of a new spirit for the Israelites.

A number of the themes associated with the Spirit found in the OT prophetic texts considered in chapter two, as well as language from Deuteronomy, appear in the first chapter of *Jubilees*.[4] The book begins with a description of a revelation given to Moses on Mount Sinai, not only giving him the Law, but also predicting Israel's transgression and eventual return. The book describes what God revealed to Moses following a forty-seven day period on the mountain: "[T]he Lord showed him what (had happened) beforehand as

---

[3] For a brief but helpful discussion of the date of the document, as well as bibliography and other introductory issues, see James C. VanderKam, *The Book of Jubilees* (Guides to Apocrypha and Pseudepigrapha; Sheffield: Sheffield Academic, 2001).

[4] For a brief discussion of Deuteronomic language in Jubilees 1, see Rodney Alan Werline, *Penitential Prayer in Second Temple Judaism: The Development of a Religious Institution* (Early Judaism and Its Literature 13; Atlanta: Scholars, 1998), 110-13; see also Daniel J. Harrington, "Interpreting Israel's History: The *Testament of Moses* as a Rewriting of Deut 31-34," in *Studies on the Testament of Moses* (ed. G. W. E. Nickelsburg; SBLSCS 4; Cambridge: Society of Biblical Literature, 1973), 59-70, esp. 61-62.

well as what was to come." (*Jub.* 1:4).[5] A similar description of the revelation as "what is first and what is last and what is to come" appears toward the end of the first chapter (*Jub.* 1:26), thus marking off the prologue and framework within which one ought to read the work. Inside this inclusio the writer focuses on Israel's transgression against the Law and the nation's eventual restoration. This description of Israel's fall and restoration is significant in that it often draws on a number of the texts considered above, particularly Deuteronomy and Ezekiel, as well as some of the key themes that appear in those books.

Immediately following the instruction to Moses to write down the revelation that he is about to receive, the Lord tells him that Israel will transgress the covenant, bringing down judgment upon the nation. In his description of this transgression, the writer draws on the language of Deuteronomy 30, noting, "So it will be that *when all of these things befall them* they will recognize that I have been more faithful than they in all their judgments and in all their actions" (*Jub.* 1:6, emphasis mine; cf. Deut 30:1). The language of Deuteronomy continues to appear in the next section, which describes in greater detail how the people of Israel will forsake their God and therefore suffer punishment. Again the Lord predicts the rebelliousness of Israel, drawing on language from Deuteronomy 30 and 31:[6]

> Now you write this entire message which I am telling you today, because I know their defiance and stubbornness (cf. Deut 31:27) even before I bring them into the land which I promised by oath to Abraham, Isaac, and Jacob (cf. Deut 30:20): 'To your posterity I will give the land which flows with milk and honey'. When they eat and are full, they will turn to foreign gods – to ones which will not save them from any of their afflictions (cf. Deut 31:20). (*Jub.* 1:7-8)

Just as Deuteronomy itself writes from the perspective of an inevitable turning away on the part of Israel, *Jubilees* picks up the theme, "predicting" the transgression that leads to the unleashing of the curses on the people. In addition to the language from Deuteronomy 30 and 31, the book also uses language and imagery reminiscent of Deuteronomy 28. The Israelites will serve other gods who become an affliction to them (*Jub.* 1:9) and as a result they will fall into the hands of their enemies (*Jub.* 1:10).[7]

Most intriguing in light of the analysis of Deuteronomy given in chapter two above is where the author locates the source of the error for the Israelites, as well as the prescription for restoration and renewal. Following a description of the Israelites' abandonment of the sanctuary God prepared for them, *Jubilees* asserts that they will build altars to idols, reflecting the condition of

---

[5] All translations are taken from James C. VanderKam, trans., *The Book of Jubilees* (CSCO 511; Paris: Aedibus E. Peeters, 1989), with modifications as discussed in n. 8 below.

[6] See again Harrington, "Interpreting Israel's History," 61-62.

[7] Cf. the description of the curses in Deut 28:15-68, esp. vv. 25, 36.

their hearts: "They will sacrifice their children to the demons and to every product (conceived by) their erring hearts" (*Jub.* 1:11, modified).[8] Just as Deuteronomy and several of the Prophets locate the root of Israel's problem in the heart, so also *Jubilees* portrays the heart as the source of their transgression and the organ that God must fix in order for them to follow his commandments.[9] This theme of the heart recurs four more times after *Jub.* 1:11, but not before the writer presents the climax of the curses.

As in Deuteronomy 28, for *Jubilees* the final result of Israel's sins is the scattering of the tribes of Israel from the land. Following a description of God's sending of the prophets to rebuke Israel, God tells Moses, "I will deliver them into the control of the nations for captivity for *booty*, and for being devoured. I will remove them from the land and disperse them among the nations" (*Jub.* 1:13, original emphasis; cf. Deut 28:64). As we saw in chapter two, the scattering of Israel appears both as an inevitable threat in Deuteronomy and as one of the major problems that Ezekiel addresses in his oracles.

With v. 15 *Jubilees* begins to describe the restoration of Israel after its sin and scattering among the nations. Once again the writer emphasizes the necessity of conversion of the heart, drawing on the language of the Shema: "After this they will return to me from among the nations with all their hearts, all their souls, and all their strength" (*Jub.* 1:15, modified).[10] Although the book uses the common combination of heart, soul, and strength, the emphasis remains primarily on the heart, as one can see both from the description of their sin as a "work of the error of their heart" (*Jub.* 1:11, modified) and from Moses' plea for mercy, which we will discuss presently. Before turning to this plea, though, we must highlight a number of important themes that appear in the first description of Israel's repentance and restoration.

First, the repentance of the Israelites will result in the re-gathering of the nation from its exile. *Jubilees* uses language that we have already seen in several of the oracles of Ezekiel: "Then I will gather them from among all the nations" (*Jub.* 1:15; cf. Ezek 11:17; 36:24). Second, in addition to the assurance of restoration to the land, *Jubilees* also promises some of the eschatological conditions that appear in Isaiah: "I will rightly disclose to them abundant peace. I will transform them into a righteous plant with all my heart and

---

[8] In personal communication, VanderKam informs me that he consistently translates the Ethiopic *lebb* as "mind" because that is what it and its Hebrew cognate mean. Because most standard translations of the OT still render the Hebrew לב as "heart," I have modified his translation by consistently using "heart" for "mind" in order to make the connection with the OT texts considered in chapter two more apparent, while acknowledging that in both the OT and *Jubilees* "mind" may be a better translation. Ultimately, the translation makes little difference since the connection between the texts is based on the Hebrew and Ethiopic cognates, not a translation.

[9] See the excursus on the "heart" on pp. 35-38 above.

[10] Cf. Deut 6:4-5; see also Deut 4:29-30; 30:2.

with all my soul" (*Jub.* 1:15b-16a; cf. Isa 32:17). Finally, drawing again on the language of Deuteronomy, Jubilees reassures the Israelites that "They will become a blessing, not a curse" (*Jub.* 1:16; the "blessing" and "curse" motif is ubiquitous in Deuteronomy, esp. chapters 27-30). Although we cannot say for certain at what point in the eschatological framework the writer of *Jubilees* saw himself, the fact that the work takes up the language of the prophets and still portrays it as a reality yet to be accomplished suggests an as yet unfulfilled expectation on the part of the writer.[11] Most significant for the present study is the way in which the writer describes the restoration of Israel.

Following God's prediction of the scattering and eventual restoration of the nation, Moses makes a plea on behalf of his people: "Lord my God, do not allow your people and your heritage to go along in the error of their hearts, and do not deliver them into the control of the nations with the result that they rule over them lest they make them sin against you" (*Jub.* 1:19, modified). Like Deuteronomy and Ezekiel, *Jubilees* highlights the significance of the heart as the source of Israel's sins and the resultant curses. The book also makes a prescription for correcting their waywardness similar to that of Ezekiel. Moses pleads, "May your mercy, Lord, be lifted over your people. Create for them a *just spirit*" (*Jub.* 1:20, emphasis mine). The closest parallel to this language in the OT is to be found in Psalm 51:10, "Create in me a clean heart, O God, and put a new spirit within me." Indeed, a little further on in *Jubilees*, the conjunction of heart and spirit reappears, as Moses requests, "Create for them a pure heart and a holy spirit" (*Jub.* 1:21, modified). Given the broader context with its emphasis on the scattering of Israel and the restoration of the nation, the text may well also envision the restoration promised by Ezekiel, which also emphasizes the renewal of heart and spirit. Indeed, the fact that the writer describes God's act of delivering the Israelites from the Egyptians suggests that he expects a similar deed to rescue Israel after its exile.

After Moses' plea *Jubilees* describes another prediction by God of the future restoration of Israel, not surprisingly drawing on Deuteronomic language and the motif of the heart. After Israel's turning away, the writer asserts, "After this they will return to me in a fully upright manner and with all (their) hearts and all (their) souls. I will cut away the foreskins of their hearts and the foreskins of their descendants' hearts" (*Jub.* 1:23a, modified). As we saw

---

[11] For a similar judgment, see Michael A. Knibb, "The Exile in the Literature of the Intertestamental Period," *HeyJ* 17 (1976): 253-72, esp. 266-67. Cf. also Werline, *Penitential Prayer in Second Temple Judaism*, 113: "These omissions [of reference to Israel's return from Babylon and the rebuilding of the Temple] are tantamount to a total dismissal of the era of restoration and the early Second Temple period as an era of sin. Consequently, the author believes that the fulfillment of Deuteronomy 4 and 30 refers to his own time and not to the Persian period."

in chapter two, one of the primary remedies for Israel's sin in Deuteronomy is the "circumcision of the heart," which we see reappear here in *Jubilees*.[12] More interesting for the present study, though, is the way in which the author develops the motif and connects it with the prophetic promise of the gift of a new spirit. Immediately following the prediction of the circumcision of the heart, Jubilees states, "I will create a holy spirit for them and will purify them in order that they may not turn away from me from that time forever" (*Jub.* 1:23b).[13] The healing of Israel's heart, then, comes about through the creation of a new spirit for the people, not unlike Ezekiel's promise that the Israelites would receive a "new spirit" (Ezek 18:31; 36:26). This creation of a "holy spirit" most likely refers to the purification of the human spirit or a change in the disposition of the recipients to obey the commandments since nowhere in the passage does the author refer to God's own Spirit.[14]

The creation of this "holy spirit" for Israel not only empowers Israel to follow the commandments of the Lord, however. In addition, it reestablishes a covenantal relationship between God and the people. After God makes the promise of the spirit, he goes on to declare, "I will become their father and they will become my children. All of them will be called children of the living God. Every angel and every spirit will know them. They will know that they are my children and that I am their father in a just and proper way and that I love them" (*Jub.* 1:24b-25). Here *Jubilees* brings together a number of prophetic and Deuteronomic themes: the creation of a holy spirit for the people heals their hardness of heart and makes them children of God once again.

---

[12] See Deut 10:16 and 30:6, as well as the discussion of these texts in the excursus in chapter two above. Deuteronomy is not the only OT text to locate Israel's problem in the heart – the theme also appears in Jer 31:31-34; 32:37-41; Ezek 11:19-20; 36:26-28. In each of these texts, the new or transformed heart that God gives to the people is connected with restoration to the land. See chapter two above for further discussion of the latter two texts from Ezekiel.

[13] For a brief discussion of the relationship between this verse and Ezekiel 36 that sees Jubilees as referring to the renewal of the human spirit rather than the outpouring of God's own Spirit, see Johannes Sijko Vos, *Traditionsgeschichtliche Untersuchungen zur paulinischen Pneumatologie* (Assen: Van Gorcum, 1973), 51. See also Friedrich Wilhelm Horn, *Das Angeld des Geistes: Studien zur paulinischen Pneumatologie* (Göttingen: Vandenhoeck & Ruprecht, 1992), 39, 146. The question of the relationship between the renewal of the human spirit and the giving of God's own Spirit is a difficult one, as one can see in various texts of the OT. As we saw in chapter two, Ezekiel 11 and 18 speak of God creating a new spirit for the Israelites, but Ezekiel 36, 37 and 39 refer to God putting his own Spirit within them. Similarly, the penitential Psalm 51 follows the petition for God to "put a new and right spirit within me" (Ps 51:10b) with the request that God "not take [his] holy spirit from me" (Ps 51:11b).

[14] See Barry D. Smith, "The Spirit of Holiness as Eschatological Principle of Obedience in Second-Temple Judaism," in *Christian Beginnings and the Dead Sea Scrolls* (ed. Craig A. Evans and John J. Collins; Acadia Studies in Bible and Theology; Grand Rapids: Baker Academic, 2006), 76-78.

The phrase "children of the living God" most likely alludes to Hosea 1:10 (2:1 [LXX]), which also describes Israel's restoration after a period of sin and punishment.[15] Moreover, the writer describes this restored relationship in terms of God's "just" or "righteous" way with Israel, a concept which we saw frequently associated with the Spirit in Isaiah and which plays a central role in Galatians.

Jubilees, then, presents a fascinating development of the prophetic motifs discussed in chapter two above. In answer to the question with which we closed the first chapter, *Jubilees*, like Deuteronomy before it, envisions the scattering of Israel as an accomplished fact and holds out hope for the reversal of Israel's misfortunes. Although the text does not clearly refer to God's own Spirit, it nevertheless describes the remedy for Israel's sin as the giving of a spirit that in several ways resembles the prophecies of Ezekiel, especially Ezekiel 11 and 18. This new spirit repairs the Israelites' hardened heart and brings them into a filial relationship of righteousness with the God of Israel. Based on the language of "creating" a new spirit, it seems most likely that *Jubilees* picks up the theme of renewal or purification of the human spirit more than endowment with the divine Spirit. Nevertheless, the context still suggests that it connects this renewal with the restoration of Israel.

The Treatise on the Two Spirits: The Spirits of Truth and Injustice

Although it does not offer an explicit description of an eschatological restoration of Israel, the *Treatise on the Two Spirits*, a subsection of the Community Rule found at Qumran cave one, shares a number of similarities with *Jubilees*.[16] Like *Jubilees*, the *Treatise* seems to envision God creating a spirit for the sons of light rather than imparting a portion of his own Spirit. Moreover, the document describes the reward for the children of light in terms that evoke the creation, and indeed the basic anthropology of the text alludes to the crea-

---

[15] Cf. James M. Scott, *Adoption as Sons of God: An Exegetical Investigation into the Background of ΥΙΟΘΕΣΙΑ in the Pauline Corpus* (WUNT 2/48; Tübingen: Mohr/Siebeck, 1992), 109.

[16] On the eschatological nature of the document, see Karl Georg Kuhn, "New Light on Temptation, Sin, and Flesh in the New Testament," in *The Scrolls and the New Testament* (ed. Krister Stendahl; New York: Harper and Brothers, 1957), 94-113; on the ambiguity of the word "spirit" in the treatise, see Marco Treves, "The Two Spirits of the Rule of the Community," *RevQ* 3 (1961): 449-52; P. Wernberg-Møller, "A Reconsideration of the Two Spirits in the Rule of the Community (1 Q Serek III,13 - IV, 26)," *RevQ* 3 (1961): 413-41. For more recent discussion, see Robert P. Menzies, *The Development of Early Christian Pneumatology with special reference to Luke-Acts* (JSNTSup 54; Sheffield: Sheffield Academic, 1991), 78-80 and Mark Adam Elliott, *The Survivors of Israel: A Reconsideration of the Theology of Pre-Christian Judaism* (Grand Rapids: Eerdmans, 2000), 400-08.

tion story. Finally, the text associates the spirit of truth with several concepts we have already seen both in the OT prophetic corpus and in *Jubilees*.

The treatise begins in the middle of column III of 1QS. Following a description of the requirements for entry into the community, the text sets forth the Instructor's duty to teach the sons of light concerning the two spirits: "The Instructor should instruct and teach all the sons of light about the nature of all the sons of man, concerning all the ranks of their spirits, in accordance with their signs, concerning their deeds in their generations, and concerning the visitation of their punishments and the times of their reward" (1QS 3.13-15a).[17] After setting forth God's sovereignty over all of creation, the treatise resumes its treatment of the two spirits: "[God] created man to rule the world and placed within him two spirits so that he would walk with them until the moment of his visitation: they are the spirits of truth and of deceit" (1QS 3.17b-19a). Note how the treatise refers to humankind's original task of governing the world given at creation. As we shall see, this appeal to creation finds a parallel in the description of the reward for those who follow the spirit of truth and of the renewal at the "appointed end." It is also worth noting that in the immediate context the rule describes those who follow this spirit as "sons of justice (צדק)" (1QS 3.22). As we have seen both in several of the OT prophetic texts and in *Jubilees*, the treatise connects following the right spirit with righteousness.[18]

In addition to the connection between the spirit and righteousness, the treatise also emphasizes the theme of a right heart and the action of this spirit in enabling Israelites to obey God's laws. Beginning in Col. IV, the *Treatise* states, "These are their paths in the world *to enlighten the heart of man* (להאיר בלבב איש), straighten out in front of him all the paths of true justice (דרכי צדק אמת), establish *in his heart* (לבבו) respect for the precepts of God" (1QS 4.2-3a, emphasis mine). Like *Jubilees*, the *Treatise* also locates the problem of human sinfulness in the heart and prescribes a following of the right spirit to restore humanity to the ways of God. It is difficult to determine whether the document refers to God's Spirit or to the human spirit. On the one hand, most

---

[17] Unless otherwise noted, translations are taken from Florentino García Martínez and Eibert J. C. Tigchelaar, *The Dead Sea Scrolls: Study Edition* (2 vols.; Grand Rapids: Eerdmans, 1997-98).

[18] For arguments for and against readings of the spirits as cosmic powers, see Arthur E. Sekki, *The Meaning of Ruah at Qumran* (SBLDS 110; Atlanta: Scholars, 1989), 196-200. Sekki sides with the majority of scholars who treat the spirits as "simply spiritual dispositions and nothing more." The question is a complex and much-debated one that we cannot settle here. As noted above in n. 13, the blurring of lines between the renewing of the human spirit and the gift of God's own Spirit occurs already in the OT (e.g. Ps 51:10-11). As I will argue below, the allusions to Isaiah 11 suggest at least some relationship between the spirits of the just ones and God's own Spirit.

of the references to "spirit" in the treatise seem to refer to the human spirit.[19] On the other hand, the text draws on language from Isaiah 11 to describe this spirit: "a spirit of meekness, of patience, generous compassion, eternal goodness, intelligence, understanding, potent wisdom which trusts in all the deeds of God and depends on his abundant mercy" (1QS 4.3-4). The language of understanding, intelligence, and wisdom reflects the description of the Spirit in Isaiah 11:2: "The Spirit of the LORD shall rest on him, the spirit of *wisdom* and *understanding*, the spirit of *counsel* and *might*, the spirit of *knowledge* and the fear of the LORD" (emphasis mine).[20] These parallels suggest that the *Treatise* describes an eschatological reality, and the continuing exposition of the behavior of those who follow the spirit of truth confirms this reading in at least two ways.

First, as we have already seen, the *Treatise* expects the spirit to enable the sons of truth to obey God's commands from the heart: the paths of the sons of truth are to "establish in [humankind's] heart respect for the precepts of God" (1QS 4.2b-3a). Those who walk by this spirit, then, will obey God's laws with a steadfast heart; the failure to do this is exactly what Deuteronomy proposes as the source of Israel's problem.[21]

A second indication that the *Treatise* envisions an eschatological change is the language of "reward" with respect to those who follow the spirit of truth combined with imagery typically associated with eschatological abundance in the prophets: "These are the foundations of the spirit of the sons of truth (in) the world. And the reward of all those who walk in it will be healing, plentiful peace in a long life, fruitful offspring with everlasting blessings, eternal enjoyment with endless life, and a crown of glory with majestic raiment in eternal light" (1QS 4.6b-7). The language of "eternal enjoyment with endless life" points to an eschatological reward, and a number of features of this description deserve comment. First, once again we see a text that connects walking by the spirit with eschatological peace. Second, the *Treatise* promises fruitfulness, another eschatological sign of restoration found in the prophetic texts, especially Isaiah.[22] Third, as in *Jubilees*, the spirit brings about a blessing for those who follow it. Fourth and finally, in addition to this blessing those who walk in the spirit are promised a "crown of glory," which, as a

---

[19] So Sekki, *The Meaning of Ruaḥ at Qumran*, 193-219.

[20] See G. K. Beale, "The Old Testament Background of Paul's Reference to 'the Fruit of the Spirit' in Galatians 5:22," *BBR* 15 (2005): 1-38, esp. 17-18, who provides a helpful chart indicating the shared language between Isa 11:1-2 and 1QS 4.3-4, 6-7b. If the treatise intentionally alludes to Isaiah 11, then it is possible that it makes a connection between the "Spirit of the LORD" (Isa 11:2) and the renewal of the human spirit it describes, though Beale may go too far in asserting that this spirit must be God's own Spirit.

[21] See pp. 35-38 above.

[22] See again Beale, "The Old Testament Background of Paul's Reference to 'the Fruit of the Spirit' in Galatians 5:22," 18-19.

consideration of the latter part of Col. IV shows, points to a restoration of those who follow the spirit of truth that parallels the first creation.

The latter portion of 1QS 4 refers to a "visitation," which the *Treatise* describes as an eschatological time of judgment. Having described the two spirits and their continual struggle against one another, the text states, "God, in the mysteries of his knowledge and in the wisdom of his glory, has determined an end to the existence of injustice and on the appointed time of the visitation he will obliterate it for ever [*sic*]" (1QS 4.18b-19a). In contrast to the destruction of injustice "truth shall rise up forever (in) the world" (1QS 4.19). At this eschatological judgment the *Treatise* envisions a purification of the sons of truth by means of a spirit that is designated as the spirit of "holiness" and "truth." The cleansing of abomination and injustice brought about by the spirit is to lead the upright to "knowledge of the Most High" (1QS 4.22). The final description of the cleansing of the upright combines traditional restoration language with creation imagery: "For those God has chosen *for an everlasting Covenant* [*sic*] *and to them shall belong all the glory of Adam*" (1QS 4.24, emphasis mine). The action of the spirit of truth, then, is to bring about for those who follow it an everlasting covenant envisioned as a new creation, a point reaffirmed toward the end of Col. IV. Once again the *Treatise* highlights the dividedness of the human heart, noting that "Until now the spirits of truth and injustice feud in the heart of man" (1QS 4.23). A little later in 4.25 the rule affirms that the struggle is to continue until the "appointed end and the new creation" (קץ נחרצה ועשות חדשה). The reference to the "glory of Adam" earlier in the column, combined with the use of the same word (עשות) found in the summary of YHWH's creation in Gen 2:4, suggests an allusion to creation. The ultimate vindication of the sons of truth, which the spirit of truth brings about, involves a new creation.

As with *Jubilees*, we have seen a number of significant themes in the *Treatise on the Two Spirits*, though the prophetic texts alluded to are fewer in number and no explicit references to the curses of Deuteronomy appear. The *Treatise* nevertheless associates the spirit of truth with several characteristics of eschatological renewal: those who follow it are children of righteousness, the spirit of truth will set their hearts aright in order that they might be enabled to serve God in accordance with his will, and they can expect to receive peace and a blessing in fruitfulness. Moreover, the children of righteousness will participate in an everlasting covenant prepared for them by God and they will receive the glory of Adam in an act of new creation.

The Words of the Luminaries: Holy Spirit, Blessing, and Restoration

Like much of the Qumran literature, the liturgical fragments known as the *Words of the Luminaries* (4Q504) provide far less information than one would hope.[23] The fragments consist of a series of prayers to be recited on each of the days of the week. The prayers for the first six days draw on and retell the biblical history of Israel, while the prayers for the Sabbath praise God for the wonders of creation.[24] Of particular interest for the present study are fragments 1 and 2 of 4Q504, which present part of the prayer for the sixth day of the week. The text describes Israel's apostasy and punishment, followed by God's mercy and restoration of Israel to the land.[25]

Despite the fragmentary nature of the text, enough remains to show the prominence of the covenantal curses in the prayer. The text continually evokes language from Leviticus and Deuteronomy in describing Israel's sins and petitioning God for forgiveness. Beginning in Col. II of fragments 1 and 2, the prayer acknowledges the sins of Israel's fathers and appeals to God's mercy, recalling how, though he was angry with them, he chose not to destroy the people (4Q504 frgs. 1-2 col. 2.8b-10).[26] The prayer continues to appeal to God to turn back his "anger" (אף) and "rage" (חמה) from the people (4Q504 2.11; cf. Lev 26:28; Deut 29:22, 27). Recalling the mighty deeds that God did for Israel, in 2.13 the prayer suggests that these acts were intended to bring

---

[23] For a brief introduction to the fragments, see James R. Davila, *Liturgical Works* (Eerdmans Commentaries on the Dead Sea Scrolls; Grand Rapids: Eerdmans, 2000), 239-42; more extensively Daniel K. Falk, *Daily, Sabbath, and Festival Prayers in the Dead Sea Scrolls* (STDJ 27; Leiden: Brill, 1998), 59-94. Although the arguments are not conclusive either way, most scholars consider the document to be non-sectarian in origin due to paleographical evidence (which suggests a date around 150 B.C., at the very outer limits of the formation of the community), as well as to a positive description of Israel as a whole lacking explicitly sectarian language and imagery. For the latter point, see Hermann Lichtenberger, *Studien zum Menschenbild in Texten der Qumrangemeinde* (SUNT 15; Göttingen: Vandenhoeck & Ruprecht, 1980), 93 n. 1; for a fuller discussion of the issues involved, see Esther G. Chazon, "Is *Divrei Ha-Me'orot* a Sectarian Prayer?" in *The Dead Sea Scrolls: Forty Years of Research* (ed. Devorah Dimant and Uriel Rappaport; STDJ 10; Leiden: Brill, 1992), 3-17. Unless otherwise noted, translations and text are taken from García Martínez and Tigchelaar, *The Dead Sea Scrolls: Study Edition*.

[24] Davila, *Liturgical Works*, 241; see also Esther G. Chazon, "*4QDibham*: Liturgy or Literature?" *RevQ* 59 (1992): 447-55.

[25] Werline, *Penitential Prayer in Second Temple Judaism*, 148, argues that the positive reference to the return from the Babylonian exile may support a non-sectarian origin for the text or at least an origin prior to the sectarian turn in the community (if such a turn occurred).

[26] Werline (*Penitential Prayer in Second Temple Judaism*, 149) notes that line 8 reflects the description of God's anger at Mount Horeb in Deut 9:8, though the prayer emphasizes God's mercy.

about repentance so that God's Law might be planted "in our hearts" (בלבנו), most likely drawing on Jeremiah 31:33.²⁷ This implantation of the Law will result in a healing of conditions that came about as a result of the curses of Deuteronomy, namely, "madness" (שגעון), "blindness" (עורון), and "confusion" (תמהון) (4Q504 2.14; cf. Deut 28:27-28).²⁸ The prayer describes these curses as the result of Israel's iniquities (4Q504 2.15).

After a break in the fragments, Col. III again takes up the petition, appealing to Israel's status as God's "son" and describing the chastisements that the people received as fatherly correction. Drawing once more on the language of Deuteronomy, the prayer describes Israel's "evil illnesses, famine, thirst, plague, the sword," the result of breaking the covenant (4Q504 frgs. 1-2 3.8; cf. Deut 28:48, 59).²⁹ The text continually refers to God's "rage" (חמה), "wrath" (חרון), and "anger" (אף), terms associated with the punishments described in Deuteronomy (cf. Deut 29:19-29; 32:22-24). Moreover, the prayer asserts that these curses were spoken of by "Moses... and your servants the prophets" (4Q504 3.12-13). Israel's plight results from the people's disobedience to the covenant.

Following a description of God's love for and election of the people and several damaged lines, in the fifth column the prayer resumes its description of Israel's sin, possibly drawing on language from Deuteronomy: "they served a foreign god in their land. And their land, too, became a wasteland, due to their enemies" (4Q504 frgs. 1-2 col. 5.3-4).³⁰ The prayer then describes how God poured out his wrath upon Israel because of its disobedience, resulting in its expulsion from the land. Nevertheless, God does not abandon the "seed of Jacob" because of the covenant (4Q504 5.6b-8). From the perspective of the prayer, God remembered the covenant (4Q504 5.9b) he made when he brought Israel out of Egypt and showed them mercy in the places to which they were exiled. Barry Smith has recently suggested that this description of Israel's punishment and return in the prayer alludes to Leviticus 26:³¹

4Q504 frgs. 1-2 5.9b-12a	Lev 26:45
ותזכור ברית׳׳ אשר הוצאתנו לעיני הגוים ולוא עזבתנו בגוים יתחון את ישראל בכול [ה]ארצות אשר הדחתם שמהעמכה	וזכרתי להם ברית ראשנים אשר הוצאתי־אתם מארץ מצרים לעיני הגוים להיות להם לאלהים אני יהוה

---

²⁷ Cf. Werline, *Penitential Prayer in Second Temple Judaism*, 150.
²⁸ Ibid., 149.
²⁹ Ibid., 151 n. 422.
³⁰ Davila (*Liturgical Works*, 261) notes that the phrase "foreign god" occurs only in Deut 32:12 and Ps 81:10.
³¹ Translation and chart from Smith, "The Spirit of Holiness as Eschatological Principle," 80 n. 17.

| And you remembered your covenant, so that you brought us out before the eyes of the nations. And you did not leave us among the nations. And you were gracious to your people Israel in all lands to which you exiled them. | And I will remember for them the covenant of the ancestors whom I brought out of the land of Egypt before the eyes of the nations to be God to them. I am Yahweh. |

The implication seems to be that Israel had suffered under the curse of Leviticus until God chose to redeem the nation. The prayer also appears to draw upon language from Deuteronomy in describing the change that God effects in the Israelites:[32]

4Q504 5.11b-15	Deut 30:1-2
ולוא עזבתנו בגוים ותחון את עמכה ישראל בכול [ה]ארצות אשר הדחתם שמה להשיב אל לבבם לשוב עודך ולשמוע בקולכה [כ]כול אשר צויתה ביד מושה עבדכה	והיה כי־יבאו עליך כל־הדברים האלה הברכה והקללה אשר נתתי לפניך והשבת אל־לבבך בכל־הגוים אשר הדיחך יהוה אלהיך שמה ושבת עד־יהוה אלהיך ושמעת בקלו ככל אשר־אנכי מצוך היום אתה ובניך בכל־לבבך ובכל־נפשך

| And [you] did not desert us amongst the nations. You did favours to your people Israel among all [the] countries amongst whom you had exiled them, to place upon their heart to turn to you and to listen to your voice [in agreement] with all that You commanded through the hand of Moses, your servant. | So it shall be when all of these things have come upon you, the blessing and the curse which I have set before you, and you call them to mind in all nations where the LORD your God has banished you, ² and you return to the LORD your God and obey Him with all your heart and soul according to all that I command you today, you and your sons… |

God's answer to Israel's situation under the curse is to bring the nation back from exile and to put it into their hearts to obey the commandments.

Most important for the present study is the means by which God brings about this change in the Israelites. Not surprisingly in light of the material that we have surveyed thus far, the prayer connects this obedience in the heart with an outpouring of God's own Spirit: "[Fo]r you have poured your holy Spirit (רוח קודשכה) upon us, [to be]stow your blessings to us" (4Q504 5.15-16). The connection between the "blessings" and the "Spirit" most likely alludes to Isa 44:3, the only verse in the OT to associate these two together.[33] Like some of the texts we considered in chapter two above, 4Q504 interprets the outpouring of God's Spirit as a sign of Israel's redemption from the curses of

---

[32] See Davila, *Liturgical Works*, 262.

[33] See ibid. Davila's distinction between the "holy spirit" in this text and "God's spirit" in Isa 44:3 is a bit puzzling, however, given that the prayer speaks of "your (i.e. God's) spirit of holiness." Sekki (*The Meaning of Ruah at Qumran*, 79 n. 27) also recognizes the connection with Isa 44:3: "Note that the speakers in 4Q504, 1-2 view themselves as the eschatological generation of Isa 44:3." See also Smith, "Spirit of Holiness," 81 n. 18.

the Law. Additionally, the Spirit is meant to empower Israel to seek God in their time of "distress" (צר; 4Q504 5.17, 18).

The final column of the prayer continues the confession of Israel's sins and acknowledges the justice of God (4Q504 frgs. 1-2 6.4). The petitioner accepts the trials the Lord has given Israel and at the same time asks for release from these trials and an end to God's anger. Drawing on language from Leviticus, the prayer seeks atonement: "with humble heart we seek atonement for our iniquities and the iniquity of our fathers, for our rebellion and continued hostility to you" (4Q504 6.6-7; cf. Lev 26:40-41).[34] Though portions of the column are missing, the prayer seems also to request a return of the people of Israel from the various lands to which they have been exiled (4Q504 6.13-15), though certainty is impossible because of the pieces missing in the column. Nevertheless, such a reconstruction would be in keeping with what we have seen throughout the prayer, as exile was one of the primary curses of the covenant (cf. Deut 30:1, 15-20).

The *Words of the Luminaries*, then, is perhaps the clearest example we have seen thus far in the Second Temple literature to associate the gift of God's own Spirit with the restoration of Israel after its punishment for failure to keep the covenant. The prayer describes Israel's plight as a result of the communal failure to obey the covenant. Embedded within this communal prayer of penitence, the text draws on Isaiah 44 to present Israel's reception of God's holy Spirit and of the blessing as the sign that God has redeemed Israel from the curses of Leviticus and Deuteronomy in the past and as a petition for a future redemption from the curses.

4Q521: The Messiah, the Spirit, and the Eternal Kingdom

Though also fragmentary in nature, the so-called *Messianic Apocalypse* (4Q521) presents a fascinating conjunction of eschatological themes and serves as a fitting transition to the next set of texts in that it mentions a Messiah but still speaks of the outpouring of the Spirit as a communal phenomenon. Moreover, the text combines language drawn from Isaiah with references to creation/new creation.

The beginning of Col. II of the second fragment states "[for the heav]ens and the earth will listen to his anointed one (למשיחו), [and all] that is in them will not turn away from the precepts of the holy ones" (4Q521 frag. 2, 2.1-2).[35] The fragment next presents an offer of encounter with the Lord for those who "hope in their heart" (המיחלים בלבם) (4Q521 frag. 2, 2.4) and then pro-

---

[34] Werline, *Penitential Prayer in Second Temple Judaism*, 156.
[35] Unless otherwise noted, translations are taken from García Martínez and Tigchelaar, *The Dead Sea Scrolls: Study Edition*.

ceeds to describe this encounter: "For the Lord will consider the pious, and call the righteous (צדיקים) by name, and his Spirit will hover (רוחו תרחף) upon the poor, and he will renew the faithful (ואמונים יחליף) with his strength. For he will honour the pious upon the throne of an eternal kingdom (מלכות עד)" (2.5-7, modified). The text draws together themes from Isaiah and from the creation account with the words "poor" (ענוים; cf. Isa 61:1), "renew in his strength" (יחליף בכחו; cf. Isa 40:31-41:1) and "his Spirit will hover" (רוחו תרחף; cf. Gen 1:2).[36] Based on the creation imagery used to describe the hovering of the Spirit and the broader context of Second Isaiah, the eschatological vision presented by the fragment describes the deliverance that God will bring about in terms of a new creation.[37] In addition, as another aspect of this eschatological vision God will give the pious an eternal kingdom at the time of the Messiah. The fragment continues to describe the healing that will accompany this kingdom, using language similar to that of Isaiah 35. A little later the text makes a claim referring possibly to "fruit" (פר). As we saw in some of the prophetic texts in chapter two, fruit is a symbol often associated both with eschatological restoration and with the gift of the Spirit. Unfortunately this reference occurs in a damaged portion of the text, but the possibility that the hymn somehow associates the other clear eschatological themes with the bearing of fruit remains intriguing nevertheless. In line 11, the fragment continues to describe the awesome deeds that the Lord will do at that time: "and the Lord will perform marvelous acts such as have not existed" (ונכבדות שלוא היו יעשה אדני).[38] Among these great deeds are healing, raising of the dead, and the proclamation of good news to the poor (ענוים יבשר). The reference to giving life to the dead adds further support to a new creation interpretation of the text as a whole and fills out the meaning of this imagery.

We see, then, that despite its fragmentary nature, the *Messianic Apocalypse* displays a number of features with significant implications for the present study. In one brief text we find reference to an anointed one, the Spirit, new

---

[36] So Émile Puech, "Un apocalypse messianique (4Q521)," *RevQ* 60 (1992): 475-522; Craig A. Evans, "Jesus and the Dead Sea Scrolls from Qumran Cave 4," in *Eschatology, Messianism, and the Dead Sea Scrolls* (ed. Craig A. Evans and Peter W. Flint; Studies in the Dead Sea Scrolls and Related Literature; Grand Rapids: Eerdmans, 1997), 96-97; Stephen T. Um, *The Theme of Temple Christology in John's Gospel* (Library of New Testament Studies 312; Sheffield: T & T Clark, 2006), 114.

[37] Cf. Um, *The Theme of Temple Christology in John's Gospel*, 114: "The verb רחף in Gen. 1.2 characterizes the powerful activity of the Spirit during creation. The Qumran writer uses the theme of this creative power as the basis for God's ushering in the new creation by the agency of the eschatological Messiah (line 12)."

[38] Prof. Loren Stuckenbruck suggests to me that the reference to "things that were not" might also point to an act of creation on the part of God, thus reinforcing the creation motifs sounded earlier in the fragment with the reference to the hovering of the Spirit over the poor. Prof. Joel Marcus also suggests a similarity to Rom 4:17.

creation, Isaianic promises of healing and restoration, possibly the bearing of eschatological fruit, the raising of the dead and the preaching of good news to the poor. One only wishes more had been preserved, but even what little we do have proves significant for the question of the Spirit and eschatology.

The *Psalms of Solomon*: The Messiah's Spirit and the Restoration

Some of the texts we have considered thus far have been less explicit or have not at all mentioned the restoration of Israel. When we turn to the *Psalms of Solomon*, we find a much more explicit emphasis on national restoration, one that envisions the advent of a messianic ruler who is endowed with the holy Spirit. The *Psalms* present a particularly interesting study in that they draw heavily on several eschatological passages from the book of Isaiah. Moreover, like several of the texts we have already examined, a number of common themes appear in conjunction with the spirit and the restoration: righteousness, blessing, mercy, and judgment.[39]

Psalms of Solomon 17 divides into two parts, a historical portion (*Pss. Sol.* 17:1-20) describing a change in power in Israel and an eschatological portion (*Pss. Sol.* 17:21-46) entreating God for vindication, tied together by the common thread of the kingship of God and the kingship of David.[40] For the purposes of this study, the historical section does not concern us; we shall concentrate on the eschatological section with its plea for a Davidic ruler described in Isaianic terms. In *Pss. Sol.* 17:21, the psalmist begins to plead, "See, Lord, and raise up for them their king, the son of David, to rule over your servant Israel (ἐπὶ Ἰσραὴλ παῖδα σου)."[41] This king is to receive strength to perform a number of acts of judgment on the unrighteous rulers

---

[39] For general introductory issues, see R. B. Wright, "Psalms of Solomon," in *The Old Testament Pseudepigrapha* (2 vols.; ABRL; ed. James H. Charlesworth; New York: Doubleday, 1983-85), 2.639-70, from which all translations are taken. See also the helpful treatment of Gene L. Davenport, "The Anointed of the Lord in the Psalms of Solomon," in *Ideal Figures in Ancient Judaism: Profiles and Paradigms* (ed. John J. Collins and George W. E. Nickelsburg; SBLSCS 12; Chico: Scholars, 1980), 67-92. With the exception of Davenport and Max-Alain Chevallier, *L'Esprit et le Messie dans le bas-judaïsme et le Nouveau Testament* (Paris: Presses Universitaires de France, 1958), very little literature makes more than passing reference to the role of the Spirit in the *Psalms of Solomon*. See, e.g., Menzies, *Development of Early Christian Pneumatology*, 72-73 and Horn, *Das Angeld des Geistes*, 37.

[40] Cf. the similar division in Davenport, "The Anointed of the Lord in the Psalms of Solomon," 69-70.

[41] Given the other allusions to Isaiah, the use of the phrase "servant Israel" most likely draws on the same book, which describes Israel as God's servant at 42:1-4; 49:1-6; 50:4-9 and 52:13-53:12. For an extensive discussion of language from Isaiah 11 and 49 appearing in this psalm, see Chevallier, *L'Esprit et le Messie*, 12-16; see also Davenport, "The Anointed of the Lord in the Psalms of Solomon," 72-73.

who have oppressed Israel and on the sinners who have collaborated with them, driving the latter out "from the inheritance" (ἀπὸ κληρονομίας; *Pss. Sol.* 17:23).

Following the account of the judgment that the king is to bring about, the psalm then describes the positive aspect of his rule: "He will gather a holy people whom he will lead in righteousness (ἐν δικαιοσύνῃ); and he will judge the tribes of the people that have been made holy by the Lord their God" (*Pss. Sol.* 17:26). In addition to leading the people into righteousness, the messianic ruler establishes a covenantal relationship with them, one based upon their status as children of God: "For he shall know them [*sic*] that they are all children of their God (υἱοὶ θεοῦ αὐτῶν)" (*Pss. Sol.* 17:27b). The language referring to knowledge and a filial relationship suggests the prophet Hosea's notion of covenant, as seen in Hos 4:1: "Hear the word of the LORD, O people of Israel; for the LORD has an indictment against the inhabitants of the land. There is no faithfulness or loyalty, and no knowledge of God in the land."[42] As in several of the OT prophetic texts considered above, the restoration of Israel entails a reaffirmation of Israel's status as children of God.[43] Furthermore, the restoration envisions a distribution of the tribes on the land: "He will distribute them upon the land according to their tribes; the alien and the foreigner shall no longer live near them" (*Pss. Sol.* 17:28).

Beginning in v. 30 a shift takes place which, though surprising at first glance, makes sense if the psalm relies heavily upon Isaiah. As we just saw, earlier in the text the psalmist promises that the Israelites will no longer live among foreigners, but in v. 30 the psalm begins to describe an ingathering of Gentiles as well as Israelites: "And he will have gentile nations (λαοὺς ἐθνῶν) serving him under his yoke, and he will glorify the Lord in (a place) prominent (above) the whole earth" (*Pss. Sol.* 17:30a). This ingathering of the Gentiles serves as a means to bring back the scattered tribes: "And he will purge Jerusalem (and make it) holy as it was even from the beginning, (for) nations to come from the ends of the earth to see his glory, *to bring as gifts her children who had been driven out*" (*Pss. Sol.* 17:30b-31a, emphasis mine). According to the psalmist, then, God will use the Gentiles to bring about the restoration of Israel, and then both of the groups will be ruled by the Messiah: "And he will be a righteous king (βασιλεὺς δίκαιος) over them, taught by God" (*Pss. Sol.* 17:32a).[44]

---

[42] Cf. also Hos 11:1.

[43] See the discussion of Isaiah 63 on pp. 26-28 above.

[44] Cf. Davenport, "The Anointed of the Lord in the Psalms of Solomon," 75: "The king will rule not only the reconstituted people of God, but the entire earth (vss. 29-35a). Thus, his empire will exceed even that of his ancestor David." Davenport rightly goes on to argue that the object of the king's reign includes the Gentiles. Although the contexts are different, there is some affinity between the psalmist's association of the ingathering of the Gentiles and the restoration of Israel and Paul's argument in Romans 11 that the Gentile mission was

A little later in the psalm, the psalmist reiterates the inclusion of other nations under the messiah's rule: "He shall be compassionate to all the nations (πάντα τὰ ἔθνη) (who) reverently (stand) before him. He will strike the earth with the word of his mouth forever; he will bless the Lord's people with wisdom and happiness. And he himself (will be) free from sin, (in order) to rule a great people" (*Pss. Sol.* 17:34b-36a). Shortly following this description of the messiah's rule over a great people, the psalmist explains how the king receives the ability to accomplish such a task: "And he will not weaken in his days, (relying) upon his God, for God made him powerful in the holy spirit and wise in the counsel of understanding, with strength and righteousness" (*Pss. Sol.* 17:37).[45] The language of counsel, wisdom, and understanding used to describe the spirit that empowers the king draws on Isaiah 11, an important text, as we have seen, concerning the restoration of Israel.[46] The bestowal of the Spirit upon the ruler leads to the restoration of the nation: "This is the beauty of the king of Israel which God knew, to raise him over the house of Israel to discipline it" (*Pss. Sol.* 17:42).

Shortly after this statement, the psalm recounts the king's judgment, which seems to encompass more than Israel alone: "He will judge the peoples in the assemblies, the *tribes* of the sanctified. His words will be as the words of the holy ones, among sanctified *peoples*" (*Pss. Sol.* 17:43, emphasis mine). Although the word "tribes" most likely refers to Israel, the reference to "sanctified peoples" (λαῶν ἡγιασμένων) may suggest that the psalm expects other (Gentile) peoples to be subject to the king, particularly given the statement in *Pss. Sol.* 17:34 that the king will have compassion on all the nations (πάντα τὰ ἔθνη) that stand reverently before him. The concluding verses reiterate the hope of Israel at the time of this messianic rule: "Blessed are those born in those days to see the good fortune of Israel which God will bring to pass in the assembly of the tribes. May God dispatch his mercy to Israel; may he deliver us from the pollution of profane enemies" (*Pss. Sol.* 17:44-45). The coming of the messianic king, who is anointed with the Spirit described in Isaiah 11, will bring about the restoration of Israel, a restoration that incorporates all nations that stand before him in reverence and results in holiness and righteousness for the whole earth.[47]

---

meant to bring Israel to its restoration. The difference is that, whereas Paul envisions the Gentiles provoking Israel to jealousy and bringing them into Christ, the psalmist envisions the Gentiles literally bringing Israel back to the Promised Land.

[45] The Greek of 17:37b runs as follows: ὁ θεὸς κατειργάσατο αὐτὸν δυνατὸν ἐν πνεύματι ἁγίῳ καὶ σοφὸν ἐν βουλῇ συνέσεως μετὰ ἰσχύος καὶ δικαιοσύνης. Cf. Isa 11:2a (LXX): καὶ ἀναπαύσεται ἐπ' αὐτὸν πνεῦμα τοῦ θεοῦ, πνεῦμα σοφίας καὶ συνέσεως, πνεῦμα βουλῆς καὶ ἰσχύος.

[46] Strangely Chevallier (*L'Esprit et le Messie*, 15) seems to miss this connection.

[47] Cf. the summary of Davenport, "The Anointed of the Lord in the Psalms of Solomon," 85-86.

More explicitly than any other text that we have considered thus far, the *Psalms of Solomon* closely associates the Spirit with a messianic figure. The messiah's endowment with the Spirit allows him to judge righteously and to help bring about the restoration of Israel, even gathering in the Gentiles under his just rule.

The *Similitudes of Enoch*: The Lord of the Spirits and the Spirit of the Elect One

With the *Similitudes of Enoch*, we begin to consider texts whose dating is a matter of much dispute. The dating of this part of the Enoch corpus has been highly contested, with some scholars proposing dates as early as the second c. B.C. and others dates as late as the third c. A.D.[48] Therefore, we must be careful not to put too much weight on a document that may date to NT or post-NT times. Nevertheless, as with the *Testaments of the Twelve Patriarchs*, which we will discuss below, the *Similitudes* at least point to early Christian interpretations of the Spirit and probably preserve some pre-Christian Jewish traditions.

Although the Spirit does not play a prominent role in the *Similitudes*, the few places where it does appear present an interesting conjunction of themes similar to some of the ones that we have already seen.[49] Throughout the book as a whole the author discusses the "righteous," and so it is not surprising when we see the Spirit associated with the righteous and specifically with righteousness. Moreover, the Spirit appears in texts that discuss an eschatological judgment and seem also to suggest an expectation of a new creation.

The first reference to the Spirit occurs in *1 En.* 49:3; in order to get a better grasp of the Spirit's role, it will be helpful to look at the broader context of the verse, which extends at least from *1 En.* 47 to *1 En.* 51 and is part of the second major parable (*1 En.* 45-57). As Max-Alain Chevallier has suggested, the primary subject of this parable is not so much the messianic Son of Man as the last judgment.[50] The phrase "in those days" punctuates this section,

---

[48] See Christopher L. Mearns, "Dating the Similitudes of Enoch," *NTS* 25 (1979): 360-69; Michael A. Knibb, "The Date of the Parables of Enoch: A Critical Review," *NTS* 25 (1979): 345-59; J. T. Milik, ed., *The Books of Enoch: Aramaic Fragments of Qumrân Cave 4* (Oxford: Clarendon, 1976), 89-98.

[49] For an all-too brief discussion of the Spirit and the Messiah in the *Similitudes*, see Menzies, *Development of Early Christian Pneumatology*, 70-73. As with the *Psalms of Solomon*, there is a similar lacuna in discussion of the Spirit in the *Similitudes*.

[50] Chevallier, *L'Esprit et le Messie*, 18: "Contrairement à ce qu'on dit souvent, la 2ᵉ parabole n'a pas pour *sujet* la présentation du Messie-Fils de l'homme; le sujet est le jugement final, et c'est comme auteur du jugement final que le Fils de l'homme est au centre de toute la vision."

connecting the chapters in the context of the coming of the Son of Man and eschatological judgment. *1 En.* 47 first describes the prayers of the righteous ascending to heaven and requesting justice for the martyrs from the Lord of the Spirits. *1 En.* 48 then begins to describe the source of righteousness: "In that place I saw the spring of righteousness, and it was inexhaustible, and many springs of wisdom surrounded it. And all the thirsty drank from them and were filled with wisdom; and their dwelling places were with the righteous and the holy and the chosen" (*1 En.* 48:1).[51] The text then proceeds to describe the Son of Man's preexistence and role as judge. Although the writer does not explicitly connect the giving of the Spirit with the heart, the text does make mention of the problem of the heart: "He [i.e. the Son of Man] will be a staff for the righteous, that they may lean on him and not fall; and he will be the light of the nations, and he will be a hope for those who grieve in their hearts" (*1 En.* 48:4). The chapter continues to describe the wisdom that the Lord of the Spirits reveals to the righteous ones and the judgment that he will execute on their oppressors. Toward the end of the chapter, evoking imagery from Psalm 2, the writer blames the judgment of the wicked on their denial of the Lord of the Spirits and his Messiah (*1 En.* 48:10).

1 Enoch 49 then describes the power of the Chosen One, which the text once again associates with righteousness: "For he is mighty in all the secrets of righteousness; and unrighteousness will vanish like a shadow, and will have no place to stand" (*1 En.* 49:2). Following a description of the Chosen One's glory as he stands before the Lord of the Spirits comes the reference to the spirit: "And in him dwell the *spirit of wisdom and the spirit of insight*, and *the spirit of instruction and might*, and the spirit of those who have fallen asleep in righteousness" (*1 En.* 49:3, emphasis mine). The language of the passage seems to evoke the promise found in Isaiah 11: "The Spirit of the LORD shall rest on him, the *spirit of wisdom and understanding*, the spirit of counsel and *might*, the spirit of *knowledge* and of fear of the LORD" (Isa 11:2, emphasis mine).[52] As we saw in chapter two, this promise of the outpouring of the Spirit on a righteous ruler also occurs in a context that envisions an eschatological renewal of all creation. It should come as no surprise, then, that following the Enochic description of the Spirit within the Chosen One the text discusses the eschatological judgment, a resurrection of the dead, and a new creation.

Continuing the refrain "in those days," chapter 50 promises glory and honor for the righteous ones and judgment for the sinners. *1 En.* 51 then describes the glory that the righteous will receive, namely, resurrection: "In

---

[51] All translations are taken from George W. E. Nickelsburg and James C. VanderKam, *1 Enoch: A New Translation* (Minneapolis: Fortress, 2004).

[52] On the Isaianic imagery throughout *1 En.* 49, cf. Chevallier, *L'Esprit et le Messie*, 19-20 and, more briefly, Menzies, *Development of Early Christian Pneumatology*, 72.

those days, the earth will restore what has been entrusted to it, and Sheol will restore what it has received, and destruction will restore what it owes. For in those days, my Chosen One will arise, and choose the righteous and the holy from among them, for the day on which they will be saved has drawn near" (*1 En.* 51:1-2). The glory and joy of this resurrection extends not only to the righteous ones, however, but also to all the earth: "And the earth shall rejoice, *and the righteous will dwell upon it and the chosen will go upon it*" (*1 En.* 51:5, emphasis mine).

Although the mention of the Spirit within this section is brief, its position highlights its significance. *1 Enoch* 47-51 follows a chiastic pattern, punctuated by the refrain "in those days" referring to the eschatological time of judgment:

A *1 Enoch* 47: Cry of the suffering righteous for vindication

    B *1 Enoch* 48: Judgment by the Son of Man

        C *1 Enoch* 49: Power and wisdom of the Chosen One for judgment

    B' *1 Enoch* 50: Judgment by the Son of Man

A' *1 Enoch* 51: Promise of resurrection for the righteous

Located at the center of this chiastic structure, the Chosen One's endowment with the Spirit takes on added significance. Additionally, as we have seen in a few other texts both in the OT Prophets and in other Second Temple literature, the *Similitudes* draw a connection between the Spirit and righteousness and also connect these to an anointed figure.

The *Similitudes* contain two more brief references to the Spirit, both appearing once again in a context of eschatological judgment. The first occurs in *1 Enoch* 61, which begins with a description of angels measuring an area that the text refers to as the "garden of life" (*1 En.* 61:12). The measurements are carried out for the sake of the "righteous… so that they may rely on the name of the Lord of the Spirits forever and ever" (*1 En.* 61:3). Furthermore, the text describes these measurements in a way that suggests resurrection/restoration:

And these are the measures that will be given to faith, and they will strengthen righteousness. And these measures will reveal all the secrets of the depths of the earth, and those who were destroyed by the desert, and those who were devoured by beasts, and those who were devoured by the fish of the sea; *so that they may return and rely on the day of the Chosen One*, for no one will be destroyed in the presence of the Lord of the Spirits, and no one can be destroyed. (*1 En.* 61:4-5, emphasis mine)

Thus, those who die but belong to the Chosen One will be brought back, presumably to embodied life, as the description of the various spheres found later in the chapter suggests.

Before considering the end of the chapter, though, we should examine the two references to the Spirit. Shortly after the word of hope for those who have been destroyed by the various forces of nature, the text presents an eschatological occasion of worship, one that the author connects with the Spirit: "And him, at the beginning, they blessed with their voice, and they exalted and glorified him with wisdom; and they were wise in speech and in the *spirit of life*" (*1 En.* 61:7, emphasis mine). The Chosen One is then said to execute judgment on the holy ones, which leads to further worship of the Lord of the Spirits. Intriguingly, the text describes the work of the Spirit in those who worship the name of the Lord of the Spirits, describing what appears to be an impartation of the Spirit ascribed to the Chosen One in *1 En.* 49 upon those who belong to him: "And they will raise one voice, and they will bless and glorify and exalt with the spirit of faith and with the spirit of wisdom, and with (a spirit of) long suffering and with the spirit of mercy, and with the spirit of judgment and peace and with the spirit of goodness" (*1 En.* 61:11).

Although this passage shares only one characteristic with the earlier description of the Spirit of the Chosen One (wisdom), in both cases the Spirit is in some way associated with the Chosen One, and the repetition in both passages of the term "spirit" with a variety of attributes evokes the description of the Spirit of the Lord in Isaiah 11. Equally significant is the way the author uses the same language to describe the Chosen One and those who worship him (the "chosen" – *1 En.* 61:12), suggesting that there may be some relationship between the Spirit that they receive and the Spirit that the Chosen One receives. In addition, the chosen are said to dwell in "the garden of life," imagery that hearkens back to the Genesis account. This impartation of the Spirit of the Chosen One, then, accompanies a return to the conditions of Paradise. The reference earlier in the text to the return of those who have been devoured (*1 En.* 61:5), however, suggests an expectation of resurrection, especially when read in light of the description of those who worship God toward the end of the chapter: "and all flesh that with great power glorifies and blesses your name forever and ever" (*1 En.* 61:12). The reference to all flesh glorifying forever suggests that this is no simple return to Eden, but rather a new creation.

The final reference to the Spirit appears in *1 En.* 62, once again in a context of judgment and condemnation. In this chapter, which focuses primarily on the retribution of unjust rulers, the Lord of the Spirits sets up his Chosen One for those rulers to see (*1 En.* 62:1). The Lord of the Spirits then takes his seat on the throne of glory, and the text declares, "the spirit of righteousness was poured out upon him [i.e., the Chosen One]" (*1 En.* 62:2). The bestowal of the Spirit upon the Chosen One prepares him for the judgment that he then executes on the sinners and the oppressors. Following a lengthy description of this judgment, in which the Son of Man is said to sit upon the glorious throne, the *Similitudes* then depict the positive aspect of the Son of Man's enthronement for the righteous and chosen: "And the righteous and chosen will be saved on that day" (*1 En.* 62:13). Then, using language reminiscent of *1 Enoch* 61, the text describes a resurrection and new creation for the righteous, giving content to the declaration of salvation: "And the Lord of Spirits will abide over them, and with that son of man they will eat, and they will lie down and rise up for ever and ever. And the righteous and the chosen will have arisen from the earth, and have ceased to cast down their faces, and have put on the garment of glory. And this will be your garment, the garment of life from the Lord of Spirits; and your garments will not wear out, and your glory will not fade in the presence of the Lord of Spirits" (*1 En.* 62:15b-16a). The language of life, similar to that used in *1 Enoch* 61 to refer to the "garden of life," suggests that the righteous will be saved for a new creation, and once again the author connects this salvation with the bestowal of the Spirit of righteousness on the Chosen One/Son of Man (*1 En.* 62:2).

Like the *Psalms of Solomon*, the *Similitudes* closely associate the Spirit with a messianic figure, the Chosen One/Son of Man. On the other hand, the *Similitudes* do not seem to expect a national restoration of Israel. Nevertheless, they, too, draw on language from Isaiah 11 to describe the Spirit that is poured out on the Chosen One (and perhaps by extension on the chosen/righteous). Moreover, the few references to the gift of the Spirit accompany a hope for some kind of return to Eden or a "new creation."

The *Testament of Judah*: The Spirit of Sonship and Resurrection

When we turn to the *Testaments of the Twelve Patriarchs*, we face both promise and a challenge: promise, because in these texts we find some of the most interesting developments of the connection between the outpouring of the Spirit and the restoration of Israel; a challenge, because the key passages in the *Testament of Judah* and the *Testament of Levi* seem clearly to betray Christian influence.[53] We will return to the question of Christian elements in the texts in due course. Assuming for the moment that the texts do reflect Christian influence, they are nevertheless *Jewish* Christian documents and may preserve aspects of early Jewish eschatology available to Paul and his readers. Furthermore, they are also useful in that they show how some early

---

[53] For a recent introduction to the *Testaments* with bibliography, see Robert A. Kugler, *The Testaments of the Twelve Patriarchs* (Guides to Apocrypha and Pseudepigrapha; Sheffield: Sheffield Academic, 2001). For a fuller treatment of the document's textual tradition, see Jarl Henning Ulrichsen, *Die Grundschrift der Testamente der Zwölf Patriarchen: Eine Untersuchung zu Umfang, Inhalt und Eigenart der ursprünglichen Schrift* (Acta Universitatis Upsaliensis, Historia Religionum 10; Uppsala: Almqvist & Wiksell, 1991).

Christians may have interpreted the early Christian experience of the Spirit in ways similar to Paul's, whether dependently or independently. Before turning to the question of interpolations, let us first consider the text in its present form.

Testament of Judah 23-25 presents a number of fascinating images connected to the outpouring of the Spirit and the restoration of Israel. In chapter 23, the patriarch Judah laments over the sins that his descendants will perpetrate after his death: "My grief is great, my children, on account of the licentiousness and witchcraft and idolatry that you practice contrary to the kingship, following ventriloquists [*sic*], omen dispensers, and demons of deceit" (*T. Jud.* 23:1).[54] As a result of these sins, Judah warns his descendants that the God of Israel will punish them, and the list of plagues that are to come upon them are reminiscent of the curses of Deuteronomy 28:

> In response to this the Lord will bring you famine and plague, death and the sword, punishment by a siege, scattering by enemies like dogs, the scorn of friends, destruction and putrefaction of your eyes, slaughter of infants, the plunder of your sustenance, the rape of your possessions, consumption of God's sanctuary by fire, a desolate land, and yourselves enslaved by the Gentiles. (*T. Jud.* 23:3)

Many of these punishments reflect the language of Deuteronomy 28: "famine" (cf. Deut 28:48), "death" (cf. Deut 28:21), "enemies" (cf. Deut 28:25, 31, 48, 53, 55, 57, 68), "destruction" (cf. the verb in Deut 28:20, 22, 24, 45, 51); "the sword" (cf. Deut 28:22), "putrefaction of eyes" (cf. Deut 28:32; see also Lev 26:16), desolation of the land (cf. Deut 28:24,51; see also Lev 26:34-35), and slavery among the Gentiles (cf. Deut 28:32, 36, 49-51, 64).

It is not only the list of punishments that reflects the language of Deuteronomy, but also the description of the initiation of the restoration. The patriarch notes that all of these punishments will come upon his descendants "until you return to the Lord in integrity of heart (ἐπιστρέψητε πρὸς κύριον ἐν τελείᾳ καρδίᾳ), penitent and living according to all the Lord's commands (ἐν πάσαις ταῖς ἐντολαῖς τοῦ θεοῦ)" (*T. Jud.* 23:4).[55] As we have seen in Deuteronomy and in the prophets, particularly Ezekiel, the restoration of Israel is expected to come about through a transformation of the heart. Also like Eze-

---

[54] All translations for the *Testament of Judah* and the *Testament of Levi* are taken from Howard Clark Kee, "Testaments of the Twelve Patriarchs," in *The Old Testament Pseudepigrapha* (2 vols.; ABRL; ed. James H. Charlesworth; New York: Doubleday, 1983-85), 1.775-828.

[55] I have modified Kee's translation to reflect the reading τοῦ θεοῦ in Marinus de Jonge's critical edition. See M. de Jonge et al., *The Testaments of the Twelve Patriarchs: A Critical Edition of the Greek Text* (PVTG 1,2; Leiden: Brill, 1978), 76. Cf. Deut 30:10: "If you hearken to the voice of the Lord your God to keep and do all his commandments (πάσας τὰς ἐντολὰς αὐτοῦ)... if you turn to the Lord your God with your whole heart (ἐὰν ἐπιστραφῇς ἐπὶ κύριον τὸν θεόν σου ἐξ ὅλης τῆς καρδίας σου) and with your whole soul."

kiel, the *Testament of Judah* in its present form describes this transformation in part through the outpouring of the Spirit.

Testament of Judah 24 describes in greater detail the restoration promised at the end of chapter 23, portraying the advent of a messianic king anointed with the Spirit. The first verse notes that the coming of the messianic king will bring peace: "And after this there shall arise for you a Star from Jacob in peace" (*T. Jud.* 24:1). Furthermore, the coming king has the characteristic of righteousness, one that he brings with him: "And a man shall arise from my posterity like the Sun of *righteousness*, walking with the sons of men in gentleness and *righteousness*, and in him will be found no sin" (*T. Jud.* 24:1, emphasis mine). It is after this description that the passage most suspected of Christian interpolation and at the same time most intriguing for the present study appears: "And the heavens will be opened upon him to pour out the Spirit as a blessing of the Holy Father. And he will pour the Spirit of grace on you. And you shall be sons in truth, and you will walk in his first and final decrees" (*T. Jud.* 24:2-3, modified). Most commentators take the description of the opening up of the heavens as a clear Christian interpolation – although there is some precedent for the imagery of the heavens opening in Isa 64:1– reflecting the accounts of Jesus' baptism in the Synoptic Gospels, a question to which we will return presently. For the moment, let us focus rather on the cluster of images found in this passage. The outpouring of the Spirit appears in a context that emphasizes righteousness and peace. Moreover, the equation of the Spirit with a blessing in *T. Jud.* 24:2 most likely draws upon Isaiah 44:

And the heavens will be opened upon him to pour out the Spirit as a blessing (πνεύματος εὐλογίαν) of the Holy Father. And he will pour out the Spirit of grace on you. And you shall be sons in truth, and you will walk in his first and final decrees. (*T. Jud.* 24:2-3, modified)

I will place my Spirit (τὸ πνεῦμά μου) upon your seed, and my blessings (τὰς εὐλογίας μου) upon your children. (Isa 44:3 [LXX])

The similarity in language is unmistakable, if not exact.[56] Both texts join the outpouring of the Spirit with the blessing upon Israel's children.[57] The primary difference lies in the fact that in Isaiah it is God who pours out the Spirit upon the Israelites, whereas in the *Testament* it is the "Star of Jacob." Nevertheless, the ultimate source of the Spirit, as one can see in *T. Jud.* 24:2, is the Holy Father.

In addition to the connection between the Spirit and the blessing, the *Testament of Judah* also asserts that those who receive the Spirit will be "sons in

---

[56] Others have noted this connection. See Marinus de Jonge, "Christian influence in the Testaments of the Twelve Patriarchs," in *Studies on the Testaments of the Twelve Patriarchs* (ed. Marinus de Jonge; SVTP 3; Leiden: Brill, 1975), 216, following Chevallier, *L'Esprit et le Messie*, 130 n. 2.

[57] In the Isaiah text, this is clear from the preceding context; in the *Testament of Judah*, chapter 25 describes the blessing on Abraham, Isaac, and Jacob and their descendants.

truth" (*T. Jud.* 24:3). Again, the text is not clear whether those who receive the Spirit are to be sons of the messiah or sons of God, but the important point is that the Spirit establishes a filial relationship in those who receive it. Moreover, the advent of the king brings about life for humanity and righteousness for all:

This is the Shoot of God Most High; this is the fountain for the life of humanity. Then he will illumine the scepter of my kingdom, and from your root will arise the Shoot, and through it will arise the rod of righteousness for the nations, to judge and to save all that call on the Lord. (*T. Jud.* 24:4-6)[58]

A number of features in this passage call for comment. First, the text seems to hold out hope not just for Israel, but for all of humanity, as seen in the phrase "fountain for the life of humanity." Second, this righteousness comes about with the eschatological kingdom of the messiah. Third, this passage, which at the beginning draws upon the language of Joel in describing the outpouring of the Spirit (*T. Jud.* 24:2; cf. Joel 2:28-29), later picks up on the imagery of Joel, noting that the rod of righteousness will arise "to judge and to save all that call on the Lord" (cf. Joel 2:32).

After this promise of judgment and salvation, the text begins to describe a restoration of Israel using the language of resurrection: "And after this Abraham, Isaac, and Jacob will be resurrected to life and I and my brothers will be chiefs (wielding) our scepter in Israel" (*T. Jud.* 25:1). Following this statement, the text pronounces a blessing on each of the tribes of Israel, beginning with Levi.[59] After the list of blessings one finds a curious statement: "And you shall be one people of the Lord, with one language" (*T. Jud.* 25:3). The reference to one language perhaps alludes to the account of the scattering of peoples after the destruction of the Tower of Babel, suggesting that the restoration of Israel may include more than only descendants of Israel. The text proceeds to reiterate the promise of resurrection: "And those who died in sorrow shall be raised in joy; and those who died in poverty for the Lord's sake shall be made rich; those who died on account of the Lord shall be wakened to life" (*T. Jud.* 25:4). This restoration results ultimately in the everlasting worship of God by all the nations: "the impious shall mourn and sinners shall weep, but all people shall glorify the Lord forever" (*T. Jud.* 25:5).

The *Testament of Judah* describes both the endowment of a messianic figure with the Spirit and the passing of the Spirit on to a restored Israel. Moreover, this gift of the Spirit draws on prophetic texts such as Joel and Isaiah that highlight the restoration of Israel and appears in a context describ-

---

[58] Note also the affinities with the "root" and "shoot" language in Isa 11:1.

[59] The prominence given to Levi, though not surprising within the context of *T. 12 Patr.*, is surprising if the text is Christian in origin insofar as Levi does not enjoy a prominent position in the writings of the NT.

ing Israel suffering under the curses of Deuteronomy. Finally, the restoration that the *Testament* describes includes resurrection and new creation.

The *Testament of Levi*: Spirit of Holiness and New Creation

Like *Testament of Judah* 24, the eighteenth chapter of the *Testament of Levi* presents both intriguing and problematic material for the question of the Spirit's relation to restoration eschatology – intriguing because it shares the most parallels with some of the NT evidence and brings together several of the themes that we have seen thus far; problematic because of the possibility of Christian influence. Again, for the moment it will be helpful to set aside the latter question and simply look at the passage as it stands.

The chapter begins with a prediction that the priesthood of Israel will lapse, after which "the Lord will raise up a new priest to whom all the words of the Lord will be revealed" (*T. Levi* 18:2). The text goes on to describe this priest with royal imagery, suggesting that this is to be a messianic priesthood, and that the priest is to receive worship from the entire world (*T. Levi* 18:3). Following the account of the worship given to the priest, the passage begins to announce an eschatological reign of peace, drawing substantially on language from Isaiah. The advent of this priest will result in peace over all the earth, and all of creation will rejoice: "The heavens shall greatly rejoice in his days and the earth shall be glad (cf. Isa 44:23); the clouds will be filled with joy and the knowledge of the Lord will be poured out on the earth like the waters of the sea (cf. Isa 11:9)" (*T. Levi* 18:5). The arrival of the priest, then, signals a transformation of the whole of creation.

The text proceeds to describe the bestowal of the Spirit upon the priest in one of the passages most suspected of Christian influence. Once again, the language used comes from Isaiah: "And the Spirit of understanding and sanctification shall rest upon him" (*T. Levi* 18:7, modified). As in *Testament of Judah* 24, the one who receives the Spirit in turn passes it on "to those who are his sons in truth" (*T. Levi* 18:8). One interesting difference between the *Testament of Levi* and the *Testament of Judah* concerns the result of the outpouring of the Spirit. Whereas in the latter text this outpouring leads to the restoration of Israel as a whole, taking note of each of the tribes, in the former the arrival of this new, everlasting priesthood leads to the conversion of nations: "And in his priesthood the nations shall be multiplied in knowledge on the earth, and they shall be illumined by the grace of the Lord, but Israel shall be diminished by her ignorance and darkened by her grief" (*T. Levi* 18:9). Why the beginning of this priesthood should lead to a diminishment of Israel is puzzling and may point to Christian influence, but the inclusion of the nations remains intriguing in light of some of the prophetic texts we considered in chapter two above, as well as the appropriation of the theme in much of the NT literature.

The arrival of the messianic priest also results in the end of sin: "In his priesthood sin shall cease and lawless men shall rest from their evil deeds, and righteous men shall find rest in him" (*T. Levi* 18:9). This end to sin in turn leads to the restoration of creation in its original, Edenic state: "And he shall open the gates of paradise; he shall remove the sword that has threatened since Adam, and he will grant to the saints to eat of the tree of life" (*T. Levi* 18:10-11). The return to paradise is accompanied by the bestowal of the Spirit of holiness and leads to a clothing in righteousness for the saints: "The Spirit of holiness shall be upon them... Then Abraham, Isaac, and Jacob will rejoice, and I shall be glad, and all the saints shall be clothed in righteousness" (*T. Levi* 18:11, 14, modified). The Spirit, then, is connected both with new creation and with the gift of righteousness to the saints. Moreover, the connection between the Spirit and creation suggests that this Spirit is God's own Spirit and is perhaps also connected with resurrection, given the reference to Abraham, Isaac and Jacob rejoicing.

In sum, the *Testament of Levi* develops several of the themes that we have seen in other texts from the Second Temple period: the outpouring of the Spirit on a messianic figure, the renewal of creation, the resurrection of the dead, and the ingathering of the Gentiles. The extreme emphasis on the Gentiles combined with a reference to the diminishment of Israel, however, raises the question of Christian influence, whatever the Jewish origins of the text might be.[60]

Excursus: The Testaments of Judah and Levi: Christian, Jewish, or Admixture?

As already noted a number of times, using the *Testaments of the Twelve Patriarchs* as background to the NT in general is controversial due to the possibility of Christian redaction or even authorship.[61] It is important therefore to reiterate that the argument of the present study does not stand or fall with a decision about the dating of these texts. To be sure, an earlier and non-

---

[60] For a more sanguine approach to Jewish traditions in both the *Testament of Levi* and the *Testament of Judah*, see Anders Hultgård, "The Ideal 'Levite', the Davidic Messiah, and the Saviour Priest in the Testaments of the Twelve Patriarchs," in *Ideal Figures in Ancient Judaism* (ed. George W. E. Nickelsburg and John J. Collins; SBLCS 12; Chico: Scholars, 1980), 93-110.

[61] For an earlier catalog of the various stances taken on Jewish and Christian elements in the *Testament of Judah*, see Jürgen Becker, *Untersuchungen zur Entstehungsgeschichte der Testamente der Zwölf Patriarchen* (AGJU 8; Leiden: Brill, 1970), 319-23.

Christian origin for these texts would broaden the pool of evidence demonstrating the significance of the Spirit in early Jewish restoration eschatology. Nevertheless, even if the texts are Christian, they demonstrate how some early Christians interpreted the outpouring of the Spirit and dovetail with the argument I will make in the following chapters with respect to Galatians. These similarities could be explained in one of two ways. If the *Testaments* are independent of Paul, then they represent a second stream of early Christianity that interpreted the gift of the Spirit in a way similar to Paul. If the *Testaments* depend on Paul, then they may demonstrate an early interpretation of Paul's understanding of the Spirit similar to the one proposed in the present study. Before we reach any such conclusion, however, we must consider whether or not either of the *Testaments* may preserve Jewish tradition.

Due to its significance in the debate, it makes sense to begin with *Testament of Judah* 24.[62] The most outspoken proponent of completely Christian authorship of the *Testaments* has been Marinus de Jonge, who has made arguments to that effect in a number of places.[63] For the purposes of the present discussion I will limit myself to his article "Christian Influence in the Testaments of the Twelve Patriarchs" since the basic argument has remained the same. His case can be summarized briefly. First, although the language in *T. Jud.* 24:1 about the messiah's gentleness, righteousness and lack of sinfulness does not demand Christian influence as an explanation, it would not be surprising if this were the explanation.[64] This first argument, however, is specious. By de Jonge's logic, if the only manuscripts we had of Isaiah 53 dated to the third century A.D., we might be tempted to view it as a Christian text, but we would be wrong. Second, and more significant for the question of Christian influence, though, is the description of the outpouring of the Spirit in *T. Jud.* 24:2-3. A number of expressions in this section remain puzzling: the description of the Spirit of the "holy father," the attribution of the outpouring of the Spirit to the messianic figure, and the sonship of those who receive

---

[62] See de Jonge, "Christian Influence," 213: "The most important passage with regard to the problem of Christian influence is, however, T.Jud. XXIV, 2-3."

[63] The list is vast. In addition to "Christian Influence," see Marinus de Jonge, "Once More: Christian Influence in the Testaments of the Twelve Patriarchs," *NovT* 5 (1962): 311-19, Marinus de Jonge, "The Testaments of the Twelve Patriarchs: Christian and Jewish: A hundred years after Friedrich Schnapp," *NedTT* 39 (1985): 265-75, and most recently Marinus de Jonge, *Pseudepigrapha of the Old Testament as Part of Christian Literature: The Case of the Testaments of the Twelve Patriarchs and the Greek Life of Adam and Eve* (SVTP 18; Leiden/Boston: Brill, 2003), 71-83.

[64] De Jonge, "Christian Influence," 213: "As CHARLES [sic] and PHILONENKO [sic] have pointed out the expressions [in *T. Jud.* 24.1] need not be Christian, because they can be explained with the help of Ps. xlv 5, Zech. ix 9 and Ps. Sol. XVII, 36 – but, of course, it would not be surprising if they were."

the Spirit.[65] Each of these elements, suggests de Jonge, can only make sense as deriving from early Christianity. Fundamental to his argument is the parallel between *Testament of Judah* 24 and *Testament of Levi* 18. The latter passage also describes the descent of the Spirit upon a messianic figure in terms reminiscent of the accounts of Jesus' baptism in the Gospels: the heavens are opened, a fatherly voice is heard, and the Spirit is said to rest upon the figure while he is "in the water." Given the close parallels between *Testament of Levi* 18 and the Synoptic Gospels on the one hand, and between *Testament of Levi* 18 and *Testament of Judah* 24 on the other hand, both texts must reflect Christian influence: "The account in T.Jud. XXIV is shorter than the story in T. Levi but the same elements are found there, and it is *clearly* Christian too."[66]

One must admit the striking nature of the similarities between the *Testament of Levi* and the baptismal accounts of the Synoptic Gospels. On the other hand, as de Jonge himself notes, much of the language in *Testament of Judah* 24 comes directly from the OT (Psalm 45, Zechariah 9, Joel 3, and Numbers 24, among others). The use of these texts does not demand Christian influence.[67] Moreover, the parallels to Jesus' baptism are not as striking as most scholars make them out to be. As James M. Scott has argued, unlike *Testament of Levi* 18, *Testament of Judah* 24 makes no mention of a baptism or even of water.[68] Theoretically, one might argue that the text need not make explicit connections, since Christians would catch the allusion, but in this case, one must ask why the material in *Testament of Levi* 18 is so much more explicit than that in *Testament of Judah* 24. Were there varying expectations of what early Christians would and would not understand? Moreover, the language used to describe the pouring out of the Spirit is different from that of the Synoptics. Whereas the latter texts speak of the Spirit "descending" (καταβαίνω; cf. Mark 1:10 and par.) upon Jesus, the *Testament of Judah* uses the eschatological language of "outpouring" (ἐκχέω) and applies it both to the messianic figure and to Judah's sons, leading to adoption.[69] In addition, *T. Jud.* 24:1-3 flows naturally out of the material that precedes it and into the material that follows. As we saw in chapter two above, the outpouring of the Spirit often appears in contexts of restoration following Israel's suffering under the curse. Scott argues that the appearance of a messianic figure in *Testament of Judah* 24 makes sense in light of a common Sin-Exile-Restoration

---

[65] Ibid., 215.
[66] Ibid. (emphasis added).
[67] As de Jonge himself admits. See n. 64 above.
[68] See Scott, *Adoption as Sons of God*, 110.
[69] Ibid., 111.

pattern, insofar as a number of passages in the OT anticipate a new king in conjunction with the restoration of Israel.[70]

Our discussion of the *Words of the Luminaries* lends further support to Scott's case.[71] As we have seen, the prayer for the sixth day of the week follows a pattern in which Israel sins by going after foreign gods, God punishes the Israelites by scattering them among the nations, and then brings them back and restores them to the land. Most significantly, the prayer describes the return by drawing on the same language from Isa 44:3 that seems also to underlie the description in *Testament of Judah* 24. The most significant difference between the Qumran text and the *Testament of Judah* is the appearance of a messianic figure in the latter. The *Testament of Judah* may also envision an inclusion of the Gentiles, but the imagery used to describe this comes straight from the OT.[72] Apart from these differences, both texts follow a similar pattern of Israel's sin, punishment, and restoration accompanied with the outpouring of the blessing and the Spirit upon the people.

Turning to *Testament of Levi* 18, one must admit that the parallels with the Synoptic Gospels are stronger and more obvious.[73] The reference to the messianic figure in the water, the resting of the Spirit upon this figure, and the heavenly voice all have much clearer parallels to the NT descriptions of Jesus' baptism than does *Testament of Judah* 24. More significantly, in addition to the more obvious character of the similarities between the *Testament of Levi* and the Gospels, the points of commonality have no clear precedent in the OT, unlike the allegedly Christian elements in *Testament of Judah* 24. Whereas the imagery in the latter text can be explained purely from a combination of messianic and eschatological texts from the OT, the parallels in the *Testament of Levi* almost certainly derive from the baptismal accounts, though the possibility cannot be ruled out that the phrase "in the water" is the only Christian interpolation in an otherwise Jewish passage.[74]

Much more could be said about both of these texts. The question of whether the Armenian or the Greek textual tradition better represents the original version of the *Testaments* remains open. Moreover, none of these

---

[70] Ibid., 112, referring to Amos 9:11-15; Ezek 34:11-24; 37:15-28.

[71] See pp. 52-55 above.

[72] The language of a "rod of righteousness for the nations" most likely comes from Isaiah 11. See H. W. Hollander and M. de Jonge, *The Testaments of the Twelve Patriarchs: A Commentary* (SVTP 8; Leiden: Brill, 1985), 228.

[73] On these similarities see again de Jonge, "Christian Influence," 216-19; Chevallier, *L'Esprit et le Messie*, 129: "La parenté du texte de T. Lévi avec les récits du baptême de Jésus est manifeste." See also Scott, *Adoption as Sons of God*, 111 n. 234: "On the other hand, the parallel passage in TLevi 18 explicitly mentions the Spirit as resting upon the Levitic [sic] deliverer 'in the water' (v. 7)."

[74] So, apparently, Kee, "Testaments of the Twelve Patriarchs," 795 n. c. See also Hultgård, "The 'Ideal Levite,'" 104-07.

arguments conclusively shows either that *Testament of Levi* 18 is completely Christian in composition or that *Testament of Judah* 24 has no Christian influence. The purpose of this excursus is simply to demonstrate that the arguments for Christian composition of the latter text are not as strong as is often supposed, and that *Testament of Judah* 24 very likely preserves earlier Jewish tradition.[75] On this latter point even de Jonge seems to concur: "Our conclusion with regard to T. Jud. XXIV must be that this is a Christian passage in which possibly material from the Qumran sect (or a related group) has been incorporated."[76] The parallels between the *Testament of Judah* and 4Q504 indicate that it is not only "possible," but indeed "probable," and therefore we are justified in using the *Testament of Judah* as another witness to pre-Christian Jewish expectations about the Spirit, though we must do so with caution.

Hellenistic Judaism: The Spirit and no Restoration

All of the texts considered thus far represent examples of apocalyptic or sectarian Judaism. When we turn to the writings of Josephus and Philo, we encounter a significantly different picture.[77] Neither of these two writers, each in his own way characteristic of so-called Hellenistic Judaism and sharing much in common with Paul, has anything to say regarding the Spirit and the restoration of Israel. Indeed, in this area the contrast between these two writers and the other texts we have considered could hardly be more striking. Since neither figure connects the Spirit with restoration eschatology, there is no need for an in-depth treatment of the topic. Nevertheless, a brief outline of some aspects of each writer's pneumatology will highlight the difference and provide a contrasting voice to the picture we have seen thus far.

---

[75] Representative of the absolute confidence in the Christian provenance of the *Testament of Judah* is Kugler, *The Testaments of the Twelve Patriarchs*, 60: "But de Jonge (1953:89-90) points out that no matter its earlier forms, the chapter as we have it now is undeniably Christian. De Jonge is certainly correct: 24.1-6 is nothing more or less than a Christian prophecy of Jesus, a redeemer endowed with priestly and royal traits." Ulrichsen, *Die Grundschrift der Testamente der Zwölf Patriarchen*, 174, allows for the remote possibility of earlier Jewish tradition in the text, but only in *T. Jud.* 24:5-6: "Es ist möglich, jedoch höchst unsicher, daß ein bearbeitetes jüdisches Original zugrunde liegt. Es schimmert eventuell in V.5-6 durch, während V.1-4 wie ein original-christlicher Beitrag anmuten."

[76] De Jonge, "Christian Influence," 216.

[77] For a fuller discussion of these two figures, as well as other texts representative of first century Judaism, see John R. Levison, *The Spirit in First Century Judaism* (AGJU 29; Leiden; New York: Brill, 1997).

All of Josephus's references to the Spirit of God appear in the *Jewish Antiquities*.[78] By far the dominant note in his references to the Spirit is an association with prophecy. With one exception, all of the references to the Spirit that Josephus retains from the biblical texts relate to prophecy.[79] Moreover, at certain points in his retelling Josephus emphasizes the association of the Spirit with prophecy in two other ways. On a few occasions he adds references to the Spirit not found in the biblical text. So, for example, in *Ant.* 4.108 and 4.119 he modifies the story of Balaam and his ass to suggest that the Spirit inspires the speech of both Balaam and the ass.[80] In other places Josephus omits explicit references to the Spirit in the text, instead describing those upon whom the Spirit of God comes as prophets.[81] Nowhere does Josephus even hint at the connection between an outpouring of the Spirit upon the people and the restoration of Israel.

Much the same can be said of Philo, who, like Josephus, does not devote considerable attention to the OT Prophets. Space does not permit an extensive discussion of the Alexandrian's multifaceted and complex understanding of the spirit/Spirit.[82] A brief overview of two main themes will show the distance between Philo and the other texts we have considered.[83] Like Josephus, Philo puts a heavy emphasis on the Spirit's role in inspiration, which can be expressed in numerous ways. The divine Spirit empowers human beings for special tasks (*Giants* 23) and makes them in a sense superior to other human beings, if only for a time (*Giants* 24-29). The Spirit enables the mind of the human to make an ascent to wisdom and knowledge (*Planting* 23-25). Often in prophecy the Spirit takes the place of the prophet's mind, which returns when the trance is over (*Heir* 265; *Moses* 1.277; *Spec. Laws* 4.49). The Spirit of God inspires Joseph with wisdom and intelligence (*Joseph* 116-117). God fills Moses with the divine Spirit in order to give the Law (*Decalogue* 175). In addition to inspiration, another important aspect of Philo's understanding

---

[78] For a brief discussion of Josephus's understanding of the Spirit, see Menzies, *Development of Early Christian Pneumatology*, 58-61; for a more extensive discussion, see Levison *The Spirit in First Century Judaism*, *passim*.

[79] Menzies (*Development of Early Christian Pneumatology*, 59 n. 2) lists the following passages with their scriptural counterparts: *Ant.* 1.27 (Gen 1:2); *Ant.* 4.118 (Num 23:7); *Ant.* 6.222 (1 Sam 19:20); *Ant.* 6.223 (1 Sam 19:23); *Ant.* 10.239 (Dan 5:14, MT). The first text, Josephus's retelling of the first creation story in Genesis, is the only one in which the Spirit is in no way related to prophecy.

[80] Menzies, *Development of Early Christian Pneumatology*, 58.

[81] Menzies (*Development of Early Christian Pneumatology*, 60) lists the following passages: *Ant.* 4.165 = Num 27:18; *Ant.* 8.295 = 2 Chron 15:1; *Ant.* 9.10 = 2 Chron 20:14; and *Ant.* 9.168 = 2 Chron 24:20.

[82] See again Levison, *The Spirit in First Century Judaism*, *passim*.

[83] Menzies (*Development of Early Christian Pneumatology*, 63-67) treats the creation of the rational soul and prophetic inspiration as the two most important elements of Philo's pneumatology.

of the divine Spirit is its role in the creation of the soul and the mortality of human beings. God created the rational soul by breathing the divine Spirit into him at creation (*Creation* 134-35; *Alleg. Interp.* 1.33-42; *Spec. Laws* 4.123). Through this action of the Spirit of God the rational soul is fashioned in the divine image (*Planting* 18-20; cf. *Spec. Laws* 1.171). The Spirit does not remain in the human being forever, though. This temporary dwelling of the Spirit in human beings explains their mortality (*Giants* 19-21; 53-56).

Such a brief overview hardly does justice to the depth and richness of Philo's conception of the Spirit, but it must suffice for the purposes of the present work. In the writings of Josephus and Philo, two representative figures of Hellenistic Judaism, a different picture emerges from what we have seen earlier in the present chapter. In their writings one detects no hint of eschatological expectation. Indeed, one might describe an element of Philo's approach as protological or anthropological, focusing in part on the relationship between the divine Spirit and the rational soul at creation. Moreover, even though both figures emphasize the role of the Spirit in the inspiration of prophecy, neither devotes much attention to most of the writings of the OT Prophets, much less the oracles that associate the Spirit with Israel's restoration in Isaiah, Ezekiel, and Joel. Though this survey of Josephus and Philo has largely turned up negative results regarding the theme of restoration eschatology, it has not been for naught. The contrast serves to underscore the significance of restoration themes in the other texts we have considered, as well as the importance of the latter texts for understanding Paul's own interpretation of the outpouring of the Spirit.

Spirit and Restoration Eschatology in the Second Temple Period: Summary

As with the OT prophetic literature, our survey of Second Temple literature has not yielded a monolithic picture of the Spirit and restoration eschatology. Nevertheless, with the exception of Philo and Josephus, these texts take up and develop a number of the themes that appear in the prophetic texts considered in chapter two, as well as addressing the problem of exile described in Deuteronomy. Rather than simply reviewing the results of our survey, it would be helpful at this point to group the texts based on the various themes and images associated with the Spirit's eschatological role, and then to consider briefly some of the OT texts that play a prominent role in these documents.

Eight distinct themes appear in at least two of the documents discussed:

(1) A number of texts connect the Spirit or a spirit with the problem of the heart (*Jubilees*, *Words of the Luminaries*, *Testament of Judah*, *Treatise on the*

Two Spirits). It is the Spirit (of God) or a "new spirit" that enables Israel at last to obey the commandments.

(2) Closely related, several of these texts describe the problem with the heart in relation to disobedience to the Law and the resultant curse that had come upon Israel (*Jubilees, Words of the Luminaries, Testament of Judah*). In other words, as in Ezekiel, the outpouring of the Spirit or the creation of a new spirit performs the task of repairing Israel's heart, one of the key problems described in Deuteronomy.[84]

(3) A few of the documents also relate the gift of the/a spirit to the establishment of a filial relationship (*Jubilees, Psalms of Solomon, Testament of Judah*): it is by means of a new spirit or the Spirit that Israel is given the status of sonship.

(4) The Spirit is often associated with eschatological blessing (*Words of the Luminaries, Testament of Judah, Treatise on the Two Spirits*). The first two texts in particular tie the Spirit and the blessing closely together, both most likely alluding to Isaiah 44.

(5) The Spirit or a spirit appears in texts that describe the eschatological blessings associated with a number of the oracles of Isaiah (*Treatise on the Two Spirits, Messianic Apocalypse*).

(6) Several texts associate the Spirit or a spirit with resurrection and new creation (*Treatise on the Two Spirits, Messianic Apocalypse, Similitudes of Enoch, Testament of Judah, Testament of Levi*).

(7) In a number of texts, the Spirit relates to the status of righteousness (*Jubilees, Testament of Judah, Treatise on the Two Spirits, Psalms of Solomon, Testament of Levi*).

(8) Finally, the Spirit sometimes appears in the context of an ingathering of the Gentiles (*Psalms of Solomon, Testament of Levi*), although this theme is a little more tenuous in that the latter text most likely betrays Christian influence and perhaps authorship.

Each of these eight themes plays a role in Galatians. Perhaps equally significant is the OT material that appears in or influences several of these Second Temple texts. As already noted, the theme of the curse and of a problem with the heart are important in Deuteronomy, and so it is worth noting that *Jubilees*, the *Words of the Luminaries*, and the *Testament of Judah* all in one way or another see the gift of the Spirit as the solution to this double problem. Moreover, both the *Words of the Luminaries* and the *Testament of Judah* appear to allude to Isaiah 44 in their association of the Spirit with the blessing, a significant point when we turn to Gal 3:13-14. Finally, we should note the prominence of Isaiah 11 in a number of these texts (*Treatise on the Two Spirits, Psalms of Solomon, Similitudes of Enoch, Testament of Levi*). Although Paul does not seem to show much interest in Isaiah 11 in Galatians (but cf.

---

[84] Again, see pp. 35-38 above.

Rom 15:12), the pervasiveness of influence of this text adds to the evidence that eschatological expectations about the Spirit were vibrant in some streams of Second Temple Judaism. With these themes and texts in mind, we now turn to Galatians to see what light these trajectories shed on Paul's argument.

Chapter 4

New Exodus and the Spirit in Galatians 3-4: From Death to Life, From Slavery to Sonship

Introduction

In the previous two chapters we have surveyed a significant amount of material from both the OT prophetic corpus and various Jewish texts from the Second Temple period. Although these writings do not by any means present a monolithic picture, they do tend to share a number of important themes connecting the outpouring of a spirit, be it a "new spirit" or God's Spirit, with restoration eschatology.[1] Many of the texts describe this outpouring with imagery and themes taken from creation and the exodus, suggesting that the restoration of Israel will entail a new creation and/or a new exodus. Moreover, much like Deuteronomy, several of the passages we have considered suggest that Israel had come under the curse due to a failure of the heart. Likewise, several of these texts expect that God will bring about the undoing of the curse by pouring a new spirit into the hearts of the Israelites.[2] In addition, several texts describe the restoration of Israel in terms of resurrection, sometimes also with the expectation of the appearance of a messianic figure. Perhaps most importantly for this study, the vast majority of these texts present the giving of the Spirit either explicitly or implicitly as the solution to the curses of Deuteronomy, particularly as they foreshadow the exile and scattering of the tribes of Israel from the land. This emphasis on curse and exile – and on the Spirit as God's solution – will play a significant role, both positively and negatively, in the following examination of Galatians 3-4.

The goal of the present chapter, then, is to relate the material surveyed in chapters two and three to Paul's argument about the Spirit in Galatians 3-4. Τοῦτο μόνον, "this alone," Paul asks in Galatians 3:2: "Did [the Galatians] receive the Spirit through works of the Law, or through the proclamation of

---

[1] Hereafter I will simply refer to the outpouring or giving of "the Spirit" to avoid the cumbersome phrase "the Spirit/a spirit," particularly since Paul has in mind the Spirit of God throughout the letter. Nevertheless, the reader should bear in mind that some of the OT and Second Temple texts do not explicitly refer to God's Spirit.

[2] See the discussions of Ezekiel and Deuteronomy in chapter two and of the Second Temple texts in chapter three above.

faith?"³ As both Lull and Cosgrove have demonstrated, the emphatic nature of this rhetorical question indicates the importance of the answer for Paul's entire argument – the Galatians' reception of the Spirit is the point on which the whole letter hangs.⁴ While the answer that he expects is quite clear – the Galatians received the Spirit through Paul's proclamation – the significance of the Spirit for Paul is less clear. In light of the material in chapters two and three, an exegesis of select passages in Galatians 3 and 4 will show that Paul appeals to the Spirit as a sign of the inauguration of the restoration of Israel promised by the prophets and anticipated by some during the Second Temple period. Paul's interpretation, however, does not simply reproduce these expectations, but rather radically transforms them through the death and resurrection of Jesus. Just as the resurrection of Jesus completes the transformation of the metaphorical language of Ezekiel from a symbol of return from exile into literal, bodily resurrection, so, too, does it complete the transformation of the metaphorical language of the dead bones from a symbol for the exile into a literal reference to death, the true problem with the Law.⁵ So, Paul evinces both similarities to and dissimilarities from his Second Temple Jewish contemporaries and near contemporaries. Like them, he interprets the gift of the Spirit as an indication of the redemption of Israel from the curse of the Law. Unlike them, he interprets this curse as more fundamentally about death than about exile, and restoration as resurrection and new creation rather than a nationalistic return of the tribes to the land of Israel. Moreover, unlike

---

³ Unless otherwise noted, all translations of Galatians are my own.

⁴ David J. Lull, *The Spirit in Galatia: Paul's Interpretation of Pneuma as Divine Power* (SBLDS 49; Ann Arbor: Scholars Press, 1980), 25: "In the letter to the Galatians, Paul gives the term πνεῦμα a prominent position; one might say, the *most* prominent position" (original emphasis); Charles H. Cosgrove, *The Cross and the Spirit: A Study in the Argument and Theology of Galatians* (Macon: Mercer University, 1988), 41-42: "Judging from the words themselves, including the fact that Paul places the phrase 'this alone' (τοῦτο μόνον) in emphatic first position...we have a rhetorical device in Galatians 3:2 that signals a question regarded by the speaker as sufficient to decide the whole matter at hand." Cf. Sam K. Williams, *Galatians* (ANTC; Nashville: Abingdon, 1997), 82: "Throughout the whole section, sometimes quite allusively, Paul continues to connect his argument with the Galatians' experience of the Spirit (3:14, 18, 21, 29; 4:6-7). Indeed, readers of the letter can profitably regard 3:6-4:7 as Paul's effort to convince the Galatians that they can confidently rely on their experience of the Spirit as proof of their new status as 'heirs' because that experience is fully consonant with the divine plan revealed in Scripture." See also Gordon D. Fee, *God's Empowering Presence: The Holy Spirit in the Letters of Paul* (Peabody: Hendrickson, 1994), 382.

⁵ It is worth noting that this shift had already begun in Second Temple Judaism – the book of Daniel, for example, already develops Ezekiel's imagery to refer to actual bodily resurrection. See also the recent discussion in Jon D. Levenson, *Resurrection and the Restoration of Israel: The Ultimate Victory of the God of Life* (New Haven: Yale University, 2006). The key transformation that Paul brought about was the idea that one figure would be raised in the middle of history, and that others would somehow participate both anticipatorily and ultimately in that eschatological life.

the OT and Second Temple texts that combine the outpouring of the Spirit with faithfulness to the statutes and ordinances of the Law (see, e.g. Ezek 36:27), Paul puts forth the experience of the Spirit as the primary reason that the Galatians should *not* submit to circumcision and other ordinances of the Law.[6]

Methodology

Before turning to Galatians 3-4, it would be helpful to set forth some basic methodological principles for the present chapter. With a few exceptions, the main purpose of this chapter is not to argue for specific, conscious allusions on the part of Paul. As I have noted a number of times, the purpose of surveying the material from the Second Temple period was not to suggest that Paul read any or all of these texts, a suggestion that would be impossible to substantiate. Rather, the purpose was to establish one encyclopedia of Second Temple Jewish expectations regarding the Spirit and restoration eschatology that would shed light on Paul's understanding of the Spirit. The evidence surveyed in chapters two and three demonstrates that certain patterns of expectation regarding the outpouring of the Spirit and the restoration of Israel found in the prophetic texts of the OT continued to influence certain streams of Jewish thought in the Second Temple period. Again, I will argue that Paul stands within these streams and that several of the texts discussed in chapters two and three shed light on his arguments without necessitating that he was consciously alluding to any one of them.

This chapter, then, will focus on three sections of Galatians 3-4 and will approach the problem from two angles. I suggest that the "curse of the Law" discussed by Paul in Gal 3:10-14 and his emphasis on the outpouring of the Spirit make sense of one another. The association of the Spirit with the restoration or redemption of Israel suggests that the "curse" refers to the curse that Deuteronomy pronounces on disobedient Israel as a whole for breaking the covenant by transgressing the Law. Conversely, if the curse is that of Deuteronomy, once epitomized for the prophets and some intertestamental literature in terms of exile but now seen by Paul as consisting fundamentally of death,

---

[6] So, rightly, Cosgrove, *The Cross and the Spirit*, 44: "There is only one sort of dispute that the apostle's question in 3:2b could be said to sufficiently settle: a disagreement over the relationship of life in the Spirit to keeping the law. Where the Galatians connect their present experience of the Spirit with their newly adopted practice of law, Paul seeks to reveal the illogic of this by reminding them of the circumstances under which they first received the Spirit." Cf. Heinrich Schlier, *Der Brief an die Galater* (KEK 7; 12th ed.; Göttingen: Vandenhoeck & Ruprecht, 1962), 121: "Die Galater haben den Geist nicht dem Gesetz zu verdanken, sondern der Glaubenspredigt."

then this makes sense of Paul's emphasis on the Spirit and new creation (cf. Gal 6:15) as the overcoming of the curse. The chapter will begin by suggesting an allusion to Isaiah 53 in Gal 3:1-5 that sets a new exodus context for Paul's argument. We will then examine Gal 3:10-14 in detail, as well as the closely related Gal 4:1-7, demonstrating that Paul's remarks about the Spirit make most sense in light of the varied hopes in Second Temple Judaism discussed above.

Galatians 3:1-5: "Who has believed our message?"

Although he does not mention the Spirit in the first two chapters of Galatians, Paul's tone in Gal 3:1-5, as well as the answer he expects to his rhetorical questions, makes it clear that the Spirit plays a crucial role in his understanding of the nature of redemption and the problem with the Law. As several recent commentators have argued, the Galatians' experience of the Spirit is central to Paul's argument.[7] Clearly it is important for Paul that the Galatians received the Spirit through the "message of faith" rather than through "works of the Law," but how does Paul interpret this experience? While the language of the passage does not overlap with any of the Spirit texts we considered in chapters two and three, I suggest that Paul's argument nevertheless depends on and in some ways anticipates the new exodus/new creation language that comes to the forefront later in the chapter. Specifically, Paul's use of the phrase ἐξ ἀκοῆς πίστεως draws upon a number of themes found in Isaiah 53 and its wider context.

Given that the main goal of this study is not to argue for specific allusions, the suggestion that Paul intended to allude to Isaiah at this point in his argument calls for justification, particularly as it seems to hang on such a small phrase as ἐξ ἀκοῆς πίστεως. While at first glance the case appears weak, at least three factors support this proposal. First, there can be no question that Paul gave some thought to Isaiah 53, given that he cites Isa 53:1 in Rom 10:16. Second, there is the presence of Isaianic themes both prior to Gal 3:1-5 and after the passage. Many scholars recognize that Paul's description of his conversion/call in Gal 1:15 alludes at least in part to Isaiah 49.[8] More im-

---

[7] See the references to Lull and Cosgrove in n. 4 above, as well as Richard N. Longenecker, *Galatians* (WBC 41; Dallas: 1990), 101; Williams, *Galatians*, 82; J. Louis Martyn, *Galatians: A New Translation with Introduction and Commentary* (AB 33A; New York: Doubleday, 1997), 283-84.

[8] So F. F. Bruce, *The Epistle to the Galatians* (NIGTC; Exeter: Paternoster, 1982), 92; Frank J. Matera, *Galatians* (SP 9; Collegeville: Liturgical Press, 1992), 63; R. Longenecker, *Galatians*, 30; Martyn, *Galatians*, 156-57; Gerhard Ebeling, *Die Wahrheit des Evangeliums: Eine Lesehilfe zum Galaterbrief* (Tübingen: J.C.B. Mohr [Paul Siebeck], 1981), 105; James

portantly, Paul explicitly cites Isa 54:1 in the midst of the climax of this central exegetical section (Gal 4:21-5:1). Given the significance of Isaianic imagery both prior to and following Gal 3:1-5, it is reasonable to suggest that Paul intended to evoke Isaiah 53 at the outset of Galatians 3. Finally, in addition to the two factors just mentioned, the most important point is the overlap of key images from the wider context of Isaiah 53 with Galatians 1-3.

In Gal 3:1-5 Paul juxtaposes the image of Christ crucified, the outpouring of the Spirit on the Galatians, and the phrase ἐξ ἀκοῆς πίστεως. The only explicit verbal links between Gal 3:1-5 and Isaiah 53 are the root πιστ- and the noun ἀκοή; however, a number of elements in the surrounding context of Isaiah 53 dovetail with other themes in Galatians. At the broadest and most obvious level, the fourth servant song appears in the context of Deutero-Isaiah, a section replete with new exodus imagery, some of which, I will suggest shortly, plays an important part at other climactic points in Paul's argument in Galatians 3 and 4. Narrowing the focus a bit more, this servant song specifically follows a description of an exodus-like deliverance of Israel:

Depart, depart, go out from there! Touch no unclean thing; go out from the midst of it, purify yourselves, you who carry the vessels of the LORD. For you shall not go out in haste, and you shall not go out in flight; for the LORD will go before you and the God of Israel will be your rear guard. (Isa 52:11-12, NRSV)

The imagery of God going before Israel and acting as the nation's rear guard evokes the exodus narrative in which the pillar of cloud leads Israel in the wilderness and protects the Israelites from the Egyptians (see Ex 13:21-22; 14:19-20), though the text from Isaiah describes a more wondrous redemption in that the people will not need to flee. Immediately following this exhortation to leave we find the fourth servant song, which describes the brutal death of the servant, a description that resonates with Paul's reminder to the Galatians of his depiction of Christ crucified. In the midst of this description of the servant comes the verse that Paul quotes in Romans 10 and that shares some vocabulary with Gal 3:1-5:[9]

D. G. Dunn, *The Epistle to the Galatians* (BNTC; London: Cambridge, 1993), 63-64; Williams, *Galatians*, 46.

[9] Tangentially, the possible allusion to Isa 53:1 is one among many reasons that I have chosen to translate the phrase ἀκοὴ πίστεως "the message of faith." For a helpful discussion of the various possibilities, see Richard B. Hays, *The Faith of Jesus Christ: The Narrative Substructure of Galatians 3:1-4:11* (2d ed.; Grand Rapids: Eerdman's, 2002), 124-32. Also in support of this translation, see Hans-Dieter Betz, *Galatians: A Commentary on Paul's Letter to the Churches in Galatia* (Hermeneia; Philadelphia: Fortress, 1979), 128; Matera, *Galatians*, 112; Schlier, *Der Brief an die Galater*, 122; Johannes Sijko Vos, *Traditionsgeschichtliche Untersuchungen zur paulinischen Pneumatologie* (Assen: Van Gorcum, 1973), 87. For arguments in favor of translating ἀκοή as "hearing," see Bruce, *Galatians*, 149; R. Longenecker, *Galatians*, 103.

Lord, who has believed our message (τίς ἐπίστευσεν τῇ ἀκοῇ ἡμῶν)? And to whom has the arm of the Lord been revealed? (Isa 53:1)

Again, by itself this connection of one root and one noun seems tenuous, but a consideration of the broader context suggests that there may be more to the connection than meets the eye. In addition to the question of believing a message, integral to Paul's argument in 3:1-5, there is also the notion of revelation, another key theme in Galatians. Indeed, one needs little imagination to determine how Paul was likely to answer the prophet's question, "to whom has the arm of the Lord been revealed (ἀπεκαλύφθη)?" Throughout the first two chapters of Galatians Paul emphasizes again and again that the gospel and his mission came to him through a revelation of Jesus Christ (note the noun ἀποκάλυψις in 1:12 and 2:2, as well as the verb ἀποκαλύπτω in 1:16), not through human agency.

Isaiah 53:1 is not the only verse in this section of the book that uses the verb ἀποκαλύπτω. Shortly preceding the exhortation to depart and in the context of another passage that Paul knew, the text uses the verb ἀποκαλύπτω in Isa 52:10. Before we consider that verse, it is worth noting other language in Isaiah 52 that overlaps with Paul's argument in Galatians 3. Isa 52:7, also quoted by Paul in Romans 10, announces the impending salvation of Israel using terms quite significant for Paul:

I am present as a moment upon the mountains, as the feet of one announcing a message of peace (εὐαγγελιζομένου ἀκοὴν εἰρήνης), as one who announces good news (εὐαγγελιζόμενος ἀγαθά); for I will make known your salvation, saying, "Zion, your God will reign." (Isa 52:6b-7 [LXX], my translation)

The phrase "one announcing a message of peace" brings together three important themes found in Galatians at the beginning, middle, and end, respectively, of the letter: "gospel" (1:6-9), "message" (3:2-5), and "peace" (5:22; 6:16). It is also worth noting here that the word ἀποκαλύπτω appears in Isa 52:10 and in Isa 53:1, and yet in each case it translates a different Hebrew word. The translator(s) use ἀποκαλύπτω to translate the Hebrew חשף in Isa 52:10 and גלה in Isa 53:1. This suggests that if Paul is alluding to Isaiah, he most likely has the Greek textual tradition in mind.

The Isaianic passage then proceeds to announce the salvation of Zion and Jerusalem, after which the verb ἀποκαλύπτω appears again (or rather for the first time in this section): "And the Lord shall reveal (ἀποκαλύψει) his holy arm before all the nations (πάντων τῶν ἐθνῶν; cf. Paul's reference to πάντα τὰ ἔθνη in Gal 3:8), and all the ends of the earth shall see the salvation that is from God" (Isa 52:10 [LXX], my translation). The entire complex found in Isaiah 52 and the beginning of Isaiah 53 of announcing salvation to Zion/Jerusalem, the revelation of God's arm to the nations, and the brutal suffering of the servant of the Lord serves as a natural backdrop to Paul's argument throughout Galatians.

The rest of Isaiah 53 is notoriously complicated, with significant divergences between the Greek and the Hebrew tradition(s). Nevertheless, the basic picture in each version is roughly the same, depicting the suffering and eventual death of the servant on account of the sins of Israel. In addition, two more themes appear later in the chapter that figure in the argument of Galatians. First, the various Greek and Hebrew texts of Isa 53:10 make reference to a relationship between a sin offering and the establishment or prolonging of a seed:

ויהוה חפץ דכאו החלי אם־תשים אשם נפשו יראה זרע יאריך ימים וחפץ יהוה בידו יצלח: (Isa 53:10 [MT])[10]

καὶ κύριος βούλεται καθαρίσαι αὐτὸν τῆς πληγῆς ἐὰν δῶτε περὶ ἁμαρτίας ἡ ψυχὴ ὑμῶν ὄψεται σπέρμα μακρόβιον (Isa 53:10a [LXX])[11]

This verse manifests significant discrepancies between the various Greek textual traditions and the MT of Isaiah 53, but the main point does not lose its force for all the differences. In each version, the sin offering presented on behalf of (or "by" according to the Greek) the people leads to the establishment of the "seed" or "offspring," a term which figures prominently in Paul's argument in the second half of Galatians 3. The next verse in Isaiah is more complicated and the differences between the Greek and the Hebrew do matter, if Paul intended to evoke them. The MT reads: יצדיק צדיק עבדי לרבים (Isa 53:11 [MT]).[12] By contrast, according to the Greek the Lord justifies or vindicates the just/righteous one: βούλεται κύριος ἀφελεῖν ἀπὸ τοῦ πόνου τῆς ψυχῆς αὐτοῦ δεῖξαι αὐτῷ φῶς καὶ πλάσαι τῇ συνέσει δικαιῶσαι δίκαιον εὖ δουλεύοντα πολλοῖς καὶ τὰς ἁμαρτίας αὐτῶν αὐτὸς ἀνοίσει. (Isa 53:10b-11 [LXX]).[13] The combination of "seed" language and "righteousness" language in such close proximity in a text that shares other important themes with Galatians 3 suggests that Paul had the passage in mind while writing Galatians, especially given some of the similarities noted above. Nevertheless, in this case the difference between the Hebrew and the Greek clearly affects the meaning and the way Paul would have appropriated the text: is it the servant who makes many righteous by bearing the iniquities of the people, or does the Lord justify/make righteous the just/righteous one?

At least two factors suggest that Paul is alluding to Greek textual traditions, which has interesting implications not only for Gal 3:1-5, but for the

---

[10] "Yet it was the will of the LORD to crush him with pain. When you make his life an offering for sin, he shall see his offspring, and shall prolong his days; through him the will of the LORD shall prosper." (Isa 53:10, NRSV)

[11] "And the Lord desires to cleanse him from the plague; if you (pl) will give a sin offering, your (pl) soul will see a long-lived seed."

[12] "The righteous one, my servant, will make many righteous."

[13] "The Lord desires to take away from the affliction of his soul, to show him light, and to form [him] with understanding; to make righteous the righteous one who serves many well, and *he* will take away their sins."

interpretation of Galatians 3 in general. First, as noted above, the phrase ἐξ ἀκοῆς πίστεως has no equivalent in the Hebrew text as handed down by the Masoretes. Moreover, we saw that the "revelation" of the arm of God as a consistent theme appears more clearly in the Greek than in the Hebrew. When combined with the fact that Paul almost certainly cites the Greek text in Romans 10:16, these data point to the conclusion that this is the text that he primarily had in mind.[14] A second characteristic of Isaiah 53 also points in this direction. As Richard Hays has noted, in addition to the terms "righteous one" and "seed," the Greek of Isaiah 53:12 also states that the righteous one "will inherit (κληρονομήσει) many," yet another theme that appears in the argument of Galatians 3.[15] By contrast, the Hebrew speaks of God dividing for the servant a portion with the great (לכן אחלק־לו ברבים) and the servant dividing the spoils with the strong (ואת־עצומים יחלק שלל). Based on all of this evidence, we see that part of Paul's argument in Galatians, at least in broad outline, follows the grand sweep of Isaiah 52-53, especially the Greek traditions. He received his gospel not through human agency but by a revelation of Jesus Christ (Gal 1:12, 16; cf. Isa 52:7, 10; 53:1); he preached to the Galatians a message of faith (Gal 3:1-5; cf. Isa 53:1) which portrayed Jesus Christ crucified (Gal 3:1; cf. Isa 52:13-53:10); as the "seed" Christ received the "inheritance" (Gal 3:15-18; cf. Isa 53:12). This shared language gains added significance when one notes that toward the climax of Galatians 3-4 Paul cites Isa 54:1 in the context of a discussion of the promise and inheritance of Abraham (Gal 4:21-5:1).[16]

Paul's proclamation of the cross and the blessing of the nations that accompanied it, then, find at least some anticipation in the restoration oracles of Isaiah. The fact that this imagery is so prominent throughout Galatians and that the Spirit plays such an important part in his argument suggests that it would be wise to look to similar Isaianic themes in order to understand the significance of the Spirit. His apocalyptic gospel – a gospel no doubt founded

---

[14] See J. Ross Wagner, Jr., *Heralds of the Good News: Isaiah and Paul in Concert in the Letter to the Romans* (Leiden: Brill, 2002), 179 n. 81: "Paul's quotation of Isaiah 53:1a exactly follows the reading of the LXX, whose own textual tradition is univocal at this point. This is a clear example of Paul's dependence on a septuagintal text, for the LXX alone explicitly makes this verse an address to God."

[15] Hays, *The Faith of Jesus Christ*, 137; for reasons that will become clear below, I do not, however, follow Hays in interpreting Paul's citation of Habakkuk 2:4 as messianic, despite the intriguing reference to the "righteous one" in Isaiah 53.

[16] Karen H. Jobes ("Jerusalem, Our Mother: Metalepsis and Intertextuality in Galatians 4:21-31," *WTJ* 55 [1993]: 299-320, esp. 312-13) notes some of the allusions that I have suggested (Isa 53:1, 2-12), though I came to these conclusions before reading her work. Jobes helpfully captures the effect of these resonances when combined with Paul's citation of Isaiah 54 later in the epistle: "Paul's citation of Isa 54:1 sets up waves of resonance with Isaiah's proclamation of the suffering servant and Jerusalem's future that ripple through the entire *probatio* of Gal 3:1-4:31."

on the cross and resurrection of Christ – nevertheless corresponds to the promises of restoration and peace given to the people of Israel through Isaiah; at the same time Paul's gospel transforms these promises. Most fundamental in this transformation is the realization that the ultimate curse of the Law from which Israel needed redemption was not, as some of Paul's contemporaries and near contemporaries asserted, exile from the land, but rather the death sentence pronounced by Deuteronomy on those who fail to obey the covenant – historically this came upon Israel as a nation, but in the new situation Paul applies it by extension to the Gentiles who seek to come under the Law.[17] In light of this problem, we can begin to understand why Paul insists that his Gentile converts not submit to the Law, a question that he addresses more directly in Gal 3:10-14.

Galatians 3:10-14: Life and Death, The Blessing and The Curse

With its series of scriptural citations, alternating pronouns, and dense argumentation, Gal 3:10-14 presents the reader with a host of issues. Since in the present discussion I cannot provide a full exegesis of the passage, I will take up the more modest task of explaining the significance of the outpouring of the Spirit, which serves as the climax of this section, in order to make sense of the general thrust of the passage. As noted above, I intend to approach the problem from two angles, which will in turn shed light on one another. First, the association of the outpouring of the Spirit with the restoration of Israel in some of the OT prophetic literature implies that the curse of which Paul speaks is the curse pronounced by the Law on the people of Israel as a whole. Given that certain texts from the OT and Second Temple period connected the outpouring of the Spirit with redemption from the Deuteronomic curse, Paul's emphasis on the Spirit suggests that the "curse" to which he refers in Gal 3:10 and 13 is the curse pronounced by the Law on Israel. Second, if the curse is the one pronounced by Deuteronomy, Paul's emphasis on the outpouring of the Spirit makes sense and confirms that he interprets the phenomenon as the beginning of the redemption of Israel, which in his mind also entails the ingathering of the Gentiles. Nevertheless, as I will argue below, Paul's understanding of the curse differs from that of his contemporaries in that he no longer sees exile itself as the ultimate curse; rather, the eschatological life that Christ's death and resurrection brought about indicates that death itself is the

---

[17] It is important to note that in Deuteronomy death and exile are intimately related (cf. Deut 30:20); nevertheless, when speaking of the curse of the Law, Paul always uses the language of death, and never of exile. Whereas for Deuteronomy death and exile went hand in hand, for Paul exile seems to have lost its significance and to have been replaced by death as a result of sin. See further the discussion below on the relationship between death and exile.

epitome of the curse of Deuteronomy. Indeed, just as resurrection has been transformed from a metaphor for return from exile to the actual, bodily resurrection of the Messiah (and the anticipated resurrection of believers already in some sense present – cf. Gal 2:19-20), so also death no longer functions simply as a symbol for exile, but rather represents the literal, ultimate curse of the Law. This shift in emphasis, I suggest, helps to clarify the line of Paul's argument in Galatians, and fits with many of his statements about the Law in the other *Hauptbriefe*.

The pattern of argumentation in Galatians 3

Before considering 3:10-14 in detail, it would be helpful to set it in its broader context in Galatians 3. This context will help to answer the question of who are the ones under the curse of the Law. Paul's argument in this section of the epistle runs at least from 3:6 to 3:29 and consists of an extended discussion of the relationship between the promise to Abraham and the giving of the Law. Specifically, Paul contrasts the promise to Abraham that all nations would be blessed in him (3:8) with the Law that came in four hundred thirty years later (3:17) and was not able to make alive (3:21). Much of the second half of Galatians 3 develops this contrast between the Law and the promise to Abraham in order to show that the former was only temporary and did not succeed in bringing the blessing to the nations.[18] The details of the argument would lead us too far afield, but the basic point that bears on the present discussion is this: Paul contrasts the giving of the Mosaic Law with the promise to Abraham. The former had not brought about the fulfillment of the latter, and therefore something had to be done in order to extend the blessing to all the nations in fulfillment of the promise to Abraham.[19] The significance of this broad line of argument will become clearer as we consider 3:10-14 in more detail.

Turning to 3:10, the first question facing the interpreter is how the verse relates to the preceding verse, since Paul connects the two with the conjunction γάρ. As many have noted, the most natural connection between the verses is to be found in the contrast between blessing and curse.[20] Blessing

---

[18] So N. T. Wright, *The Climax of the Covenant: Christ and the Law in Pauline Theology* (Minneapolis: Fortress, 1992), 143-44; for a similar outline highlighting the historical sequence of Abraham-Moses-Christ in both 3:6-14 and 3:15-29, see Ulrich Luz, *Das Geschichtsverständnis des Paulus* (BEvT 49; Munich: Kaiser, 1968), 149.

[19] Cf. Philip F. Esler, *Galatians* (New Testament Readings; London and New York: Routledge, 1998), 188: "By dying, [Christ] destroyed the death which threatened from Sinai, so that he might allow us access to life promised earlier to Abraham."

[20] So Wright, *Climax of the Covenant*, 142, following Richard B. Hays, *Echoes of Scripture in the Letters of Paul* (New Haven: Yale University, 1989), 109; Dunn, *Galatians*, 170;

and curse appear as a consistent theme both in the Pentateuch as a whole and more narrowly within Deuteronomy.[21] In addition to this obvious connection, however, I suggest that the shift from the blessing of Abraham to the curse of the Law sets up the pattern of argumentation for the rest of the chapter: God promised to bless the nations through Abraham, the Law got in the way due to Israel's sin, and those under the Law needed to be redeemed from its curse in order that Abraham's blessing might come upon them as well as upon the Gentiles.

Galatians 3:10 and Deuteronomy 27:26

With this broader context in mind, let us now turn to consider Paul's citation of Deut 27:26 in Gal 3:10. Though the problem is difficult, the basic question is simple: how does Paul understand Deut 27:26, which seems to say that anyone who does not do all that is written in the book of the Law is under a curse, to mean that "as many as are of works of the Law" are under a curse? James M. Scott helpfully summarizes several of the positions taken on the question.[22]

One widely held opinion assumes that Paul leaves out an implied presupposition, later expressed in Gal 5:3 and 6:13: no one can actually fulfill all of the deeds of the Law, and therefore anyone who attempts to do so will inevitably come under the curse of the Law.[23] Although at first glance such an argument might seem appealing, it does not correctly represent what Paul actually says in 5:3 and 6:13. In neither verse does he state that it is impossible to keep the Law; rather, in the former verse he states that those who are circumcised are required to keep the whole Law, in the latter that those who would have the Galatians circumcised do not keep it themselves. Indeed, Paul's assertion in Philippians that he was "blameless" with regard to righteousness under the Law seriously undercuts this interpretation.[24]

---

similarly E. P. Sanders, *Paul, the Law, and the Jewish People* (Philadelphia: Fortress, 1983), 22.

[21] Gen 1:28; 3:14-18; 9:1, 25-26; 12:2-3; 18:18; 22:17-18; 27:12; Num 24:9; Deut 11:26; 30:1, 19, *et passim*.

[22] James M. Scott, "'For as Many as Are of Works of the Law Are Under a Curse' (Galatians 3.10)," in *Paul and the Scriptures of Israel* (ed. Craig A. Evans and James A. Sanders; JSNTSup 83; Sheffield: Sheffield Academic, 1993), 188-94, on which I depend for much of what follows.

[23] See, e.g., Heikki Räisänen, *Paul and the Law* (WUNT 29; Tübingen: Mohr/Siebeck, 1987), 94; so also R. Longenecker, *Galatians*, 118.

[24] A point made decades ago by Krister Stendahl, "The Apostle Paul and the Introspective Conscience of the West," in *Paul Among Jews and Gentiles and Other Essays* (Philadelphia: Fortress, 1976), 78-96 and followed by many scholars since. For a recent defense of the traditional position against Stendahl and the standard appeal to Phil 3:6, see Bruce W. Longenecker, *The Triumph of Abraham's God: The Transformation of Identity in Galatians*

Another commonly held view contends that in 3:10 Paul is condemning reliance upon the Law rather than trust in God as a means to salvation.²⁵ This anti-legalistic reading of the verse fails on two counts, however. First, the phrase "as many as are of works of the Law" does not say anything about relying upon the Law – rather, like the earlier phrase ἐκ πίστεως, it refers to the origin or identity of the ones spoken of. While this is not unrelated to the question of reliance, it is not exactly the same thing. Second, and more significantly, Deut 27:26 does not pronounce a curse on those who misguidedly seek to obey the Law, but rather on those who *fail* to obey. This second interpretation of 3:10 actually makes the verse more perplexing rather than less.

E. P. Sanders suggests that in order to understand Paul's OT citations, one should look to Paul's own words rather than to the texts themselves.²⁶ According to Sanders, Paul arrives at his position (anyone who accepts the Law is cursed) and then finds a prooftext to support it (Deut 27:26, the only passage in Scripture to connect the terms "Law" and "curse"). There is more than a grain of truth in two of Sanders' suggestions. Indeed, as I hope to show below, Paul's own words (though not just those in 3:10) are crucial for understanding how he interprets the curse, and Paul does assert that those who accept the Law are under a curse. Nevertheless, Sanders's suggestion as to why those who accept the Law are under a curse (because the Law is not faith in Christ) seems needlessly arbitrary. In 3:13 Paul speaks of the curse of the Law as something that had actually come upon a specific group of people ("us," on which see below), not as something that anyone not in Christ suffers.

According to James D. G. Dunn, the "works of the Law" to which Paul refers in 3:10 are only the badges of national identity (circumcision, food laws, and Sabbath).²⁷ The problem for Paul with these identity markers, according to Dunn, is that they restrict the grace of God and make the gospel a nationalistic program rather than the universal goal of salvation for all in Christ. It is obviously true that circumcision is a key concern for Paul in Galatians (see 2:3, 12; 5:2-3, 6; 6:12-13, 15) and that table fellowship played an important part in the dispute between Paul and Peter (2:11-21). Nevertheless, there is

---

(Nashville: Abingdon, 1998), 139-42. Although Longenecker makes an interesting case, it fails because its appeal to Romans 7 presumes that Paul there is referring to an individual, rather than to Israel's history – a point that needs to be demonstrated rather than assumed. See also Guy Waters, *The End of Deuteronomy in the Epistles of Paul* (WUNT 2.221; Tübingen: Mohr/Siebeck, 2006), 99-100.

²⁵ See Bruce, *Galatians*, 157.

²⁶ Sanders, *Paul, the Law, and the Jewish People*, 22: "I think that what Paul says in his own words is the clue to what he took the proof-texts to mean. Thus in 3:10 Paul means that those who accept the law are cursed."

²⁷ Dunn has argued for this position in a number of places. Among his other works, see Dunn, *Galatians*, 172.

no indication either in Paul's own words in 3:10 or in his citation of Deut 27:26 that by "works of the Law" he means circumcision and the other ethnic rites. On the contrary, the Deuteronomy citation pronounces a curse on those who do not do "*all* the things written in the book of the Law" (emphasis added). It is highly unlikely that this "all" refers only to ethnic boundary markers, either in Deuteronomy or in Paul's use of the verse.[28]

Other scholars such as Hans Dieter Betz and Heinrich Schlier, interpreting 3:10 in light of 3:13 and reading the genitive in the latter verse as an epexegetical genitive ("the curse which the law is"), suggest that the curse is the Law itself.[29] Such an interpretation, however, blatantly contradicts the positive statements Paul makes about the Law implicitly in Galatians (3:21a; 5:14; 6:2) and explicitly in Romans (Rom 7:7-12). Moreover, this interpretation makes no sense of the Deuteronomy citation, which does not state that the book of the Law is a curse, but rather that those who fail to do the Law will be cursed. Rather than interpreting 3:10 in light of 3:13, one should read the latter verse in light of the former. As I will argue below, the "curse of the Law" in 3:13 refers to the same curse that the Law pronounces on those who fail to observe it.[30]

Yet another interpretation has been provided by Christopher D. Stanley, who suggests that Paul's use of Deut 27:26 serves as a threat rather than as a statement of an accomplished fact.[31] On Stanley's reading, Paul uses the text to warn the Galatians that if they do not obey all of the Law's commandments, then they will come under a curse. One could cite Gal 5:3 in support of this proposal, but evidence closer to 3:10 points in the opposite direction. In 3:13 Paul speaks of the curse as something that had come upon "us" and from which Christ redeemed "us" – rather than a potentiality, Paul speaks of the curse as a present reality from which Christ has redeemed some. Although the curse of the Law remains a potential threat for Gentiles prior to their taking up the Law, Paul's statement in 3:10 suggests that as soon as they come under the Law they will be under its curse.

---

[28] Cosgrove, *The Cross and the Spirit*, 53-54, also points out that any distinction between "works of the Law" and "the Law" makes no sense in light of Paul's critique of the Law itself in 3:12.

[29] Betz, *Galatians*, 149, citing approvingly Schlier, *Der Brief an die Galater*, 136: "Der Fluch des Gesetzes ist der Fluch, den das Gesetz bringt und in diesem Sinne dann auch selbst ist." This view finds more recent support in Fee, *God's Empowering Presence*, 391-92.

[30] See similarly Williams, *Galatians*, 89: "This curse that persons are 'under' is not the Law itself but rather the disasters that the Law forewarns will befall those who break the commandments"; B. Longenecker, *Triumph*, 144 also rightly interprets the genitive "curse of the Law" as a subjective genitive, the curse which the Law pronounces.

[31] Christopher D. Stanley, "'Under a Curse': A Fresh Reading of Galatians 3.10-14," *NTS* 36 (1990): 481-511, esp. 501.

In his commentary J. Louis Martyn proposes another interpretation of the curse, starting with the hypothesis that Paul formulates his argument vis-à-vis the exegetical sermons of his opponents in Galatia.[32] On Martyn's reading Paul takes Deut 27:26 from the arguments of his opponents but sets it in the framework of his own understanding of the gospel. In light of this gospel Paul eliminates the distinction between those who do and do not observe the Law and asserts that the curse falls on both alike. Summarizing Paul's interpretation of Deut 27:26, Martyn writes:

The Law does not have the power to bless. It is the Law's business to pronounce a curse, and, by attending both to one of the Teachers' major texts and to [Paul's] exegesis of it, you will see that the Law's curse falls both on those who are observant and on those who are not. By pronouncing a curse, the Law establishes a sphere of inimical power that is universal.[33]

I fail to see how this reading of Gal 3:10 escapes the same charge of arbitrariness that Martyn levels at other readings of the verse. What is exegetically precise about reading a verse to mean the opposite of what it says based on one's understanding of the gospel?[34]

More recently, Timothy Gombis has suggested that in order to understand the citation of Deut 27:26 in Gal 3:10, we must interpret the former verse in light of its immediate narrative context in Deuteronomy 27.[35] According to that context, Deuteronomy pronounces a curse on *individuals* within Israel who "commit heinous sins, such that they are to be cut off from Israel."[36] Because of this emphasis on the individual, the corporate exile-restoration interpretation of the citation does not work. There are problems with Gombis's reading, however. First, it does not account for the mixed nature of Paul's citation. If the only significant context for understanding Paul's interpretation of the Deuteronomy citation is Deut 27:15-26, as Gombis suggests, then why does Paul append a phrase to the citation that recurs throughout Deuteronomy 28-30? Second, Gombis's own reading of the passage does not square with the interpretation he gives the citation. According to Gombis, the context of

---

[32] Martyn, *Galatians*, 309-11.

[33] Ibid., 311.

[34] Martyn (*Galatians*, 309-10) claims to reject readings of 3:10 that say Paul simply lost his way because "Paul shows that he is an extraordinarily precise and subtle exegete." To support this claim, Martyn cites E. P. Sanders's observation (*Paul and Palestinian Judaism: A Comparison in Patterns of Religion* [Philadelphia: Fortress, 1977], 483-84) that by quoting Gen 15:6 and Hab 2:4 Paul has brought together the only two verses in Scripture that bring together the terms "righteousness" and "faith." Again, I fail to see how this linking of verses by keywords demonstrates exegetical precision – to be sure, such a discovery is impressive in an age without concordances, but I hardly consider it exegetically insightful.

[35] Timothy G. Gombis, "The 'Transgressor' and the 'Curse of the Law': The Logic of Paul's Argument in Galatians 2-3," NTS 53 (2007), 81-93.

[36] Ibid., 84 n. 10.

Deuteronomy describes heinous sins committed in secret.[37] Yet on his reading, the "offense" Paul describes is table fellowship with Gentiles. One might debate whether such a practice constituted a heinous sin, but it most certainly was not committed in secret.[38] More importantly, though, Gombis's interpretation fails to explain why the Spirit plays such a significant role in Paul's discussion of the curse and redemption.

Having surveyed these various interpretations of Gal 3:10, one can see the complexity of the question. Any solution to this *crux interpretum* must be offered with humility and due caution. With such caution in mind, I suggest that James Scott and N. T. Wright have independently pointed a clear way forward in the interpretation of the verse, though I will offer some modifications to their proposals.[39] Both scholars have independently suggested that Paul read Deut 27:26 in the broader context of Deuteronomy 27-30 (or 32 in Scott's case) to show that the curse had indeed come upon Israel as a whole and could be seen most clearly in the exile and in the failure of a full restoration as promised by the Prophets.[40] In what follows, I propose to strengthen the first part of the argument (that Paul believed that the curse had come upon Israel as a whole) and to modify the second part (that the curse Paul had in mind was the exile). An understanding of the curse as that which the Law pronounces, but focused on death rather than exile, makes sense of Paul's appeal to the Spirit. At the same time such a reading acknowledges the radical, transformative nature of the cross in Paul's thinking and distinguishes his views from those of some of his near contemporaries.

As both Hays and Scott point out, Paul does not cite Deut 27:26 in isolation, but rather combines it with part of another verse from Deuteronomy, ei-

---

[37] Ibid., 91.

[38] Esler (*Galatians*, 93-116) argues that prohibitions of table fellowship were related to the laws against idolatry.

[39] Martyn (*Galatians*, 310) mistakenly puts both Scott and Wright into the category of those who assume Paul has an unstated premise that no one can observe the whole Law, despite the fact that both deny this and put forth proposals focusing on the status of Israel as a nation, rather than on the individual's failure to observe the commandments. As I will show, this corporate understanding of the curse both does justice to Deuteronomy and reflects the understanding of at least some Second Temple Jews.

[40] Scott's argument rests on firmer ground since he analyzes a number of Second Temple texts that show the continued understanding on the part of at least some Jews that they were still under the curse of Deuteronomy. The latter point stands regardless of Waters' critique of Scott that most Second Temple Jews did not read Deuteronomy 27-30 as a separate unit. See Waters, *The End of Deuteronomy*, 36-42, and the whole of his chapter two. The important point on which I agree with Wright and Scott is that Paul himself read Deuteronomy 27-30 as a whole, pointing to the curse of Deuteronomy that had come upon Israel. I differ from them in that I do not believe that Paul's argument comes naturally out of the flow of Deuteronomy 30, even if it addresses the problem expressed in this section of Deuteronomy and other Second Temple texts that allude to it.

ther 28:58 or 29:19b.⁴¹ This combination indicates that Paul does not read Deut 27:26 as an isolated prooftext, but rather reads it in the broader context of Deuteronomy 27-30.⁴² Deuteronomy 27 describes the ceremony for the establishment of the covenant on Mount Ebal. Deuteronomy 28 then enumerates the blessings for obedience and the curses for disobedience of the covenant, with the accent heavily on the curses.⁴³ Significantly, two curses in particular occur again and again: exile and death/destruction.⁴⁴

After recounting a part of the exodus story, Deuteronomy 29 returns to the possibility of curse for those who disobey. The Hebrew of v. 18 seems to

---

⁴¹ Hays (*Echoes*, 43) proposes the former, whereas Scott ("For as Many as are of Works of the Law," 194-95) considers both to be possible, noting that the phrase γεγράμμενα ἐν τῷ βιβλίῳ τοῦ νόμου τούτου recurs throughout Deuteronomy 27-32 like a leitmotif (28:58, 61; 29:19, 20, 26; 30:10). It is unclear to me, however, why Scott extends the section to Deuteronomy 32, given that the last occurrence of the phrase appears in Deuteronomy 30, and that this chapter suffices to prove his point that Deuteronomy portrays the curse as something that inevitably came upon Israel. For arguments in favor of Deut 29:19b rather than Deut 28:58 as the second verse that Paul draws on in his citation, see Dietrich-Alex Koch, *Die Schrift als Zeuge des Evangeliums* (BHT 69; Tübingen: Mohr/Siebeck, 1986), 164 and 266.

⁴² Hays restricts the unit to Deuteronomy 27-28, whereas Scott prefers Deuteronomy 27-32. I have chosen to split the difference simply because the phrase "written in the book of this Law" to which Scott appeals occurs in Deuteronomy 28-30 and there is no clear indication that Paul here intends to evoke all of Deuteronomy 27-32. Extending the unit through Deuteronomy 30 suffices and actually makes more sense in the context of Paul's argument in Gal 3:10-14, as I will show shortly. Wright (*Climax of the Covenant*, 140-46) also suggests Deuteronomy 27-30 as the context of the citation, though not (explicitly) by way of the combined citation. Both Wright and Scott rely on Martin Noth, *The Laws in the Pentateuch and Other Studies* (trans. D. R. AP-Thomas; Edinburgh and London: Oliver & Boyd, 1966), 118-31, who approaches the question from this angle, though without considering how Deuteronomy was taken up in subsequent Jewish literature. Furthermore, Wright's and Scott's proposals differ from Noth's in that the latter suggested that Paul used Deuteronomy as an analogy rather than as referring to an actual curse upon Israel. See also Koch, *Die Schrift als Zeuge des Evangeliums*, 163, who suggests that Paul's modification of the citation from Deuteronomy 27 has the effect of including all the curses in Deuteronomy 28-30, as well as the lengthy discussion in Waters, *The End of Deuteronomy*, 80-86. Waters suggests that elements from a variety of verses – Deut 28:58; 29:20, 21, 28; 30:10 (all LXX) – influenced Paul's combined citation. Further, he argues on this basis that Paul read Deuteronomy 27-30 as a unit, unlike most other Second Temple Jews (in Waters's estimation).

⁴³ There are almost four times as many verses devoted to the curses as to the blessings – cf. Deut 28:1-14 and 28:15-68.

⁴⁴ With respect to exile, Scott ("For as Many as are of Works of the Law," 195) cites Deut 28:32, 36, 37, 41, 48, 63, 64, 68, to which I would add v. 21; with respect to death/destruction, see Deut 28:20-22, 24, 26, 45, 48, 51, 61, 63, 66, with the repeated use of the words ἀπόλλυμι and ἐξολεθρεύω. It is worth noting that a few of these verses (28:21, 48, 63) combine the curse of exile with that of death/destruction, a connection that appears again toward the end of Deuteronomy 30.

suggest that the disobedience of one man or family could potentially bring judgment upon the whole of the nation:[45]

והיה בשמעו את־דברי האלה הזאת והתברך בלבבו לאמר שלום יהיה־לי כי בשררות לבי אלך למען ספות הרוה את־הצמאה:

The lines that follow seem to suggest that God will single out the family or tribe that disobeyed for punishment, noting that the Lord will blot out their names and that they will be singled out for evil/distress (רעה) according to the curses written in the book of the Law (29:20-21). The rest of the paragraph, however, proceeds to speak as though the curses will come upon the whole people of Israel.[46] The succeeding generation is to look at the curses that have come upon the land and realize that the people and the land were cursed because of their failure to obey the Law.

If Deuteronomy 29 speaks ambiguously about whether or not the curse will come upon all the people, the beginning of Deuteronomy 30 leaves no questions, describing both the blessings and the curses as inevitable in v. 1. After the curse has come upon Israel, however, Deuteronomy holds out the promise that God will bring the Israelites back and restore them, circumcising their hearts and enabling them to keep the commandments (Deut 30:6). The latter part of the chapter then describes the choice set before the Israelites in terms of life and death (Deut 30:15). Obedience will lead to life and prosperity in the land; if Israel's heart turns away, however, then they will "utterly perish" (אבד תאבדון; ἀπωλείᾳ ἀπολεῖσθε), drawing on the language that recurs throughout Deuteronomy 28.[47] Finally, the last exhortation of Deuteronomy

---

[45] "And it shall be with the one who hears the words of this oath and blesses himself, saying in his heart, 'There will be peace for me, even if I walk in the stubbornness of my heart,' so that he sweeps away the moist and the dry" (Deut 29:18, MT). Jeffrey H. Tigay (*Deuteronomy* [The JPS Torah Commentary; Philadelphia: The Jewish Publication Society, 1996], 280) notes a number of possibilities for interpreting the phrase "sweeps away the moist and the dry." It could refer to all the possessions of an individual, or it could refer to those of the entire nation.

[46] Tigay (*Deuteronomy*, 281) notes that the list in Deut 29:19-28 moves from the individual to the largest unit: "Perhaps that list is merely suggestive, implying all units of society, from the smallest on up, and verses 19-28 are meant to be understood elliptically: verse 19 describes the punishment of the smallest unit, the individual, and Moses then skips over the fate of the intermediate-sized units, which is in principle the same, so as to conclude with the climactic fate of the largest unit, the entire nation." Cf. also Patrick D. Miller, *Deuteronomy* (IBC; Louisville: John Knox, 1990), 210-11: "In a different way, the text shows an awareness of the individual as part of a larger whole when it refers to an act of stubborn disobedience and describes it as 'a root bearing poisonous and bitter fruit' that sweeps away 'moist and dry alike.' While the expressions are somewhat enigmatic, they suggest the picture of a disobedience that grows and whose outcome is bitter fruit, not only for the individual who disobeys but eventually for the whole community, 'moist and dry alike' serving apparently as an image for totality."

[47] Deut 30:18; cf. Deut 28:20, 22, 24, 45, 51.

30 brings together the concepts of life and death with blessing and curse: "I call heaven and earth to witness against you today that I have set before you life and death, the blessing and the curse" (Deut 30:19a). The NRSV obscures the meaning by translating the last phrase "life and death, blessings and curses" despite the fact that both the Hebrew (הברכה והקללה) and the Greek (τὴν εὐλογίαν καὶ τὴν κατάραν) speak of a singular blessing and curse with the article. Repeating and modifying the substance of Deut 30:15 and coming at the end of Deuteronomy 27-30, the synonymous parallelism ("life and death, blessing and curse") suggests a close association between "blessing" and "life" on the one hand and "curse" and "death" on the other. The curses of Deuteronomy are encapsulated under the category "death."[48]

Such then is the basic outline of Deuteronomy 27-30 with its emphasis on blessing and curse, life and death. Clearly Deuteronomy itself speaks of the blessing and the curse as something that would and did inevitably come upon Israel. The question remains, though, whether Jews contemporary with Paul and, more importantly, Paul himself thought that this curse had come and remained upon Israel. A brief review of a few of the Second Temple texts we studied in chapter three will show that at least some Second Temple Jews believed that the curse had come upon Israel and in some cases had remained in effect.

As we saw above in chapter three, *Jubilees* takes up much of the language of Deuteronomy, particularly reiterating the point that Deuteronomy 30 makes, namely, that the curse would inevitably fall upon Israel.[49] Moreover, the book presents an expectation of restoration in terms of the creation of a new spirit for the Israelites.[50] The fact that this promise appears with no ref-

---

[48] Cf. Esler, *Galatians*, 191: "Deuteronomy summarises the curse more in terms of death than exile (Deut. 30.15-20)." So also Joel Marcus, "'Under the Law': The Background of a Pauline Expression," *CBQ* 63 (2001): 72-83, esp. 78: "Those who [refuse God's revelation of the Torah] will be punished by death, presumably the same death that is threatened in the Torah's covenant curses (Deuteronomy 27-28)." The argument of Todd A. Wilson (*The Curse of the Law and the Crisis in Galatia: Reassessing the Purpose of Galatians* [WUNT 2.225; Tübingen: Mohr/Siebeck, 2007], 36) seems to be heading in this direction. The concept of death is not unrelated to exile, however, as the following verse clearly shows: "so that you may live in the land that the LORD swore to give to your ancestors" (Deut 30:20). Nevertheless, my point is that death and exile could both be used to describe the curse, an important point when considering Paul's discussion in Gal 3:10-14. Members of the NT Seminar at the University of Durham and Ellen Davis independently alerted me to the possibility that the article, both in Hebrew and in Greek, may indicate a class ("blessing" and "curse") rather than a specific blessing and curse. Nevertheless, later readers could still draw from this association the conclusion that the ultimate curse of the Law is death.

[49] See pp. 43-44 above.

[50] *Jubilees* also demonstrates a shift in traditional expectation, however, in that it describes Israel's inheritance in terms of the whole earth rather than simply the land. See *Jub.* 22:11b, 13. Paul seems to be aware of a similar tradition (see Rom 4:13).

erence to its fulfillment suggests that for the writer of Jubilees the curse remained on Israel and the return to the land had not yet taken place or at least remained incomplete. Although the *Psalms of Solomon* do not refer to Deuteronomy as explicitly as *Jubilees*, they nevertheless also speak of an as yet unmet restoration of the people of Israel to the land. The psalmist speaks of the messianic king's mission to regather the scattered tribes. Finally, the *Testament of Judah*, like *Jubilees*, also alludes to the curses of Deuteronomy, speaking of them as something that had come upon the people and from which the people still need redemption.[51]

The question of whether Paul believed that the curse remained in effect in his day is easier to answer, insofar as he seems to say as much in Gal 3:10 and 13. First, in 3:10 he states that "as many as are of works of the Law are under a curse." He speaks of the curse not as a threat, but as an established reality. Second, if he did not believe that the curses had come upon Israel, then his statement that Christ redeemed "us" from the Law's curse would make no sense. In a moment we will once again consider how Paul interpreted the substance of the curse. Before answering this question, let us continue to work through Gal 3:11-12.

Galatians 3:11 and Habakkuk 2:4

Having asserted that the curse of Deuteronomy has come upon the nation as a whole, and that as a result those who seek to enter this covenant come under the curse, Paul proceeds to contrast the true way to life and righteousness (faith) with the way that fails to lead to life by citing two more Scriptural verses.

In Gal 3:11, Paul argues from the premise that no one is made righteous by the Law to the conclusion that there must be another way to righteousness/life set forth by Scripture.[52] My reading of this verse depends on taking the verb δῆλον in Gal 3:11 with the second ὅτι rather than the first, which, though very much a minority position, makes better sense of the verse, and results in a translation such as, "Now because no one is made righteous by the Law be-

---

[51] For further discussion of these texts, as well as additional texts from the Second Temple period that witness to the persistence of the curse upon Israel, see chapter three above. See also Scott, "For as Many as are of Works of the Law," 197-213; the clearest texts to which Scott points are Dan 9:11 and Bar 1:20.

[52] That Paul sees the terms "righteousness" and "life" as interrelated is apparent not only from the flow of 3:10-14, but also from Gal 2:15-21, where he moves seamlessly from talking about righteousness to living through Christ, as well as in the statement of Gal 3:21b: "If a law had been given that could make alive, then righteousness would indeed be from the Law." See Bruce, *Galatians*, 162.

fore God, it is clear that 'the righteous one will live by faith.'"[53] In other words, the Habakkuk citation does not lead Paul to deduce that righteousness does not come from the Law, as practically every English translation suggests. Rather, Paul has already asserted that the Law does not make righteous (Gal 2:16) and explains why in 3:10: "as many as are of works of the Law are under a curse." Based on this understanding that the Law does not bring righteousness or life, Paul cites a verse that was already interpreted eschatologically in his day to present the alternative way to life and righteousness.[54]

Recently Andrew Wakefield has proposed an alternative to the traditional view that Gal 3:11-12 refers to eschatological life. He proposes that in these verses Paul contrasts Habakkuk and Leviticus as two ways of living: "What seems to be developing is not, as we might have expected, a choice between life and death, but rather a choice between life and life – between a life of blessing, characterized by the Spirit and righteousness and faith, and a life under curse, characterized by law."[55] Wakefield makes an interesting case, but ultimately it is unpersuasive. Although the first use of the term "life" in Galatians does refer to daily conduct (Gal 2:14), a number of the other occurrences of "life" terminology in the epistle refer to eschatology and soteriology (cf. Gal 3:21b; 5:25; 6:8).[56] Moreover, it is not clear, as Wakefield suggests, that Lev 18:5 refers to a way of life, either in its original setting or in later interpretative traditions.[57] To cite just one text to which we will return below, Ezek 20:11 seems to interpret Leviticus as offering the blessing of life as a result of keeping the commandments: "And I gave to them my ordinances and

---

[53] For detailed arguments in favor of this reading, see Andrew H. Wakefield, *Where to Live: The Hermeneutical Significance of Paul's Citations from Scripture in Galatians 3:1-14* (Academia Biblica 14; Atlanta: Society of Biblical Literature, 2003), 162-67, who notes that for the most part English speaking scholarship has not so much denied as ignored the possibility of such a reading. The two exceptions he cites are Wright, *Climax of the Covenant*, 149 n. 42, who credits research assistant Chris Palmer, and Richard B. Hays, *The Letter to the Galatians* (NIB 11; Nashville: Abingdon, 2000), 259, who follows Wakefield on this point.

[54] The classic discussion of the eschatological reading of Habakkuk in Second Temple literature is Augustin Strobel, *Untersuchungen zum Eschatologischen Verzögerungsproblem: Auf Grund der Spätjüdisch-Urchristlichen Geschichte von Habakuk 2,2 FF.* (NovTSup 2; Leiden: Brill, 1961). More recently and focusing on Paul's use of the text, see the helpful discussion of Francis Watson, *Paul and the Hermeneutics of Faith* (Edinburgh: T & T Clark, 2004), 127-63, as well as Rikki E. Watts, "'For I Am Not Ashamed of the Gospel': Romans 1:16-17 and Habakkuk 2:4," in *Romans and the People of God: Essays in Honor of Gordon D. Fee on the Occasion of His 65th Birthday* (ed. Sven K. Soderlund and N. T. Wright; Grand Rapids: Eerdman's, 1999), 3-25.

[55] Wakefield, *Where to Live*, 144; see also 169-71; cf. B. Longenecker, *Triumph*, 164-65 on the significance of the shared "life" terminology in Leviticus and Habakkuk.

[56] Gal 5:25 is the most telling in that it speaks of both the life given by the Spirit and conduct led by the Spirit: "If we live by the Spirit, let us also conduct ourselves by the Spirit."

[57] For a fuller discussion of the following, see Watson, *Paul and the Hermeneutics of Faith*, 315-23.

I made known to them my regulations, all of which a human being will do them and will live by them" (Ezek 20:11 [LXX], my translation). As Watson perceptively notes, the ambiguity as to whether the "living" refers to conduct or reward becomes clearer if one compares this verse with Ezekiel 18:

> If a person is righteous, and does justice and righteousness, and does not eat upon the mountains or lift up his eyes to the idols of the house of Israel... and walks in my statutes and has kept my decrees, acting with integrity: he is righteous, he shall surely live... says the Lord YHWH. (Ezek 18:5-9)[58]

This passage unambiguously speaks of life as a reward for obedience to the commandments, and later texts from the Second Temple period confirm that at least some Jews saw eschatological life as a reward for obedience to the commandments.[59]

The eschatological dimension of the Habakkuk citation, then, is a key to its function in Paul's argument, since indeed the whole argument is eschatological.[60] As I have argued in the previous two chapters and will demonstrate further below, the outpouring of the Spirit, which came about for the Galatians on the basis of the message of faith (cf. 3:2, 5), serves as an eschatological sign of the inauguration of the new creation. Paul's citation of Habakkuk, then, rests on two premises. First, as noted above, the Law has no power to make righteous or to give life (3:10; cf. also 3:21b). Second, the outpouring of the Spirit came about through the proclamation of faith (3:2, 5). Because the Spirit was given through the proclamation of the eschatological faith, it is this faith that will characterize those who have been brought from death to life, which coheres with an eschatological interpretation of Habakkuk 2:4 that was common in Paul's day.[61]

---

[58] The citation and translation are from Watson, *Paul and the Hermeneutics of Faith*, 321, with the Hebrew transliteration removed.

[59] See also Simon J. Gathercole, "Torah, Life, and Salvation: Leviticus 18:5 in Early Judaism and the New Testament," in *From Prophecy to Testament: The Function of the Old Testament in the New* (ed. Craig A. Evans; Peabody: Hendrickson, 2004), 131-50.

[60] Cosgrove, *The Cross and the Spirit*, 56, rightly notes the eschatological character of faith for Paul's argument: "Faith is conceived here as an eschatological reality, which enters the world with God's action in Christ."

[61] Cf. the inability of the Law to make alive in Gal 3:21 with Paul's statements elsewhere about the Spirit's power to make alive (Rom 8:11; 2 Cor 3:6, which contrasts the Spirit with the letter and uses the same verb found in Gal 3:21, ζῳοποιέω). As I noted above in n. 15, I do not find Hays's proposal (*The Faith of Jesus Christ*, 134-38, and more recently "Apocalyptic Hermeneutics: Habakkuk Proclaims 'The Righteous One,'" in *The Conversion of the Imagination: Paul as Interpreter of Israel's Scripture* [Grand Rapids: Eerdmans, 2005], 101-18) that Paul interprets Habakkuk 2:4 as a messianic text persuasive. Although Hays raises some intriguing parallels and the possible allusions to Isaiah 53, esp. the Greek textual tradition, might point in this direction, the flow of the argument in 3:6-14 seems to me to work differently. Paul speaks in 3:9 about those who are "of faith" receiving the blessing. He then asserts that those who are "of the Law" are under a curse, after which comes the Habakkuk

There is another feature of the book of Habakkuk, however, that may also have contributed to Paul's selection of this text. In a recent essay Rikki Watts demonstrates how the broader context of Habakkuk sheds considerable light on Paul's use of Hab 2:4 in Romans.[62] Although the article focuses on how Habakkuk and Romans each address issues of theodicy, it also points to one aspect of Habakkuk that helps to explain why Paul would appeal to it in Galatians. The first complaint in the book (Hab 1:1-4) laments God's indifference in the face of the prophet's suffering, climaxing (על־כן; διὰ τοῦτο) in a question about the ineffectiveness of the Law (תורה; νόμος) to restrain wickedness (Hab 1:4). Many commentators suggest that Habakkuk's complaint concerns failure in the enforcement of the Law, whether by God himself or by his appointees.[63] Given that the verb תפוג in Hab 1:4 is intransitive, however, J. Gerald Janzen and Marshall D. Johnson argue that the prophet describes a defect in the Law itself.[64] The first half of the verse reads as follows:

על־כן תפוג תורה ולא־יצא לנצח משפט (Hab 1:4a)[65]

Therefore the Law is weakened and judgment does not go out forever (my translation).

If this latter interpretation of the Law itself as "weak" is correct, or at least accurately represents how Paul understood the text, then one can see much more clearly why he would gravitate to Habakkuk in order to make his case.[66]

---

citation. Reading the "righteous one" as a messianic title disrupts the flow of the argument, which contrasts the curse upon those who "are of works of the Law" with the blessing that comes to those who are "of faith" (3:9) and the life that the righteous receive by faith (3:11). Even acknowledging for the sake of argument that those who participate in Christ would thereby be made righteous through Christ's faithfulness, one still wonders whether Paul's readers would have made such a connection based on the immediate context. See Martyn, *Galatians*, 313-14; Williams, *Galatians*, 91.

[62] Watts, "Not Ashamed of the Gospel," 3-25.

[63] See, e.g., J. J. M. Roberts, *Nahum, Habakkuk, and Zephaniah* (OTL; Louisville: Westminster/John Knox, 1991), 90; O. Palmer Robertson, *The Books of Nahum, Habakkuk, and Zephaniah* (NICOT; Grand Rapids: Eerdmans, 1990), 140.

[64] J. Gerald Janzen, "Eschatological Symbol and Existence in Habakkuk," *CBQ* 44 (1982): 394-414; Marshall D. Johnson, "The paralysis of torah in Habakkuk i 4," *VT* 35 (1985): 257-66. It should be noted, however, that the two disagree on the substance of this "Law," the former identifying it with the prophetic word, the latter with the book of the Law in Deuteronomy. Watts rightly argues that the term תורה in this case most likely refers to the book of the Law for two reasons. First, this is the more common connotation of the word. Second, the association of תורה with משפט in both Deuteronomy and Habakkuk suggests that the prophet has the book of the Law in mind, not the prophetic word. See Watts, "Not Ashamed of the Gospel," 6 *et passim*.

[65] The LXX translates the phrase לנצח as εἰς τέλος, which may point to an eschatological interpretation of the verse.

[66] This is the conclusion that Watts ("Not Ashamed of the Gospel," 6) draws with respect to Romans, but the point holds equally, *mutatis mutandis*, for Galatians. Interestingly, if one accepts the modified punctuation of Gal 3:11 suggested above, the verse follows a similar

In this regard, it is worth noting that in Rom 8:3 Paul describes the Law as "weakened through the flesh," although the word Paul uses (ἀσθενέω) does not correspond to the Greek of Hab 1:4 (διασκεδάζω).

One final feature of the Habakkuk citation bears more emphasis. Following the lead of Sanders, Martyn sees the significance of Hab 2:4 primarily in its association of righteousness with faith, a feature that the text shares only with Gen 15:6 in the rest of the OT.[67] Given the overall thrust of the argument, however, I suggest that the text's use of "life" language is equally important for Paul's case.[68] Paul's discussion of "righteousness/justification" in Gal 2:15-21 also stresses the significance of the life that he lives, or rather that Christ lives in him, in 2:19-20. Furthermore, the primary contrast in 3:10-14 is one between curse and life, and different means of attaining this life – by faith (eschatologically revealed in Paul's view) according to Habakkuk, or by doing the works of the Law (which Israel had historically failed to do in Paul's view) according to Leviticus. The fact that the Law cannot make alive (3:21b) combined with the conviction that his gospel is in line with the promises of God leads Paul to point to the Habakkuk text to demonstrate that God had already promised through the prophets a different means of attaining life.

Galatians 3:12 and Leviticus 18:5

In contrast to the righteousness that comes from faith, in Gal 3:12 Paul quotes once more from the Pentateuch, this time from Lev 18:5.[69] Many scholars have understood Paul's quotation to contrast the "doing" of the Law with righteousness that comes from "faith."[70] On the surface such a reading seems accurate; however, if the reading of Deuteronomy proposed above correctly interprets Paul's statement, then the emphasis may not fall so much on the "doing" of the Torah as on the source of life. Is there another reading that makes sense of the Leviticus quotation in concert with the Deuteronomy citation?

Once again, I think the line of argument opened up by Wright and supported independently by the work of Frank Thielman points in the right direc-

---

pattern to Habakkuk, which begins with the ineffectiveness of the Law (1:4) but then offers hope to the righteous on the basis of faith.

[67] Sanders, *Paul and Palestinian Judaism*, 483-84; Martyn, *Galatians*, 310, 12.

[68] On the significance of "life" terminology in this verse and the connection between Habakkuk and Leviticus in this regard, see Matera, *Galatians*, 119, 124. See also Wakefield, *Where to Live*, 132-45, on the centrality of "life" in the chiastic structure of Gal 3:6-14.

[69] Despite the lack of a quotation formula, it is clear that Paul is citing Scripture, particularly since he cites the same verse with a formula in Rom 10:5. See Betz, *Galatians*, 147.

[70] So, e.g., Betz, *Galatians*, 147-48; R. Longenecker, *Galatians*, 120; Matera, *Galatians*, 124; Sanders, *Paul, the Law, and the Jewish People*, 22.

tion, though it needs some modification. Thielman suggests that the key to understanding Paul's citation of Lev 18:5 is the broader context of the verse, pointing specifically to the end of chapter 18 and the recital of the curses in Leviticus 26. Both these passages pose the threat of the curse for disobedience to the Torah in the form of expulsion from the land (see Lev 18:24-28; 26:14-43). Moreover, Thielman speaks (broadly) of various Second Temple texts that see the curse of exile as having come about and in some cases remaining in effect.[71]

While in many ways persuasive, Thielman's analysis pins too much on the broader context of Leviticus without taking into consideration the tradition of interpretation of Lev 18:5 in particular.[72] Joel Willitts makes up for this deficiency in the arguments of Wright and Thielman by analyzing the citation of the verse in the biblical books of Ezekiel and Nehemiah, as well as in the Damascus Document.[73]

Leviticus 18:5 in Ezekiel 20

Ezekiel 20 presents a retelling of the exodus from Egypt, cast as an indictment of the sins of Israel's ancestors. Even before the exodus from Egypt, writes Ezekiel, the Israelites remained stubborn and refused to put away the idols of Egypt and failed to obey the commandments of the Lord (Ezek 20:5-8).[74] Despite the Lord's decision to pour out his wrath on Israel, however, he proceeds nevertheless to rescue Israel from Egypt and make a covenant with them. It is here that Ezekiel first alludes to Lev 18:5 within a few short verses.[75] First, he describes the initial giving of the covenant:

---

[71] Frank Thielman, *From Plight to Solution: A Jewish Framework for Understanding Paul's View of the Law in Galatians and Romans* (NovTSup 61; Leiden: Brill, 1989), 71-72.

[72] Thielman's suggestion that Paul has the entire context of Leviticus 18-26 is less convincing than the proposal that in citing Deut 27:26 combined with Deut 29:19 Paul intended to evoke Deuteronomy 27-30 more broadly since the latter proposal has the strength of the combined citation drawing from (at least) two different parts of the book, whereas Paul does not combine Lev 18:5 with any other part of Leviticus.

[73] Joel Willitts, "Context Matters: Paul's Use of Leviticus 18:5 in Galatians 3:12," *TynBul* 54 (2003): 105-22, on which I have relied heavily for the following discussion of Ezekiel and Nehemiah.

[74] It is interesting to note that in v. 8 God resolves to pour out his wrath even "in the midst of the land of Egypt (!)"; according to Ezekiel, then, Israel's rebellion calling down the wrath of God stretches back even before the exodus. The parallels with Paul's understanding of Israel subject to sin from the beginning are intriguing, as well as instructive. The fact that Ezekiel could speak of Israel's sinful state from the beginning and yet continue to use the language of restoration suggests that the joining together of these two concepts in Paul's own thought not only is not contradictory, but also has prophetic precedent.

[75] The way I have phrased the matter presupposes that both P and H precede Ezekiel, contrary to traditional source critical analyses of the Pentateuch. For arguments in favor of the priority of P and H, see Jacob Milgrom, *Leviticus 1-16: A New Translation with Introduction*

καὶ ἔδωκα αὐτοῖς τὰ προστάγματά μου καὶ τὰ δικαιώματά μου ἐγνώρισα αὐτοῖς ὅσα ποιήσει αὐτὰ ἄνθρωπος καὶ ζήσεται ἐν αὐτοῖς. (Ezek 20:11 [LXX])	καὶ φυλάξεσθε πάντα τὰ προστάγματά μου καὶ πάντα τὰ κρίματά μου καὶ ποιήσετε αὐτά ἃ ποιήσας ἄνθρωπος ζήσεται ἐν αὐτοῖς. (Lev 18:5 [LXX])
And I gave to them <u>my ordinances</u> and I made known to them my regulations, all of which <u>a human being will do them and will live by them</u>.	And you will keep all <u>my ordinances</u> and all my judgments and you will do them all, by which <u>a human being doing them will live by them</u>.

Almost immediately following the giving of the covenant, Ezekiel describes the Israelites' failure to live up to the commandments, again echoing the Leviticus citation: "and they did not walk [in the commandments] and they rejected my regulations, which a human being will do them and live by them" (Ezek 20:13b [LXX], my translation).[76] The result is that God once again decides to pour out his wrath upon Israel in order to annihilate them (Ezek 20:13c). It is worth noting that Ezekiel describes the first generation of Israel earning the curse before they even arrive in the land. While Ezekiel can describe this curse in terms of exile insofar as that generation never entered the land, like Deuteronomy, Ezekiel also uses the language of destruction or annihilation.[77] Finally, Ezekiel 20:21 once again refers to Lev 18:5: "And they rebelled against me, and their children did not walk in my ordinances and they did not keep my regulations to do them, which a human being will do them and live by them"(Ezek 20:21a).[78] In addition to the first generation that left Egypt, the second wilderness generation also failed to obey the statutes and ordinances, thus calling the curses upon themselves.

As Willitts briefly notes, Ezekiel 20 shares a number of words and themes with Ezekiel 36, suggesting that the two chapters mutually interpret one another.[79] The latter explains the former, indicating why Israel failed to obey

---

and Commentary (AB 3; New York: Doubleday, 1991), 3-35; *idem, Leviticus 17-22: A New Translation with Introduction and Commentary* (AB 3A; New York: Doubleday, 2000), 1361-64; and earlier Avi Hurvitz, *A Linguistic Study of the Relationship Between the Priestly Source and the Book of Ezekiel: A New Approach to an Old Problem* (Paris: J. Gabalda, 1982); for arguments in favor of a traditional Wellhausian dating, see Ernest Nicholson, *The Pentateuch in the Twentieth Century: The Legacy of Julius Wellhausen* (Oxford: Clarendon, 1998), esp. 196-221; Robert Polzin, *Late Biblical Hebrew: Toward an Historical Typology of Biblical Hebrew Prose* (HSM 12; Missoula: Scholars, 1976), esp. 85-122.

[76] καὶ οὐκ ἐπορεύθησαν καὶ τὰ δικαιώματά μου ἀπώσαντο ἃ ποιήσει αὐτὰ ἄνθρωπος καὶ ζήσεται ἐν αὐτοῖς.

[77] ἐξαναλίσκω; see Deut 28:21; cf. also Leviticus 26:22.

[78] καὶ παρεπίκρανάν με καὶ τὰ τέκνα αὐτῶν ἐν τοῖς προστάγμασίν μου οὐκ ἐπορεύθησαν καὶ τὰ δικαιώματά μου οὐκ ἐφυλάξαντο τοῦ ποιεῖν αὐτά ἃ ποιήσει ἄνθρωπος καὶ ζήσεται ἐν αὐτοῖς.

[79] Willitts ("Context Matters," 116 n. 34) lists "ordinances, commandments, dwelling in the land, doing, observing, walking in God's ways, knowledge of God among the nations," to which I would add the sanctifying/profaning of God's name (cf. 20:22 and 36:23).

God's ordinances (the absence of the Spirit in the heart) and promises the remedy needed for restoration. While both of these texts speak of restoration in terms of return to the land, Ezekiel 20 uses the language of "annihilation" to describe the outpouring of God's wrath and Ezekiel 36 uses imagery of "new creation" to describe the restoration.[80] While in its original context these texts most likely referred to an actual return to the land, one can see how Paul might read both texts to refer to an actual death and resurrection through the lens of the apocalyptic Christ event. Although Paul gives no explicit indications that he read Lev 18:5 in light of Ezekiel 20, the possibility is at least suggestive.[81]

Leviticus 18:5 in Nehemiah 9

Like Ezekiel 20, Nehemiah 9 also alludes to Lev 18:5, this time in the context of a prayer of confession and supplication by certain Levites to the God of Israel following the return to the land.[82] Like the Ezekiel passage, this prayer recites the history of God's covenantal relationship with Israel, though the prayer begins with creation (Neh 9:6) and does not pinpoint the beginning of Israel's fall as early as Ezekiel does. Nevertheless, Nehemiah does note the stubbornness of the wilderness generation, which leads them to seek to return to their slavery in Egypt (9:17). Despite this, God had compassion on the people and made his covenant with them, bringing them into the land and subduing the nations before them (9:17-25).[83] Nevertheless, in spite of the Lord's compassion and fidelity, the Israelites continued to rebel, and it is in this context that the allusion to Leviticus occurs:

---

[80] For "annihilation" see Ezek 20:13; for "new creation" imagery, see Ezek 36:34-35.

[81] Koch (*Die Schrift als Zeuge des Evangeliums*, 45) argues that Paul in fact never cites Ezekiel. Nevertheless, as I will argue below, the imagery of God sending the Spirit into the heart, if not drawn directly from Ezekiel, most likely reflects traditions stemming from Ezekiel 36.

[82] For arguments in favor of a pre-exilic date for H, see again Milgrom, *Leviticus 17-22*, 1361-64.

[83] It is interesting to note that Nehemiah associates the direction of God's own Spirit with the exodus event: "You gave your good spirit to instruct them, and did not withhold your manna from their mouths, and gave them water for their thirst" (Neh 9:20, NRSV). Note the similarity in language with Isa 44:3: "For I will pour water on the thirsty land, and streams on the dry ground; I will pour my spirit upon your descendants, and my blessing on your offspring."

ἐν ταῖς ἐντολαῖς σου καὶ ἐν τοῖς κρίμασί σου ἡμάρτοσαν <u>ἃ ποιήσας αὐτὰ ἄνθρωπος ζήσεται ἐν αὐτοῖς</u>. (Neh 9:29 [LXX])

καὶ φυλάξεσθε πάντα τὰ προστάγματά μου καὶ πάντα τὰ κρίματά μου καὶ ποιήσετε <u>αὐτά ἃ ποιήσας ἄνθρωπος ζήσεται ἐν αὐτοῖς</u>. (Lev 18:5 [LXX])

They [the Israelites] sinned in your commandments and in your judgments, <u>which a human being doing them will live by them</u>.

And you will keep all my ordinances and all my judgments and you will do them all, by <u>which a human being doing them will live by them</u>.

As a result of this disobedience, God eventually punished Israel, sending the nation into exile. Moreover, according to the prayer of the Levites in Nehemiah, even after the return to the land the people still suffered under the punishment of God: "See, we are slaves today and [also] the land which you gave to our fathers to eat its fruit" (Neh 9:36 [LXX], my translation).[84] In Nehemiah's day, as in Ezekiel's day, at least some of the people of Israel saw the curse of Leviticus still in effect. Equally important when considering Galatians, the prayer speaks of the curse in terms of "slavery," another important term that gains significance in the latter half of Galatians 3.[85]

Again, Galatians 3:12 and Leviticus 18:5

What, then, is the significance of this biblical tradition for the interpretation of Galatians? To be sure, we cannot know for certain whether Paul interpreted Leviticus 18:5 in light of these two passages; nevertheless, it would be hard to imagine him being unaware of them.[86] Indeed, this biblical tradition, much like the Second Temple traditions surrounding the curses of Deuteronomy 27-30, sheds much light on how Paul most likely interpreted the verse. Moreover, it is worth noting that the two citations in Gal 3:10 and 12 are connected by the keywords "to do them" (3:10: τοῦ ποιῆσαι αὐτά; 3:12: ὁ ποιήσας αὐτά), suggesting that Paul saw them as mutually informative, each pointing to Israel's continued status under the curse of the Law. As with the Deuteronomy citation in Gal 3:10, then, Paul cites Leviticus in Gal 3:12 to emphasize

---

[84] ἰδού ἐσμεν σήμερον δοῦλοι καὶ ἡ γῆ ἣν ἔδωκας τοῖς πατράσιν ἡμῶν φαγεῖν τὸν καρπὸν αὐτῆς.

[85] Willitts also examines a citation of Lev 18:5 in the Damascus Document which uses the verse in a positive sense as pointing to its eschatological fulfillment in the DSS community. See Willitts, "Context Matters," 114-17.

[86] Willitts ("Context Matters," 110) makes a similar judgment: "The evidence of inner-biblical exegesis in later Jewish tradition, admittedly, cannot prove that Paul read Leviticus 18:5 in the same way Ezekiel, Nehemiah, or the Dead Sea Scroll community have [*sic*]. However, it seems reasonable to propose that Paul's use of the Leviticus 18:5 clause in Galatians 3:12 is accordant with this later interpretative tradition."

Israel's continued status under the curse of the Law. With all of this information in mind, we turn finally to address what exactly this curse is.

Galatians 3:13 and the "Curse of the Law"

In Gal 3:13, there are at least three pressing exegetical questions to resolve. To whom does the first person pronoun ἡμᾶς refer? What does the curse of Deuteronomy consist of for Paul? And how does the cross redeem "us" from the curse?

To begin with the question of the pronoun, given that Paul interprets the curse as that of the Mosaic Law still upon the people of Israel, the best interpretation of the first-person pronoun is that it refers to Jewish Christians who have been redeemed from the curse of the Law. Three additional factors support this conclusion. First, the last occurrence of the pronoun ἡμᾶς preceding this one (2:16) also refers to Jewish Christians, and the line of argument in Galatians 3 proceeds directly from that statement.[87] Second, if the "curse of the Law" of Gal 3:13 is not the Law itself, but rather the curse that the Law pronounces on the people as a whole for disobeying and breaking the covenant, then it would make no sense for the "us" to refer to Gentiles, since they were never under the Law.[88] Third, the flow of the argument from 3:13 to 3:14 suggests a distinction between the "we" of 3:13 and the "Gentiles" of 3:14a.[89]

---

[87] Betz, *Galatians*, 148 n. 101.

[88] So, rightly, Betz, *Galatians*, 148 and 136: "the Galatians were not 'under the Torah' at the beginning of their Christian life, nor are they law observers now." So also B. Longenecker, *Triumph*, 90-95; Matera, *Galatians*, 120; J. B. Lightfoot, *St. Paul's Epistle to the Galatians* (London: Macmillan, 1874), 139; and much earlier, Thomas Aquinas (*Commentary on Saint Paul's Epistle to the Galatians* [trans. F. R. Larcher; Aquinas Scripture Series 1; Albany: Magi Books, Inc., 1966], 88): "He was made a curse for us not only to remove a curse but also to enable the Gentiles, who were not under the curse of the Law, to receive the blessing promised to Abraham"; *pace* Martyn, *Galatians*, 317-18 and 335. Martyn's assertion in his comment on "Theological Pronouns" that "the expression 'in our behalf' (3:13) always has for Paul the universal dimension of Christ's atoning death, just as the gift of the Spirit is universal for all Christians (3:14)" simply begs the question. Moreover, he offers no examples to substantiate his claim. Cf. Gal 4:21, where Paul refers to the Galatians as "you who are desiring to be under the Law" (οἱ ὑπὸ νόμον θέλοντες εἶναι), implying that previously Paul's addressees were not under it. This latter verse also tells against Waters's argument that Paul considers all, Jew and Gentile alike, under the Law. See Waters, *The End of Deuteronomy*, 100-103.

[89] Cf. recently Michael Bachmann, "Zur Argumentation von Galater 3.10-12," NTS 53 (2007) 524-44, here 534: "Schon wenn man den sich eben an V. 13 unmittelbar anschließenden Finalsatz in Betracht zieht, nämlich: 'damit zu den Völkern der Segen Abrahams gelange in Christus Jesus' (V. 14a), gewinnt man den Eindruck, hier solle mit ἔθνη ein deutlich weiterer Horizont beschrieben werden als zuvor mit dem zweifachen Wir. Sonst

To say that those Christ redeemed in 3:13 are Jewish Christians still leaves unanswered the question of what the curse entails. As I have hinted at a number of times, even though Paul agreed with some other Second Temple Jews that Israel remained under the curse, his experience of the Christ event transformed his understanding of the curse's content. Unlike some of his contemporaries who still believed Israel to be in exile, Paul interpreted the curse through the controlling metaphor of life and death – or rather, through the actual phenomenon of life and death.[90] Such a reading of the curse has at least three distinct advantages: (1) it makes better sense of the inner logic of Galatians; (2) it fits with the general thrust of Deuteronomy 27-30, which itself summarizes the blessing and the curse in terms of life and death; and (3) it fits with Paul's interpretation of the Law in the other *Hauptbriefe*.

To begin with the inner logic of Galatians, the whole thrust of 3:10-14 points to a contrast between life and curse.[91] If the result of redemption from the curse is (eschatological) life, then naturally the result of the curse is death. In addition, in Paul's first statements about the Law in the epistle (2:15-21), he speaks in terms of death and life: "I through the Law died to the Law that I might live to God" (Gal 2:19).[92] He then proceeds to speak of his co-crucifixion with Christ and Christ's life in him. Again, later in the epistle he speaks of the problem with the Law in terms of life: "For if a Law had been given *that was able to make alive*, then righteousness would indeed be from the Law" (3:21b, emphasis mine).[93] This verse is crucial, in that Paul explicitly states what the problem with the Law is and why his followers should not submit to it: it has no power to give life. By contrast, the Spirit, as expressed in Gal 6:8 as well as other Pauline epistles, leads to eschatological life: "For the one who sows to his own flesh from the flesh will reap corruption; but the one who sows to the Spirit from the Spirit will reap eternal life" (Gal 6:8).[94]

As noted above, in addition to exile or the scattering of the tribes, the other main curse of Deuteronomy is death.[95] Again and again, Deuteronomy 28

---

hätte man es in V. 13-14a ja nahezu mit einer Tautologie zu tun, mit der natürlich das ἵνα nicht eben gut zusammenpassen würde."

[90] This, I suggest, is a way to keep the strengths of the so-called Exile-Restoration scheme (the redemption of Israel from the curse of the Law) while avoiding its primary weakness (exile language that does not feature prominently, if at all, in Paul's thought). See Willitts, "Context Matters," 120-21 n. 47.

[91] See again Wakefield, *Where to Live*, 132-38; see also Don Garlington, "Role Reversal and Paul's Use of Scripture in Galatians 3.10-13," *JSNT* 65 (1997): 85-121.

[92] ἐγὼ γὰρ διὰ νόμου νόμῳ ἀπέθανον, ἵνα θεῷ ζήσω.

[93] εἰ γὰρ ἐδόθη νόμος ὁ δυνάμενος ζῳοποιῆσαι, ὄντως ἐκ νόμου ἂν ἦν ἡ δικαιοσύνη. Cf. Paul's reference to the life-giving power of the Spirit in 2 Cor 3:6.

[94] ὅτι ὁ σπείρων εἰς τὴν σάρκα ἑαυτοῦ ἐκ τῆς σαρκὸς θερίσει φθοράν, ὁ δὲ σπείρων εἰς τὸ πνεῦμα ἐκ τοῦ πνεύματος θερίσει ζωὴν αἰώνιον.

[95] See n. 44 and n. 48 above.

refers to Israel's destruction; the chapter refers to death even more than it does to exile.[96] Moreover, when summing up the choice that Moses sets before the Israelites, Deuteronomy itself uses the categories of life and death to epitomize the blessing and the curse: "I call heaven and earth to witness against you today that I have set before you life and death, the blessing and the curse" (Deut 30:19, NRSV, slightly modified).

One might raise the objection that Deut 30:20 once again puts the accent on exile: "for that means life to you and length of days, so that you may live in the land that the LORD swore to give to your ancestors, to Abraham, to Isaac, and to Jacob." In order to understand Paul's interpretation, it is important to highlight the connection between death and exile that occurs frequently in the OT. In describing Adam and Eve's punishment Genesis 3 speaks both of their death and of their expulsion from Eden, a kind of exile. As we have already seen, Deuteronomy often connects death and exile when enumerating the curses for disobedience (Deut 28:21, 63). The prophet Hosea describes the scattering of the tribes of Israel as the dismemberment of a corpse and return from exile in terms of resurrection (Hosea 5:14-6:2).[97] Finally, the great prophecy of Ezekiel concerning the valley of dry bones also uses the image of death as a symbol for exile and resurrection as a symbol for return (Ezek 37:1-14). By speaking of death rather than exile as the curse, Paul has in a sense taken a metaphor that once referred to exile and made it the true referent of the curse.[98] It is important, however, not to press this distinction between exile and death too far. As Jon D. Levenson has argued, the ancient Israelite understanding of death was much broader than our contemporary notions, and among some Jews at least it also encompassed exile as well as various other maladies.[99]

Finally, an understanding of the curse as death rather than exile makes sense in light of Paul's statements in the other *Hauptbriefe* concerning the problem with the Law and the role of the Spirit. Even though both Deuteronomy and Leviticus speak of exile or scattering as the ultimate curse, Paul nowhere explicitly uses the language or imagery of exile. Rather, the problem

---

[96] Deuteronomy refers to destruction 11 times: Deut 28:20-22, 24, 26, 45, 48, 51, 61, 63, 66; to exile, 9 times: Deut 28:21, 32, 36, 37, 41, 48, 63, 64, 68.

[97] I owe this reference to Dr. Brant Pitre.

[98] One might suggest that this shift already began in the OT Prophets, and not simply in the valley of bones imagery. The promises of new creation in Isaiah (Isa 65:17) and Ezekiel (see Ezek 36:30-38, as well as the lengthy description of the new temple with Edenic imagery in Ezekiel 40-48), among others, imply a problem with the old creation, namely death. In addition, some Second Temple literature (see chapter three above on the *Similitudes of Enoch* and the *Testament of Judah*), as we have seen and will discuss again below, also connects redemption from the curses of Deuteronomy with resurrection, suggesting that the curse is at least in part death.

[99] See Levenson, *Resurrection and the Restoration of Israel*, 156-65 et passim.

with the Law, always exacerbated by sin, is death. In 1 Cor 15:56, Paul writes, "Now the sting of death is sin, and the power of sin is the Law." In other words, Sin uses the Law to mete out death to those who transgress it (a point elaborated at much greater length and detail in Romans). Similarly 2 Cor 3:6b states that "the letter kills, but the Spirit makes alive."[100] In Romans 5 Paul again emphasizes death rather than exile as the consequence of sin: "But the Law came in so that trespass might increase; but where sin abounded, grace abounded all the more, so that just as sin reigned *in death*, so also grace might reign through righteousness unto *eternal life* through Jesus Christ our Lord" (Rom 5:20-21, emphasis mine). In Romans 7 Paul makes the connection even more explicit. First in 7:5-6, he contrasts the death-dealing power of the Law with the giving of the Spirit: "For while we were in the flesh, the sinful passions, which were aroused by the Law, were at work in the members of our body to bear fruit for death. But now we have been released from the Law, having died to that by which we were bound, so that we serve in newness of the Spirit and not in oldness of the letter."[101] A little later in the chapter he continues with the theme: "Now I once lived apart from the Law, but when the commandment came in sin came back to life, and I died and the commandment *which was unto life* for me was found to be *unto death*; for sin taking the opportunity through the commandment deceived me and through it *killed me*" (Rom 7:9-11, emphasis mine).[102] This last citation is particularly significant in that the phrase "the commandment which was unto life" most likely alludes to Lev 18:5.[103] Throughout the *Hauptbriefe*, then, the ultimate curse of the Law, brought about through sin, is death.[104]

This understanding of the curse as death in turn sheds light on Paul's statement about Christ becoming a curse for "us" and how he understood that

---

[100] Again, note the contrast with Galatians 3:21b, where Paul states implicitly that the Law cannot "make alive."

[101] Cf. Rom 8:2, in which Paul states, "For the law of the Spirit of life in Christ Jesus has set you free from the law of sin and death."

[102] The whole of Romans 7, which deals with the problem with the Law, speaks in terms of life and death rather than exile and return.

[103] See Joseph A. Fitzmyer, *Romans: A New Translation with Introduction and Commentary* (AB 33; New York: Doubleday), 468; James D. G. Dunn, *Romans 1-8* (WBC 38A; Dallas: Word, 1988), 384.

[104] Interestingly Wright (*Climax of the Covenant*, 149) recognizes death as the primary curse of the Law: "The covenantal overtones [in Gal 3:11-12] are emphasized again by the word 'live': 'life' is the chief blessing of the covenant, as death is its chief curse (Deuteronomy 30.15)." Nevertheless, he continues to focus on exile as the primary evidence of the Law's failure. The passages cited above suggest that for Paul death has replaced exile as the ultimate curse of the Law. In private conversation, Wright expressed his openness to death as the primary curse of the Law, noting that he would use "exile" as a cipher for being under the curse of the Law. It might be more helpful to use the language of "curse" as a catchall, since this is the term Paul uses and since it is less misleading than "exile."

death as redemptive. Strictly speaking, the crucifixion was not an exile, but rather the death penalty – precisely the ultimate curse of the Law. Redemption for Paul, then, comes about through being crucified with Christ and rising with him to new life (Gal 2:19-20). Again, the key image in speaking of redemption for Paul is not exile and restoration, but rather death and resurrection. Nevertheless, one can (and should) still interpret these images in light of the prophetic promises of restoration for two reasons. First, some of these texts speak not only of return from exile, but also of new creation, an image that came to be understood more concretely in at least some Second Temple texts in terms of resurrection from the dead.[105] Second, Paul's emphasis on the promise of the Spirit makes the most sense in light of many of the prophetic and Second Temple texts that portray the outpouring of the Spirit as the inauguration of the restoration of Israel.

Galatians 3:14 and the promise of the Spirit

With Gal 3:14 Paul brings his argument around full circle, tying up at least provisionally the issues raised in 3:1-9 regarding the outpouring of the Spirit and the blessing of the Gentiles.[106] It would be helpful at this point to recall the broad pattern of argumentation throughout Galatians 3 discussed above: the giving of the Law did not result in the blessing of the nations promised to Abraham. The flow of the argument in Gal 3:6-14 conforms to this pattern: God promised to bless all nations through Abraham (3:8-9); however, because of Israel's disobedience, the Law pronounced a curse upon the nation as a whole (3:10-12), as well as any who chose to identify themselves with the Law (3:10a); therefore, Christ died on the cross in order to redeem those still under the curse of the Law (3:13) so that the blessing promised to Abraham might at last come upon the nations and upon Israel (3:14).

And here, at last, we return once again to the question of the Spirit, the primary focus of this study. As with Gal 3:13, we will address three main issues in this verse. Why does Paul associate the Spirit with the blessing of Abraham? How, more broadly, does Paul interpret the Spirit experience of the Galatians? Finally, does the first-person plural verb λάβωμεν still refer solely to Jewish Christians, or has Paul's outlook broadened at this point?[107]

---

[105] See again Isa 65:17, as well as Ezek 36:30-38 and the lengthy description of the new temple with Edenic imagery in Ezekiel 40-48; *T. Jud.* 25:1-2. See also Levenson, *Resurrection and the Restoration of Israel*, 156-65, who provocatively argues that Israel's hope in actual bodily resurrection began earlier than the standard historical critical account and that it went hand-in-hand with hopes for national restoration.

[106] Cf. Martyn, *Galatians*, 323-34.

[107] When speaking about Paul's understanding of the role of the Spirit for Jewish and Gentile Christians, I am making no claims about the Galatian congregations, which most likely were primarily, perhaps even exclusively, Gentile in origin. My use of these terms

To begin with the question of the relationship between the blessing and the Spirit, Hays suggests that Paul made this connection via Isa 44:3, the only passage in the OT that associates the Spirit with the blessing:[108]

For I will give water among thirst to those who walk in a desert; I will place my Spirit upon your seed (τὸ πνεῦμά μου ἐπὶ τὸ σπέρμα σου), and my blessings upon your children (τὰς εὐλογίας μου ἐπὶ τὰ τέκνα σου). (Isa 44:3 [LXX])

As Hays notes, the passage does not speak about Abraham, but rather Israel. Nevertheless, a number of factors speak in favor of this connection. First, in addition to the language shared between Isa 44:3 and Galatians (τὸ πνεῦμα, τὸ σπέρμα, τὰς εὐλογίας), the text refers to the Lord as Israel's redeemer (ὁ ῥυσάμενος, Isa 44:6), highlighting the redemption of the nation and fitting with the general thrust of Gal 3:10-14. Second, the text appears in the broader context of the latter half of the book of Isaiah, which speaks not only of the redemption of Israel, but also of the ingathering of the Gentiles, which dovetails with the promise to Abraham that Paul has in mind in Galatians 3.[109]

Two other passages in Deutero-Isaiah mention Abraham, each one interesting for different reasons. First, Isa 41:8, which also appears in the context of an oracle that refers to the Lord as Israel's redeemer (ὁ λυτρούμενος, 41:14), addresses Israel as the "seed of Abraham" (σπέρμα Ἀβρααμ) – the same term that Paul uses in Gal 3:29 (τοῦ Ἀβραὰμ σπέρμα) to refer to all those who have been baptized into Christ.[110] Deutero-Isaiah, then, closely connects Israel and Abraham, suggesting that if Paul is alluding to Isa 44:3, he could well have

---

describes rather theological categories for Paul's understanding of the gospel and its implications for Jews and Gentiles. Cf. the recurring phrase "to the Jew first and also to the Greek" in Romans.

[108] Hays, *The Faith of Jesus Christ*, 182-83; *idem, Galatians*, 261. So also F. F. Bruce, "The Spirit in the Letter to the Galatians," in *Essays on Apostolic Themes: Studies in honor of Howard M. Ervin* (ed. P. Elbert; Peabody: Hendrickson, 1985), 214. Interestingly, Martyn, *Galatians*, 323 n. 121, notes this passage, but does not explore the significance of its context for Paul's argument. See also James M. Scott, *Adoption as Sons of God: An Exegetical Investigation into the Background of ΥΙΟΘΕΣΙΑ in the Pauline Corpus* (WUNT 2.48; Tübingen: J.C.B. Mohr [Paul Siebeck], 1992), 179 n. 205.

[109] See Isa 42:1, 6; 49:6; 55:5. On the significance of Deutero-Isaiah for Paul's understanding of the Spirit, though without reference to the Gentiles, cf. Vos, *Paulinische Pneumatologie*, 92-93: "Wenn man schließlich nach den genaueren alttestamentlich-jüdischen Voraussetzungen für das Geist verständnis von Gal 3,6-14 fragt, dann ist auf Deuterojesaja hinzuweisen. Auch für Deuterojesaja galt, wie wir sahen, daß der Bundessegen, die den Vätern verheißene Fruchtbarkeit des Gottesvolkes, nur Wirklichkeit werden kann durch einen wunderbaren Schöpfungsakt Gottes, der in der Gabe des Geistes vollzogen wird. Auch für Deuterojesaja bedeutete dieser Schöpfungsakt Gottes die Durchbrechung der Grenzen des alten Bundesvolkes. Es ist denn auch kaum zufällig, daß Paulus sich etwas weiter, in 4,27, ausdrücklich auf diesen Propheten beruft."

[110] The connection gains added significance when one notes that the phrase σπέρμα Αβρααμ appears only three times in the OT, in Isa 41:8, Ps 104:6 (LXX), and 2 Chron 20:7.

done so in the context of associating Israel and Abraham together. This addresses Hays's concern that Isaiah 44 does not speak directly about Abraham – the promise to Abraham is closely tied to the fate of Israel.

Second, Isa 51:2 also speaks of Abraham, again in a context that speaks of the salvation of Israel. At least three features of this text are worth noting. First, the text specifically refers to God's blessing of Abraham (εὐλόγησα αὐτὸν). Second, like many of the texts associated with the Spirit that we considered in chapter two, Isaiah 51 describes Israel's deliverance in terms of a new creation, returning to an Edenic state (ὡς παράδεισον, Isa 51:3 [LXX]). Third, the text envisions not only deliverance for Israel, but also a spreading out of God's justice to the nations (εἰς φῶς ἐθνῶν, Isa 51:4).

In addition to the broader context in Second Isaiah, it is worth revisiting the use of Isa 44:3 in two other Second Temple texts. Both the *Words of the Luminaries* and the *Testament of Judah* allude to Isa 44:3 in a context similar to that of Galatians 3. As noted above, the Qumran text alludes to this Isaianic verse in describing an already accomplished deliverance of Israel.[111] Initially, the text refers to Israel's disobedience and the resultant punishment: "and they served a foreign god in their land and also their land was desolated by their enemies, for Your wrath [was pour]ed forth, and Your rages of anger with the fire of Your jealousy, so as to eradicate it of anyone passing by or returning" (4Q504 1-2v recto 3-6a).[112] In contrast to Israel's waywardness, the prayer then describes God's faithfulness to "the seed of Jacob" (זרע יעקוב, a term also shared with Isaiah 44, though again no reference is made to Abraham).[113] Rather than abandon Israel among the nations, God brought them back from their dispersion. The prayer continues: "You were gracious toward Your people Israel among all [the] lands where You had driven them, in order to bring it back into their heart to return to You and to listen to Your voice" (4Q504 1-2v recto 11b-13).[114] Following this account of the mercy God showed to Israel, the prayer describes how God brought this about through the outpouring of his holy Spirit, using language similar to that found in Isa 44:3: "You have poured out Your holy *spirit* (יצקתה את רוח קודשכה) upon us, [to b]ring Your *blessings* (ברכתיכה) to us" (4Q504 1-2v recto 15-16, emphasis mine).[115] Portrayed as an already accomplished fact, the redemption of Israel from the curse comes about through God's pouring out of his own holy Spirit.

---

[111] See pp. 52-55 above.

[112] The translation is taken from James R. Davila, *Liturgical Works* (Eerdmans Commentaries on the Dead Sea Scrolls; Grand Rapids: Eerdmans, 2000), 260.

[113] Technically, Isa 44:3 does not have the phrase "seed of Jacob" (זרע יעקוב), but rather refers to "your seed" (זרעך). Nevertheless, from the context the phrase clearly refers to Jacob's seed. The phrase זרע יעקוב occurs only three times in the OT (Isa 45:19; Jer 33:26; Ps 22:24), and in none of these instances is it connected with the Spirit.

[114] Davila, *Liturgical Works*, 260.

[115] Ibid.

Like the *Words of the Luminaries*, the *Testament of Judah* also uses language similar to that found in Isa 44:3 to describe Israel's redemption. As noted in chapter three above, *Testament of Judah* 23 describes how Israel suffered under the curses of Deuteronomy 28 and 30, scattered among the nations due to the nation's unfaithfulness to the Lord. After the unleashing of the curse, however, the text holds out hope that God will show mercy to Israel and restore its fortunes. At the time of God's mercy a messianic figure will appear, and at that time God will pour forth his Spirit upon this prince, who in turn is to pour it out on Israel: "And the heavens will be opened upon him to pour out *the spirit as a blessing* of the Holy Father. And he will pour the spirit of grace on you" (*T. Jud.* 24:2-3b, emphasis mine).[116] Chapter 24 of the *Testament of Judah* is, of course, one of the passages that many scholars consider to be rife with Christian redaction. This may or may not be the case.[117] Regardless, the fact that the connection of the Spirit and the blessing appears in the *Words of the Luminaries* demonstrates that the *Testament of Judah* at the very least may preserve earlier Jewish traditions about the outpouring of the Spirit and the redemption of Israel from the curse of the Law.

Following this description, the text proceeds to depict the resurrection of the patriarchs Abraham, Isaac, and Jacob, and to promise a kingdom to the sons of Israel (25:1-2). Though the text does not explicitly speak of a "promise," it does seem to present this outpouring of the Spirit as the fulfillment of the promise to Abraham, intriguingly reinterpreting it in terms of resurrection. If, as I have suggested, one of the underlying presuppositions of Paul's argument in Gal 3:10-14 is Christ's resurrection and the eschatological life that it brings, and if the *Testament of Judah* represents a tradition that may have been available to Paul, then the connection between the Spirit and the promise to Abraham begins to make more sense.[118]

Isaiah 44 may not be the only text that informs Paul's understanding of the Spirit, however. In addition to this text, I suggest that the expectations set forth first in Ezekiel 36 and carried on in later Jewish literature may also shed light on his understanding of the gift of the Spirit. As we saw in chapters two

---

[116] On the allusion to Isaiah 44, see Marinus de Jonge, "Christian influence in the Testaments of the Twelve Patriarchs," in *Studies on the Testaments of the Twelve Patriarchs* (ed. Marinus de Jonge; SVTP 3; Leiden: Brill, 1975), 216, following Max-Alain Chevallier, *L'Esprit et le Messie dans le bas-judaïsme et le Nouveau Testament* (Paris: Presses Universitaires de France, 1958), 130 n. 2.

[117] For arguments in favor of the text preserving Jewish tradition, see the excursus on pp. 69-73 above.

[118] Again, see the excursus in chapter three above for more detailed arguments against Christian redaction. To recapitulate the arguments briefly: 1. nothing in this section of the *Testament* demands Christian influence – the key images all appear in various parts of the OT, most of which are not especially prominent in the NT; 2. the significant structural parallels with 4Q504 suggest at the very least that the text preserves early Jewish traditions.

and three above, Isaiah 44 is just one of a variety of OT texts that expect the outpouring of the Spirit in conjunction with Israel's restoration and that influenced the expectations of at least some Second Temple Jews. It is at least plausible, then, to suggest that texts such as Ezekiel 36 also influenced Paul's understanding of the Spirit, even if Paul never explicitly cites this passage.[119] At the very least, I will argue below that traditions stemming from Ezekiel 36 inform Paul's language of God sending the Spirit into "our hearts" in Gal 4:4-6. Given the likelihood of this influence and the close relationship between Gal 3:13-14 and 4:4-6, a connection with Ezekiel in Gal 3:14 becomes more plausible.[120]

Before turning to Galatians 4, however, we must briefly consider one final question. Does Paul once again use the first-person plural in Gal 3:14 to refer only to Jewish Christians, or has it taken on a broader referent, namely, Jew and Gentile alike in Christ? As Norman Young has noted, the referent of first-person plurals in Paul in general and in Galatians in particular is a vexed question, although the issue can be stated simply.[121] Some scholars take the first-person pronoun in Gal 3:13 to refer to Christian Jews, whereas the verb in Gal 3:14 refers to Christians more broadly.[122] Others take the first-person throughout Galatians 3-4 to refer to Jewish and Gentile Christians inclusively.[123]

The one position that Young does not discuss, and the one for which I will argue here, is that throughout Gal 3:13-14 Paul uses the first person to refer to Jewish Christians. To be sure, there can be no question that Paul holds that all believers receive the Spirit. Moreover, the way that Gal 3:14 brings to an initial close the line of thought begun in 3:1-5, where Paul asks the Galatians if they received the Spirit by works of the Law or by the proclamation of faith, might lead one to infer that Paul has broadened his outlook to include both Jewish and Gentile Christians. At least three factors, however, suggest

---

[119] See n. 81 above.

[120] The connection between Gal 3:13-14 and 4:4-6 is acknowledged by many. For relevant discussions, see, among others, Hays, *The Faith of Jesus Christ*, 75-82 and B. Longenecker, *Triumph*, 90-95.

[121] Norman H. Young, "Pronominal Shifts in Paul's Argument to the Galatians," in *Ancient History in a Modern University, Vol 2: Early Christianity, Late Antiquity and Beyond* (ed. T. W. Hillard *et al.*; 2 vols.; Grand Rapids: Eerdmans, 1998), 2.205-15.

[122] For a list of scholars advocating this position see Terence L. Donaldson, "The 'curse of the Law' and the Inclusion of the Gentiles: Galatians 3.13-14," *NTS* 32 (1986): 94-112, 107 n.3, who himself favors the position, and Young, "Pronominal Shifts," 206 n. 6, who opposes it.

[123] See again Young, "Pronominal Shifts," 206-07 for a list of those who hold to this interpretation.

that this second use of the first-person pronoun might refer once again to Jewish Christians.[124]

First, as I have already argued, the first-person pronoun in Gal 3:13 refers to Jewish Christians, and so one might expect Paul to continue to use the first person in this way.[125] Indeed, if he meant to shift from Jewish Christians to Gentile Christians to Christians as a whole in 3:13-14, one might expect a signal such as the use of "all" in v. 14 to clarify that he had all Christians in mind at that point. Second, this reading makes sense of the two purpose clauses in 3:14: both clauses are the result of Christ's redemptive act, but the first clause describes (primarily) the outcome for the Gentiles – they have at last received the blessing of Abraham – and the second clause describes (primarily) the outcome for Jewish Christians – they have at last received the Spirit for which they had longed.[126] Finally, insofar as Gal 3:14 brings full circle the argument beginning in 3:1, by emphasizing that even "we Jewish Christians" received the promise of the Spirit "through faith," Paul brings home the point that the gift of the Spirit does not come about through works of the Law.[127]

Galatians 4:1-7: From Slavery to Sonship

As suggested above, Gal 3:10-14 must be read in the broader context of Gal 3:6-29, and indeed 3:1-4:7, one of whose primary themes is the contrast between the promise to Abraham and the function of the Law in Israel's history. Like 3:10-14, Gal 4:1-7 must be understood within this schema, though it highlights themes that play more prominently in the rest of the epistle. Again, as with 3:10-14, a full exegesis would be beyond the scope of the present work, and so I will focus on the points most relevant to understanding the function of the Spirit in Paul's argument.

---

[124] In general agreement with Wright, *Climax of the Covenant*, 154.

[125] Young's argument ("Pronominal Shifts," 207) that "it is difficult to exclude Gentiles from the redemptive activity of Jesus described in 3.13 and 4.5" fails to convince because it assumes (wrongly) that taking the "us" of Gal 3:13 as referring to Christian Jews excludes Gentiles from the redemption. The point is not that Gentiles are excluded from redemption – on the contrary, the point is that for Paul the Jews had to be redeemed from the curse in order for salvation to extend even to the Gentiles.

[126] Again, this is not to suggest that Paul believed only Jewish Christians had received the Spirit (cf. 3:2) – it is rather a matter of the emphasis in this verse.

[127] *Pace* Donaldson, "The 'curse of the Law'," who argues that the final "we" of the passage is inclusive based on a common pattern in 3:10-14, 23-28, and 4:1-7. While I agree with Donaldson that these three sections of Galatians share a common pattern, I would suggest that the pattern involves the eschatological redemption of Israel/Jewish Christians being inextricably bound up with the ingathering of the Gentiles. See further below.

Many commentators recognize 4:1-7 as a discrete unit, indicated by the inclusio of the words "slave" and "heir";[128] however, the phrase λέγω δέ also signals that Paul means to expand upon the preceding material (cf. the similar expression in 3:17). In order to understand the example that Paul uses in 4:1-7, then, it is crucial to determine how these verses relate to what precedes them. First we must understand the force of the inheritance analogy in Gal 4:1-2 and then explore the parallels between Gal 4:1-7 and Gal 3:23-29.

The inheritance analogy in Galatians 4:1-2

The standard reading of Gal 4:1-7, found in many commentaries, takes the first two verses of this passage to refer to a general Greco-Roman legal custom of guardianship as an illustration of the status of humanity as a whole before the sending of Christ. As Betz describes it:

According to this institution the *paterfamilias* appoints one or more guardians for his children who are entitled to inherit his property after his death. During the time in which the heir (ὁ κληρονόμος) is a minor (νήπιος) he is potentially the legal owner (ὁ κύριος) of the inheritance, but he is for the time being prevented from disposing of it. Although he is legally (potentially) the owner of it all, he appears not to be different from a slave (οὐδὲν διαφέρει δούλου). To be sure, this comparison must be taken *cum granu salis* [*sic*].[129]

Betz's final comment is indicative of the difficulties that face the usual interpretation.[130] The illustration is far from perfect, and while it is true that analogies need not be perfect, if there exists a reading that makes better sense of the comparison, then such an interpretation should be favored.

James Scott has challenged this *opinio communis* and proposed an alternative reading that better connects the analogy with the application. Scott points to two major difficulties with the standard reading. First, as even those who accept the standard reading acknowledge, Paul's statement that the heir is no better off than a slave is an exaggeration.[131] Second and more importantly, the common reading of 4:1-2 leaves two glaring discrepancies between the illustration and its application in 4:3-7: "(1) The Father in vv. 3-7 is presented as alive and active, sending his own Son and adopting others, whereas the hy-

---

[128] So Betz, *Galatians*, 202; Martyn, *Galatians*, 384; Scott, *Adoption as Sons of God*, 121.

[129] Betz, *Galatians*, 202-03, who is representative of the majority reading of the illustration.

[130] Cf. the assessment of R. Longenecker, *Galatians*, 164: "It is difficult to determine exactly what legal system Paul had in mind when he said, 'but he is under guardians and administrators until the time set by the father.' It is entirely possible, in fact, that Paul, being more interested in application than precise legal details, made the specifics of his illustration conform to his purpose." See also Matera, *Galatians*, 148-49; Schlier, *Der Brief an die Galater*, 188-89; Williams, *Galatians*, 107-08; Dunn, *Galatians*, 210-11; Bruce, *Galatians*, 192-93.

[131] So Betz, *Galatians*, 202-03; R. Longenecker, *Galatians*, 162 ("hyperbole for the sake of the illustration"); Martyn, *Galatians*, 387.

pothetical father in v. 2 is presumed dead, his minor heir now standing under guardians until the time set by the father in his will. (2) Divine adoption in v. 5 is compared with Greco-Roman guardianship in v. 2."[132] The application in vv. 3-7 says nothing about leaving the status of minority, as the Greco-Roman custom would dictate. These two difficulties, among others, have led one interpreter to suggest that vv. 4-7 constitute an interpolation.[133] In order to account for these discrepancies, Scott proposes an alternative reading of the illustration, taking it to refer to Israel's status in Egypt at the time of the exodus. In support of this case he points to six exegetical oversights of the standard reading, of which I find the following four most compelling.[134]

First, Scott suggests that the term "heir," rather than referring to a figure in an abstract legal principle, describes the "seed of Abraham" in Gal 3:29, though shifting from those in Christ to Israel as collective heir.[135] Second, there is no evidence to suggest that the word νήπιος is a *terminus technicus* for a legal minor.[136] Likewise the interpretation of the expression κύριος πάντων as a legal term rests on very slim evidence. Scholars adduce only one papyrus to support a legal interpretation of the phrase, and in that papyrus the phrase κύριος πάντων is modified to refer clearly to the estate; Paul's usage of the phrase, by contrast, is unqualified. On Scott's reading the term more likely refers to a Jewish tradition that Israel was to inherit the whole world.[137] Fourth and finally, the argument that προθεσμία is a technical legal term also rests on very slight evidence.[138] A better reading takes the term to overlap with the χρόνος to which Paul refers in Gal 4:1 and 4, i.e. the time between the giving of the Law and the sending of the Son.

---

[132] Scott, *Adoption as Sons of God*, 123-24.

[133] J. C. O'Neill, *The Recovery of Paul's Letter to the Galatians* (London: Penguin Books, 1972), 56, as cited by Scott, *Adoption as Sons of God*, 124-25.

[134] Scott, *Adoption as Sons of God*, 126-49, followed by Sylvia C. Keesmaat, *Paul and his Story: (Re)Interpreting the Exodus Tradition* (JSNTSup 181; Sheffield: Sheffield Academic, 1999), 158-67. For some helpful corrections of Scott's position, see Scott J. Hafemann, "Paul and the Exile of Israel in Galatians 3-4," in *Exile: Old Testament, Jewish, and Christian Conceptions* (ed. James M. Scott; JSJSup 56; Leiden: Brill, 1997), 331-54, and the discussion below.

[135] Scott, *Adoption as Sons of God*, 128-29. Further arguments in favor of such a reading will be provided in the discussion of 4:1-2 below.

[136] Ibid., 129-30.

[137] Ibid., 130-35, citing *Jub.* 22:11b, 13; 32:19, as well as Rom 4:13a. On this point see also Dunn, *Galatians*, 211.

[138] According to Scott (*Adoption as Sons of God*, 140 n. 74), "The closest example which was found seems to be Lucian *Abdic.* 11, in which a grown man asserts in court that the προθεσμία of his father's authority has passed, because his father had disowned him. Here, however, προθεσμία has nothing to do with coming of age, much less with a date of termination for a guardianship."

As I will argue below, Scott's interpretation, though in need of modification, makes better sense of the flow of Paul's argument. The fundamental insight of Scott's proposal lies in the suggestion that the "heir" of Gal 4:1 does not refer to some generic legal example, but rather specifically to Israel as Abraham's original (collective) heir.[139] Rather than speaking broadly of humankind or a generalized legal principle, the figure of the heir under guardians and stewards refers to Israel in its condition under the Law. One might ask, however, how the reference to "we" in Gal 4:3 relates to the description of Israel's history in 4:1-2. I propose the following reading: in Gal 4:3 Paul appeals to his Jewish lineage, reminding the Galatians that just as throughout Israel's history the nation was under guardians, so too Paul and his fellow Jews, being a part of that history prior to the coming of Christ, were under guardians and subject to the στοιχεῖα. As I will argue below, the "guardians" of 4:2 are not equivalent to the στοιχεῖα. Rather, Israel's status under the guardians demonstrates that the nation was no better off than the Gentiles. This recapitulates Paul's point about the pedagogue in Gal 3:23: the pedagogue is not a bad thing, but demonstrates that Israel needs a guardian because of its status under sin (Gal 3:22). All of this serves as an explanation of why Paul's Gentile Christian followers should not begin observing the Law: for Gentile Christians to turn to the Law is tantamount to a return to slavery, insofar as the Law did not prevent Israel from falling into sin (cf. Gal 3:22).

Galatians 4:1-7 and Galatians 3:23-29

It is significant that Paul already touches on the theme of Israel under the Law in Gal 3:23-29.[140] Indeed, several parallels suggest a close connection between 4:1-7 and 3:23-29.[141] In 3:23-24 Paul speaks of Israel's status before the coming of the faith as a time of guardianship "under the Law." In 3:25 he then asserts that "we" (i.e. Jewish Christians) are no longer "under the pedagogue" now that faith has come. As proof of Israel's newfound freedom Paul points to the sonship of Galatian Christians in 3:26, which leads into the equality of Jews and Gentiles in Christ, capped by the reassurance that those who belong to Christ are Abraham's seed and therefore heirs. Similarly, in 4:1-3 Paul speaks of Israel's status under guardianship for a set time. In 4:4-5

---

[139] Ibid., 128-29.

[140] The suggestion that the heir refers to Israel throughout its history under the Law is Hafemann's correction ("Paul and the Exile of Israel," 335-39) of Scott's interpretation (*Adoption as Sons of God*, 145-49) of 4:1-2 as referring to Israel at the time of the first exodus.

[141] For a table delineating the parallels between these two sections of the epistle, see Dunn, *Galatians*, 210. See also Schlier, *Der Brief an die Galater*, 188 and Fee, *God's Empowering Presence*, 400 on 4:1-7 as a recapitulation of 3:23-29 and Matera, *Galatians*, 155 on 4:1-7 as a recapitulation of 3:22-29.

the "fullness of time" marks the sending of the Son to redeem Jews under the Law, who thereby receive adoption as sons. Similar to 3:26, in 4:6 Paul points to the sonship of the Galatians as proof of the redemption of Israel. Finally, in 4:7 he brings home the significance of the argument by reminding the individual Galatians that they are now sons and therefore heirs (cf. 3:29). Such, then, is the broad outline of 4:1-7; we turn now to the details of the argument.

Galatians 4:1-2: the heir under guardians and stewards

In addition to the parallels between 4:1-7 and 3:23-29 just noted, two factors speak in favor of taking the "heir" of 4:1 to refer to Israel rather than a generic legal example. First, unlike Gal 3:15, where Paul states that he is speaking "according to human example" (κατὰ ἄνθρωπον), in 4:1 he gives no indication that he is drawing on a legal precedent.[142] Second, when read in light of later Jewish tradition reflected in *Jubilees*, Sirach, and Romans that Israel was to inherit the world, understanding the heir of 4:1 as referring to Israel makes sense of the puzzling phrase κύριος πάντων ὤν: Israel as the heir of Abraham stood to inherit the world, but throughout its historical period of guardianship under the Law it had not yet come into this inheritance.[143] One might object to this reading on the grounds that Paul would not refer to Israel as the heir, least of all so shortly after referring to the Galatians as heirs in Christ, but Scott notes that in Romans Paul can and does still refer to ethnic Israel as the heirs of the promises to Abraham.[144]

Taking the heir to refer to Israel helps to make better sense of the rest of the imagery. As a whole, Gal 4:1-2 describes Israel's historical condition under the Law, a period in which the prophets on occasion referred to the nation as a νήπιος.[145] Indeed, in two books of the OT prophetic corpus the terms νήπιος and νηπιότης appear in the context of a description of Israel's rebellion

---

[142] Scott, *Adoption as Sons of God*, 130.

[143] See Scott, *Adoption as Sons of God*, 130-35, citing *Jub.* 32:19; Sir 44:19-23; and Rom 4:13. Such a reading of the phrase κύριος πάντων ὤν undercuts Scott's reading of 4:1-2 as referring to the first exodus, however, insofar as Israel did not inherit the entire world at that time. The phrase makes more sense in context if the language of the "heir" refers to Israel's (unfulfilled) status as Abraham's heir throughout its history. Presumably, it is this role that *Jubilees* and Sirach (and Paul) have in mind, since at the time of the writing of these documents Israel had not yet inherited the entire world.

[144] Ibid., 129 n. 27, citing Rom 9:4 in which Paul says that Israelites have "the covenants" and "the promises." It is worth noting that this reference also comes after a section expounding the status of believers as heirs in Romans 8.

[145] See the excursus below. In addition to the texts treated therein, Hafemann ("Paul and the Exile of Israel," 338 n. 24) points to Jer 3:24ff.; 22:21; 31:19; 32:30; Ezek 23:3, 8, 19, 21; Mal 2:14ff., though these texts refer more broadly to Israel's "youth" (νηότης) without using the term νήπιος or νηπιότης.

and slavery to idols. Israel's slavery under the Law explains why the heir "is no better than a slave." In other words, just as prior to the coming of Christ the Gentiles were enslaved, both under sin (3:22) and under the "elements of the cosmos" (4:9), so too Israel, the heir, was enslaved and continues to be enslaved as long as it remains a νήπιος; therefore the heir (Israel) is no better off than the slave (the Gentiles), even though by right of inheritance the heir is destined to be "lord of all." Instead, the heir is kept under "guardians and stewards" until the time appointed by the father – the parallel between the guardians and stewards of 4:2 and the pedagogue of 3:24-25 is hardly accidental and adds further support to an identification of the heir as Israel. Based on this parallel, it would seem that the "guardians and stewards" of 4:2 correspond to the Law. This reading tightens the connection between 4:1-2 and 4:3-7: the "set time" of 4:2 corresponds to the "fullness of time" of 4:4, at which point God ("the father" of 4:2) intervenes to rescue Israel from her slavery.

Excursus: Israel as νήπιος, idolatry, and the knowledge of God

Although Scott suggests that the word νήπιος functions as an allusion to the first exodus via Hos 11:1, to assert a conscious allusion based on one word is tenuous at best.[146] Moreover, as Hafemann argues, if the term alludes to any kind of exodus, it is most likely to a second exodus as envisioned by various texts in the prophets.[147] A closer consideration of the term νήπιος as well as its cognate "childhood" (νηπιότης) in other parts of the prophetic corpus demonstrates the appropriateness of the term for Paul's exposition of Israel's time in virtual slavery (cf. 4:1, "no better than a slave"). In addition to νήπιος at Hos 11:1, the cognate form νηπιότης appears earlier in Hosea 2:17 (LXX), as well as in Ezekiel 16:22, 43, 60.

Like Hos 11:1, Hos 2:17 (LXX) describes the time of Israel's exodus from Egypt as the "days of her childhood (τὰς ἡμέρας νηπιότητος)." Of equal significance is the fact that this designation appears in the context of an oracle of judgment that leads eventually to the redemption of Israel. In 2:10-13 (2:12-16 [LXX]), the Lord condemns Israel for her harlotry in going after the idols of the land.[148] In 2:14-15 (2:17-18 [LXX]), the prophet then speaks of God luring Israel out into the wilderness "according to the days of her childhood" (τὰς ἡμέρας νηπιότητος) to win her back to himself. By this intervention God will remove the names of idols from Israel's lips and make a new covenant with them (2:17-18). Intriguingly, in that covenant God will betroth Israel to

---

[146] So Keesmaat, *Paul and his Story*, 159.

[147] See n.140 above.

[148] Interestingly, Hos 2:11 (2:13 [LXX]) speaks of God doing away with Israel's various festivals and celebrations. Although the language is not the same, the parallel with Paul's concern over the Galatians' infatuation with similar celebrations in Gal 4:10 is intriguing.

himself, among other ways, "in righteousness" (ἐν δικαιοσύνῃ), "in mercy" (ἐν ἐλέει), and "in faithfulness" (ἐν πίστει) (2:19-20 [LXX]). As a result of this new covenant, Israel will "know the Lord" (ἐπιγνώσῃ τὸν κύριον) (2:20 [LXX]). Although Hosea does not explicitly refer to Israel as being in slavery, still less in slavery to the Law, it does associate Israel's status as an infant with sin and punishment.

Hosea 11 shares not only the language of "child/childhood" with Hos 2:17 (LXX), but also some of the other themes found in Hosea 2 as a whole. As in Hosea 2, when God called Israel as a "child" (νήπιος) out of Egypt, Israel went astray after idols and after the Baals of the land. The idolatry of the nation then leads to punishment (11:6-7), but once again a punishment that eventually ends in mercy. God promises not to destroy Israel, but rather to have compassion on the nation. Moreover, God's mercy results in a relationship of knowledge between God and Israel, though this time it is the former who knows the latter. In contrast to Israel and Judah's lying and wickedness, at the time of their redemption "now God knows them (ἔγνω αὐτοὺς ὁ θεός) and they shall be called God's holy people" (Hos 11:12). This last phrase is particularly striking in light of Paul's description of the change in status that occurred for the Galatians when they came to believe in Christ: "But now that you know God, or rather have come to be known by God (μᾶλλον δὲ γνωσθέντες ὑπὸ θεοῦ)" (Gal 4:9).

Finally, Ezekiel 16 also uses the language of childhood to describe Israel at the time of the exodus and the making of the covenant. The chapter as a whole presents an indictment of Israel for her abominations and idolatry, in spite of her covenantal relationship with the Lord. The oracle begins by recounting the mercy that God showed on Israel at its birth (νηπιότης), which then serves as the basis for the indictment of the nation. Throughout the chapter, oracles against idolatry are punctuated by reminders of God's mercy on Israel in "the days of [her] childhood" (τὰς ἡμέρας τῆς νηπιότητος) (Ezek 16:22). Again in 16:43 God promises to bring judgment upon Israel because of a failure to recall "the day of [her] childhood (τὴν ἡμέραν τῆς νηπιότητος)." Finally, in 16:60, following a lengthy account of the punishments destined for Israel, God promises to remember the covenant he made with Israel "in the days of [her] childhood" (ἐν ἡμέραις νηπιότητος) and to show mercy to her. God will make an everlasting covenant and the result will once again be knowledge of the Lord: "and you will know that I am the Lord" (καὶ ἐπιγνώσῃ ὅτι ἐγὼ κύριος) (Ezek 16:62 [LXX]).

In each of these three passages (Hosea 2, Hosea 11, and Ezekiel 16), we see a pattern that bears striking similarities to the broad outline of Galatians 4:1-11. Each of the texts refers to Israel's "childhood" (cf. the description of the "heir" as νήπιος in Gal 4:1). References to this "childhood" always occur in the context of Israel's lapse into idolatry (cf. the enslavement of Jewish

Christians prior to the sending of the Son and the Spirit in Gal 4:3-6). Finally, following this idolatry God has mercy on Israel and calls her into a relationship of knowledge with him (cf. Gal 4:9). Although it might be going too far to suggest that Paul consciously alludes to any or all of these texts in Galatians 4, it is plausible that they constitute a stock motif describing Israel's history as a period of infancy and slavery to idols, something that the Law failed to remedy. Such a pattern helps to make sense not only of the first part of Gal 4:1-7, but also of the broader outline of Gal 4:1-11. The redemption of the νήπιος leads to knowledge of God – a knowledge, no doubt, that Paul would insist belongs to Jewish Christian and Gentile Christian alike, insofar as both have been redeemed from some form of idolatry (Gal 4:9).

Galatians 4:3-7: New Exodus and the Spirit

In light of the foregoing discussion it is hardly adequate then to speak of Gal 4:1-2 as a matter of "typology" (so Scott) or even as an "analogy" (so Hafemann).[149] Rather, these verses describe the circumstances of Israel as a whole under the Law prior to God's sending of the Son. In Gal 4:3-7, Paul then asserts that he and his fellow Jewish Christians had participated in this history prior to their redemption: just as Israel throughout its history was under guardians, when Paul and his fellow Jewish Christians were νήπιοι (i.e. before the coming of Christ and their reception of the Spirit), they were no better off than slaves, but rather were under the elements of the cosmos.[150] Based on the analysis given above, Paul's choice of the word νήπιοι does not simply hearken back to Gal 4:1 – it also alludes to Israel's history of idolatry, which helps to make sense of his statement in Gal 4:3 concerning the elements of the cosmos. Although most commentators take the verse to refer to Jew and Gentile alike, with a minority I suggest that in Gal 4:3, as in Gal 3:13, Paul again uses the first person plural to refer to himself and his fellow Jewish Christians.[151] Two points support this suggestion. First, the analysis

---

[149] Scott, *Adoption as Sons of God*, 149-51 *et passim*; Hafemann, "Paul and the Exile of Israel in Galatians 3-4," 339.

[150] Here again I side with Hafemann, "Paul and the Exile of Israel in Galatians 3-4," 339-41 against Scott, *Adoption as Sons of God*, 149-57. The latter takes 4:3-7 as referring to humankind in general, but such a reading fails to recognize the significance of the parallels between 4:1-7 and 3:23-29, as well as the relationship between the redemption of Israel and the ingathering of the Gentiles. Moreover, it makes no sense to say with Scott (*Adoption as Sons of God*, 173) that Gentile Christians were ever "under the Law."

[151] So rightly R. Longenecker, *Galatians*, 164; cf. Matera, *Galatians*, 149: "The first person plural is emphasized by *kai hēmeis* ('even we') and can be understood in either an exclusive sense ('we Jewish Christians') or an inclusive sense ('we Jewish and Gentile Christians'). While most commentators prefer the latter interpretation, Paul's use of 'you' in v. 6 suggests that the 'we' in this verse should be taken in an exclusive sense: we Jewish Christians. Thus Paul is talking about the situation of his kinsmen just as he does in 2:16 (*kai*

above suggests that the terms νήπιοι and νηπιότης connote Israel's idolatrous history.¹⁵² Second, in Gal 4:9 Paul asserts that by submitting to the Torah the Galatians would be returning to slavery under the elements of the cosmos. In other words, even though the Law acted as a guardian over Israel, the nation's history showed it to be enslaved to sin and idolatry. By turning to the Law, Paul's Gentile Christian followers would be abandoning the Spirit which leads to freedom in order to serve under the Law, which had failed to keep Israel from falling into idolatry.¹⁵³

Before we proceed to consider the rest of Gal 4:1-7, two clarifications are in order. First, by saying that Paul refers only to Jewish Christians in 4:3, I am not suggesting that he did not believe that Gentiles, too, were under the elements – the very fact that he speaks of them returning again (ἐπιστρέφετε πάλιν) to the elements in 4:9 implies that they were once under the same or similar powers.¹⁵⁴ Second, in arguing that Paul viewed the Jews under the elements, I am not suggesting that he equated the elements with the Law, thereby implying that the Gentiles, too, were at one point under the Law. Rather, I maintain that being "under the Law" for Paul is one way of being under the elements (shocking though it no doubt sounded to his fellow Jews), a way that the Galatian Christians were seeking to embrace (Gal 4:21). Being under the Law would not and could not prevent either Israel or the Gentiles from falling into the slavery of idolatry, as the reference to Israel's "infancy" in 4:1 and 3 implies.

---

hēmeis, 'even we'); 3:13; and 3:23-24." See also Dunn, *Galatians*, 212, though he takes the verse to represent the beginning of a shift to a more generalized "we" including Jew and Gentile alike in Christ; Bruce (*Galatians*, 193) also suggests that v. 3 most likely refers specifically to Christians of Jewish descent; Williams (*Galatians*, 109) suggests that the we must "at least *include* Jews" (original emphasis). *Pace* Schlier, *Der Brief an die Galater*, 193 and Martyn, *Galatians*, 388.

¹⁵² In this regard it is interesting to note that the two occurrences of the root in Hosea appear in a context which highlights Israel's going after Baal (Hos 2:13, 17 [15, 19 LXX]; 11:2), a word that connotes a master or owner. These motifs resonate with Paul's use of the imagery of slavery.

¹⁵³ Intriguingly, this interpretation has some similarities with Paul's diatribe against self-satisfied Jewish criticism of the Gentiles in Romans 1-3. Paul's language about the heir being no better off than the slave in 4:1-2 corresponds to Jews being no better off than the Gentiles. Despite its possession of the Law, Israel had been enslaved to sin and idolatry throughout its history. Such an interpretation also fits with the reading of Galatians 5-6 offered below, in which the works of the flesh are the result of living in the old age of the Law rather than in the new age of the Spirit.

¹⁵⁴ Incidentally, the shift in Gal 4:8 to the second person may also support the argument that in 4:1-7 the "we" refers to Jewish Christians.

The fullness of (the) time

This slavery to the elements was to last only until the "fullness of (the) time came" (Gal 4:4). As many commentators note, the phrase "fullness of time" represents a common motif in early Jewish and Christian eschatology.[155] Among Jewish texts, 1QpHab 7.2 refers to the appointed time prophesied in Hab 2:3 as "the consummation of the era (נמר הקץ)."[156] Likewise, the penitential prayer of Daniel 9, which anticipates the redemption of Israel in light of Jeremiah's prophecy of the 70 years of punishment, speaks of those years as the "number of years... to fill" (מספר השנים... למלאות) (Dan 9:2). Among early Christian texts, perhaps the most significant is Mark 1:15, in which Jesus proclaims "the time is fulfilled (πεπλήρωται ὁ καιρός) and the kingdom of God has come near." The connection between fulfillment of time and the kingdom is particularly noteworthy, given that later in Galatians Paul makes one of the few references in his letters to the kingdom of God (Gal 5:21), and specifically in conjunction with inheritance language, a key theme in Gal 4:1-7. It is interesting to note, moreover, that in 4:4 Paul once again uses the term χρόνος. Given the connection between 4:1-2 and 4:3-7, the articular form τοῦ χρόνου should be taken as anaphoric: the fullness of the heir's time as a νήπιος (4:1) under the guardianship of the Law ends with the sending of the Son and the Spirit.[157]

The sending of the Son

At this fullness of time God (the "father" of 4:2) sends his son to redeem "those under the Law." As most commentators note, the phrase "born of a woman" refers to the humanity of Jesus, a bit puzzling here in that it does not seem to play a significant role in the argument. More clearly significant (and debated) is the designation "born under the Law (γενόμενον ὑπὸ νόμον)," which some take as an equivalent to "under the elements." Martyn, for example, asserts that for Paul the Law and the elements have been fused together, such that all human beings are under the power of the Law and of the elements.[158] Similarly, Scott suggests that "those under the Law" in 4:5 refers to all human beings, based on the parallelism between 4:5a and 4:5b ("those under the Law," "we might receive adoption as sons"), as well as parallels

---

[155] Betz, *Galatians*, 206; Scott, *Adoption as Sons of God*, 161-62; Bruce, *Galatians*, 194; Williams, *Galatians*, 111; Dunn, *Galatians*, 213-14; R. Longenecker, *Galatians*, 170; Matera, *Galatians*, 150; Schlier, *Der Brief an die Galater*, 194-95.

[156] In this regard, it is significant that Paul cites Habakkuk 2 in Gal 3:11. Indeed, a reading of "fullness of time" as referring to eschatological fulfillment supports the suggestion that Paul interprets Habakkuk 2:4 eschatologically.

[157] So Hafemann, "Paul and the Exile of Israel in Galatians 3-4," 341; see also Bruce, *Galatians*, 194.

[158] Martyn, *Galatians*, 390; see also Betz, *Galatians*, 208.

between 4:1-7 and 3:10-14.[159] Moreover, he suggests that the general nature of the ἡμεῖς in Gal 4:3 supports this interpretation, insofar as Paul speaks of humankind in general throughout 4:3-7.

Scott's and Martyn's proposals run into a number of difficulties, however. As noted above, a strong case can be made for taking the ἡμεῖς of Gal 4:3 to refer more narrowly to Jewish Christians (though not implying that Gentiles were not under the elements). In addition, as Scott himself notes, the only other occurrence of the phrase οἱ ὑπὸ νόμον in the Pauline corpus (1 Cor 9:20-21) refers to Jews.[160] Indeed, it is puzzling that Scott appeals to Gal 4:21 to support his case: "Paul clearly addresses the Galatian Gentiles, those who want to undergo supplementary circumcision after conversion, as οἱ ὑπὸ νόμον θέλοντες εἶναι (4:21)."[161] The very logic of this verse points in exactly the opposite direction. Precisely by seeking circumcision, the Galatians are seeking to come under the Law – a status that they did not have prior to circumcision. Moreover, the parallels with Gal 3:10-14 need not imply that Paul has all of humanity in mind in 4:4-5. On the contrary, if the interpretation of 3:10-14 provided above is correct, then the most natural reading of Gal 4:4-5 would be to take "those under the Law" to refer once again to Jewish Christians.[162] Such a reading, though not without its own difficulties, fits well with the rest of the passage, and makes the connection between 4:1-7 and 3:10-14 clearer.[163]

The two main difficulties with this reading concern the relationship between Gal 4:5a and 4:5b and the relation of 4:7 to the rest of the passage as a whole. To begin with 4:5, it might seem natural to take the verb ἀπολάβωμεν to refer to all believers; two considerations, however, point in a different direction. First, the parallels between 3:13-14 and 4:5 (both use the verb ἐξαγοράζω and a form of λαμβάνω/ἀπολαμβάνω in speaking of redemption from

---

[159] Scott, *Adoption as Sons of God*, 172-74.

[160] Ibid., 173.

[161] Ibid.

[162] Not insignificantly, in addition to pointing back to Gal 3:13, Paul's use of the term ἐξαγοράζω with its connotations of buying back from slavery most likely points to Israel's slavery under the elements in Gal 4:3, thus confirming that Paul refers to Jewish Christians in that verse. In the undisputed Pauline epistles, the verb only occurs in these two verses. The language of "buying back" may hint at further exodus imagery, although the verb does not appear in the LXX. On the relationship between Gal 3:13-14 and 4:4-5, see Betz, *Galatians*, 207, though I believe Betz poses too sharp a dichotomy between the two passages. A more reasonable explanation is that Paul focuses on different aspects of the redemption in each passage. See again Hays, *The Faith of Jesus Christ*, 75-82.

[163] B. Longenecker, *Triumph*, 92, puts it well: "In this way, Gal. 4.4-5 reveals the following chronological series of events: (1) the situation of Israel is the context into which God's son was 'sent', in order that (2) that same situation might be redeemed, with the result that (3) salvation might be offered on a universal scale, beyond the exclusive boundaries of the people Israel."

the Law /the curse of the Law) suggest that the two passages should be read together. If as argued above the verb λάβωμεν in 3:14 refers primarily to Jewish Christians, then it should not be at all surprising for Paul to use the verb again to refer to himself and his fellow Jewish Christians.[164] Second, the shift between first and second person in 4:5-6 makes a distinction between the two groups natural, if not absolutely necessary.[165] If Paul were referring to all Christians in 4:5, then one might expect him to maintain the use of the first person plural throughout 4:6.[166] As it stands, the way that Paul alternates between first and second person suggests a different explanation based on the interrelationship between the ingathering of the Gentiles and the outpouring of the Spirit, which we will discuss further below.[167]

Although Paul focuses primarily on Jewish Christians in Gal 4:1-7, this does not mean that he thinks Gentiles were any better off prior to the sending of the son. As noted above, the fact that he speaks in 4:9 about the Galatians *returning* to serve the elements implies that they, too, were once slaves.[168] Moreover, his appeal to their newfound status as sons (4:6) also implies a former slavery, such that it would make sense for him to address them in 4:7 as no longer slaves but sons. In addition to these considerations, as has been noted several times, Gal 4:1-7 follows a pattern similar to Gal 3:10-14, which begins with the problem of "those under the Law" and ends with the ramifica-

---

[164] Again, though, one must be careful not to take this focus on Jewish Christians in 4:5 to be exclusive. Just as in 3:14 Paul focuses on the reception of the Spirit by Jewish Christians while acknowledging that Gentiles, too, receive the Spirit, so too in 4:5 he focuses on the adoption of Jewish Christians, all the while maintaining that Gentiles, too, have been adopted by God (cf. 3:26; 4:6-7).

[165] Cf. R. Longenecker, *Galatians*, 172: "If vv 4-5, however, are a confessional portion that stems from early Jewish Christendom, as we propose, then 'those under the law' of v 5a and 'we' of v 5b are to be seen in parallel fashion...with the result that what is said about God's activity in these two cases should also be taken as roughly parallel. The statements, then, are probably to be interpreted as complementary facets of what Jewish believers in Jesus had experienced: (1) redemption from both the law's condemnation (cf. 3:13) and the law's supervision (cf. 3:23-25), and (2) reception of a new relationship with God, which involved primarily the enjoyment of full sonship rights."

[166] That others saw this difficulty is evident from the manuscript evidence: several MSS have a second person plural pronoun (ὑμῶν) modifying καρδίας rather than the first person plural, trying to bring the pronoun into harmony with the verb ἐστε. The reading ἡμῶν is the most likely reading, however, based both on early and multiple manuscript evidence and on *lectio difficilior*. See Bruce M. Metzger (ed.), *A Textual Commentary on the Greek New Testament* (New York: United Bible Societies, 1994), 526.

[167] As noted above with respect to Gal 3:14, one might also expect Paul to use some qualifying adjective such as "all" to indicate that he was referring to Jew and Gentile in Christ alike.

[168] In this regard, it is worth noting that in 4:1-2 Paul speaks of both the heir and the slave, seeming to refer to two different groups. If the heir refers to Israel, then the slave most naturally refers to the Gentiles.

tions for both Gentile Christians (blessing) and Jewish Christians (the Spirit).[169] Now that Jewish Christians, who were no better off than slaves (4:1), have been redeemed from the curse of the Law, Gentile Christians, who once were actual slaves (4:8), are now sons and fellow heirs with their Jewish Christian brethren.[170] Again, it is worth noting how similar this pattern is to that found in 3:23-29, especially the shift from Jewish freedom from the pedagogue in 3:25 to Gentile Christians' status as sons in 3:26. In keeping with the pattern of argument throughout 3:1-4:7, now that Jewish Christians have finally been redeemed from the Law, Gentile Christians, too, are no longer slaves, but sons and fellow heirs (cf. 3:29). Conversely, now that Gentiles have been welcomed into the people of God and the blessing of Abraham, Jewish Christians have at last received the Spirit promised by God through the prophets.

The outpouring of the Spirit

Taking Gal 4:5 as a whole to refer to Jewish Christians, then, how does Paul's shift to the second person in 4:6 fit into the argument? Again, the parallels with 3:13-14, as well as 3:24-26, are instructive. To begin with the former passage, just as 3:13-14 climaxes in the outpouring of the Spirit, so does 4:6. Perhaps more significantly, the structural parallels with 3:23-29 helps to explain the sense of the conjunction ὅτι. Paul begins by describing Israel's status under the Law as a pedagogue (3:23). In 3:25, he then asserts that with the coming of faith (or "the faith") Jews are no longer under the pedagogue. As proof of this (note the explanatory γάρ of 3:26), he points to the Galatian Christians' status as sons. The explanatory significance of the inclusion of the Gentiles in 3:26 suggests that the ὅτι of 4:6 should be taken in a causal sense. The argument runs as follows: the fact that the Gentiles have been incorporated into Christ demonstrates the inauguration of the eschatological age. One significant feature of this age, witnessed to by both the prophetic literature and some Second Temple texts, was the outpouring of the Spirit into the heart.[171] Because God has opened the way for Gentiles to enter the people of God, the Jews have at last received the promise of the Spirit, which the Law itself had failed to bring about. With the redemption of Jewish Christians from the curse of the Law (3:13; 4:5), God inaugurates the eschatological age that entails the inclusion of the Gentiles and the gift of the Spirit.

The significance of the outpouring of the Spirit specifically into the hearts of Jewish Christians makes most sense in light of the prophetic and Second

---

[169] Again, this is not to say that only the Gentiles received the blessing and only the Jews received the Spirit – it is a matter of what Paul is emphasizing in this part of the argument.

[170] See Hafemann, "Paul and the Exile of Israel in Galatians 3-4," 348.

[171] See, e.g., Ezek 36:26-27 and *Jub.* 1:22-25, and the discussion of these and other texts in chapters two and three above.

Temple background of the Spirit imagery in Gal 4:6. Two key OT texts serve as the primary backdrop of Paul's language about the Spirit. Commentators have noticed connections in language between 4:6 and Ezekiel 36:[172]

> A new *heart* I will give you, and a new *spirit* I will put within you; and I will remove from your body the *heart* of stone and give you a *heart* of flesh. I will put my *Spirit* within you, and make you follow my statutes and be careful to observe my ordinances. (Ezek 36:26-27, NRSV, modified, emphasis added)

This passage, as well as traditions that developed out of it, most likely represents a key part of the background to Paul's statement in Gal 4:6: "God sent the *Spirit* of his Son into our *hearts* crying, 'Abba, Father!'" Given the close linguistic and thematic resonances between the two passages, the restoration eschatology of the broader context of the Ezekiel passage should inform our interpretation of Paul's statement about the Spirit.[173] Although many commentators note the connections between Gal 4:6 and Ezekiel 36, often they do not recognize the significance of the latter passage for Paul's argument as an answer to the problem of Deuteronomy.[174] One of the key problems repeated again and again throughout Deuteronomy is a failure of the heart.[175] Prophecies such as this one in Ezekiel, as well as the closely related Jeremiah 31, serve as the answer to this problem of the heart and speak of the redemption of Israel. In this light, the shift back to the first person in 4:6b fits with the line of Paul's argument: God sent his son to redeem those under the Law (Jewish Christians) in the eschatological age, which results in the extension of the blessing to the Gentiles and the long-anticipated outpouring of the Spirit into the hearts of Jewish Christians. Furthermore, the logic of this verse reflects Paul's earlier formulation in 3:14 that the outpouring of the Spirit is integrally connected to the extension of the blessing to the Gentiles.

Less often noted, but no less significant for Paul's understanding of the outpouring of the Spirit, is Isaiah 63. Although Paul does not explicitly cite the text, a number of parallels with Gal 4:1-7 suggest that Paul interpreted the gift of the Spirit in terms of a new exodus:

> But *they rebelled and grieved his holy Spirit*; therefore he became their enemy; he himself fought against them. Then they remembered the days of old, of Moses his servant. Where is the one who brought them up out of the sea with the shepherds of his flock? *Where is the one*

---

[172] See chapter two above for a fuller discussion of Ezekiel 36, as well as other texts relating to the spirit in Ezekiel. On the connection between Galatians 4 and Ezekiel 36, see Martyn, *Galatians*, 391-92; see also Walther Zimmerli, *Ezekiel 2* (trans. James D. Martin; Hermeneia; Philadelphia: Fortress, 1983), 252; much earlier, Aquinas, *Galatians*, 119; strangely, Dunn (*Galatians*, 220) connects Galatians 4 with Ezekiel 37, but not Ezekiel 36.

[173] It is also worth noting that Ezekiel 36 most likely lies in the background of Paul's discussion of the writing of the "letter of Christ" in 2 Cor 3:3.

[174] So, e.g., Martyn, *Galatians*, 391-92.

[175] See Deut 4:25-29; 6:4-6; 10:12, 16; 26:16; 28:47, 65, 67; 30:1-10, as well as the excursus in chapter two above.

who put within them his holy Spirit, who caused his glorious arm to march at the right hand of Moses, who divided the waters before them to make for himself an everlasting name, who led them through the depths? Like a horse in the desert, they did not stumble. Like cattle that go down into the valley, the Spirit of the LORD gave them rest. Thus you led your people, to make for yourself a glorious name. Look down from heaven and see, from your holy and glorious habitation. Where are your zeal and your might? The yearning of your heart and your compassion? They are withheld from me. *For you are our father, though Abraham does not know us and Israel does not acknowledge us; you, O LORD, are our father*; our Redeemer from of old is your name. Why, O LORD, do you make us stray from your ways and *harden our heart,* so that we do not fear you? Turn back for the sake of your servants, for the sake of the tribes that are your heritage. Your holy people took possession for a little while; but now our adversaries have trampled down your sanctuary. We have long been like those whom you do not rule, like those not called by your name. (Isa 63:10-19, NRSV, modified, emphasis added)

A number of features in this text call for comment.[176] First, the passage speaks not only of the Spirit's activity, but of God putting the holy Spirit within the Israelites (ὁ θεὶς ἐν αὐτοῖς τὸ πνεῦμα τὸ ἅγιον, 63:11 [LXX]). Second, the prayer of repentance pleads for a new act of redemption based on the paradigmatic redemption of the exodus. Third, the petition stresses God's role as father – one of the key features in the climax of Gal 4:4-6. Fourth, the text also puts an emphasis on the hardness of Israel's heart, perhaps drawing on the tradition of Deuteronomy that sees Israel's problem as one of the heart. Finally, the Greek text speaks of the goal of this redemption as inheritance: "that we might inherit a small part of your holy mountain" (ἵνα μικρὸν κληρονομήσωμεν τοῦ ὄρους τοῦ ἁγίου σου; Isa 63:18 [LXX]).[177]

In addition to Ezekiel 36 and Isaiah 63, as we saw in chapter three above, similar themes appear in a number of documents from the Second Temple pe-

---

[176] For a fuller discussion of this section of Isaiah, see pp. 26-28 above.

[177] One other factor may lend support to the possibility that traditions stemming from Isaiah 63 lie in the background of Gal 4:1-7. Isaiah 63 seems to appear in other parts of the Pauline tradition in Ephesians 4 and Hebrews 13. Significantly, both texts only allude to Isaiah, rather than citing it explicitly. Ephesians 4:30 alludes to Isa 63:10, exhorting the recipients of the letter "do not grieve the holy Spirit of God (μὴ λυπεῖτε τὸ πνεῦμα τὸ ἅγιον τοῦ θεοῦ)." Although the lexical connections are not many, the phrase "holy Spirit" is rare in the OT, and only Isa 63:10 refers to people causing some offense to God's holy Spirit: "but they disobeyed and provoked his holy Spirit (παρώξυναν τὸ πνεῦμα τὸ ἅγιον αὐτοῦ)." Similarly, the Epistle to the Hebrews draws on language from Isaiah 63 at the end of the exhortation, when it refers to Jesus as the "great shepherd of the sheep" (τὸν ποιμένα τῶν προβάτων τὸν μέγαν) (Heb 13:20; cf. Isa 63:11 [LXX]). Although both of these texts are most likely later than Galatians, they at least demonstrate that Isaiah 63 was known and drawn upon in early Christian tradition, and more specifically in Pauline circles. In referring to Ephesians and Hebrews, I make no claims about the authorship of either epistle. I simply appeal to them as texts in the Pauline tradition, the former more so than the latter. G. K. Beale ("The Old Testament Background of Paul's Reference to 'the Fruit of the Spirit' in Galatians 5:22," *BBR* 15 (2005): 1-38, esp. 13) also notes the possible allusions to Isaiah 63 in Ephesians and Hebrews.

riod. Most significantly, *Jub.* 1:22-25 alludes to Ezekiel's promise of the sending of a new spirit into the heart and combines it with a renewed relationship of sonship. Similarly, *T. Jud.* 24:1-6 associates the outpouring of the Spirit with a filial relationship. Although this text does not refer to the heart explicitly, the preceding chapter describes a return to the Lord in "integrity of heart" in the context of Israel's disobedience to the Law.[178] Finally, although the *Words of the Luminaries* does not refer to "sonship," it does also speak of the Spirit in relation to a problem of the heart. The appearance of this constellation of themes in both OT texts and the Second Temple period confirms that this is the most appropriate context within which to understand Paul's reference to God's sending of the Spirit into the hearts of believers. Moreover, the expectation of sonship in *Jubilees* and the *Testament of Judah* suggests that an emphasis on Jewish Christians' new status as sons would be in keeping with at least some Second Temple Jewish expectations.

No longer a slave but a son

With 4:7 Paul provisionally concludes not only the smaller subsection of Gal 4:1-7, but also the longer argument begun at Gal 3:1, shifting to the second person singular to bring home the import of his argument for each Galatian Christian personally.[179] Once again Paul reminds the Galatians that, as a result of the redemption of Israel from the curse of the Law, Gentile Christians, too, are now sons in Christ through the Spirit. The consistent reference to Israel's slavery under the Law serves to demonstrate to the Galatians why they should not seek to submit to the Law – to do so would be to return to the slavery from which they have been freed.

Galatians 4:1-7: Summary

As we have seen, Gal 4:1-7, like Gal 3:10-14, makes sense in light of a pattern in which the redemption of Israel and the blessing/inclusion of the Gentiles are interrelated. As in Gal 3:10-14, the primary object of Paul's redemption language in 4:5 is Jewish Christians, the only ones who in any real sense were under the Law. This reading fits with the line of argument throughout Galatians 3, in which Paul wrestles with the relationship between the giving of the Law and the promise to Abraham. Once again, the Spirit serves as the sign of the eschatological age, though in 4:1-7 Paul elaborates on the simple reception of the Spirit in 3:14. Paul interprets the outpouring of the Spirit specifically into the heart as an indication that at long last God has begun the redemption of Israel promised in various parts of the prophetic corpus.

---

[178] Cf. Scott, *Adoption as Sons of God*, 179.

[179] On Gal 4:7 as the conclusion to the larger argument beginning at Gal 3:1, see Betz, *Galatians*, 211; Luz, *Geschichtsverständnis*, 282; R. Longenecker, *Galatians*, 175.

The Outpouring of the Spirit and the Galatian Situation

One of the great strengths of Martyn's magisterial commentary on Galatians is the care he takes to read the letter in light of the situation in Galatia, and more specifically vis-à-vis the outlook of the "Teachers."[180] Before turning to Galatians 5-6, it would be worth considering briefly how Paul's argument relates to his opponents' position. Despite the obvious differences, it seems likely that Paul and his opponents would share at least some common assumptions about the Spirit. In particular, Paul's opponents would be amenable to many of the expectations traced out in chapter three above, especially since some of the texts (e.g., *Jubilees*) strongly emphasize the importance of keeping the Law. Moreover, some of these texts connect the keeping of the Law with the gift of the Spirit.[181] Indeed, according to Martyn the Teachers asserted that Gentiles would receive the Spirit through proper exegesis of Scripture and observance of the Law, perhaps drawing on a tradition reflected in *Jub.* 1:22-25.[182] At root, then, the point of contention between Paul and the Teachers comes down to how the Galatians received and should continue to live out their life in the Spirit. For Paul, the Spirit comes by means of the proclamation of the gospel of the crucified Christ (Gal 3:1-5). Moreover, the gospel alone has the power to guide the Galatians' life in the Spirit. Most likely part of the appeal of the Teachers' instruction was the guidance that the Law would give the Galatians for ordering their daily life.[183] Paul thus tries to make clear in Galatians 5 and 6 that the Spirit they received through the proclamation of the gospel is the only guidance the Galatians need.

Conclusion

As we have seen, Paul's argument with respect to the Spirit in Galatians 3-4 is the result of a confluence of factors and ideas including Scripture, the history of Israel's (corporate) failure to obey the commands of Torah, and Paul's and the Galatians' experience of the eschatological outpouring of the Spirit.[184]

---

[180] See Martyn, *Galatians*, 27-34, 41-42, *et passim*. "Teachers" is the neutral term Martyn uses to refer to "the Christian-Jewish evangelists who came into Paul's Galatian churches after his departure" (*Galatians*, 588).

[181] Martyn, *Galatians*, 286 n. 17.

[182] Ibid., 123, 286 n. 17.

[183] Ibid., 302-06; cf. John M. G. Barclay, *Obeying the Truth: A Study of Paul's Ethics in Galatians* (Studies of the New Testament and its World; Edinburgh: T. & T. Clark, 1988), 68-72.

[184] It may come as a surprise that the present chapter does not discuss Gal 4:21-5:1, with its citation of Isa 54:1 in 4:27 and reference to those "born according to the flesh" and those "born according to the Spirit" 4:29. The reason for this is simple: although Paul refers to the

Scripturally, Paul interprets the Galatians' reception of the Spirit in light of the prophetic promises of an outpouring of God's Spirit at the time of Israel's restoration, though he has redefined this restoration in terms of resurrection and new creation with no emphasis on a nationalistic return to the land. At the same time, he interprets this outpouring in terms of the promise to Abraham that all nations would be blessed in his seed. This promise to Abraham, combined with Israel's history of failure to obey the Law, leads to the dichotomy he sets up between the Spirit and the Law. The latter not only excluded the Gentiles, thus limiting the blessing of Abraham to the people of Israel; it also had failed to produce the life that it held out, only bringing about death, the ultimate curse of the Law (3:10-14, 21; cf. Deut 30:19). The outpouring of the Spirit, then, brings about two things for Paul. First, it opens up the blessing of Abraham to the Gentiles, while at the same time inaugurating the eschatological age promised by the prophets. Second, it gives believers initial participation in the eschatological life brought about through the death and resurrection of Jesus. An aspect of both of these results, again anticipated in some of the prophetic promises concerning the Spirit, is the ability to serve God faithfully from the heart. It should come as no surprise, then, that following his lengthy argument against doing the Law in Galatians 3-4, Paul turns to the implications of life in the Spirit for daily living in Galatians 5-6.

Spirit in passing, it does not play a central role in the argument, and does not add much to the arguments in 3:10-14 and 4:1-7 – rather, it seems to presuppose them. Nevertheless, it is significant that toward the climax of the central section of the epistle, Paul cites a text from Isaiah with eschatological overtones similar to the ones I have suggested as fundamental to Paul's earlier arguments about the Spirit.

Chapter 5

New Creation and the Spirit in Galatians 5-6: Bearing Fruit Unto Eternal Life

Introduction

The preceding chapter argued that Paul's emphasis on the Spirit in Galatians 3-4 makes the most sense in light of the various eschatological expectations about the Spirit in the Second Temple period. What remains for the present study is to show how this context makes sense of Paul's continued emphasis on the Spirit in the exhortations of Galatians 5-6.

The question of how these last two chapters of Galatians relate to the rest of the epistle has been the subject of much debate in the history of modern biblical scholarship. John Barclay provides a helpful overview of the various stances taken by scholars with respect to this relationship.[1] Representative of the most extreme position, J. C. O'Neill considers Gal 5:13-6:7 to be an interpolation totally unrelated to the rest of the epistle and not from the hand of Paul.[2] Less extreme, though still emphasizing the discontinuity between this section and the rest of the epistle, Martin Dibelius argues that this section presents paraenesis, which he defines as a series of wisdom teachings unrelated to one another and to their broader context.[3] A third group of scholars suggests that the moral teaching serves as a preemptive argument against possible objections to Paul's view of the Law presented in the earlier parts of the epistle.[4] Finally, the apparently strange conjunction of Paul's antinomian argument in chapters 3 and 4 with the moral injunctions of chapters 5 and 6 has led some to suggest that Paul addresses two different groups, a strict nomist party and a libertine party.[5]

---

[1] This paragraph relies heavily on John M. G. Barclay, *Obeying the Truth: A Study of Paul's Ethics in Galatians* (Studies of the New Testament and its World; Edinburgh: T. & T. Clark, 1988), 9-26.

[2] J. C. O'Neill, *The Recovery of Paul's Letter to the Galatians* (London: Penguin Books, 1972), 65-71.

[3] Martin Dibelius, *Die Formgeschichte des Evangeliums* (Tübingen: Mohr/Siebeck, 1959), 239.

[4] See, e.g., Franz Mussner, *Der Galaterbrief* (HTKNT 9; Freiberg: Herder, 1974), 364-65.

[5] See, e.g., J. H. Ropes, *The Singular Problem of the Epistle to the Galatians* (HTS 14; Cambridge: Harvard University, 1929), modifying and expanding on the earlier arguments of

Against these positions, Barclay makes a compelling case for an integral relationship between the paraenetic material in Galatians 5-6 and the rest of the epistle, taking into account some of the strengths and weaknesses of other readings that seek to understand the letter as a unified whole.[6] Although he makes a number of observations in this regard, I would like to highlight two of Barclay's suggestions. First, he points to the concentration of vices relating to communal strife in Gal 5:25 to suggest that this section of the epistle is directed specifically to the situation in Galatia.[7] Whether the divisions in the Galatian church arose from or simply were exacerbated by the agitators, it is clear from early on in the epistle that communal division was a primary concern for Paul (see esp. Gal 2:15-21).[8] Second, Barclay notes that the Spirit/flesh dichotomy so central to Galatians 5 continues a theme that begins earlier in the epistle (see Gal 3:3; 4:29).[9]

These two points suggest a fundamental continuity throughout the letter, which, I will suggest, makes sense in light of the eschatology of Galatians. As I argued in the first three chapters, the outpouring of the Spirit serves as a sign of the in-breaking of the eschatological age, both in Second Temple Jewish sources and in Paul's own thought. It is *prima facie* likely, then, that Paul's continued emphasis on the Spirit depends upon the eschatological underpinnings of his argument.[10] As in Galatians 3-4, eschatological language appears periodically in the last two chapters of the epistle. Four terms in particular merit our attention. In Gal 5:2-12, which serves as a transition from Galatians 3-4 to the final hortatory section of the epistle, Paul connects the Spirit with the expectation of "righteousness." As we saw in chapters 3 and 4 righteousness functions as an eschatological category, both in OT and intertestamental texts and in Paul's own thought. Similarly, in Gal 5:21 Paul warns the Galatians that those who practice the works of the flesh will not inherit the "kingdom of God," a term that was closely connected to eschatology in the early Christian movement.[11] Third, in Gal 6:8 Paul associates life in the

---

Wilhelm Lütgert, *Gesetz und Geist: Eine Untersuchung zur Vorgeschichte des Galaterbriefes* (Beiträge zur Förderung christlicher Theologie; Gütersloh: C. Bertelsmann, 1919).

[6] A similar case had been made earlier by Richard B. Hays, "Christology and Ethics in Galatians: the Law of Christ," *CBQ* 49 (1987): 268-90.

[7] Barclay, *Obeying the Truth*, 152-54. On the same point, see again Hays, "Christology and Ethics in Galatians," 286.

[8] On the question of the genesis of the discord, see Barclay, *Obeying the Truth*, 154. The connection with Gal 2:15-21 is my own.

[9] Ibid., 178-82.

[10] For a helpful article dealing with this issue, see Walt Russell, "The Apostle Paul's Redemptive-Historical Argumentation in Galatians 5:13-26," *WTJ* 57 (1995): 333-57.

[11] See, e.g., Mark 1:15, which connects the fulfillment of time with the approach of the kingdom. Cf. David J. Lull, *The Spirit in Galatia: Paul's Interpretation of Pneuma as Divine Power* (SBLDS 49; Ann Arbor: Scholars Press, 1980), 175: "Other evidence that Paul identi-

Spirit with reception of "eternal life," a phrase which confirms our earlier argument that the life Paul describes in Galatians 3 is eschatological. Finally, in Gal 6:15 Paul closes the letter by denying the significance of both circumcision and uncircumcision in comparison with the "new creation," yet another key eschatological term.[12] This periodic appearance of eschatological language at climactic points in the argument suggests that the entire letter is set within an eschatological framework and that Paul's instructions on daily life grow naturally from his understanding of the outpouring of the Spirit that he articulates in Galatians 3-4.[13]

Methodology

As was the case in chapter four, the purpose of the present chapter as a whole is not to argue for allusions to specific OT texts or to other texts from the intertestamental period. Rather, the goal is to demonstrate that general Jewish expectations about the outpouring of the Spirit – which appear in a variety of Second Temple texts – illuminate Paul's argument insofar as his instructions for daily life spring forth naturally from the eschatological gift of the Spirit. Based on the general eschatological expectations traced in chapters two and three and on the connection between the present section and Paul's argument in Galatians 3-4, I will argue that the paraenetic material serves as an integral part of an eschatological whole whose basic premise is the gift of the Spirit.

The present chapter, then, will provide exegetical treatments of the remaining passages in which the Spirit plays a significant role in Galatians 5-6. I will begin by discussing the connection between the Spirit and the hope of righteousness in Gal 5:2-6. I will then consider the Spirit/flesh dualism of 5:13-26 in light of its eschatological context.[14] In contrast to older ap-

---

fied the time of the Spirit as the 'last age' is the association of the Spirit with the kingdom of God."

[12] See, e.g., Isa 65:17-18. David W. Kuck, "'Each Will Bear his Own Burden': Paul's Creative Use of an Apocalyptic Motif," *NTS* 40 (1994): 289-97, esp. 295-96, gives a similar list of eschatological imagery in Galatians, including the element of judgment in Gal 6:7-9.

[13] I borrow the term "daily life" from J. Louis Martyn, *Galatians: A New Translation with Introduction and Commentary* (AB 33A; New York: Doubleday, 1997), 502, who rightly suggests that Paul has more in mind in Galatians 5 than what is commonly referred to as "morals" or "ethics."

[14] Throughout the present chapter, I will strive for consistency in the use of upper and lower case letters with respect to the terms "flesh" and "Spirit." As will become clear, I refer to "flesh" with a lower-case "f" because I do not find the arguments in favor of reading the term as a cosmological power compelling, at least not in the Letter to the Galatians. By contrast, most of the occurrences of the term "Spirit" in Galatians refer to God's own Spirit, and so I will continue to spell it with an upper case "s."

proaches that see an anthropological spirit/flesh dichotomy, I will suggest that the contrast Paul draws refers to the change in and overlap of the ages.[15] The "flesh" side of this contrast refers to human frailty prior to the coming of the Spirit; the "Spirit" side, however, refers not to an anthropological aspect of human nature but rather to God's own Spirit. We will then consider Paul's "kingdom" language and the "fruit of the Spirit," both of which relate to eschatological expectation. Finally, the relationship between the Spirit and eternal life in 6:7-10 will round out the discussion, confirming the connection between the curse of the Law and death for which I argued in chapter four.

Galatians 5:2-6: Awaiting the Hope of Righteousness by the Spirit

Before considering Galatians 5-6, we must address two formal questions regarding the structure of the epistle. First, does Paul's previous argument end at 4:31 or at 5:1? Second, does the hortatory section of the epistle begin at 5:1 (or 5:2, depending on where one sees the end of the argument in Galatians 3-4) or at 5:13? With regard to the first question, although 5:1 may serve as a kind of transition to the following section, it seems best to take it primarily as concluding Gal 4:21-31.[16] Paul's allegory of Sarah and Hagar highlights language of "freedom" and "slavery," which leads naturally into the final exhortation of 5:1 to bring the argument to a provisional close. In addition, the conjunction οὖν in 5:1b makes more sense as signaling the conclusion of the preceding argument than as beginning a new section. Moreover, the sudden imperative and emphatic "I" in Gal 5:2 marks the beginning of a new (though closely related) subsection.

With respect to the second question, it seems best to take Gal 5:2-12 as a transitional section that shifts the discussion from the problem with the Law to practical instructions about how the Galatians ought to order their daily

---

[15] For a helpful, albeit dated, history of research on the question of this dualism, see Robert Jewett, *Paul's Anthropological Terms: A Study of their Use in Conflict Settings* (AGJU 10; Leiden: Brill, 1971), 49-95.

[16] With Martyn, *Galatians*, 432-33; Sam K. Williams, *Galatians* (ANTC; Nashville: Abingdon, 1997), 124-25; Richard B. Hays, *The Letter to the Galatians* (NIB 11; Nashville: Abingdon, 2000), 306; J. B. Lightfoot, *St. Paul's Epistle to the Galatians* (London: Macmillan, 1874), 185; against Heinrich Schlier, *Der Brief an die Galater* (KEK; Göttingen: Vandenhoeck & Ruprecht, 1949), 228; Mussner, *Der Galaterbrief*, 334; James D. G. Dunn, *The Epistle to the Galatians* (BNTC; London: Cambridge, 1993), 260-61; Hans-Dieter Betz, *Galatians: A Commentary on Paul's Letter to the Churches in Galatia* (Hermeneia; Philadelphia: Fortress, 1979), 251-52; Richard N. Longenecker, *Galatians* (WBC 41; Dallas: 1990), 223; Frank J. Matera, *Galatians* (SP 9; Collegeville: Liturgical Press, 1992), 180.

life.¹⁷ Several features in the text point in this direction. Paul once again refers to circumcision and the doing of the Law (5:2-3), two key themes in Galatians 3-4. He then contrasts righteousness from the Law with righteousness from Christ on the basis of faith and through the Spirit (5:4-5; cf. 2:21). In 5:6, he introduces the term ἀγάπη, which will serve as one of the key themes throughout the rest of the epistle.¹⁸ In 5:7-12, Paul once again exhorts the Galatians not to listen to the agitators since their message nullifies the scandal of the cross (5:11) before transitioning into his concrete instructions for the Galatians.

Although Gal 5:2-12 stands together as a unified whole, 5:2-6 pertains most directly to the present study of the Spirit in Galatians, and so we will focus on this section. These verses recapitulate Paul's argument to this point, coming to a climax and transitional point in 5:6.¹⁹ In 5:2-3, Paul returns to the question of circumcision, one of the primary indicators of submission to the Law to which Paul objects. Paul warns the Galatians that Christ will be of no benefit to them if they submit to the Law. Although he does not use the language of curse again in chapter 5, the sentiments expressed are similar to those found in Gal 3:10 and the repetition of the warning signals its importance for Paul. In another parallel to Gal 3:10, Paul asserts that those who have themselves circumcised are obligated to do the entire Law (5:3; cf. the reference to "all the things written in the book of the Law" in 3:10). It is hardly a coincidence that Paul once again uses the term "to do" (ποιῆσαι) with reference to the Law, a term that has already appeared in his citation of Lev 18:5 and that Paul will contrast with "fulfillment" of the Law in Gal 5:14.²⁰

---

¹⁷ So, rightly, Matera, *Galatians*, 185: "In a word, this section recalls what has preceded and foreshadows what will come." See also Martyn, *Galatians*, 467-69. Commentators who see 5:1-12 (or 5:2-12) as the beginning of a new section include Betz, *Galatians*, 253-55; Lightfoot, *Galatians*, 203 (at least the discussions of critical issues between the treatment of 5:1 and 5:2 suggests that Lightfoot considers 5:2 to be the beginning of a new section); Hays, *Galatians*, 311 seems to include 5:2-12 with 5:13-6:10; those who see the section as the conclusion to the preceding argument include R. Longenecker, *Galatians*, 221-22; Dunn, *Galatians*, 261; Schlier, *Der Brief an die Galater*, 229; Mussner, *Der Galaterbrief*, 366. It is important to remember, however, that the problem with the Law never remains too far from the discussion. See, e.g., Gal 5:18.

¹⁸ Paul uses the verb ἀγαπάω earlier in the letter at Gal 2:20, but this is the first occurrence of the noun. See R. Longenecker, *Galatians*, 229-30; Betz, *Galatians*, 263; Matera, *Galatians*, 183; Mussner, *Der Galaterbrief*, 353-54; Hays, *Galatians*, 314; Charles H. Cosgrove, *The Cross and the Spirit: A Study in the Argument and Theology of Galatians* (Macon: Mercer University, 1988), 148.

¹⁹ On the connections between Gal 5:1-6 and Gal 3:28, see Wolfgang Harnisch, "Einübung des neuen Seins: Paulinische Paränese am Beispiel des Galaterbriefs," *ZTK* 84 (1987), 279-96, esp. 285.

²⁰ See R. Longenecker, *Galatians*, 227; Dunn, *Galatians*, 266-67; Matera, *Galatians*, 181; Mussner, *Der Galaterbrief*, 347-48; Martyn, *Galatians*, 470-71.

This use of ποιέω recalls one of the climaxes of his argument in 3:10-14, reminding the Galatians of the ever-present reality of the curse of the Law upon those who submit to it. Reaching further back in his argument, Paul then warns those who would achieve righteousness "in the Law" (5:4) that they have been cut off from the grace of Christ (cf. Gal 2:21a). Because righteousness cannot come from the Law (cf. 2:21 and 3:21b), those who seek righteousness in the Law not only do so in vain – they forfeit the grace they received through the cross of Christ.

In Gal 5:5-6, Paul then presents the alternative in which he wishes the Galatians to remain steadfast: the righteousness that one receives from the Spirit on the basis of faith. Using the first person pronoun ἡμεῖς in the emphatic first position, he highlights the contrast between those who would attain righteousness under the Law and those who are made righteous by means of the Spirit.[21] A number of features in v. 5 relate to the earlier parts of Paul's argument. Three key terms from Galatians 3 reappear in this short verse: the Spirit, faith, and righteousness. For this reason, some commentators see 5:5-6 as a summary of Gal 2:15-4:7.[22] The dative form πνεύματι recalls the dative appearing in 3:3, reminding the Galatians of how their life in Christ began. The phrase ἐκ πίστεως has already appeared a number of times (2:16; 3:7, 8, 9, 11, 12, 22, 24), always in contrast (whether explicitly or implicitly) with the works of the Law as the basis of righteousness.

In addition to these connections, it is significant that Paul describes righteousness as the object of eschatological hope (ἐλπίδα δικαιοσύνης ἀπεκδεχόμεθα), since this is the only verse in Galatians to speak of a future hope.[23] When combined with the connections that we saw in chapter two between righteousness and the outpouring of the Spirit in Isaiah, this association in Gal 5:5 lends further support to the eschatological reading of Galatians 3-4 provided above. At least two passages from Isaiah which we considered in chapter two tie the Spirit to righteousness.[24] Isaiah 32 describes the desolation of Israel due to the Israelites' sins before describing the nation's restoration by

---

[21] See R. Longenecker, *Galatians*, 228-29, though Longenecker takes the pronoun "we" to continue to refer to Jewish Christians; given the exhortations of the last two chapters and Paul's indifference to circumcision in 5:6, it seems best to take this first person pronoun to be more inclusive; see also Hays, *Galatians*, 313; Dunn, *Galatians*, 269; Matera, *Galatians*, 182; Mussner, *Der Galaterbrief*, 349.

[22] R. Longenecker, *Galatians*, 228-29; Betz, *Galatians*, 262-64; although Hays does not explicitly suggest that these verses summarize what has gone before, he does suggest that the terms "Spirit" and "faith" retain the connotations that they have accrued throughout the epistle (2:16; 3:1-14, 22-26; 4:6-7). See Hays, *Galatians*, 314; Martyn, *Galatians*, 472 also seems to imply a similar connection.

[23] Reading δικαιοσύνης as an epexegetical genitive with Martyn, *Galatians*, 472, 478-79; see also Hays, *Galatians*, 313; Dunn, *Galatians*, 270.

[24] See pp. 18-19 and 24-25 above for a fuller discussion of these two oracles.

means of the outpouring of the Spirit: "until a Spirit from on high is poured out on us, and the wilderness becomes a fruitful field" (Isa 32:15, NRSV, modified). Immediately following this outpouring, the nation will be blessed with the righteousness that was lacking due to Israel's sins: "Then justice will dwell in the wilderness, and righteousness abide in the fruitful field" (Isa 32:16, NRSV). Moreover, this righteousness is to lead to peace (Isa 32:17), yet another key theme that appears in Gal 6:16.

In a similar way, the giving of the Spirit in Isaiah 59 addresses the lack of righteousness in Israel. As we saw in chapter two, the first two-thirds of the chapter describes the state of sin among the Israelites, twice highlighting the lack of righteousness among the people (Isa 59:9; 14). In answer to this lack the Lord goes forth as a warrior wearing righteousness as a breastplate in order to redeem Zion. The oracle culminates in God describing his covenant to the prophet: "And as for me, this is my covenant with them, says the LORD: my *Spirit* which is upon you, and my words which I have put in your mouth, shall not depart out of your mouth" (Isa 59:21, NRSV, modified, emphasis added). In both these oracles, the eschatological outpouring of the Spirit accompanies God's act to redress the lack of righteousness among the people.

As we saw in chapter three above, this connection between the Spirit and righteousness extends also to some texts in the Second Temple period. The opening chapter of *Jubilees*, in which God promises Moses that he will create a new spirit for the Israelites to bring them back from their exile, twice highlights the righteousness to accompany Israel's restoration:[25]

When they seek me with all their heart and with all their soul, I shall reveal to them an abundance of peace in *righteousness*. (*Jub.* 1.15b, emphasis added)

And they [the Israelites] will all be called 'sons of the living God.' And every angel and spirit will know and acknowledge that they are my sons and I am their father in uprightness and *righteousness*. (*Jub.* 1:25, emphasis added)

In *Jubilees* as in Isaiah, "righteousness" functions as an eschatological category. Moreover, in two of the passages that we considered from the *Similitudes of Enoch*, the Spirit that God pours out upon the Elect One is associated

---

[25] For a fuller discussion of *Jubilees* 1, see chapter three above. Translations are taken from Orville S. Wintermute, "The Book of Jubilees" in *The Old Testament Pseudepigrapha* (2 vols.; ABRL; ed. James H. Charlesworth; New York: Doubleday, 1983, 1985), 2.35-142. Wintermute's translation expresses the "righteousness" language more clearly than James C. VanderKam, trans., *The Book of Jubilees* (CSCO 511; Paris: Aedibus E. Peeters, 1989): "I will rightly disclose to them abundant peace" (*Jub.* 1:15b); "They will know that they are my children and that I am their father in a just and proper way and that I love them" (*Jub.* 1:25b). Cf. the translation of R.H. Charles, *The Book of Jubilees, or The Little Genesis* (London: Adam and Charles Black, 1902): "And I shall disclose to them abounding peace with righteousness" (*Jub.* 1:16a); "[T]hey will know that these are My children, and that I am their Father in uprightness and righteousness, and that I love them" (*Jub.* 1:25b).

with righteousness. In *1 Enoch* 49 the outpouring of the Spirit appears in the context of a promise of deliverance/new creation for the "righteous ones" and following a vision of the "fountain of righteousness" (*1 En.* 48:1). *1 Enoch* 62 describes the outpouring of the "spirit of righteousness" on the Elect One, leading to new creation. Finally, the *Psalms of Solomon* also associate the giving of the Spirit to the messianic ruler in some way with righteousness: "And he will not weaken in his days, (relying) upon his God, for God made him powerful in the holy spirit and wise in the counsel of understanding, with strength and righteousness" (*Pss. Sol.* 17:37). The entirety of this psalm describes the advent of a messianic king and the regathering of the people of Israel, two eschatological events stemming from the OT prophetic literature.

These motifs common to Isaiah and to some Second Temple Jewish texts suggest that Paul's argument continues in the eschatological key present throughout Galatians 3-4. In addition, the language Paul uses in Gal 5:5-6 further confirms this eschatological character. As Hays notes, Paul's use of the words "hope" (ἐλπίς) and "eagerly expecting" (ἀπεκδεχόμεθα) hints at eschatological themes that he treats more explicitly in other epistles. Eschatological hope is not a pronounced motif in Galatians; nevertheless, the way Paul speaks of "expectation" and "hope" in other letters (most elaborately in Rom 8:18-25, but also in 1 Cor 1:7 and Phil 3:20) helps to clarify what Paul means by the "hope of righteousness."[26] This language, combined with the connection between 5:2-12 and 5:13-6:10, suggests that one must read the end of the epistle, indeed the entirety of the epistle, in light of its eschatological framework.[27]

That Gal 5:13-6:10 is integrally related to the transitional section 5:2-12 can be seen most clearly in Paul's summary statement in 5:6: "For in Christ Jesus neither circumcision counts for anything nor uncircumcision, but rather faith working through love." As noted above, this verse is the first in which Paul uses the noun ἀγάπη, signaling the shift to his discussion of the daily life that flows from faith working itself out in love. The word ἀγάπη reappears at the beginning of the exhortation in 5:13 and as the first among the list of the virtues constituting the "fruit of the Spirit" in 5:22, both times in contrast to behavior that Paul condemns among the Galatians. Moreover, following as it does upon his discussion of the inefficacy of the Law, this statement prepares the way for the alternative vision he offers to the Galatians.[28]

---

[26] Hays, *Galatians*, 313-14; see also Matera, *Galatians*, 182; Dunn, *Galatians*, 270; Schlier, *Der Brief an die Galater*, 233 n. 1; Lightfoot, *Galatians*, 204.

[27] Although eschatological expectation is muted, then, it is not altogether absent, contrary to the preface to the first edition of J. Christiaan Beker, *Paul the Apostle: The Triumph of God in Life and Thought* (1st ed.; Philadelphia: Fortress, 1980), x.

[28] So Russell, "Redemptive-Historical Argumentation," 338: "This contrast signals that the following relational discussion harnesses the *antithetical contrasts* between Paul's community and the Judaizers' seen in 3:1-5:5. Specifically, the antithesis discussed in 5:1-5 of

Galatians 5:13-26: The Spirit and the Flesh

The conjunction γάρ in Gal 5:13 suggests a connection between this part of Paul's argument and what immediately precedes it. Indeed, the continued use of terms from earlier sections of the epistle implies continuity in Paul's argument that demands a reading of his exhortations in light of the whole.[29] Although some translations have taken the occurrence of "flesh" in 5:13 to refer to the passions or general sinful desires, the position of the verse between the transitional section 5:2-12 and Paul's statement about the Law in 5:14 points in another direction.[30] As we have just seen, in the former section Paul insists that the Galatians eschew circumcision of the flesh, since it will result in their being cut off from Christ. In 5:14 Paul speaks of the fulfillment of the Law in terms of love. Given its placement between a warning against circumcision and a statement about the fulfillment of the Law, the reference to the flesh in 5:13 must include circumcision as part of its meaning (cf. Gal 3:3), with the broader connotation pointing to the weakness of flesh in the old age.[31] This proposal finds further confirmation if one considers the use of the term "call" that immediately precedes 5:13. While urging the Galatians to shun those who would have them circumcised in 5:7-10, Paul warns them that the course of action proposed by the agitators is "not from *the one who called* you" (οὐκ ἐκ τοῦ καλοῦντος ὑμας; 5:8b, emphasis mine), using the same language that appears in 5:13. This combination of factors suggests that rather than completely shifting to an understanding of flesh as a cosmic power, the term continues to carry its association with the Law and the old age even in 5:13-26. Indeed, as Russell notes, the structure of 5:13b-c parallels the structure of 5:6:[32]

---

the freedom of Paul's gospel versus the bondage of the Judaizers' nongospel is continued in the relational discussion of 5:6-6:16" (original emphasis).

[29] A number of terms in 5:13 appear earlier in the epistle: ἐλευθερία (Gal 2:4; 5:1; cf. also the use of the adjective ἐλεύθερος throughout 4:21-31); καλέω (1:6; 5:8); σάρξ (1:16; 2:16, 20; 3:3; 4:23, 29); ἀγάπη (5:6). See Betz, *Galatians*, 272; R. Longenecker, *Galatians*, 239; Dunn, *Galatians*, 286-87; and especially Matera, *Galatians*, 192-93. These connections, which continue throughout the argument of 5:13-6:10, cast doubt on O'Neill's theory (*Recovery*, 65-71) that this section is an interpolation unrelated to the rest of the epistle.

[30] The NRSV ("self-indulgence") and the NIV ("the sinful nature") both provide periphrastic (and slightly misleading) translations of σάρξ.

[31] It is interesting in this regard to compare Paul's discussion of the resurrection in 1 Corinthians 15:50ff. In vv. 50-55 of that chapter Paul asserts that weak flesh and blood cannot inherit the kingdom of God (a phrase similar to that found in Gal 5:21), which he defines in terms of resurrection. After this discussion he then briefly notes the problem of the Law, associated as it is with sin. I am indebted to David Moffitt for this connection.

[32] Russell, "Redemptive-Historical Argumentation," 339. I have modified Russell's translation on 339, "you do not have your freedom," to "do not use your freedom," in line with his own suggested translation on 338.

5:6a For in Christ Jesus neither circumcision nor uncircumcision means anything...
    5:13b do not use your freedom for an opportunity for the flesh, ...
5:6b but faith working through love.
    5:13c but through the love [sic] serve one another.

To be sure, "flesh" in this exhortation means more than simply circumcision, as one can see from the list of vices associated with the flesh in 5:19-21. Nevertheless, it is important to recognize that for Paul these vices are symptomatic of a larger phenomenon associated with the old age, of which circumcision is a part.

Excursus: The "Flesh" as a power?

In his landmark commentary on Galatians, J. Louis Martyn argues on the basis of his apocalyptic reading of the letter that in chapter 5 Paul describes a battle between two cosmic powers, "the Flesh" and "the Spirit."[33] As part of his case Martyn draws attention to the original military connotation of the word ἀφορμή in 5:13, as well as the antagonism (ἀντίκειται) that Paul describes between the flesh and the Spirit in 5:17.[34] Hays extends Martyn's argument to include Paul's use of στοιχέω in 5:25, suggesting that these three terms (ἀφορμή, ἀντίκειται, and στοιχέω) confirm Martyn's argument.[35] Martyn's reading has much to commend it. There can be no doubt that Paul sees an antagonism between flesh and Spirit. Moreover, Martyn does well to move beyond the older view that Galatians 5 refers to an internal anthropological dualism between flesh and spirit – Paul does not refer to the "spirit" (lower case "s") as part of human nature, but rather to the Spirit (upper case "s") of God in most of the occurrences of πνεῦμα throughout the letter. His argument for the use of military metaphors, however, founders on two points. First, he reads too much into a few words, a point that becomes apparent when one considers other places where Paul uses the same terms. Second, although he recognizes that the Spirit in Galatians 5 refers to God's Spirit as it does earlier in the epistle, he fails to recognize a similar continuity in Paul's use of the term "flesh."

To begin with the terminology, Martyn's reading of ἀφορμή as a base of military operations seems to depend on the use of Thucydides, who antedates Paul by several centuries.[36] While it is conceivable that the word retained this connotation in Paul's day, his own use of the term in other contexts suggests that this is not the meaning he has in mind. The word appears twice in 2 Corinthians and in neither case does it seem to have the military connotation Mar-

---

[33] See Martyn, *Galatians*, 524-36 *et passim*.
[34] Ibid., 485, 94. I have chosen here to refer to "flesh" with a lower-case "f" because I am not convinced that Paul considers "flesh" to be a power, as Martyn suggests.
[35] Hays, *Galatians*, 321.
[36] Martyn, *Galatians*, 485.

tyn gives it in Galatians. In 2 Cor 5:12, Paul writes, "we are not commending ourselves to you again but rather giving you an opportunity (ἀφορμήν) to boast about us." Nothing in the context suggests that Paul has military imagery in mind. Likewise in 2 Cor 11:12 Paul uses the term twice, again with the connotation of "opportunity": "What I am doing I will keep doing so that I might remove the opportunity (ἀφορμήν) from those who wish for an opportunity (ἀφορμήν) that they might be found like us in that in which they boast about." Once again, the term does not carry any military connotation, but refers simply to an opportunity for some action. The best example to support Martyn's case comes from Romans 7, where the noun appears two more times. In Rom 7:8, Paul writes, "Sin taking the opportunity (ἀφορμήν) through the commandment brought about in me every desire." Three verses later, he writes, "For sin taking the opportunity (ἀφορμήν) deceived me through the commandment and killed me through it" (Rom 7:11). Of the five occurrences of the word that we have considered, only this last one makes good sense of the original military connotation, but even this instance does not demand such a reading.[37]

A similar case can be made for the verb στοιχέω. Neither of the two occurrences outside of Galatians (Rom 4:12 and Phil 3:16) suggests military imagery, and even the other use of the word in Galatians (6:16) does not have any such connotation.[38] The only word that may imply military imagery is the verb ἀντίκειμαι in Gal 5:17. There can be no question that this verb connotes some kind of opposition, and that theoretically it could even imply some kind of a battle. The question remains, though, whether such a reading necessitates that σάρξ be interpreted as a power. A consideration of the term's range of meaning in the rest of the epistle suggests that such an interpretation goes beyond the evidence.

In this regard, Martyn's analysis fails in that it does not sufficiently consider the continuity in Paul's use of the term "flesh" throughout Galatians. The first reference to the flesh/Spirit dichotomy occurs in Gal 3:3, and there it

---

[37] Martyn refers only to these last two occurrences in a footnote, citing Paul W. Meyer, "The Worm at the Core of the Apple," in *The Conversation Continues: Studies in Paul and John in Honor of J. Louis Martyn* (ed. Robert T. Fortna and Beverly R. Gaventa; Nashville: Abingdon, 1990), 62-84, to bolster his argument, although Meyer makes no reference to the noun ἀφορμή. Although it is true that "Sin" appears as a personified power in Romans 7, it is better to err on the side of caution when extrapolating backward from a later letter to make sense of what Paul means in an earlier one.

[38] Martyn refers only to ἀντίκειμαι and ἀφορμή in his commentary, making nothing of στοιχέω, but Hays includes it among the military metaphors found in Galatians 5. See n. 35 above.

most likely alludes to the Galatians' desire for circumcision.[39] The contrast reappears in Gal 4:23 and 29, where it has a double-meaning of physical descent from Abraham and entry into the covenant via circumcision. Although Gal 5:2-12 does not use the term "flesh," it is significant that it is in this section immediately following the flesh/Spirit contrast in Gal 4:29 that Paul makes his first explicit reference to the ritual of circumcision (Gal 5:3).

This transitional section sets up the extended discussion of the flesh/Spirit contrast in Gal 5:13-26, which also goes back and forth between references to the "flesh" and references to the Law. Paul's first warning against submitting to the flesh occurs in 5:13: "Only do not use your freedom as an opportunity for the flesh." Immediately following this warning, Paul speaks of the fulfillment of the Law through love. This alternation between "flesh" and "Law," which continues throughout this section, suggests that the two are intimately related. Indeed, the way Paul alternates between flesh and Law in 5:13-26, combined with the contrasts he sets up between the Spirit and the Law, suggests that Law and flesh are bound up together as belonging to a former age characterized by human weakness (cf. the reference to the "fullness of time" in Gal 4:4). One can see a similar phenomenon in 5:17-18. Paul first describes the conflict between the flesh and the Spirit, and then goes on to draw the conclusion that the Galatians, provided they are led by the Spirit, are "no longer under the Law."[40] The flesh and the Law continue to be allied, but not in the sense that they are both powers warring against the Spirit. Rather, they belong together to the old age (cf. Gal 3:23-25; 4:5-6) in which frail humanity was tempted by the "desire of the flesh" to do the "works of the flesh." To say this is not to deny that Paul believed humans experienced temptation, or even that frail humanity was not opposed to the Spirit – it is only to suggest that to turn the weakness of fallen humanity into a personified power is to read too much into the text.

When Paul refers to the flesh in 5:13-26, then, he is not portraying it as a power; rather, he continues to think of the flesh as bound up with the Law in redemptive-historical terms, as part of the era of human frailty that led humans to give in to their desires.

Galatians 5:13-15: Fulfilling the Law

As some scholars note, Gal 5:13-15 introduces Paul's discussion of the flesh/Spirit conflict in vv. 13-26, forming a bookend in conjunction with vv. 25-26 around 5:16-24. Barclay perceptively notes the likelihood that in this

---

[39] For a lengthier discussion of the following points, see again Russell, "Redemptive-Historical Argumentation," 333-57 and *idem*, *The Flesh/Spirit Conflict in Galatians* (Lanham: University Press of America, 1997), esp. 119-41.

[40] See again Russell, "Redemptive-Historical Argumentation," 348.

introductory section we catch a glimpse of one of the problems in the Galatian community that Paul wishes to address.[41] The concentration of words connoting strife and communal discord both in the introduction and in the vice list of 5:19-21 suggests that, whether the arrival of the agitators precipitated the situation or merely exacerbated it, division was plaguing the Galatian churches. In order to combat this infighting Paul, paradoxically in light of his earlier description of slavery to the Law, enjoins the Galatians to become slaves of one another through love (διὰ τῆς ἀγάπης δουλεύετε ἀλλήλοις).

Perhaps even more surprisingly Paul grounds his exhortation in a quotation from Leviticus, asserting that all the Law is "fulfilled" in the one word "You shall love your neighbor as yourself" (Gal 5:14, citing Lev 19:18). Given the apparently negative picture of the Law that he has presented thus far in the epistle, it seems strange that he should now speak of a fulfillment of the Law.[42] A couple of points help to make sense of the quotation. First, 5:14 is not the first time that Paul appeals to the Law positively to support his argument. In 4:21 he prefaces the climactic allegory of Sarah and Hagar by asking his readers, "You who wish to be under the Law, don't you hear the Law?"[43] This question indicates that in Galatians the Law does not have an unequivocally negative connotation for Paul; on occasion he can even bring it in to support his own point. Second, one should note Paul's careful choice of language: in contrast to his earlier warnings that the Galatians not seek to "do" the Law, in this verse he speaks of a "fulfillment" of the Law. As Barclay notes, this connection between the words πληρόω and νόμος is altogether absent in the OT.[44] Moreover, in every instance in which Paul employs the verb "to fulfill" it refers to Christian fulfillment of the Law; when speaking of Jewish Law observance, he uses the language of "doing" or "observing."[45] These data lead Barclay to suggest that Paul chose the language of "fulfillment" precisely because of its ambiguity: it allows Paul to assert that Christians fulfill the true purpose of the Law without observing it in each and every one of its details.[46]

---

[41] Barclay, *Obeying the Truth*, 152-55; see also Hays, "Christology and Ethics in Galatians," 286, who cites Bernard Hungerford Brinsmead, *Galatians - A Dialogical Response to Opponents* (SBLDS 65; Atlanta: Scholars, 1982), 167-68.

[42] It is important to recall, however, that Paul does say or imply positive things about the Law in Gal 3:21 and 4:21. Moreover, if the argument in chapter four above with regard to the στοιχεία is correct, then Paul's view of the Law might not be as negative as many suggest – the Law is insufficient to empower humans to live rightly, but it is not a malevolent power.

[43] Hays, *Galatians*, 322.

[44] Barclay, *Obeying the Truth*, 138-42.

[45] See ibid., 139, citing Betz, *Galatians*, 275 and Stephen Westerholm, "On Fulfilling the Whole Law (Gal. 5:14)," *SEÅ* 51-52 (1986): 229-37 in support.

[46] Barclay, *Obeying the Truth*, 140-41; see also Westerholm, "On Fulfilling the Whole Law (Gal. 5:14)," 235; see also the recent correctives to this approach offered by Todd A.

There is a further ambiguity in Paul's language that Barclay does not mention. The verb πληρόω in 5:14 appears in the passive voice, leaving open the question of who has fulfilled the Law. Although most commentators understand the verb as a gnomic use of the perfect tense, implying that the Law is generally fulfilled when one loves one's neighbor as oneself, Hays suggests that Paul reads the verse from Leviticus as a prophetic promise fulfilled by Christ: "the Law *has been fulfilled* in one word."[47] Several features of the text commend this reading. First, it would be in keeping with Paul's attribution of prophetic promises to Christ first, and then by extension to those in Christ (cf. Gal 3:16, 29). Second, the only other occurrence of the verb ἀγαπάω in Galatians describes Christ's death, an incarnate example of the love described in Lev 19:18 as understood by Paul.[48] Third, reading the verse christologically also establishes a deeper continuity throughout the latter half of the epistle. In Gal 4:4, Paul speaks of the "fullness of time" (τὸ πλήρωμα τοῦ χρόνου) with respect to the sending of the Son as the fulfillment of God's purposes. Reading 4:4 and 5:14 together makes sense of the fulfillment language in a way that also prepares for the third instance of fulfillment language in Gal 6:2.[49] Moreover, reading the Leviticus citation christologically also makes better sense of 6:2. As Barclay rightly argues, the "Law of Christ" in 6:2 refers to the Mosaic Law "as it is redefined through Christ."[50] Paul's exhortation to the Galatians to fulfill the Law of Christ is based on Christ's own fulfillment of the Law through his sacrificial death. As Hays notes, such a reading would entail Paul interpreting the phrase ἐν ἑνὶ λόγῳ as an eschatological prophecy. In this regard, it is significant that Paul does not refer to the verse as a "commandment" but rather as a "saying."[51] Christ through his self-sacrificial death (Gal 2:20b) fulfills the prophetic saying of Scripture (Lev 19:18). The note of fulfillment, particularly as it is related to Gal 4:4, once again suggests that the argument of Galatians 5-6 builds on the preceding argument and flows from the same eschatological perspective.

Wilson, *The Curse of the Law and the Crisis in Galatia: Reassessing the Purpose of Galatians* (WUNT 2.225; Tübingen: Mohr/Siebeck, 2007), 104-12.

[47] Hays, *Galatians*, 323-24; Martyn (*Galatians*, 489-90) makes a similar argument; against Dunn, *Galatians*, 289; Matera, *Galatians*, 193.

[48] Hays, *Galatians*, 323.

[49] Barclay (*Obeying the Truth*, 139) draws a connection between 4:4 and 5:14, but does not read the latter verse christologically.

[50] Ibid., 125-42; the quotation comes from 141. Again, Barclay's argument would be strengthened by a christological reading of Gal 5:14.

[51] Hays, *Galatians*, 324.

Galatians 5:16-18: The Spirit and the flesh

With Gal 5:16 Paul sets forth the contrast between the Spirit and the flesh more explicitly, beginning with an exhortation to walk by the Spirit. Once again, the linguistic connections between this section of the epistle and Galatians 3-4 prove illuminating. Paul enjoins the Galatians to "walk by the Spirit and you will not complete the desire of the flesh." This juxtaposition of "flesh" and "Spirit" recalls the opening of the central section of the epistle in which Paul first draws a contrast between the two: "having begun in the Spirit (πνεύματι) are you now being completed in the flesh (σαρκὶ ἐπιτελεῖσθε)" (Gal 3:3)? It is worth noting that Paul uses the verb τελέω in 5:16, a word clearly related to ἐπιτελέω in 3:3. The similarity in word choice, combined with the strong verbal connections we saw between 5:13 and the earlier parts of the epistle and the interchangeability of Law and flesh throughout this section, suggests that "flesh" bears the same connotation here: it is tied to the old age, the age of the Law that did not empower Israel to fulfill God's commands. In this regard it is interesting to note that in 1 Cor 10:6 Paul describes Israel's problem in the wilderness as one of "desire" (ἐπιθυμέω; cf. ἐπιθυμία in Gal 5:16).

This reading of the flesh as referring to the old age helps to make sense of the following two verses, notorious for the difficulties they pose to interpreters. Galatians 5:17 presents the reader with a number of questions: to what does the "flesh" refer? What is the nature of the desire of the flesh and that of the Spirit? And what exactly does Paul mean by saying "so that the things that you will, these things you do not do"? In keeping with the approach that I have been developing thus far, I suggest that the "flesh" still refers to human frailty as it exists prior to the coming of the Spirit and in the present age apart from the Spirit. That the weakness of the flesh is connected to the old age, the age of the Law, is confirmed by Gal 5:18, in which Paul reverts to contrasting life in the Spirit and life under the Law.

The conjunction γάρ in 5:17 signals that what follows elaborates on Paul's statement in v. 16, "you will certainly not complete the desire of the flesh."[52] The Galatians will not submit to this desire because the flesh's desire is against the Spirit, and the Spirit's is against the flesh (Gal 5:17ab). The reason for this desire, Paul proceeds to explain, is that "these [i.e. the flesh and the Spirit] are opposed to one another" (ταῦτα γὰρ ἀλλήλοις ἀντίκειται) (Gal 5:17c). Thus far, the connection between vv. 16 and 17 makes sense. The

---

[52] Cf. the similar analysis of Jan Lambrecht, "The Right Things You Want to Do: A Note on *Galatians* 5,17d," *Bib* 79 (1998): 515-24, esp. 516, although Lambrecht's reading of the verse fails due to his overemphasis on the parallels between Romans 7 and Galatians 5 and insufficient consideration of the importance of the context of Galatians 5.

difficulty comes with the last phrase of 5:17, which has been variously interpreted.

Barclay provides three standard interpretations of the phrase.[53] Some have taken the verse to describe an inner conflict between the flesh and the Spirit that frustrates the believer's desire to do good.[54] As Barclay notes, this interpretation fails in that it blatantly contradicts Paul's statement in 5:16 that those who walk by the Spirit will not complete the flesh. A second reading takes the verse as describing not the victory of the flesh over the Spirit, but rather a stalemate between the two.[55] Again, though, a stalemate fails to make sense of Paul's confidence in 5:16, a confidence which continues through to 5:18: "if you are led by the Spirit, you are not under the Law." Finally, a third interpretation takes the final clause as asserting that the Spirit succeeds in quenching the desire of the flesh, taking the phrase "whatever you want" (ἃ ἐὰν θέλητε) to refer to fleshly desire.[56] According to Barclay, the problems of this third solution "lie in accommodating the central clause ('these are opposed *to each other*') and explaining why 'whatever you want' should be taken as 'what the flesh desires'."[57] Of these two objections, the latter is more compelling than the former. With respect to the first objection, even if the Spirit overcomes the desires of the flesh, this still implies some kind of opposition between the two. The second objection, however, makes a good point: nothing in the context suggests that the phrase "whatever you want" refers to the desire of the flesh, but rather it seems like a general description of complete autonomy. As Barclay puts it, "The warfare imagery is invoked not to indicate that the two sides are evenly balanced but to show the Galatians that they are already committed *to* some forms of activity (the Spirit) and *against* others (the flesh). The Galatians need have no fear that Paul's talk of 'freedom' and 'following the Spirit' will leave them without moral direction in a structureless existence 'doing whatever they want'."[58] In other words, one might paraphrase the last half of Gal 5:17 as follows: "these [i.e. the Spirit and the flesh] are opposed to one another, so that (despite your freedom!) you are not free to do whatever you want." This broader interpretation would obviously also exclude the desire of the flesh, but only insofar as it excludes complete autonomy.

In Gal 5:18, Paul brings his reflections on the desire of the flesh to bear on the main question he has been addressing throughout the epistle: why the Ga-

---

[53] Barclay, *Obeying the Truth*, 112-19.
[54] So, e.g., R. A. Cole, *The Epistle of Paul to the Galatians* (TNTC 9; Grand Rapids: Eerdmans, 1975), 158; Herman N. Ridderbos, *The Epistle of Paul to the Churches of Galatia* (NICNT; Grand Rapids: Eerdmans, 1956), 203-04.
[55] So Schlier, *Der Brief an die Galater*, 249-50; Betz, *Galatians*, 278-79.
[56] See Jewett, *Paul's Use of Anthropological Terms*, 106-07.
[57] Barclay, *Obeying the Truth*, 114.
[58] Ibid., 115 (original emphasis).

latians should not submit to the Law. As we have come to expect by now, the reason for this relates to the Spirit, and it can be expressed in a variety of ways. At the beginning of the central section of the epistle, Paul asks if the Galatians "received the Spirit" on the basis of works of the Law or of the message of faith (Gal 3:2). Here in Galatians 5, he uses different language to express the significance of the Spirit's role in the Christian life: "If you are *led by* the Spirit, you are not under the Law" (Gal 5:18, my emphasis). The shift in emphasis can be easily explained. Whereas in Galatians 3 Paul wants to remind his readers that their reception of the Spirit did not come from the Law but from the preaching of the gospel, here he focuses on the practical implications of the guidance of the Spirit for daily life. As Barclay has persuasively argued, it is likely that one of the reasons the Galatians may have been attracted to submitting to the Law is for the concrete guidance it gave them with regard to ordinary life.[59] By emphasizing the guidance of the Spirit, then, Paul is advocating an alternative means of knowing how one ought to act.

As we saw in chapter four above, the primary context for interpreting the significance of the outpouring of the Spirit in Galatians 3-4 is the various prophetic and intertestamental texts that envision an eschatological new exodus. Given the connections already demonstrated between Galatians 5 and the earlier parts of the epistle, we should not be surprised that such a background also sheds light on Paul's ethical exhortation.

The motif of being led by the Spirit appears in a number of texts that refer either simply to the first exodus or to the exodus as a type of a new exodus to come.[60] The prayer of confession of Nehemiah 9 speaks both of the pillar of cloud guiding the Israelites through the wilderness and of God giving his "good Spirit" to instruct them (Neh 9:12, 20).[61] Likewise, the lament prayer in Isaiah 63 considered in chapter two above also speaks of the Spirit guiding the Israelites in the wilderness: "The Spirit came down from the Lord and guided them; thus you led your people to make a glorious name for yourself"

---

[59] Ibid., 68-72 *et passim*. On p. 70 Barclay writes, "If Gentiles were attracted to the Jewish law this was probably at least partly because of the detailed instruction it contained for the conduct of ordinary life." Betz (*Galatians*, 8-9) proposes a similar explanation for the Galatians' attraction to the Law.

[60] For a discussion of this motif vis-à-vis Romans, see Sylvia C. Keesmaat, *Paul and his Story: (Re-)Interpreting the Exodus Tradition* (JSNTSup 181; Sheffield: Sheffield Academic, 1999), 55-65 *et passim*.

[61] See William N. Wilder, *Echoes of the Exodus Narrative in the Context and Background of Galatians 5:18* (Studies in Biblical Literature 23; New York: Peter Lang, 2001), 138-48 for a fuller discussion of this passage; cf. the similar interpretation recently proposed in Wilson, *The Curse of the Law*, 125-37. Wilson's proposal would be more persuasive if there were stronger lexical connections between Galatians and the Pentateuchal texts he cites in his analysis.

(Isa 63:14).⁶² This description of the guidance of the Spirit is not simply a recollection, however, but also a plea that God might intervene again to guide the Israelites in a new exodus. As argued above in chapter four, it is likely that language and motifs stemming in part from Isaiah 63 play an important role in Paul's argument in Gal 4:4-6, based both on the number of keywords that overlap between the two books and on the influence the Isaiah text had on other early Christian literature (Ephesians, Hebrews).⁶³ Given this influence, it seems likely that Paul's reference to being "led by the Spirit" in Gal 5:18 draws on similar exodus imagery.

A recent study by William Wilder proposes a more specific allusion to Ps 143:10 (142:10 [LXX]) in Gal 5:18.⁶⁴ Two main features of Galatians and the Psalm verse speak in favor of this allusion. First, scholars agree that Paul quotes or alludes to Psalm 142 (LXX) twice (Gal 2:16; cf. Rom 3:20).⁶⁵ Second, Ps 142:10 (LXX) shares a basic pattern with Paul's line of argument in 5:17-18. Both texts speak directly or indirectly of doing God's will and both texts refer to the guidance of the Spirit:⁶⁶

(a) δίδαξόν με τοῦ ποιεῖν τὸ θέλημά σου ὅτι σὺ εἶ ὁ θεός μου·
(b) τὸ πνεῦμά σου τὸ ἀγαθὸν ὁδηγήσει με ἐν γῇ εὐθείᾳ.
(a) Teach me to do your will, because you are my God.
(b) Your good Spirit will lead me in a level land.

The similarity with the pattern of Gal 5:17d-18a is suggestive:

(a) ἵνα μὴ ἃ ἐὰν θέλητε ταῦτα ποιῆτε.
(b) εἰ δὲ πνεύματι ἄγεσθε
(a) So that you may not do whatever you want.
(b) But if you are led by the Spirit.

It is not simply the guidance by the Spirit that overlaps between these two passages, but also the notion of doing someone's will, either positively doing God's will (τοῦ ποιεῖν τὸ θέλημά σου) according to the Psalm or not doing "whatever you want" (μὴ ἃ ἐὰν θέλητε ταῦτα ποιῆτε) according to Paul.

In addition to these lexical and thematic parallels, Wilder also argues that the Psalm reflects an exodus typology that dovetails with the imagery of Gala-

---

⁶² For a fuller discussion of Isaiah 63, see pp. 26-28 above. Cf. also Wilder, *Echoes of the Exodus Narrative*, 130-38.

⁶³ See pp. 127-28 above.

⁶⁴ Wilder notes that he is not the first to recognize this parallel. Thomas Aquinas (*Commentary on Saint Paul's Epistle to the Galatians* [trans. F. R. Larcher; Aquinas Scripture Series 1; Albany: Magi Books, Inc., 1966], 171-72) makes the same connection.

⁶⁵ See Betz, *Galatians*, 118 n. 48; Hays, *Galatians*, 240-41; Martyn, *Galatians*, 252-53; Schlier, *Der Brief an die Galater*, 89; Dunn, *Galatians*, 140.

⁶⁶ The diagram comes from Wilder, *Echoes of the Exodus Narrative*, 184, though I have modified his translation of τὸ πνεῦμά σου τὸ ἀγαθὸν ὁδηγήσει, which he renders "Let your good Spirit lead me," despite the fact that ὁδηγήσει is an indicative verb.

tians 5. A number of features of the psalm, particularly when compared to other psalms such as Psalm 23, reflect this typology, but for our purposes it is the Spirit that plays the most crucial part.[67] In particular, Psalm 142 (LXX) shares language that we already saw above with respect to two other OT texts alluding to the exodus. Like Isaiah 63, Ps 142:10 (LXX) describes the Spirit's guidance of the psalmist using the verb ὁδηγέω, the same word that occurs in Isa 63:14 to describe the Spirit's leading of the Israelites in the wilderness. As Wilder notes, these are the only two verses in the LXX that bring together the words πνεῦμα and ὁδηγέω; likewise, in the OT only Ps 142:10 (LXX) and Neh 9:20 use the phrase "good Spirit" to describe God's Spirit, the latter verse also in the context of a retelling of Israel's exodus from Egypt.[68] Based on these connections, as well as other exodus motifs in the psalm, Wilder suggests that Paul's allusion to the psalm in Gal 5:18 uses exodus typology to describe the Galatians' experience of the Spirit and freedom from the Law.[69] No doubt, such a reversal would have been scandalous to Paul's Jewish contemporaries. In effect, Paul takes the paradigmatic event of Israel's freedom and turns it into that from which believers are saved.

The shocking nature of his use of the exodus tradition, however, is in keeping with Paul's argument in Galatians 3 and 4. In the Sarah and Hagar allegory (Gal 4:21-31), he has already made the stunning association of Sinai with slavery. The revisionary nature of Paul's argument is not unique to Galatians 5, but pervades the entire epistle. Moreover, despite the startling transformation of Paul's hermeneutic, the exodus imagery fits with the eschatological character of the argument up to this point in the letter. Although Psalm 143 does not explicitly describe restoration eschatology in the same way as some of the Isaianic oracles, its use of exodus motifs in the context of a plea for salvation fits with the Isaianic background of the earlier sections of Galatians. In particular, if the exodus imagery in Psalm 142 (LXX) draws on traditions such as that of Isaiah 63, then it is likely that the psalm contains an implicit restoration eschatology. Regardless of whether or not the psalmist or the later compiler of the Psalms drew a connection between the two, it is reasonable to think that Paul would have seen such connections. As noted in chapter four, there is some evidence to suggest that Isaiah 63 played an important role in early Christianity, particularly in Pauline circles.[70] Paul's argument in Galatians 5, then, flows naturally from the eschatological framework that undergirds the entire epistle. The outpouring of the Spirit on the

---

[67] See ibid., 148-59 for a lengthy discussion of the possible exodus background to Psalm 142:10 (LXX).

[68] Ibid., 149.

[69] Ibid., 177.

[70] See above, p. 128 n. 177. See also Wilder, *Echoes of the Exodus Narrative*, 164 n. 23 and 166 n. 41.

Galatians when they heard the message of faith signaled the beginning of the restoration of Israel. As a part of this restoration that has begun, the Spirit enables believers to do God's will in a way that historically Israel had failed to do under the Law.

Equally important for understanding how Paul uses the term "flesh" is the second half of 5:18: "you are not under the Law." Before we consider the relationship between the Law and the flesh, however, we must understand its role with respect to the Galatians' freedom. In the exodus typology that Paul sets up the Law is that from which the Galatians have been freed by the Spirit.[71] Although this description of the Law certainly would have been controversial among Second Temple Jews, it fits with the way Paul uses the phrase ὑπὸ νόμον throughout Galatians. In Gal 3:23 he refers to the Jews as guarded and locked up under the Law until the revealing of (the) faith. Later he uses language that originally had connotations of buying someone out of slavery to describe Jesus' redemption of those "under the Law" (Gal 4:5). The final part of the central section of the epistle, Gal 4:21-5:1, begins with Paul addressing the Galatians as those "who wish to be under the Law" and ends with an exhortation not to "submit again to the yoke of slavery" (5:1). Given this association of the Law with slavery, we should not be surprised to find the second half of 5:18 describing the Law as that from which God has freed the Galatians.[72] Once again it is worth noting the way Paul shifts back and forth between contrasting the Spirit and the flesh and the Spirit and the Law. This alternation suggests that the flesh and the Law are intimately related as both belonging to the old age. The close connection between Law and flesh becomes clearer in the next several verses.

Galatians 5:19-21: The works of the flesh

Galatians 5:19-21 presents one of several vice lists in Paul (cf. Rom 1:18-32; 1 Cor 6:9-10). Some commentators have taken this list as pointing to a two-front problem confronting Paul in Galatia, particularly due to the references to fornication, impurity, idolatry, and so forth.[73] On this reading the Galatian churches consisted of both rigorous nomists and libertines. Galatians 3-4 is thought to address the former group, whereas Galatians 5-6 offers moral exhortation to those who are living loosely. This reading fails, however, based on the strong connections that we have seen between Galatians 3-4 and Galatians 5-6. These connections suggest that Paul addresses a single problem in

---

[71] Ibid., 180-82 *et passim*.

[72] Technically Paul does not say that the Galatians have been freed from the Law, but the whole thrust of the passage implies a connection between the Law and slavery. On the question of whether this slavery is directly to the Law, see the discussion of the "guardians" on pp. 118-19 above.

[73] See the works of Ropes and Lütgert cited in n. 5 above.

Galatians as a whole, not two separate groups.[74] Moreover, unlike letters such as 1 Corinthians and Romans, the text gives no indication that Paul is addressing two different groups.[75] How then do the "works of the flesh" relate to Paul's argument and the Galatian situation?

To this point in the letter, whenever Paul has referred to "works" (ἔργα) they have always been coupled with the Law (Gal 2:16 [3x]; 3:2, 5, 10). Given the way Paul shifts back and forth between the flesh and the Law in Gal 5:13-18, we may reasonably infer that the works of the flesh and the works of the Law, while certainly not identical, are nevertheless related.[76] Again, the connection makes the most sense if Paul understands both the flesh and the Law as entities that belong to the old age, from which the Galatian Christians have been rescued (cf. Gal 1:4). The works of the flesh are those things to which humans unaided by the Spirit resort. It is significant that Paul lists the works of the flesh immediately after he has stated that the Galatians are not under the Law provided that they are led by the Spirit. When they were under the Law, Jews were unable to do the will of God and to resist the desires of the flesh (cf. 1 Cor 10:6, although that verse refers to a period just prior to the giving of the Law).

In different ways the arguments of Barclay and Russell support this reading. Barclay notes with respect to vice lists, "it would be foolhardy to take them in any simple way as a direct reflection of the sins of the person or community addressed."[77] Rather, vice lists in general, and this one in particular, reflect traditional catalogues of sins, some of which may or may not apply to the situation at hand. Despite this caution, Barclay asserts that the specific nature of this list, emphasizing as it does sins involving communal strife, most likely reflects the situation Paul was addressing in Galatia.[78]

The list is framed on one side by five commonly listed vices ("fornication, impurity, licentiousness, idolatry, and sorcery") and on the other by two more general vices ("drunkenness and carousing"). In between these two sets ap-

---

[74] Theoretically, one could attribute the thematic unity to Paul's theology rather than to the problem he is addressing; however, the connection that Paul makes between "flesh" and "circumcision" in Gal 6:12-13 so closely after the discussion of "works of the flesh" suggests an integral link throughout the epistle. Moreover, Paul seems to have only one group of opponents in mind (Gal 6:12: "those who would compel you to be circumcised"). Again, it is possible that he misread the situation, but it is more likely that only one group was causing the trouble in Galatia, and that Paul was addressing the inroads of that group. In this regard, it is significant that Gal 2:15-21 addresses both the question of righteousness and the question of unity, and that the two seem to be closely related.

[75] See, e.g., Romans 14; 1 Corinthians 7-8.

[76] Cf. Matera, *Galatians*, 200: "*Ta erga tou sarkos* also recalls *ta erga tou nomou* (2:16; 3:2, 5, 10). The two expressions, though different, are related to each other by the concept of 'doing'"; see also R. Longenecker, *Galatians*, 252-53; Dunn, *Galatians*, 301.

[77] Barclay, *Obeying the Truth*, 152-53.

[78] Ibid., 153.

pear eight vices, more than half of the list, reflecting conflict within the community: "hostilities, strife, jealousy, wrath, rivalry, division, factions and envy." This proportion of vices is more striking when one compares Galatians with other vice lists in Paul. A bit surprisingly 1 Cor 6:9-10 lists no vices related to communal strife, but rather focuses on more typical vices (fornication, idolatry, thievery, etc.). Although Rom 1:29-31 lists several sins that could relate to conflict (envy, strife, gossip, slander), the proportion of these sins compared to others is not nearly as high as the corresponding proportion in Galatians. Moreover, the vice list in Romans does not seem to reflect the actual situation in Rome, but rather the depravity of humankind after the Fall. Based on this evidence, it is safe to conclude with Barclay that one of the primary problems that Paul addresses in Galatians is communal discord. The point gains further support when one notes that the discussion of the flesh/Spirit dichotomy in 5:19-21 is bookended by instructions concerning division in the community: in Gal 5:15 Paul warns the Galatians not to "devour" one another lest they be consumed and in Gal 5:26 he admonishes them not to be envious of one another.[79]

That the vice list should include not only these sins leading to community conflict but also more common sins involving lust, idolatry, and the like is also significant. If Paul had only wanted to address disunity among the Galatians, he could have simply listed the middle eight vices. By framing them in the broader context of more common vices and by placing them in relation to the flesh, Paul points out the inadequacy of the Law in dealing with sin. The use of the term "flesh" once again points to the old age before the coming of the Spirit when human beings could not do the will of God – a fact demonstrated by Israel's history. Russell puts the point well:

What Paul is *not* saying in Gal 5:19-21 is that the Christian Judaizers or pious Jews presently do all of the sins that he enumerates in this list of pagan vices. Rather Paul's point is that the list of sins in vv. 19-21 is a litany of the deeds of those who live according to the standards of the σάρξ. Apparently, this was somewhat true of Israel during the Mosaic Law era (e.g., Rom 2:17-24). Israel was "in the flesh" and "under Torah" when she manifested these pagan-like behaviors which are so "evident" (φανερά in [Gal] 5:19a). Neither Torah nor circumcision prevented the practice of these fleshly deeds (cf. Eph 2:3). Neither will they prevent the Galatians from *continuing to do* these deeds if they attach themselves to Israel (4:21; 5:1-4; 6:12-13).[80]

In other words, the vice list seems to function as a prophetic critique of Israel apart from the gift of the Spirit.[81] Like Rom 2:17-24, the vice list in Gal 5:19-

---

[79] See ibid.; cf. Hays, "Christology and Ethics in Galatians," 286.
[80] Russell, *The Flesh/Spirit Conflict in Galatians*, 161, original emphasis.
[81] One might ask whether such a critique stands in tension with the exodus typology, insofar as the typology seems to suggest that Israel *was* led by the Spirit. While it is true that these texts imply some sort of guidance by the Spirit, Israel's failure to obey the Law (see, e.g., Neh 9:29) indicates that this guidance was in some sense incomplete or inadequate. The

154   Chapter 5: New Creation and the Spirit in Galatians 5-6

21 suggests that the Law was unable to restrain Israel as a whole from committing the sins listed in order to discourage the Galatians from submitting to the Law. The intended goal is the same as that of Galatians 3-4, though the approach differs slightly. Whereas the previous chapters emphasize the curse of death that came upon those who submitted to the Torah, Galatians 5 reminds the Galatians that the Law will not enable them to fulfill God's will.

That all of this must be understood in an eschatological context can be seen by the way that Paul concludes the vice list before moving on to describe the fruit of the Spirit: "I am warning you just as I warned you before, that those who do such things will not inherit the kingdom of God" (5:21b).[82] The terms "inherit" and "kingdom of God" both bear eschatological connotations, suggesting that this whole section of the epistle continues the line of thought begun in Galatians 3 and 4.[83] The prominence given to the language of "inheritance" in these chapters (3:18, 29; 4:1, 7, 30) further confirms the continuity of the argument, especially since inheritance is tied both directly and indirectly to the Spirit.[84] In Gal 3:14 Paul speaks of those who have been redeemed receiving the "promise of the Spirit." In 3:18 he then speaks of Abraham receiving the inheritance through "promise" rather than through the Law. Although "promise" in this verse probably bears a different connotation than in 3:14, the proximity of the two uses is significant, particularly since later in the epistle Paul uses the terms "promise" and "Spirit" interchangeably (cf. Gal 4:23 and 4:29). Earlier in the epistle the inheritance is bound up with the promise and the Spirit; it should come as no surprise, then, that Paul warns that those who do the deeds of the flesh will not inherit the kingdom of God. As we saw in chapter two above, Isa 44:1-6, which describes the outpouring of the Spirit, frames this eschatological event within two statements about God's kingship over Israel.[85] In addition, the emphasis on inheritance once again confirms that Paul's argument throughout the letter rests upon an eschatological understanding of the Christ event and the outpouring of the Spirit, as one can see also from the list of the fruit of the Spirit in 5:22-23.[86]

---

prophetic and Second Temple Jewish expectations of an eschatological outpouring of the Spirit point to the insufficiency of the external guidance of the Spirit during the exodus, while still using the image as a type of what is to come.

[82] See Kuck, "Each Will Bear his Own Burden," 296.

[83] On the eschatological nature of "kingdom" and "inheritance" language, see Hays, *Galatians*, 327; Matera, *Galatians*, 202; Schlier, *Der Brief an die Galater*, 255.

[84] The continued use of inheritance language, especially in conjunction with the Spirit, is significant, even if the nuances of the term vary from verse to verse. On the differences, see R. Longenecker, *Galatians*, 258.

[85] See pp. 20-22 above on Isa 43:14-44:8.

[86] Cf. Isa 54:3; 57:13 (LXX); 60:21; 61:7; 65:9. Of these verses, the most striking is Isa 60:21: "And your people will be all righteous (πᾶς δίκαιος), and they will inherit (κληρονομήσουσιν) the land forever, guarding the planting, the works of his hands, for glory" (Isa

Galatians 5:22-23: The fruit of the Spirit

The motif of fruitfulness as part of eschatological restoration runs through a number of texts in the OT Prophets, as well as other literature from the Second Temple period. G. K. Beale has shown that a few of these texts combine the expectation of fruitfulness with the outpouring of the Spirit and with the blossoming of virtue in Israel.[87]

As we saw in chapter two, a number of oracles in Isaiah connect the outpouring of the Spirit at the restoration of Israel with the establishment of righteousness and other virtues, but here I will focus on Isaiah 11, 32, and 57. Isaiah 11 is the first oracle in the canonical form of Isaiah that describes the outpouring of the Spirit, in this case upon a messianic ruler. Although the text does not use the language of fruit (καρπός), it does speak of a branch shooting forth from the stump of Jesse, imagery that suggests fruitfulness. The oracle then describes the Spirit coming to rest upon the ruler and bringing about virtues similar to those Paul describes in Galatians, righteousness (δικαιοσύνη) and truth or faithfulness (ἀλήθεια). Originally applied to an eschatological ruler, the text was later applied to all the people in some Second Temple Jewish texts, as we shall see below.[88] Moreover, the latter half of Isaiah 11 draws implications for the people as a whole on the basis of the outpouring of the Spirit on the ruler, describing the restoration of the former in terms of a new creation and a new exodus.[89]

Isaiah 32:9-14 describes Israel's desolate condition as the result of its sins before offering hope in the form of the outpouring of the Spirit in 32:15-20. Unlike Isaiah 11, this oracle refers to the people as a whole and uses clearer imagery of fruitfulness, though once again it does not use the same term (καρπός) as Gal 5:22. Nevertheless, the oracle of woe admonishes the listeners to mourn for the failure of the "pleasant fields" (ἀγροῦ ἐπιθυμήματος) and the "harvest of the vine" (ἀμπέλου γενήματος) (Isa 32:12). This barrenness is said to last until the "Spirit from on high comes upon" the readers (Isa 32:15). When this event takes place the land will once again bear fruit.[90] This fruitfulness, however, results in blessed life:

Then justice will dwell in the wilderness, and righteousness abide in the fruitful field. The effect of righteousness will be peace, and the result of righteousness, quietness and trust for-

---

60:21 [LXX], my translation). Note how the text combines righteousness, inheritance, and planting imagery.

[87] G. K. Beale, "The Old Testament Background of Paul's Reference to 'the Fruit of the Spirit' in Galatians 5:22," *BBR* 15 (2005): 1-38.

[88] Cf. ibid., 15 and see below on the *Treatise on the Two Spirits*.

[89] For a fuller discussion of the text, see pp. 15-17 above.

[90] The Hebrew text states literally that "the wilderness will become a garden" (והיה מדבר לכרמל; Isa 32:15). The Greek versions take the word for "garden" to be a place name.

ever. My people will abide in a peaceful habitation, in secure dwellings, and in quiet resting places. (Isa 32:16-18, NRSV)

Particularly significant with respect to Galatians is the mention of "righteousness" (δικαιοσύνη) and "peace" (εἰρήνη), since the latter appears as a fruit of the Spirit in Gal 5:22.[91]

Perhaps the most significant Isaianic oracle to consider as possible background to Paul's use of the term "fruit of the Spirit" in Gal 5:22 is Isaiah 57, an oracle that shares much in common with Galatians 5. Like Isaiah 11 and Isaiah 32, Isaiah 57 describes a restoration of Israel following punishment for its sins. As we noted in chapter two, the reference to the Spirit in this oracle occurs only in the Greek versions.[92] That at least some of these versions were known to the Pauline tradition, however, can be seen from the allusion to Isaiah 57 in Eph 2:17. More significantly for the point under discussion, the Hebrew text also refers to God creating "fruit" (נוב), and as Beale notes, several important Greek versions not only refer to the Spirit but also make mention of "fruit" (καρπός) in Isa 57:18b-19a: "and I gave to him true comfort [*and*] *for the mourners, (I am the one) creating fruit* [{καὶ} τοις πενθουσιν αυτον, κτιζων καρπον]: peace upon peace to them that are far off and to them that are near."[93] Moreover, the oracle mentions the first three virtues that follow "love" in Paul's list of the "fruit of the Spirit" in Gal 5:22-23. Isaiah describes God as the one who "gives patience (μακροθυμία) to the discouraged" (Isa 57:15; cf. Gal 5:22). The outpouring of God's Spirit will result in "peace" (εἰρήνη) for those who are near and those who are far off (Isa 57:19; cf. Gal 5:22). The final verse of the oracle notes that the wicked will have no "rejoicing" (χαίρειν), implying that the righteous will receive it together with the peace that God proclaims to them (Isa 57:21; cf. Gal 5:22).

Another feature of Isaiah 57 not noted by Beale suggests that this oracle, or at least traditions stemming from it, inform Paul's description of the fruit of the Spirit. As we have already seen numerous times, inheritance plays a significant role in Paul's argument throughout the letter, particularly in the transition between the vice list and the list of the fruit of the Spirit. It is all the more striking in light of this that Isa 57:13 contrasts the wicked who will be swept away with those who cling to God: "Those who cling to [God] shall

---

[91] For a fuller discussion of Isaiah 32, see pp. 18-19 above; cf. Beale, "The Old Testament Background of Paul's Reference to 'the Fruit of the Spirit' in Galatians 5:22," 3-6.

[92] See pp. 23-24 above.

[93] Beale, "The Old Testament Background of Paul's Reference to 'the Fruit of the Spirit' in Galatians 5:22," 6. The Greek reflects the witnesses of Aquila and Symmachus as cited by Beale with some modification: the Göttingen text seems to read αυτον rather than αυτου and καρπον rather than καρπος. The form αυτον makes the phrase more difficult to translate, but the basic point remains that several important Greek witnesses reflect "fruit" as a part of this eschatological phenomenon and connect it with the outpouring of the Spirit.

inherit [God's] holy mountain (κληρονομήσουσιν τὸ ὄρος τὸ ἅγιόν μου)" (Isa 57:13 [LXX], my translation).

The inheritance language in Isaiah has added significance in that this is not the only passage that connects inheritance and the Spirit. As we have seen, Isaiah 63, which retells Israel's deliverance from Egypt as part of a plea for a new deliverance, describes the Spirit's guidance of Israel in the wilderness and then presents a plea to God as father that Israel might gain an inheritance.[94] Using language very similar to that of Isa 57:13, the lament declares: "Return for the sake of your slaves, for the sake of the tribes of your inheritance, that we might inherit a small part of your holy mountain (ἵνα μικρὸν κληρονομήσωμεν τοῦ ὄρους τοῦ ἁγίου σου)" (Isa 63:17b-18 [LXX], my translation). The juxtaposition of Spirit and inheritance language in two texts that connect the Spirit with restoration eschatology suggests that a similar eschatological framework shapes Paul's use of inheritance language in Gal 5:19-23.

A consideration of some Second Temple texts that develop these themes further confirms the likelihood of this context for Paul's argument. Two texts in particular merit attention with respect to the expression "fruit of the Spirit" in Gal 5:22. As we saw above in chapter three, the *Treatise on the Two Spirits* from Qumran draws on the language of some of the prophetic texts we have been considering.[95] Specifically, the *Treatise* appropriates the oracle of Isaiah 11 and applies it more generally to an eschatological community of all those who follow the "spirit of truth."[96] Beginning at column IV of 1QS, the text describes the paths of human beings who are led by each of the two spirits. The description of the "spirit of truth" draws on language from Isaiah 11:

It is a spirit of meekness, of patience, of generous compassion, eternal goodness, intelligence, understanding, potent wisdom which trusts in all the deeds of God and depends on his abundant mercy; a spirit of knowledge in all the plans of action, of enthusiasm for the decrees of justice, of holy plans with firm purpose, of generous compassion with all the sons of truth, of magnificent purity which detests all unclean idols, of unpretentious behaviour with moderation in everything, of prudence in respect of the truth concerning the mysteries of knowledge. (1QS 4.3-6)[97]

---

[94] Beale ("The Old Testament Background of Paul's Reference to 'the Fruit of the Spirit' in Galatians 5:22," 12-15) recognizes the significance of Isaiah 63 for Galatians, but does not note the prominence of inheritance language in both Isa 57:13 and Isa 63:17-18.

[95] For a fuller discussion of the *Treatise*, see ibid., 16-18 and pp. 48-51 above.

[96] Beale ("The Old Testament Background of Paul's Reference to 'the Fruit of the Spirit' in Galatians 5:22," 16) suggests that the "spirit of truth" refers to the divine "Spirit," due in part to the allusion to Isaiah 11. The question is a difficult one to resolve based on the complexity of the two-spirit concept at Qumran. For our purposes, however, the most significant aspect of the *Treatise* is the conjunction of spirit-language with virtues and fruitfulness, as well as new creation and everlasting life.

[97] Translation taken from Florentino García Martínez and Eibert J. C. Tigchelaar, *The Dead Sea Scrolls: Study Edition* (2 vols.; Grand Rapids: Eerdmans, 1997, 1998).

The *Treatise* then proceeds to describe the rewards that will accrue to the "sons of truth," those who "walk in [the spirit]," among them "peace," "fruit," "everlasting blessing," and "endless life" (1QS 4.7). The combination of so many terms that overlap with many of the themes of Galatians, occurring as they do in an eschatological context, strengthens the argument that Paul understands the καρπός in Gal 5:22 as part of the eschatological conditions that accompany the outpouring of the Spirit.

Similarly the *Testament of Judah* describes an outpouring of the Spirit in the context of an eschatological restoration and the bestowal of virtues on restored Israel. A ruler is said to arise from the tribe of Judah who walks in "gentleness and righteousness" (ἐν πραότητι [*sic*] καὶ δικαιοσύνη; *T.Jud.* 24:1). The ruler is described as a "shoot (βλαστός)," a term that connotes fruitfulness, and the shoot is said to be a "fountain offering life to all" (ἡ πηγὴ πᾶσι παρέχουσα ζωήν; *T.Jud.* 24:4). Moreover, the ruler brings righteousness to the nations and salvation to "all that call on the Lord," most likely an allusion to Joel 2, which also serves as one source for the eschatological outpouring of the Spirit earlier in *Testament of Judah* 24. Once again we see a text connecting this eschatological outpouring with fruitfulness and the bestowal of virtues, some of which (πραότης, δικαιοσύνη) overlap with virtues that Paul refers to in Galatians.

In light of these associations between the Spirit, fruitfulness, and virtue in both the prophetic literature of the OT and some Second Temple texts, Paul's reference to the "fruit of the Spirit" in Gal 5:22-23 makes the most sense as a continuation of the eschatological argument that he has been mounting throughout the epistle. Once again the Spirit serves as the sign and source of the in-breaking of the eschatological age. Beale may go too far in insisting that Paul consciously alludes to Isaiah 57 in these texts, but it is highly likely that the themes presented there and in other parts of Isaiah form one important component in his understanding of the fruit of the Spirit.[98] The fact that most of the texts considered above also speak of or allude to a new creation strengthens the case, particularly in light of Paul's emphasis on "new creation" in Gal 6:15.

Paul concludes the catalogue of the fruit of the Spirit with the enigmatic phrase κατὰ τῶν τοιούτων οὐκ ἔστιν νόμος (Gal 5:23). Is the sense of the text "The Law is not against such things" or is it "against such things there is no law"?[99] Given the way that Paul consistently uses νόμος throughout Galatians to refer to the Mosaic Law, the statement most likely is intended as a subtle jab at the Torah observance endorsed by Paul's opponents, particularly

---

[98] Beale, "The Old Testament Background of Paul's Reference to 'the Fruit of the Spirit' in Galatians 5:22," 25-30.

[99] These translations need not be mutually exclusive – Paul could be saying that no law condemns the fruit of the Spirit, with the Mosaic Law as the primary target of the statement.

when read in light of Paul's fulfillment language in Gal 5:14.[100] The Law is not against such virtues because the Law is fulfilled in the one saying, "You shall love your neighbor as yourself." As many have noted, Paul's ironic statement glosses over other matters that the Law endorses, most obviously circumcision and food laws. Nevertheless, if, as Barclay has argued, Paul was addressing the Galatians' felt need for guidance in moral matters, the statement meets Paul's needs: it is life in the Spirit that provides everything the Galatians need to live uprightly.[101]

Galatians 5:24-26: Crucifying the flesh, living by the Spirit

With Gal 5:24-26 Paul brings to a close his general discussion of the work that the Spirit produces in believers before providing more concrete application of these virtues. Once again Paul connects the work of the Spirit and the believer's freedom from the flesh with the death and resurrection of Christ. Using the shocking language of crucifixion, Paul asserts that those who belong to Christ have "crucified the flesh with its passions and desires" (Gal 5:24). As we saw in chapter four above, the language of death and life functions as one of the central images in the epistle, and Paul's continued use of this language confirms the interrelatedness between this part of the argument and the earlier parts of the epistle. At the same time, these verses make more explicit the connection between the cross and the Spirit in Paul's thought, tying together the crucifixion of the flesh with life in the Spirit.

It is significant that Gal 5:24-25 follows a pattern similar to Gal 2:19b-20:

I have been crucified with Christ;	Those who belong to Christ have crucified the flesh with its passions and desires.
I no longer live, but Christ lives in me. (Gal 2:19b-20a)	If we live by the Spirit, let us order our lives by the Spirit. (Gal 5:24-25)

These parallels suggest that Christ lives in believers by means of the Spirit (cf. Rom 8:9-11). Furthermore, they confirm that the practical advice Paul presents in Galatians 5-6 is intertwined with the eschatological framework he provides earlier in the epistle. Believers can be free from the works of the flesh and bring forth the fruit of the Spirit only because of the death and resurrection of Christ. It is through these eschatological events (and therefore not

---

[100] Betz, *Galatians*, 288 translates the phrase "no law is against such things"; Dunn, *Galatians*, 313 notes that most commentators render the phrase "against such as these...there is no law," but suggests that a reference to the Torah is "probably inescapable in the context of the letter." Based on a comparison with Rom 2:25-29, Hays, *Galatians*, 328 seems to take "Law" to refer to the Torah.

[101] See Barclay, *Obeying the Truth*, 122-25.

through the Law) that Christians can order their lives rightly before God.¹⁰² The emphasis on life (εἰ ζῶμεν πνεύματι) also bears mention, since the verb ζάω bears eschatological connotations in other significant parts of the epistle (Gal 2:19-20; 3:10-14; cf. ζῳοποιέω in 3:21b). It is this eschatological life in which believers participate that grounds their behavior. Before giving concrete positive advice, however, Paul once again exhorts them to avoid the characteristics of those in the flesh: boasting, provoking, and stirring up envy (Gal 5:26).

Galatians 6:1-2: Correction in the Spirit of Gentleness

Paul's continued use of "spirit" language in Gal 6:1-2 suggests that his exhortations ought to be read in light of the discussion of the Spirit in Galatians 5. These instructions, thought by many commentators to be a random collection of paraenesis, actually flow naturally from the groundwork Paul lays in Galatians 5 and make sense if one of the primary problems in the Galatian church was disunity.¹⁰³ Unity is a result of the Spirit whose fruit includes peace, patience, and gentleness, a gentleness that Paul now urges his listeners to embody in their life together.

Given that the vast majority of Paul's references to πνεῦμα in Galatians refer to the Spirit of God, the term πνευματικοί in Gal 6:1 does not indicate a subset of the community that is vaguely "spiritual," but rather it reminds the Galatians that they have all (note the plural ὑμεῖς) received the outpouring of the Spirit.¹⁰⁴ As people of the Spirit, the Galatians should not fall into the works of the flesh, accusing or mocking a brother or sister who falls into sin. Rather, in the Spirit of gentleness they ought to restore the person, knowing that they themselves are equally capable of falling into sin.

As part of his practical advice to the congregation Paul uses "fulfillment" language for the third time in the epistle, thus connecting their behavior to what God has done to bring about the era of the Spirit and to Christ's own fulfillment of the Law. Galatians 4:4 describes God's sending of the Son in the "fullness of time," a phrase which in Second Temple Judaism and early Christianity suggested the in-breaking of a new age.¹⁰⁵ As argued above, the fulfillment of the Law in Gal 5:14 refers both to Christians' fulfillment of the

---

[102] It is possible that Paul's use of the verb στοιχέω both here and in Gal 6:16 serves as a contrast to the Galatians' prior enslavement to the στοιχεῖα described in Gal 4:3, 9.

[103] See Barclay, *Obeying the Truth*, 36-74 and 155-70.

[104] So Gordon D. Fee, *God's Empowering Presence: The Holy Spirit in the Letters of Paul* (Peabody: Hendrickson, 1994), 460-61; Hays, *Galatians*, 332; R. Longenecker, *Galatians*, 273; Matera, *Galatians*, 213.

[105] See pp. 123 above.

Law through the love commandment and to Christ's fulfillment of the Law in his self-sacrificial death. By using a compound of the verb πληρόω and by modifying the phrase τὸν νόμον by the genitival phrase "of Christ," Paul draws an even closer connection between the Galatians' "filling to the full" of the Law with Christ's fulfillment of the Law.[106] The compound form of the verb (ἀναπληρώσετε) may also point to a distinction between Christ's fulfillment of the Law and that of the Galatians, suggesting that the latter depends on the former. Martyn proposes the following helpful paraphrase: "Bear one another's burdens, and in this way you yourselves will repeat Christ's deed, bringing to completion in your communities the Law that Christ has already brought to completion in the sentence about loving the neighbor."[107]

This reading assumes that the "Law" in question refers once again to the Mosaic Law. Although such a claim might seem startling at first given Paul's largely negative portrayal of the Law throughout the epistle, two factors support this interpretation.[108] First, as mentioned above, the note of fulfillment of the Law in 6:2 recapitulates Paul's reference to fulfillment in 5:14. Moreover, as Barclay suggests, both verses highlight fulfillment of the Law through taking on the role of a slave (5:13: "through love become slaves of one another"; 6:2: "bear one another's burdens").[109] In addition, since the "whole Law" of 5:14 refers to the Mosaic Law, then the "Law of Christ" in 6:2 most likely also refers to the Mosaic Law, though as it has been redefined by Christ's self-sacrificial death.[110] This argument gains further support if Paul understood the fulfillment of the Law in Gal 5:14 as a prophetic, Christological fulfillment.[111]

Galatians 6:7-8: Reaping Eternal Life

Paul's last reference to the flesh/Spirit dichotomy in Galatians sums up the outcomes for those who "sow to the flesh" and for those who "sow to the Spirit," and it confirms the connection between the Spirit and life that we have seen to this point. "The one who sows to his own flesh," Paul writes, "will reap corruption" (Gal 6:8a). Although some translators have taken this

---

[106] Cf. Fee, *God's Empowering Presence*, 458-64.
[107] Martyn, *Galatians*, 547-48.
[108] For what follows see Barclay, *Obeying the Truth*, 126-42. See also Hays's modification of his earlier position ("Christology and Ethics in Galatians," 286-88) that the "Law of Christ" is a "structure of existence" in Hays, *Galatians*, 333-34; idem, "Three Dramatic Roles: The Law in Romans 3-4," in *The Conversion of the Imagination: Paul as Interpreter of Israel's Scripture* (Grand Rapids: Eerdmans, 2005), 85-100, esp. 88 n. 9.
[109] Barclay, *Obeying the Truth*, 131-32.
[110] Ibid., 132.
[111] See above and Hays, *Galatians*, 322-24; Martyn, *Galatians*, 489-90.

verse to describe carnal sins,[112] by now it should be clear that this is not the primary connotation of "flesh" throughout most of Galatians. To be sure, Paul believes that confidence in the flesh will result in the typical sins found among the Gentiles (Gal 5:19-21), as well as in Israel apart from the indwelling of the Spirit. Nevertheless, "sowing to the flesh" does not simply mean engaging in sinful behavior. On the contrary, it means placing confidence in circumcision and the works of the Law. This has been the thrust of the argument from as far back as Gal 3:3, where Paul first contrasts the Spirit and the flesh in the context of an argument against the works of the Law.[113] That "sowing to the flesh" should result in corruption according to Paul fits with the connection between the curse of the Law and death that we saw in chapter four above.[114] As we saw there, the problem with the Law for Paul is that it could not give life (Gal 3:21b) and that therefore those under the Law were under the curse of death.

By contrast, those who "sow to the Spirit, from the Spirit will reap eternal life" (Gal 6:8b). The expression "eternal life" (ζωὴ αἰώνιον), though not common in Paul, most often carries eschatological connotations when it appears. It is also significant that eternal life is often contrasted with corruption and death, suggesting that it connotes resurrection as well.[115] Such a connotation would be in keeping with Paul's description in Gal 2:19-20 of Christ living in him. Moreover, it would connect this concluding exhortation with the rest of the epistle. It is the Spirit that leads to the eschatological life that the Law, dealing as it does with the flesh, cannot bring (Gal 3:21b). We see a consistency, then, throughout Paul's argument. The choice that Paul holds out to his readers ironically reflects the choice held out in Deuteronomy 30: life and death, the blessing and the curse. But whereas according to Deuteronomy God gives life to those who keep the Law and death to those who disobey it, according to Paul the Spirit gives the eternal life that the Law failed to produce throughout Israel's history. As in Galatians 4 and 5, Paul presents a

---

[112] Cf. the NIV: "The one who sows to please his sinful nature."

[113] This association of flesh with Torah and circumcision continues in the postscript written in Paul's own hand (Gal 6:12-13). If "flesh" in Gal 6:8 means "sinful nature" or something of the sort, it would make very little sense both in the immediate context and in the context of the letter as a whole.

[114] One might contrast Paul's contemporary Philo, who saw circumcision both symbolically and practically as an antidote to sinful desires. See, e.g., *Spec. Laws* 1.9. For a helpful comparison of Paul and Philo on circumcision with respect to Romans, see John M. G. Barclay, "Paul and Philo on Circumcision: Romans 2.25-9 in Social and Cultural Context," *NTS* 44 (1998): 536-56.

[115] See Rom 2:7; 5:21 (which leads into the discussion of dying and rising with Christ in baptism); 6:22-23 (which contrast eternal life with death). Paul's association of the Spirit with life may also have roots in the prophecy of Ezekiel 37 (see especially Ezek 37:5-6). For one fascinating text connecting "sowing" imagery with the gathering of "the fruit of life" (καρπὸν ζωῆς) see Hos 10:12.

revisionary picture of the Law and its promises to bless and to give life. To "sow to one's own flesh" is to return to the era of the Law which only brought judgment and death; to "sow to the Spirit" is to inhabit the new creation (cf. Gal 6:15) that brings about eternal life.

Conclusion

"The one who sows to the Spirit, from the Spirit will reap eternal life" (Gal 6:8b). One could argue that this brief phrase encapsulates Paul's message about the Spirit in Galatians. We saw in chapter four above that for Paul the era of the Law failed to bring about the blessing promised to Abraham and only brought judgment and death. To remain in that era or to return to it by practicing circumcision and the works of the Law is to return to judgment and death. It is only by means of the Spirit that believers are freed from the old age and from the Law to receive the eschatological life that the Law could not give. In the present chapter we have seen how Paul develops this theme with regard to the daily life of the community. The life that the Spirit gives is not some abstract principle; rather, it is the empowerment the Galatians need to order their lives properly (Gal 5:22-25). All of this stems from the transition from the old age to the new age. The outpouring of the Spirit has begun to bring about the new creation in which believers bear fruit that leads to eternal life. As in Galatians 3-4, Paul draws this imagery from a variety of prophetic texts and motifs that promise the restoration of Israel, motifs that continued to play a role in eschatological expectation during the Second Temple period. Once again, however, he transforms the motifs through the lens of the cross. Through the cross believers have crucified the flesh and thus died to the Law so that through the Spirit they might live to God.

Chapter 6

Conclusion: The Spirit and the Restoration of Israel

Summary

This study began with the question of the significance of the Spirit for Paul's argument in Galatians 3-6, taking its cue from Paul's rhetorical question in Gal 3:2. The only thing that Paul wants to know from the Galatians is how they received the Spirit. To his mind, the answer to this question settles the debate about Gentile submission to the Law. In order to answer why this is the case, we have traversed a significant amount of material.

In chapter two, we explored the connection between the outpouring of the Spirit and restoration eschatology in three books of the OT. Although by no means the only important element of restoration eschatology in the OT, the sending of the Spirit does represent one significant strand in the promises that describe the redemption of Israel. The texts representative of this strand are not monolithic, but rather provide a variety of images to describe Israel's redemption: new creation, new exodus, the fatherhood of God, peace and righteousness, and resurrection, to name just a few. Perhaps most importantly for the present study, the majority of these texts seem to reflect the position that Israel has undergone punishment because of her sins, but at the same time they hold out hope that God will once again redeem his people.

The Second Temple literature that we considered in chapter three shows that the curses of Leviticus and Deuteronomy posed a significant problem in the centuries leading up to the early Christian movement. Like the prophetic literature, these texts do not present a monolithic picture – rather, they provide a variety of images associating the outpouring of the Spirit with restoration eschatology. Despite this variety, the texts that we considered develop several of the themes that we found in the OT. A number of these texts refer to the problem of the heart and the promise that God will put a new spirit within the hearts of the Israelites so that they might do his will. Moreover, this infusion of a new spirit into the heart often is expected to result in a filial relationship with God. Many of the texts considered also hold out hope that God will provide the eschatological gifts of righteousness and peace. These terms often appear in the context of descriptions of a new creation, sometimes explicitly connected with resurrection. Finally, many of these texts describe not only eschatological renewal, but also the arrival of a messianic figure who helps to inaugurate the age of restoration and redemption. Several texts use the language of Isaiah 11 to describe the way that the Spirit of God comes to rest on this figure, who in turn pours out the Spirit onto the people. The writings of Josephus and Philo stood in marked contrast to those of apocalyptic/sectarian Judaism, highlighting the importance of the latter in interpreting this element of Paul's understanding of the Spirit.

In chapter four we came to the heart of the argument, both Paul's (Galatians 3-4) and my own. It is at the beginning of Galatians 3 that Paul asks the rhetorical question about the Galatians' reception of the Spirit. Careful attention to the three main passages that focus on the Spirit in Galatians 3-4 confirmed the significance of restoration eschatology in the epistle.

First, we saw that the introductory section of Gal 3:1-5, as well as its surrounding context, draws heavily upon the language of restoration eschatology, particularly in the book of Isaiah. The way that Paul draws on this eschatology also has an apocalyptic character in the sense that he considers his gospel to be something revealed by God. Nevertheless, Paul's apocalyptic gospel is not totally discontinuous with Israel's history and the prophetic promises.[1] On the contrary, many of the central themes of Paul's message (that it is hidden and only revealed by God to whom he wills, that it involves the proclamation of good news of peace, that it is to be revealed in the sight of the Gentiles, that it involves suffering and an inheritance) can be found in the oracles of Deutero-Isaiah. This is not to say that Paul simply read these things off the scroll and reached the obvious conclusion that they had been fulfilled in his day – his understanding of Isaiah was retrospective and made sense to him only after he had experienced the risen Christ. It is to say, however, that Paul believed his apocalyptic gospel was the beginning of God's fulfillment of the promises made to Israel through the prophets. These promises make sense to Paul looking backwards through the death and resurrection of Christ, and it is in light of the Christ event that he can confidently assert that God has begun to bring them to pass.

---

[1] In this regard, I agree with J. Louis Martyn that Paul's gospel is fundamentally apocalyptic insofar as it is something revealed. I disagree, however, with Martyn's insistence that Paul's apocalyptic rules out the significance of Israel's history. Paul draws the very language of apocalyptic from the prophets and so connects his gospel with the promises of the OT, even if the manner in which they were fulfilled is unexpected, indeed shocking. See J. Louis Martyn, *Galatians: A New Translation with Introduction and Commentary* (AB 33A; New York: Doubleday, 1997), 97-105 *et passim*; *idem*, *Theological Issues in the Letters of Paul* (Nashville: Abingdon, 1997), *passim*. For a helpful criticism of this dichotomy between apocalyptic and salvation history, see James D. G. Dunn, "How New was Paul's Gospel? The Problem of Continuity and Discontinuity," in *Gospel in Paul: Studies on Corinthians, Galatians and Romans for Richard N. Longenecker* (ed. L. Ann Jervis and Peter Richardson; JSNTSup 108; Sheffield: Sheffield Academic, 1994), 367-88, esp. 382-85.

Second, our consideration of Gal 3:10-14 led us to conclude that the "curse" in 3:10, 13 refers to the curse pronounced by the Law on Israel as a whole for breaking the covenant. In contrast to others who have taken this position such as N. T. Wright and James Scott, however, I have suggested that, unlike some of his contemporaries, Paul does not understand the curse in terms of exile from and return to the land, but rather in terms of death and life.[2] Paul, reading Israel's story through the lens of the death and resurrection of Jesus, emphasizes the other primary description of the curse in Deuteronomy, namely death (cf. Deut 30:15-20). In other words, though Paul believed himself and his fellow Jews to be under the curse of Deuteronomy, it was not exile from the land of Israel that demonstrated this condition, but rather the continued dominion of death. Throughout Israel's history, according to Paul, the Law had failed to provide the life that it held out as the primary covenantal blessing. As Paul notes in Gal 3:21, righteousness does not come from the Law because the Law is unable to make alive. The Spirit, by contrast, makes alive (cf. 2 Cor 3:6) and provides the eschatological life that the Law had failed to give.

Even though Paul eschews the language of return to the land in favor of the language of life and death, he nevertheless connects the outpouring of the Spirit with the restoration of Israel, as one can see from his emphasis on the blessing. As we saw in chapters three and four, the *Words of the Luminaries* and the *Testament of Judah* both allude to the oracle of Isaiah 44 to describe God's rescue of Israel from the curses of Leviticus and/or Deuteronomy by pouring out the Spirit and the blessing. So, when Paul describes the result of Christ's redemptive death as the reception of the Spirit and the blessing, he is thinking in the categories of restoration eschatology. Moreover, we saw that Paul understood the redemption of Israel and outpouring of the Spirit to be intertwined with the ingathering of the Gentiles, though he understands this ingathering metaphorically. It has to do not with a movement of Gentiles to the land of Israel, but rather with their inclusion in the people of God through Christ.

Finally, Gal 4:1-7 presents a similar schema to 3:10-14 in that the focus of Paul's redemption language is on Christian Jews, though that redemption seems to be dependent on the inclusion of the Gentiles (Gal 4:6). One significant new element in this passage vis-à-vis Gal 3:10-14 is Paul's reference to God sending the Spirit of his Son into "our hearts." As we saw in chapters two and three, the heart represents the locus of the problem for Israel in many

---

[2] James M. Scott, "'For as Many as are of Works of the Law are Under a Curse' (Galatians 3.10)," in *Paul and the Scriptures of Israel* (ed. Craig A. Evans and James A. Sanders; JSNTSup 83; Sheffield: Sheffield Academic, 1993), 187-221, esp. 214-15; N. T. Wright, *The Climax of the Covenant: Christ and the Law in Pauline Theology* (Minneapolis: Fortress, 1992), 146 *et passim*.

prophetic and Second Temple texts, as well as in Deuteronomy. Given the connotations that the combination of the Spirit and the heart has in Ezekiel and Isaiah, as well as some Second Temple Jewish literature, Paul's reference to the heart confirms that the Spirit serves as the sign of God's redemption of Israel from the curse. Moreover, these texts often speak not only of the restoration of Israel, but also of God's empowering Israel to do his will. Given this common association, it makes sense that the last third of the letter should address matters of conduct for the Galatians and do so in a way that draws upon the eschatological implications of the Galatians' reception of the Spirit.

Chapter five explored the ways in which Paul's exhortation in Galatians 5-6 continues to draw upon the eschatological framework that informs the central part of the epistle. We began by noting a number of features of the text that point to the eschatological underpinnings of the argument: Paul's talk of the "hope of righteousness" (Gal 5:6), his language about not inheriting the kingdom of God (5:21b), the expectation of eternal life (6:8), and the climactic reference to "new creation" (6:15). Moreover, we saw that this section of the epistle develops the flesh/Spirit contrast that makes its first explicit appearance in Galatians 3-4, suggesting a closer relationship between these two sections of the epistle than some interpreters have recognized. Given the close connection between the flesh and the Law both in Galatians 3 and in the exhortation of the epistle, we concluded that Paul's flesh/Spirit dichotomy refers primarily to a contrast between the old age of the Law and the new age of the Spirit.

Several features of Galatians 5-6 point in this direction. First, the beginning of the transitional section in Gal 5:2-6 encapsulates and summarizes Paul's argument to that point, contrasting the eschatological hope grounded in the outpouring of the Spirit with reliance on circumcision and acts of Torah. This transitional section turns explicitly to the question of circumcision, one that has been prominent (though implicit) since the early parts of the epistle. Second, Paul's continued use of fulfillment language (Gal 5:14; cf. 4:4) points to both the continuity between Galatians 3-4 and Galatians 5-6 and the transition from the old age of the Law to the new age of the Spirit. In that new age, the love commandment of Leviticus has been fulfilled and redefined by Christ's self-sacrifice on the cross. This cross-shaped love represents the first and foundational fruit of the Spirit brought forth in believers (Gal 5:22). Third, the way that Paul alternates between "flesh" and "Law" in 5:16-18, and indeed throughout 5:13-26, implies that the two are intimately related in his argument, especially in light of the connection between flesh and circumcision in Gal 3:1-5. This connection continues into the postscript of the letter (Gal 6:12), suggesting its fundamental importance for Paul.

A second, equally significant connection between Galatians 3-4 and Galatians 5-6 concerns Paul's emphasis on life and death. The emphasis on life and death found throughout the central part of the epistle continues in the hortatory section as the basis of the Galatians' daily life: "If we live (ζῶμεν) by the Spirit, let us also order our lives (στοιχῶμεν) by the Spirit" (Gal 5:25). Paul's final reference to the Spirit of God in Galatians again highlights the contrast between corruption and eternal life: "For the one who sows to his own flesh from the flesh will reap corruption, but the one who sows to the Spirit from the Spirit will reap eternal life" (Gal 6:8). The Spirit serves as the source of eternal life, the life that the Law had held out (Deut 30:15, 19) as a promise but failed to provide throughout Israel's history.

Major Contributions

Having reviewed the argument, we can now point to five major contributions of the present study. These contributions relate to Paul's pneumatology vis-à-vis other Second Temple Jewish thought, the question of the curse of the Law, the blessing of Abraham, the importance of the categories of "life" and "death," and the coherence of Galatians.

Paul, the Spirit, and Second Temple Judaism

As we saw in chapter three, a number of Jews in the Second Temple period took up various themes from the OT Prophets to describe their hope for an outpouring of the Spirit that would accompany God's restoration of Israel. The texts we considered do not present a monolithic picture of how this expectation was to play out, but they do share enough similarities to suggest that certain patterns of eschatological hope in the OT continued well into the Second Temple period. Various images of the Spirit from Isaiah, Ezekiel, and Joel continued to influence the imagination of some Jews in this period, though as we saw there were some exceptions. The writings of Josephus and Philo, two representatives of high literary Hellenistic Jewish culture, show no interest in the kinds of eschatological hope more characteristic of the apocalyptic and sectarian literature that formed the bulk of chapter three. Rather, these two focus primarily on the Spirit's role in inspiration and prophecy. Though certain similarities exist between Paul's conception of the Spirit and those of Philo and Josephus (e.g., the association between the Spirit and prophecy in 1 Corinthians 12-14), with regard to eschatological expectation Paul's pneumatology has more in common with texts such as *Jubilees, 1 Enoch*, and the *Psalms of Solomon*, as well as some writings from Qumran, than with figures such as Philo and Josephus.

The Words of the Luminaries, the Curse of the Law, and the Outpouring of the Spirit

In chapter four I suggested that the outpouring of the Spirit and the blessing in Gal 3:14 must be understood in terms of redemption from the curse of the Law. Richard Hays and James Scott have suggested that the primary text for understanding the way that Paul connects the outpouring of the Spirit with the blessing is Isa 44:3, the only text in the OT to use the words "blessing" and "Spirit" together.[3] The only Second Temple text to which Scott could point to show that Isaiah 44 exerted influence on Second Temple Judaism, however, was the *Testament of Judah*. Because of widely held suspicion of Christian influence on (or even authorship of) the document, especially with respect to chapter 24, this argument was on shaky ground.

Our comparison of the *Words of the Luminaries* with Galatians and the *Testament of Judah*, however, presents two interrelated contributions to the discussion. As I argue in both chapter three and chapter four, the allusion to Isa 44:3 in the Qumran text has two implications. First, it is likely that the allusion to Isaiah in the *Testament of Judah* reflects an earlier Jewish tradition, and so cannot be so easily dismissed as Christian redaction. It is reasonable to say, therefore, that both texts point to the kind of expectations that at least some Jews held during the late Second Temple period. Second, both the *Words of the Luminaries* and the *Testament* allude to the Isaianic oracle in the context of a description of Israel suffering under the curses of Leviticus and/or Deuteronomy. Again, this confirms that at least some Second Temple Jews continued to anticipate the outpouring of the Spirit at the time when God would redeem Israel from the curse(s) of the Law. The existence of this tradition and the fact that Paul uses "blessing" and "Spirit" language prominently in Gal 3:10-14 indicates that he saw the outpouring of the Spirit on believers as the beginning of God's restoration of Israel after centuries of suffering under the curse.

The Outpouring of the Spirit and the Blessing of Abraham

The blessing to which Paul refers, of course, is the blessing of Abraham, but the connection between the promise to Abraham and the Spirit has for some time remained puzzling. Though Isa 44:3 may account for the conjunction of the blessing and the Spirit in Gal 3:14, the text does not explain Paul's reference to Abraham. A closer consideration of the role of Abraham in the oracles of Deutero-Isaiah has helped to clarify the connection. As we saw in chapter three, Abraham appears in two texts closely related to Isaiah 44. In

---

[3] Scott, "'For as Many as are of Works of the Law'," 215 n. 96; Richard B. Hays, *The Faith of Jesus Christ: The Narrative Substructure of Galatians 3:1-4:11* (2nd ed.; Grand Rapids: Eerdman's, 2002), 182-83.

Isaiah 41 God comforts the people of Israel, referring to them as the "seed of Abraham." The oracle goes on to offer redemption and to describe the pouring out of water in the desert for the people, much like the pouring out of springs in Isaiah 44. Similarly Isaiah 51 makes reference to Abraham, using wilderness imagery similar to that of Isaiah 44 to describe Israel's plight and his deliverance of the people. The oracle also refers to God blessing Abraham and to a salvation that extends not only to Israel but also to the nations. The prominence of Abraham in these two oracles closely related to Isaiah 44 helps to explain Paul's association of the Spirit with the blessing of Abraham. Moreover, it also clarifies the connection between the redemption of Israel and the extension of the blessing to the nations. To borrow language from Romans, God's blessing comes "to the Jew first and also to the Greek." For Paul it is because God has acted to redeem Israel by pouring out the eschatological Spirit that the blessing can now go out to the Gentiles as well.

The Curse of the Law and Life and Death

Although I have followed Scott and Wright in taking the curse of Gal 3:10, 13 to refer to the curse pronounced by the Law, the present investigation led me to redefine the content of the curse. We saw in chapters three and four that a number of Second Temple Jewish texts spoke of Israel as still under the curse and awaiting a return to the land. Paul, by contrast, rarely (if ever) uses the language of exile and return. Rather, as I have suggested throughout, the key categories for Paul are life and death. One of the main problems with the Law is that it could not "make alive" (Gal 3:21b), whereas the primary benefit of the Spirit is "eternal life" (Gal 6:8). As we saw in chapter four, the main contrast throughout Gal 3:10-14 is one between life and curse, which implies that one can epitomize the content of the curse with the term "death."

In addition, such a reading actually fits with Deuteronomy's own summary statement: "I call heaven and earth to witness against you today that I have set before you life and death, the blessing and the curse" (Deut 30:19).[4] Whereas some Second Temple Jews saw the problem as exile in one form or another, for Paul the death and resurrection of Christ completed the process that had already begun with Ezekiel 37 and Daniel 12, shifting the emphasis from return to the land to bodily resurrection and life. The fact that Paul's thought on the matter is a development of an already present Jewish theme suggests that he sees the cross and resurrection as God's way of keeping his promises to

---

[4] This is not to say that the only curse for Deuteronomy is "death." Rather, all of the curses of Deuteronomy 27-30 may be categorized in some way as "death," just as all of the blessings fall under the category "life." It is significant in this regard that in Gal 3:10-14 Paul emphasizes both eschatological life and the reception of the blessing. See again Jon D. Levenson, *Resurrection and the Restoration of Israel: The Ultimate Victory of the God of Life* (New Haven/London: Yale, 2006), *passim*.

Israel. As I suggested in chapter four, this is a way to keep the strengths of the so-called Exile-Restoration scheme (the redemption of Israel from the curse of the Law) while avoiding its primary weakness (over-reliance on exile language that does not figure prominently, if at all, in Paul's thought).[5]

Life and Death, the Spirit, and the Coherence of Galatians

Finally, this emphasis on life and death and its relation to the outpouring of the Spirit lends a greater coherence to Galatians as a whole. The imagery of life and death appears again and again at climactic points in Paul's argument. In the *propositio* of Gal 2:15-21, Paul speaks of dying to the Law and living to God (see especially Gal 2:19-20, where the verb ζάω appears five times). Eschatological life is one of the primary motifs in Paul's discussion of the curse of the Law in Gal 3:10-14. Paul grounds his moral exhortation in Galatians 5-6 on the basis of the eschatological life that believers have through the Spirit (Gal 5:25), and he closes the exhortation by reminding his readers of the consequences of living in the flesh and living in the Spirit: the one leads to corruption, the other to eternal life (Gal 6:8).

Although throughout the letter Paul rarely speaks explicitly of "eternal life" (Gal 6:8 being the exception), the idea of Christ living in him (Gal 2:19-20) makes the most sense in terms of eschatological life. It is also significant in this regard that Paul opens the epistle with a reference to Christ's resurrection (Gal 1:1) and closes it by emphasizing the significance of the new creation (Gal 6:15). Even though these terms do not occur in the rest of the letter, their appearance at the beginning and at the end of the letter serves as a frame through which to interpret Paul's references to life, especially when they appear to have eschatological connotations. Relating this to the primary question of the present study, the significance of eschatological life for Paul explains why the Spirit plays such an important role in his argument and indicates a greater coherence between Galatians 3-4 and Galatians 5-6. In Galatians 3-4 Paul argues that the Spirit imparts the eschatological life that the Law could not bring; in Galatians 5-6, that as a result of this eschatological life the Spirit provides the Galatians with the fruit necessary to order their lives rightly before God, something that the Law had also failed to provide.

---

[5] Cf. Joel Willitts, "Context Matters: Paul's Use of Leviticus 18:5 in Galatians 3:12," *TynBul* 54 (2003): 105-22, esp. 120-21 n. 47.

Areas for Further Research

While the present study provides answers to some important questions with regard to Galatians, it has also opened up a number of avenues that deserve further exploration.

Galatians and Romans

As we saw at the beginning of chapter four, Paul's argumentation throughout much of Galatians seems to rely significantly, albeit implicitly, on Isaiah. The most interesting aspect of this dependence is the clustering of these passages around Isaiah 52-53. Several times we noted that the oracles to which Paul alludes in Galatians often correspond to texts that he cites explicitly in Romans. This correlation suggests a closer relationship between the two letters that bears further study.

The Commandments of God

One question to which the present study has not found a satisfactory answer concerns the relationship between the outpouring of the Spirit and obeying the commandments of God. As noted in chapter two, some of the key passages in the OT Prophets that refer to the outpouring of the Spirit envision the Spirit empowering Israel to obey God's commandments and statutes (see especially Ezekiel 36 and 37). This part of Jewish eschatological expectation seems not to have influenced Paul's ministry – on the contrary, Paul is adamant that his churches should not practice the "works of the Law." One possible explanation for this stance is the significance of the ingathering of the Gentiles *as Gentiles* for Paul's eschatology, an expectation that relied on certain parts of Isaiah that envision the ingathering of the Gentiles. Nevertheless, Paul's stance against his congregations doing the works of the Law remains a puzzle in need of a solution, especially since other aspects of his pneumatology depend on texts that combine the sending of the Spirit with obedience to the commandments.

Reconciliation and the Spirit

Finally, although it has not played a central role in the present study, the relationship between the Spirit and unity reflects a major theme in Paul's theology that bears more exploration. As Barclay and Hays note, the vice list in Gal 5:19-21 is distinguished in its emphasis on conflict and strife, indicating that this was a major problem in Galatia.[6] This observation should come as no surprise when one considers how prominent the theme is in many of the Pauline epistles. The most obvious example is the Corinthian correspondence, in which Paul emphasizes a unity in diversity that is grounded in the Holy Spirit (see especially 1 Corinthians 12). But the motif appears in other epistles as well, including those considered by many to be Deutero-Pauline. In Romans 14-15 Paul addresses the question of unity of Jew and Gentile in Christ, and twice he grounds it in the Holy Spirit (see Rom 14:17; 15:13). Likewise Ephesians discusses the same unity, referring to the dividing wall that Christ broke down in his flesh (Eph 2:14). Later in the epistle the author grounds the unity of Christians in the Holy Spirit (Eph 4:4). As the examples from Romans, Galatians, and 1 Corinthians show, this emphasis on unity in Ephesians is a natural development and continuation of Paul's earlier thought. Future treatments of Paul's theology ought to pay closer attention to this theme and its connection to the Spirit. Such research could contribute to a deeper understanding of an important aspect of Paul's thought, namely, the relationship between reconciliation among human beings and reconciliation between human beings and the God of Israel.

---

[6] John M. G. Barclay, *Obeying the Truth: A Study of Paul's Ethics in Galatians* (Studies of the New Testament and its World; Edinburgh: T. & T. Clark, 1988), 152-54; Richard B. Hays, "Christology and Ethics in Galatians: the Law of Christ," *CBQ* 49 (1987): 268-90.

Bibliography

Allison, Dale C., Jr. *The New Moses: A Matthean Typology*. Minneapolis: Fortress, 1993.
Aquinas, Thomas. *Commentary on Saint Paul's Epistle to the Galatians*. Translated by Larcher, F. R. Aquinas Scripture Series 1. Albany: Magi Books, Inc., 1966.
Bachmann, Michael. "Zur Argumentation von Galater 3.10-12." *New Testament Studies* 53 (2007): 524-44.
Baltzer, Klaus. *Deutero-Isaiah*. Hermeneia. Minneapolis: Fortress, 2001.
Barclay, John M. G. "Mirror-reading a Polemical Letter: Galatians as a Test Case." *Journal for the Study of the New Testament* 31 (1987): 73-93.
–. *Obeying the Truth: A Study of Paul's Ethics in Galatians*. Studies of the New Testament and its World. Edinburgh: T. & T. Clark, 1988.
–. "Paul and Philo on Circumcision: Romans 2.25-9 in Social and Cultural Context." *New Testament Studies* 44 (1998): 536-56.
Barton, John. *Oracles of God: Perceptions of Ancient Prophecy in Israel after the Exile*. New York: Oxford University, 1986.
Beale, G. K. "Peace and Mercy Upon the Israel of God: The Old Testament Background of Galatians 6,16b." *Biblica* 80 (1999): 204-23.
–. "The Old Testament Background of Paul's Reference to 'the Fruit of the Spirit' in Galatians 5:22." *Bulletin for Biblical Research* 15 (2005): 1-38.
Becker, Jürgen. *Untersuchungen zur Entstehungsgeschichte der Testamente der Zwölf Patriarchen*. Arbeiten zur Geschichte des Antiken Judentums und des Urchristentums VIII. Leiden: Brill, 1970.
Beker, J. Christiaan. *Paul the Apostle: The Triumph of God in Life and Thought*. 1st ed. Philadelphia: Fortress, 1980.
Belleville, Linda L. "'Under the Law': Structural Analysis and the Pauline Concept of Law in Galatians 3:21-4:11." *Journal for the Study of the New Testament* 26 (1986): 53-78.
Betz, Hans-Dieter. *Galatians: A Commentary on Paul's Letter to the Churches in Galatia*. Hermeneia. Philadelphia: Fortress, 1979.
Blenkinsopp, Joseph. *Ezekiel*. Interpretation: A Bible Commentary for Teaching and Preaching. Louisville: John Knox, 1990.
–. *Isaiah 1-39: A New Translation with Introduction and Commentary*. Edited by Freedman, David Noel and William Foxwell Albright. Anchor Bible 19. New York: Doubleday, 2000.
–. *Isaiah 40-55: A New Translation with Introduction and Commentary*. Anchor Bible 19A. New York: Doubleday, 2002.
–. *Isaiah 56-66: A New Translation with Introduction and Commentary*. Anchor Bible 19B. New York: Doubleday, 2003.
Block, Daniel I. *The Book of Ezekiel: Chapters 1-24*. New International Commentary on the Old Testament. Grand Rapids: Eerdmans, 1997.
–. *The Book of Ezekiel: Chapters 25-48*. New International Commentary on the Old Testament. Grand Rapids: Eerdmans, 1997.
Brinsmead, Bernard Hungerford. *Galatians – A Dialogical Response to Opponents*. Society of Biblical Literature Dissertation Series 65. Atlanta: Scholars, 1982.

Bruce, F. F. *The Epistle to the Galatians*. New International Greek Testament Commentary. Exeter: Paternoster, 1982.
–. "The Spirit in the Letter to the Galatians." Pages 36-48 in *Essays on Apostolic Themes: Studies in honor of Howard M. Ervin*. Edited by Elbert, P. Peabody: Hendrickson, 1985.
Charles, R. H., *The Book of Jubilees, or The Little Genesis*. London: Adam and Charles Black, 1902.
Charlesworth, James H., ed. *The Old Testament Pseudepigrapha*. 2 vols. Anchor Bible Reference Library. New York: Doubleday, 1983, 1985.
Chazon, Esther G. "*4QDibham:* Liturgy or Literature?" *Revue de Qumran* 59 (1992): 447-55.
–. "Is *Divrei Ha-Me'orot* a Sectarian Prayer?" Pages 3-17 in *The Dead Sea Scrolls: Forty Years of Research*. Edited by Dimant, Devorah and Uriel Rappaport. Studies on the Texts of the Desert of Judah 10. Leiden: Brill, 1992.
Chevallier, Max-Alain. *L'Esprit et le Messie dans le bas-judaïsme et le Nouveau Testament*. Paris: Presses Universitaires de France, 1958.
–. *Souffle de Dieu: le Saint-Esprit dans le Nouveau Testament*. Point Théologique 26. Paris: Éditions Beauchesne, 1978.
Childs, Brevard S. *Isaiah*. Old Testament Library. Louisville: Westminster/John Knox, 2001.
Ciampa, Roy E. "Scriptural Language and Ideas." Pages 41-57 in *As it is Written: Studying Paul's Use of Scripture*. Edited by Stanley E. Porter and Christopher D. Stanley. Society of Biblical Literature Symposium Series 50. Atlanta: Society of Biblical Literature, 2008.
Clements, R. E. *Isaiah 1-39*. New Century Bible. Grand Rapids: Eerdmans, 1980.
Cole, R. A. *The Epistle of Paul to the Galatians*. Tyndale New Testament Commentary 9. Grand Rapids: Eerdmans, 1975.
Cosgrove, Charles H. *The Cross and the Spirit: A Study in the Argument and Theology of Galatians*. Macon: Mercer University, 1988.
Crenshaw, James L. *Joel: A New Translation with Introduction and Commentary*. Anchor Bible 24C. New York: Doubleday, 1995.
Davenport, Gene L. "The Anointed of the Lord in the Psalms of Solomon." Pages 67-92 in *Ideal Figures in Ancient Judaism: Profiles and Paradigms*. Edited by Collins, John J. and George W. E. Nickelsburg. Society of Biblical Literature Septuagint and Cognate Studies 12. Chico: Scholars, 1980.
Davila, James R. *Liturgical Works*. Eerdmans Commentaries on the Dead Sea Scrolls. Grand Rapids: Eerdmans, 2000.
Davies, W. D. *Paul and Rabbinic Judaism: Some Rabbinic Elements in Pauline Theology*. 4th ed. Philadelphia: Fortress, 1980.
–. "Paul and the New Exodus." Pages 443-63 in *The Quest for Context and Meaning*. Edited by Craig A. Evans and Shemaryahu Talmon. Leiden: Brill, 1997.
Davies, W. D., and Dale C. Allison, Jr. *A Critical and Exegetical Commentary on the Gospel according to Saint Matthew*. International Critical Commentary on the Holy Scriptures of the Old and New Testaments 27. 3 Vols. Edinburgh: T. & T. Clark, 1988-1997.
Dibelius, Martin. *Die Formgeschichte des Evangeliums*. 3rd ed. Tübingen: J.C.B. Mohr (Paul Siebeck), 1959.
Dodd, C. H. *According to the Scriptures: The Sub-structure of New Testament Theology*. New York: Scribner, 1952.
Donaldson, Terence L. "The 'curse of the Law' and the Inclusion of the Gentiles: Galatians 3.13-14." *New Testament Studies* 32 (1986): 94-112.
Dumbrell, William J. "Spirit and Kingdom of God in the Old Testament." *The Reformed Theological Review* 33 (1974): 1-10.
Dunn, James D. G. "Works of the Law and the Curse of the Law (Galatians 3.10-14)." *New Testament Studies* 31 (1985): 523-42.
–. *Romans 1-8*. Word Biblical Commentary 38A. Dallas: Word Books, 1988.

–. *The Epistle to the Galatians*. Black's New Testament Commentary. London: Cambridge, 1993.
–. "How New was Paul's Gospel? The Problem of Continuity and Discontinuity." Pages 367-88 in *Gospel in Paul: Studies on Corinthians, Galatians, and Romans for Richard N. Longenecker*. Edited by Jervis, L. Ann and Peter Richardson. Journal for the Study of the New Testament: Supplement Series 108. Sheffield: Sheffield Academic, 1994.
Ebeling, Gerhard. *Die Wahrheit des Evangeliums: Eine Lesehilfe zum Galaterbrief*. Tübingen: J. C.B. Mohr (Paul Siebeck), 1981.
Eco, Umberto. *A Theory of Semiotics*. Bloomington: Indiana University, 1976.
Elliott, Mark Adam. *The Survivors of Israel: A Reconsideration of the Theology of Pre-Christian Judaism*. Grand Rapids: Eerdmans, 2000.
Esler, Philip F. *Galatians*. New Testament Readings. London and New York: Routledge, 1998.
Evans, Craig A. "Jesus and the Dead Sea Scrolls from Qumran Cave 4." Pages 91-100 in *Eschatology, Messianism, and the Dead Sea Scrolls*. Edited by Craig A. Evans and Peter W. Flint. Studies in the Dead Sea Scrolls and Related Literature. Grand Rapids: Eerdmans, 1997.
Evans, Craig A., and James A. Sanders, eds. *Paul and the Scriptures of Israel*. Journal for the Study of the New Testament: Supplement Series 83. Sheffield: Sheffield Academic, 1993.
Falk, Daniel K. *Daily, Sabbath, and Festival Prayers in the Dead Sea Scrolls*. Edited by Florentino García Martínez and A. S. Van der Woude. Studies on the Texts of the Desert of Judah 27. Leiden: Brill, 1998.
Fee, Gordon D. *God's Empowering Presence: The Holy Spirit in the Letters of Paul*. Peabody: Hendrickson, 1994.
Fitzmyer, Joseph A. *Romans: A New Translation with Introduction and Commentary*. Anchor Bible 33. New York: Doubleday, 1992.
Frey, Jörg. "Die paulinische Antithese von »Fleisch« und »Geist« und die palästinisch-jüdische Weisheitstradition." *Zeitschrift für die neutestamentliche Wissenschaft und die Kunde der älteren Kirche* 90 (1999): 45-77.
García Martínez, Florentino and Eibert J. C. Tigchelaar. *The Dead Sea Scrolls: Study Edition*. 2 vols. Grand Rapids: Eerdmans, 1997, 1998.
Garlington, Don. "Role Reversal and Paul's Use of Scripture in Galatians 3.10-13." *Journal for the Study of the New Testament* 65 (1997): 85-121.
Gathercole, Simon J. "Torah, Life, and Salvation: Leviticus 18:5 in Early Judaism and the New Testament." Pages 131-50 in *From Prophecy to Testament: The Function of the Old Testament in the New*. Edited by Craig A. Evans. Peabody: Hendrickson, 2004.
Gombis, Timothy G. "The 'Transgressor' and the 'Curse of the Law': The Logic of Paul's Argument in Galatians 2-3." *New Testament Studies* 53 (2007): 81-93.
Greenberg, Moshe. *Ezekiel 1-20: A New Translation with Introduction and Commentary*. Anchor Bible 22. Garden City: Doubleday, 1983.
–. *Ezekiel 21-37: A New Translation with Introduction and Commentary*. Anchor Bible 22A. New York: Doubleday, 1997.
Hafemann, Scott J. "Paul and the Exile of Israel in Galatians 3-4." Pages 329-71 in *Exile: Old Testament, Jewish, and Christian Conceptions*. Edited by James M. Scott. Supplements to the Journal for the Study of Judaism 56. Leiden: Brill, 1997.
Hahn, Scott Walker and John Sietze Bergsma. "What Laws Were 'Not Good'? A Canonical Approach to the Theological Problem of Ezekiel 20:25-26." *Journal of Biblical Literature* 123 (2004): 201-18.
Hanson, Paul D. *Isaiah 40-66*. Interpretation: A Bible Commentary for Teaching and Preaching. Louisville: John Knox, 1995.
Harnisch, Wolfgang. "Einübung des neuen Seins: Paulinische Paränese am Beispiel des Galaterbriefs." *Zeitschrift für Theologie und Kirche* 84 (1987): 279-96.

Harrington, Daniel J. "Interpreting Israel's History: The *Testament of Moses* as a Rewriting of Deut 31-34." Pages 59-70 in *Studies on the Testament of Moses*. Edited by G. W. E. Nickelsburg, Jr. Society of Biblical Literature Septuagint and Cognate Studies 4. Cambridge: Society of Biblical Literature, 1973.

Haufe, Günter. "Das Geistmotiv in der paulinischen Ethik." *Zeitschrift für die neutestamentliche Wissenschaft und die Kunde der älteren Kirche* 85 (1994): 183-91.

Hays, Richard B. "Christology and Ethics in Galatians: the Law of Christ." *Catholic Biblical Quarterly* 49 (1987): 268-90.

–. *Echoes of Scripture in the Letters of Paul*. New Haven: Yale University, 1989.

–. *The Letter to the Galatians. The New Interpreter's Bible* 11. Nashville: Abingdon, 1999.

–. *The Faith of Jesus Christ: The Narrative Substructure of Galatians 3:1-4:11*. 2nd ed. Grand Rapids: Eerdman's, 2002.

–. "Three Dramatic Roles: The Law in Romans 3-4." Pages 85-100 in *The Conversion of the Imagination: Paul as Interpreter of Israel's Scripture*. Grand Rapids: Eerdmans, 2005.

–. "Apocalyptic Hermeneutics: Habakkuk Proclaims 'The Righteous One.'" Pages 101-18 in *The Conversion of the Imagination: Paul as Interpreter of Israel's Scripture*. Grand Rapids: Eerdmans, 2005.

Horn, Friedrich Wilhelm. *Das Angeld des Geistes: Studien zur paulinischen Pneumatologie*. Göttingen: Vandenhoeck & Ruprecht, 1992.

Hurvitz, Avi. *A Linguistic Study of the Relationship Between the Priestly Source and the Book of Ezekiel: A New Approach to an Old Problem*. Paris: J. Gabalda, 1982.

Isaac, E. "1 (Ethiopic Apocalpyse of) Enoch." Pages 5-89 in *The Old Testament Pseudepigrapha*. Edited by James H. Charlesworth. 2 vols. Anchor Bible Reference Library. New York: Doubleday, 1983, 1985.

Janzen, J. Gerald. "Eschatological Symbol and Existence in Habakkuk." *Catholic Biblical Quarterly* 44 (1982): 394-414.

Jewett, Robert. *Paul's Anthropological Terms: A study of their Use in Conflict Settings*. Arbeiten zur Geschichte des Antiken Judentums und des Urchristentums 10. Leiden: Brill, 1971.

Jobes, Karen H. "Jerusalem, Our Mother: Metalepsis and Intertextuality in Galatians 4:21-31." *Westminster Theological Journal* 55 (1993): 299-320.

Johnson, Marshall D. "The paralysis of torah in Habakkuk i 4." *Vetus Testamentum* 35 (1985): 257-66.

Jonge, Marinus de. "Once More: Christian Influence in the Testaments of the Twelve Patriarchs." *Novum Testamentum* 5 (1962): 311-19.

–. "Christian influence in the Testaments of the Twelve Patriarchs." Pages in *Studies on the Testaments of the Twelve Patriarchs*. Edited by Marinus de Jonge. Studia in Veteris Testamenti Pseudepigrapha 3. Leiden: Brill, 1975.

–. "The Testaments of the Twelve Patriarchs: Christian and Jewish: A hundred years after Friedrich Schnapp." *Nederlands Theologisch Tijdschrift* 39 (1985): 265-75.

–. *Pseudepigrapha of the Old Testament as Part of Christian Literature: The Case of the Testaments of the Twelve Patriarchs and the Greek Life of Adam and Eve*. Studia in Veteris Testamenti Pseudepigrapha 18. Leiden: Brill, 2003.

Jonge, Marinus de, H. W. Hollander, H. J. de Jonge, and Th. Korteweg. *The Testaments of the Twelve Patriarchs: A Critical Edition of the Greek Text*. Pseudepigrapha Veteris Testamenti Graece 1.2. Leiden: Brill, 1978.

Joyce, Paul. *Divine Initiative and Human Response in Ezekiel*. Journal for the Study of the Old Testament: Supplement Series 51. Sheffield: Sheffield Academic, 1989.

Kee, Howard Clark. "Testaments of the Twelve Patriarchs." Pages 775-828 in *The Old Testament Pseudepigrapha*. Edited by James H. Charlesworth. 2 vols. Anchor Bible Reference Library. New York: Doubleday, 1983, 1985.

Keesmaat, Sylvia C. *Paul and his Story: (Re-)Interpreting the Exodus Tradition*. Journal for the Study of the New Testament: Supplement Series 181. Sheffield: Sheffield Academic, 1999.
Knibb, Michael A. "The Exile in the Literature of the Intertestamental Period." *Heythrop Journal* 17 (1976): 253-72.
–. "The Date of the Parables of Enoch: A Critical Review." *New Testament Studies* 25 (1979): 345-59.
–. "Isaianic Traditions in the Apocrypha and Pseudepigrapha," in *Writing and Reading the Scroll of Isaiah: Studies of an Interpretive Tradition*. Edited by Craig C. Broyles and Craig A. Evans. Supplements to Vetus Testamentum 70.2. Leiden: Brill, 1997.
Koch, Dietrich-Alex. *Die Schrift als Zeuge des Evangeliums*. Beiträge zur historischen Theologie 69. Tübingen: J.C.B. Mohr, 1986.
Kugler, Robert A. *The Testaments of the Twelve Patriarchs*. Guides to Apocrypha and Pseudepigrapha. Sheffield: Sheffield Academic, 2001.
Kuck, David W. "'Each Will Bear his Own Burden': Paul's Creative Use of an Apocalyptic Motif." *New Testament Studies* 40 (1994): 289-97.
Kuhn, Karl Georg. "New Light on Temptation, Sin, and Flesh in the New Testament." Pages 94-113 in *The Scrolls and the New Testament*. Edited by Krister Stendahl. New York: Harper and Brothers, 1957.
Ladd, George E. "The Holy Spirit in Galatians." Pages 211-16 in *Current Issues in Biblical and Patristic Interpretation*. Edited by G. F. Hawthorne. Grand Rapids: Eerdmans, 1975.
Lambrecht, Jan. "The Right Things You Want to Do: A Note on *Galatians* 5,17d." *Biblica* 79 (1998): 515-24.
Levenson, Jon D. *Resurrection and the Restoration of Israel: The Ultimate Victory of the God of Life*. New Haven: Yale University, 2006.
Levison, John R. *The Spirit in First Century Judaism*. Arbeiten zur Geschichte des antiken Judentums und des Urchristentums 29. Leiden; New York: Brill, 1997.
Lichtenberger, Hermann. *Studien zum Menschenbild in Texten der Qumrangemeinde*. Studien zur Umwelt des Neuen Testaments 15. Göttingen: Vandenhoeck & Ruprecht, 1980.
Lightfoot, J. B. *St. Paul's Epistle to the Galatians*. London: Macmillan, 1874.
Longenecker, Bruce W. *The Triumph of Abraham's God: The Transformation of Identity in Galatians*. Nashville: Abingdon, 1998.
Longenecker, Richard N. *Galatians*. Word Biblical Commentary 41. Dallas: Word Books, 1990.
Lull, David J. *The Spirit in Galatia: Paul's Interpretation of Pneuma as Divine Power*. Society of Biblical Literature Dissertation Series 49. Ann Arbor: Scholars Press, 1980.
Lust, Johan. *Ezekiel and His Book: Textual and Literary Criticism and their Interrelation*. Leuven: Leuven University, 1986.
Lütgert, Wilhelm. *Gesetz und Geist: Eine Untersuchung zur Vorgeschichte des Galaterbriefes*. Beiträge zur Förderung christlicher Theologie. Gütersloh: C. Bertelsmann, 1919.
Luz, Ulrich. *Das Geschichtsverständnis des Paulus*. Beiträge zur evangelischen Theologie 49. Munich: Kaiser, 1968.
Ma, Wonsuk. *Until the Spirit Comes: The Spirit of God in the Book of Isaiah*. Journal for the Study of the Old Testament: Supplement Series 271. Sheffield: Sheffield Academic, 1999.
Marcus, Joel. *The Way of the Lord: Christological Exegesis of the Old Testament in the Gospel of Mark*. Louisville: Westminster/John Knox, 1992.
–. "Mark--Interpreter of Paul." *New Testament Studies* 46 (2000): 473-87.
–. "'Under the Law': The Background of a Pauline Expression." *Catholic Biblical Quarterly* 63 (2001): 72-83.
Martyn, J. Louis. *Galatians: A New Translation with Introduction and Commentary*. Anchor Bible 33A. New York: Doubleday, 1997.
–. *Theological Issues in the Letters of Paul*. Nashville: Abingdon, 1997.

Matera, Frank J. "The Culmination of Paul's Argument to the Galatians: Gal. 5.1-6.17." *Journal for the Study of the New Testament* 32 (1988): 79-91.
–. *Galatians*. Sacra Pagina 9. Collegeville: Liturgical Press, 1992.
Mearns, Christopher L. "Dating the Similitudes of Enoch." *New Testament Studies* 25, (1979): 360-69.
Meier, John P., *A Marginal Jew. Rethinking the Historical Jesus. Volume Two: Mentor, Message, and Miracles*. Anchor Bible Reference Library. New York: Doubleday, 1994.
Menzies, Robert P. *The Development of Early Christian Pneumatology with special reference to Luke-Acts*. Edited by David Hill. Journal for the Study of the New Testament: Supplement Series 54. Sheffield: Sheffield Academic, 1991.
Merk, Otto. "Der Beginn der Paränese im Galaterbrief." *Zeitschrift für die neutestamentliche Wissenschaft und die Kunde der älteren Kirche* 60 (1969): 83-104.
Metzger, Bruce M. (ed.) *A Textual Commentary on the Greek New Testament*. 2nd ed. New York: United Bible Societies, 1994.
Meyer, Paul W. "The Worm at the Core of the Apple." Pages 62-84 in *The Conversation Continues: Studies in Paul and John in Honor of J. Louis Martyn*. Edited by Robert T. Fortna and Beverly R. Gaventa. Nashville: Abingdon, 1990.
Milgrom, Jacob. *Leviticus 1-16: A New Translation with Introduction and Commentary*. Anchor Bible 3. New York: Doubleday, 1991.
–. *Leviticus 17-22: A New Translation with Introduction and Commentary*. Anchor Bible 3A. New York: Doubleday, 2000.
Milik, J. T., ed. *The Books of Enoch: Aramaic Fragments of Qumrân Cave 4*. Oxford: Clarendon, 1976.
Miller, Patrick D. *Deuteronomy*. Interpretation: A Bible Commentary for Teaching and Preaching. Louisville: John Knox, 1990.
Mulka, Arthur L. "'Fides Quae Per Caritatem Operatur' (Gal 5,6)." *Catholic Biblical Quarterly* 28 (1966): 174-88.
Murray, Robert. *The Cosmic Covenant: Biblical Themes of Justice, Peace and the Integrity of Creation*. London: Sheed & Ward, 1992.
Mussner, Franz. *Der Galaterbrief*. Herders theologischer Kommentar zum Neuen Testament 9. Freiberg: Herder, 1974.
Nelson, Richard D. *Deuteronomy: A Commentary*. Old Testament Library. Louisville: Westminster/John Knox, 2002.
Nicholson, Ernest. *The Pentateuch in the Twentieth Century: The Legacy of Julius Wellhausen*. Oxford: Clarendon, 1998.
Nickelsburg, George W. E. *Jewish Literature Between the Bible and the Mishnah: A Historical and Literary Introduction*. Philadelphia: Fortress, 1981.
Noth, Martin. *The Laws in the Pentateuch and Other Studies*. Translated by AP-Thomas, D. R. Edinburgh and London: Oliver & Boyd, 1966.
O'Neill, J. C. *The Recovery of Paul's Letter to the Galatians*. London: Penguin Books, 1972.
Oropeza, B. J. "Echoes of Isaiah in the Rhetoric of Paul: New Exodus, Wisdom, and the Humility of the Cross in Utopian-Apocalyptic Expectations." Pages 87-112 in *The Intertexture of Apocalyptic Discourse in the New Testament*. Edited by Duane F. Watson. Society of Biblical Literature Symposium Series 14. Atlanta: Society of Biblical Literature, 2002.
Oswalt, John N. *The Book of Isaiah: Chapters 40-66*. New International Commentary on the Old Testament. Grand Rapids: Eerdmans, 1998.
Pao, David W. *Acts and the Isaianic New Exodus*. Wissenschaftliche Untersuchungen zum Neuen Testament 2.130. Tübingen: J.C.B. Mohr (Paul Siebeck), 2000.
Philip, Finny. *The Origins of Pauline Pneumatology*. Wissenschaftliche Untersuchungen zum Neuen Testament 2.194. Tübingen: J.C.B. Mohr (Paul Siebeck), 2005.

Pitre, Brant. *Jesus, the Tribulation, and the End of the Exile: Restoration Eschatology and the Origin of the Atonement*. Wissentschaftliche Untersuchungen zum Neuen Testament 2.204. Tübingen: J.C.B. Mohr (Paul Siebeck), 2005.
Polk, Timothy. *The Prophetic Persona: Jeremiah and the Language of Self*. Journal for the Study of the Old Testament: Supplement Series 32. Sheffield: Sheffield Academic, 1984.
Polzin, Robert. *Late Biblical Hebrew: Toward an Historical Typology of Biblical Hebrew Prose*. Harvard Semitic Monographs 12. Missoula: Scholars, 1976.
Puech, Émile. "Un apocalypse messianique (4Q521)." *Revue de Qumran* 60, no. 15 (1992): 475-522.
Räisänen, Heikki. *Paul and the Law*. 2nd ed. Wissenschaftliche Untersuchungen zum Neuen Testament 29. Tübingen: J.C.B. Mohr (Paul Siebeck), 1987.
Ridderbos, Herman N. *The Epistle of Paul to the Churches of Galatia*. New International Commentary on the New Testament. Grand Rapids: Eerdmans, 1956.
Roberts, J. J. M. *Nahum, Habakkuk, and Zephaniah*. Old Testament Library. Louisville: Westminster/John Knox, 1991.
Robertson, O. Palmer. *The Books of Nahum, Habakkuk, and Zephaniah*. New International Commentary on the Old Testament. Grand Rapids: Eerdmans, 1990.
Robson, James. *Word and Spirit in Ezekiel*. Library of Hebrew Bible/Old Testament Studies 447. New York/London: T&T Clark, 2006.
Ropes, J. H.. *The Singular Problem of the Epistle to the Galatians*. Harvard Theological Studies 14. Cambridge: Harvard University, 1929.
Russell, Walt. "The Apostle Paul's Redemptive-Historical Argumentation in Galatians 5:13-26." *Westminster Theological Journal* 57 (1995): 335-57.
–. *The Flesh/Spirit Conflict in Galatians*. Lanham: University Press of America, 1997.
Sanders, E. P. *Paul and Palestinian Judaism: A Comparison of Patterns of Religion*. Philadelphia: Fortress, 1977.
–. *Paul, the Law, and the Jewish People*. Philadelphia: Fortress, 1983.
–. *Jesus and Judaism*. Philadelphia: Fortress, 1985.
Schlier, Heinrich. *Der Brief an die Galater*. Kritisch-Exegetischer Kommentar über das Neue Testament 7. 13th ed. Göttingen: Vandenhoeck & Ruprecht, 1965.
Schweitzer, Albert. *The Mysticism of Paul the Apostle*. Translated by William Montgomery. 2nd ed. Baltimore: Johns Hopkins University, 1953.
Scott, James M. *Adoption as Sons of God: An Exegetical Investigation into the Background of ΨΙΟΘΕΣΙΑ in the Pauline Corpus*. Wissentschaftliche Untersuchungen zum Neuen Testament 2.48. Tübingen: J.C.B. Mohr (Paul Siebeck), 1992.
–. "'For as Many as are of Works of the Law are Under a Curse' (Galatians 3.10)." Pages 187-221 in *Paul and the Scriptures of Israel*. Edited by Evans, Craig A. and James A. Sanders. Journal for the Study of the New Testament: Supplement Series 83. Sheffield: Sheffield Academic, 1993.
–, "Paul's Use of the Deuteronomic Tradition." *Journal of Biblical Literature* 112 (1993): 645-65.
–. ed. *Exile: Old Testament, Jewish, and Christian Conceptions*. Supplements to the Journal for the Study of Judaism 56. Leiden: Brill, 1997.
–, ed. *Restoration: Old Testament, Jewish, and Christian Perspectives*. Supplements to the Journal for the Study of Judaism 72. Leiden: Brill, 2001.
Seitz, Christopher R. *Isaiah 1-39*. Interpretation: A Bible Commentary for Teaching and Preaching. Louisville: John Knox, 1993.
Sekki, Arthur E. *The Meaning of Ruah at Qumran*. Society of Biblical Literature Dissertation Series 110. Atlanta: Scholars, 1989.
Smith, Barry D. "The Spirit of Holiness as Eschatological Principle of Obedience in Second-Temple Judaism." Pages 75-99 in *Christian Beginnings and the Dead Sea Scrolls*. Edited

by Craig A. Evans and John J. Collins. Acadia Studies in Bible and Theology. Grand Rapids: Baker Academic, 2006.
Stanley, Christopher D. "'Under a Curse': A Fresh Reading of Galatians 3.10-14." *New Testament Studies* 36 (1990): 481-511.
–. "'Pearls Before Swine': Did Paul's Audiences Understand his Biblical Quotations?" *Novum Testamentum* 41 (1999): 124-44.
–. *Arguing with Scripture: The Rhetoric of Quotations in the Letters of Paul.* New York/London: T&T Clark, 2004.
Stendahl, Krister. "The Apostle Paul and the Introspective Conscience of the West." Pages 78-96 in *Paul Among Jews and Gentiles and Other Essays.* Philadelphia: Fortress, 1976.
Strobel, Augustin. *Untersuchungen zum Eschatologischen Verzögerungsproblem: Auf Grund der Spätjüdisch-Urchristlichen Geschichte von Habakuk 2,2 FF.* Supplements to Novum Testamentum 2. Leiden: Brill, 1961.
Stuart, Douglas. *Hosea-Jonah.* Word Biblical Commentary 31. Waco: Word Books, 1987.
Thielman, Frank. *From Plight to Solution: A Jewish Framework for Understanding Paul's View of the Law in Galatians and Romans.* Supplements to Novum Testamentum 61. Leiden: Brill, 1989.
Tigay, Jeffrey H. *Deuteronomy.* The JPS Torah Commentary. Philadelphia: The Jewish Publication Society, 1996.
Treves, Marco. "The Two Spirits of the Rule of the Community." *Revue de Qumran* 3, (1961): 449-52.
Turner, Max M. *Power from on High: The Spirit in Israel's Restoration and Witness in Luke-Acts.* Journal of Pentecostal Theology: Supplement Series 9. Sheffield: Sheffield Academic, 1996.
Ulrichsen, Jarl Henning. *Die Grundschrift der Testamente der Zwölf Patriarchen: Eine Untersuchung zu Umfang, Inhalt und Eigenart der ursprünglichen Schrift.* Acta Universitatis Upsaliensis, Historia Religionum 10. Uppsala: Almqvist & Wiksell, 1991.
Um, Stephen T. *The Theme of Temple Christology in John's Gospel.* Library of New Testament Studies 312. Sheffield: T & T Clark, 2006.
VanderKam, James C. trans., *The Book of Jubilees.* Corpus Scriptorum Christianorum Orientalium 511. Paris: Aedibus E. Peeters, 1989.
–. *The Book of Jubilees.* Guides to Apocrypha and Pseudepigrapha. Sheffield: Sheffield Academic, 2001.
Vos, Johannes Sijko. *Traditionsgeschichtliche Untersuchungen zur paulinischen Pneumatologie.* Assen: Van Gorcum, 1973.
Wagner, J. Ross, Jr. *Heralds of the Good News: Isaiah and Paul in Concert in the Letter to the Romans.* Leiden: Brill, 2002.
Wakefield, Andrew H. *Where to Live: The Hermeneutical Significance of Paul's Citations from Scripture in Galatians 3:1-14.* Academia Biblica 14. Atlanta: Society of Biblical Literature, 2003.
Waters, Guy. *The End of Deuteronomy in the Epistles of Paul.* Wissentschaftliche Untersuchungen zum Neuen Testament 2.221. Tübingen: J.C.B. Mohr (Paul Siebeck), 2006.
Watson, Francis. *Paul and the Hermeneutics of Faith.* Edinburgh: T & T Clark, 2004.
Watts, John D. W. *Isaiah 1-33.* Word Biblical Commentary 24. Waco: Word Books, 1985.
Watts, Rikki E. *Isaiah's New Exodus and Mark.* Wissenschafltiche Untersuchungen zum Neuen Testament 2.88. Tübingen: J.C.B. Mohr (Paul Siebeck), 1997.
–. "'For I Am Not Ashamed of the Gospel': Romans 1:16-17 and Habakkuk 2:4." Pages 3-25 in *Romans and the People of God: Essays in Honor of Gordon D. Fee on the Occasion of His 65th Birthday.* Edited by Sven K. Soderlund and N. T. Wright. Grand Rapids: Eerdman's, 1999.
Werline, Rodney Alan. *Penitential Prayer in Second Temple Judaism: The Development of a Religious Institution.* Early Judaism and Its Literature 13. Atlanta: Scholars, 1998.

Wernberg-Møller, P. "A Reconsideration of the Two Spirits in the Rule of the Community (1 Q Serek III,13 - IV, 26)." *Revue de Qumran* 3 (1961): 413-41.
Westerholm, Stephen. "On Fulfilling the Whole Law (Gal. 5:14)." *Svensk exegetisk årsbok* 51-52 (1986): 229-37.
Westermann, Claus. *Isaiah 40-66*. Translated by Stalker, David M. G. Old Testament Library. Philadelphia: Westminster, 1969.
Widengren, Geo. "Yahweh's Gathering of the Dispersed." Pages in *In the Shelter of Elyon: Essays on Ancient Palestinian Life and Literature in Honor of G. W. Ahlström*. Edited by W. Boyd Barrick and John R. Spencer. Journal for the Study of the Old Testament: Supplement Series 31. Sheffield: Sheffield Academic, 1984.
Wilder, William N. *Echoes of the Exodus Narrative in the Context and Background of Galatians 5:18*. Studies in Biblical Literature 23. New York: Peter Lang, 2001.
Wilk, Florian. *Die Bedeutung des Jesajabuches für Paulus*. Göttingen: Vandenhock & Ruprecht, 1998.
Williams, Sam K. "Justification and the Spirit in Galatians." *Journal for the Study of the New Testament* 29 (1987): 91-100.
–. *Galatians*. Abingdon New Testament Commentary. Nashville: Abingdon, 1997.
Willitts, Joel. "Context Matters: Paul's Use of Leviticus 18:5 in Galatians 3:12." *Tyndale Bulletin* 54 (2003): 105-22.
–. "Isa 54,1 in Gal 4,24b-27: Reading Genesis in Light of Isaiah." *Zeitschrift für die neutestamentliche Wissenschaft und die Kunde der älteren Kirche* 96 (2005): 188-210.
Wilson, Todd A. *The Curse of the Law and the Crisis in Galatia: Reassessing the Purpose of Galatians*. Wissenschaftliche Untersuchungen zum Neuen Testament 2.225. Tübingen: J.C.B. Mohr (Paul Siebeck), 2007.
Wintermute, Orville S. "Jubilees." Pages 35-142 in *The Old Testament Pseudepigrapha*. Edited by James H. Charlesworth. 2 vols. Anchor Bible Reference Library. New York: Doubleday, 1983, 1985.
Wolff, Hans Walter. *Joel and Amos*. Translated by Janzen, Waldemar, S. Dean McBride, Jr., and Charles A. Muenchow. Hermeneia. Philadelphia: Fortress, 1977.
Wright, N. T. *The Climax of the Covenant: Christ and the Law in Pauline Theology*. Minneapolis: Fortress, 1992.
–. *The New Testament and the People of God*. Christian Origins and the Question of God 1. Minneapolis: Fortress, 1992.
–. "Justification and Eschatology in Paul and Qumran: Romans and 4QMMT." Pages 104-32 in *History and Exegesis: New Testament Essays in Honor of Dr. E. Earle Ellis for his 80th Birthday*. Edited by Sang-Won (Aaron) Son. New York: T&T Clark, 2006.
Wright, R. B. "Psalms of Solomon." Pages 639-70 in *The Old Testament Pseudepigrapha*. Edited by James H. Charlesworth. 2 vols. Anchor Bible Reference Library. New York: Doubleday, 1983, 1985.
Young, Norman H. "Pronominal Shifts in Paul's Argument to the Galatians." Pages 205-15 in *Ancient History in a Modern University, Vol 2: Early Christianity, Late Antiquity and Beyond*. Edited by T. W. Hillard et al. Grand Rapids: Eerdmans, 1998.
Zimmerli, Walther. *Ezekiel 1*. Translated by Ronald E. Clements. Hermeneia. Philadelphia: Fortress, 1979.
–. *Ezekiel 2*. Translated by James D. Martin. Hermeneia. Philadelphia: Fortress, 1983.

Index of Ancient Sources

Old Testament (With Deuterocanonicals)

Genesis
1:2 — 56, 74
1:28 — 88
2:4 — 51
2:7 — 20
3 — 107
3:14–18 — 88
3:18 — 18
9:1 — 88
9:25–26 — 88
12:2–3 — 88
15:6 — 91, 100
18:18 — 88
21:10–12 — 2
22:17–18 — 88
27:12 — 88

Exodus
4:22 — 27
6:6 — 21
8:32 — 27
11:8 — 23
12 — 43
12:11 — 23
12:41 — 23
13:3–4 — 23
13:21–22 — 82
14:19–20 — 82
15:13 — 21
15:17 — 24
17:1–7 — 23
24:18 — 43

Leviticus
18–26 — 101
18:5 — 97, 100–01, 103–04, 108, 136
18:5 (LXX) — 102, 104
18:24–28 — 101
19:18 — 144–45
26 — 101
26:14–43 — 101
26:16 — 65
26:22 — 102
26:28 — 52
26:34–35 — 65
26:40–41 — 55
26:45 — 53–54

Numbers
23:7 — 74
24 — 71
24:9 — 88
27:18 — 74

Deuteronomy
4 — 35–36, 46
4:25–28 — 36
4:25–29 — 127
4:27 — 36
4:29 — 36
4:29–30 — 45
4:29–31 — 36–37
4:30–31 — 36
6:4–5 — 37, 45
6:4–6 — 127
6:10–12 — 37
6:12 — 37
9:8 — 52
10 — 37
10:12 — 37, 127
10:16 — 37, 47, 127
10:22 — 37
11:13 — 37
11:18 — 37
11:26 — 88

26	37	28:67	30, 33, 37, 127
26:16	37, 127	28:68	65, 93, 107
27	91, 93	29	93–94
27–28	93	29:18	93–94
27–30	13, 46, 92–93, 95, 101, 104, 106, 170	29:19	93–94, 101
		29:19–28	94
		29:19–29	53
27–32	93	29:20	93
27:15–26	91	29:20–21	94
27:26	88–93, 101	29:21	93
28	29–30, 33, 35–36, 40, 44–45, 65, 93–94, 106, 112	29:22	52
		29:26	93
		29:27	52
		29:28	93
28–30	91, 93	30	29–30, 35–36, 44, 46, 92–95, 112, 162
28:1–14	93		
28:1–46	37		
28:15–68	44, 93	30:1	30, 44, 55, 88, 94
28:20	65, 94		
28:20–22	93, 107	30:1–2	36, 54
28:21	65, 93, 102, 107	30:1–3	30
		30:1–5	36
28:22	65, 94	30:1–10	36–37
28:24	65, 93–94, 107	30:2	36, 45
28:25	44, 65	30:3–5	36
28:26	93, 107	30:6	30, 36–37, 47, 94
28:27–28	53		
28:31	65	30:10	36, 65, 93
28:32	36, 65, 93, 107	30:15	31, 94–95, 108, 168
28:36	44, 65, 93, 107		
28:37	93, 107	30:15–20	55, 95, 166
28:41	93, 107	30:18	94
28:45	65, 93–94, 107	30:19	88, 95, 107, 131, 168, 170
28:47	37		
28:48	53, 65, 93, 107, 127	30:20	44, 86, 95, 107
		31	44
28:49–51	65	31:20	44
28:51	65, 93–94, 107	31:27	44
28:53	65	32	93
28:55	65	32:12	53
28:57	65	32:22–24	53
28:58	93		
28:59	53	*1 Samuel*	
28:61	93, 107	19:20	74
28:62–64	36	19:23	74
28:63	93, 107		
28:64	30, 32, 45, 65, 93, 107	*2 Chronicles*	
		15:1	74
28:65	30–31, 33, 37, 127	20:7	110
		20:14	74
28:66	93, 107	24:20	74

Nehemiah

9	103, 148
9:6	103
9:12	148
9:17	103
9:17–25	103
9:20	103, 148, 150
9:29	153
9:29 (LXX)	104
9:36 (LXX)	104

Psalms

2	61
22:24	111
23	150
45	71
51	47
51:10	46–47
51:10–11	49
51:11	47
81:10	53
104:6 (LXX)	110
142 (LXX)	150
142:10 (LXX) (=MT 143:10)	149–50

Sirach

44:19–23	118

Isaiah

5:6	18
6:1	18
7:23–25	18
11	15–16, 19, 26, 49–50, 58, 61, 63–64, 76, 155–57, 165
11:1	67
11:1–2	50
11:1–9	15–17
11:1–10	16
11:1–16	15–18
11:2	50, 61
11:2 (LXX)	59
11:6–9	17, 21
11:9	16, 68
11:10	16–17
11:10–16	15
11:11	16–17
11:11–16	16
11:15	17
11:16	17
32	18, 22, 137, 155–56
32:1	18
32:9–14	18, 155
32:12	155
32:13	18
32:14	18
32:15	18, 39, 138, 155
32:15–20	18-19, 24, 28, 155
32:16	138
32:16–18	155–156
32:17	19, 46, 138
33:5	18
35	56
40–48	20
40:31–41:1	56
41	170
41:4	23
41:8	110
41:14	110
42	26
42:1	19, 110
42:1–4	57
42:1–9	19–20
42:5	19
42:5–9	20
42:6	110
42:7	26
42:9	20
43	28
43:14	21
43:14–21	20–22
43:14–44:8	20–23, 154
43:15	21
43:16–17	21
43:16–21	20–21
43:18	21
43:18–19	21
43:20	21–22
43:21	21
43:22–28	21–22
43:25	22
44	28, 55, 66, 76, 111–13, 166, 169–70
44:1–5	20–22, 28, 39
44:1–6	154
44:2	21
44:3	9, 22, 54, 72, 103, 111–12,

44:3 (cont'd)	169	57	15, 155–56, 158
44:3 (LXX)	66, 110		
44:5	22	57:1–2 (LXX)	23
44:6	21, 23, 110	57:7 (LXX)	24, 154
44:6–8	20–21	57:13 (LXX)	24, 154, 156–57
44:8	21		
44:21–23	20	57:14–21 (LXX)	23–24, 28
44:23	68	57:15 (LXX)	24, 156
45:19	111	57:16 (LXX)	24
48:6	20	57:18–19 (LXX)	156
48:12	23	57:19 (LXX)	24, 156
48:12–22	23	57:20 (LXX)	24
48:16	23, 28	57:21 (LXX)	23–24, 156
48:17–19	23	59	24, 138
48:20	23	59:1–8	24
48:20–21	23	59:9	24, 138
48:21	23	59:9–15	24
48:22 (LXX)	23	59:13	25
49	23, 58, 81	59:14	24, 138
49:1–6	57	59:15	25
49:3	19	59:15–21	24–25
49:5–6	4	59:17	25
49:6	110	59:20	25
50:4–9	57	59:21 (LXX)	25, 28
51	111, 170	59:21	25, 138
51:2	111	60:21 (LXX)	154–55
51:3 (LXX)	111	61	25–26
51:4 (LXX)	111	61:1	26, 56
52	83	61:1–11	25–26
52–53	85, 172	61:3	26
52:6–7	83	61:7	154
52:7	83	61:8	26
52:7 (LXX)	85	61:9	26
52:10	83	61:11	26
52:10 (LXX)	83, 85	63	39, 58, 127–128, 148–50, 157
52:11–12	82		
52:13–53:10	85		
52:13–53:12	58	63:7–14	26, 28
53	70, 81–85, 98	63:7–64:12	26–28
53:1	81–83, 85	63:10	26, 128
53:10	84	63:10–19	127–128
53:10 (LXX)	84	63:11 (LXX)	128
53:10–11 (LXX)	84	63:12	27
53:11	84	63:14	27, 148–50
53:12	85	63:16	27
53:12 (LXX)	85	63:17	27, 29
54	85	63:17–18	28
54:1	2, 82, 85, 130	63:17–18 (LXX)	157
54:3	154	63:18 (LXX)	128
55:5	110	63:19	28
56:1	25	64:1	66
		64:1–3	28

64:1–12	28	20	101–03
64:8	28	20:4	101
64:10–12	28	20:5–8	101
65:9	154	20:11 (LXX)	97–98, 102
65:17	19, 107, 109	20:13	103
65:17–18	134	20:13 (LXX)	102
66:22	19	20:21 (LXX)	102
		20:22	102
Jeremiah		23:3	118
1:4	4	23:8	118
3:24	118	23:19	118
4:26	18	23:21	118
22:21	118	34:11–24	72
31	38, 127	36	32–34, 47, 102–03, 112–113, 127–28, 172
31:19	118		
31:31–34	32, 47		
31:33	27, 38, 53		
32:30	118	36:16–38	32–33
32:37–41	47	36:19	32
33:26	111	36:22–23	34
38:33 (LXX)	38	36:23	34, 102
		36:24	45
Baruch		36:26	30, 32, 37, 47
1:20	96	36:26–27	29, 39, 126, 127
		36:26–28	47
Ezekiel		36:27	33, 80
8:1–3	29	36:28	33
11	29, 31–33, 47–48	36:29–30	33
		36:30–38	107, 109
11:1–13	29	36:34–35	103
11:14–21	29–31	36:35	33
11:14-25	29	36:38	34
11:15	29, 31	37	47, 127, 162, 170, 172
11:16	30		
11:16–17	30		
11:17	45	37:1–14	33–34, 107
11:19	30	37:5	34
11:19–20	39, 47	37:5–6	162
11:22–25	29	37:6	34
11:25	29	37:6 (LXX)	34, 39
16	120	37:11–14	34
16:22 (LXX)	119–20	37:14	34, 39
16:43 (LXX)	119–20	37:15–28	72
16:60 (LXX)	119–20	39	47
16:62 (LXX)	120	39:21–22	34
18	31–33, 47–48, 98	39:21–29	34–35
		39:23–24	34
18:5–9	98	39:25	34
18:30	31	39:29	35, 39
18:30–32	29, 31–32	40–48	107, 109
18:31	30–31, 37, 39, 47		

Daniel

5:14	74
9	123
9:2	123
9:11	96
12	170

Hosea

1:10	48
2	120
2:1 (LXX)	48
2:1	2
2:12–16 (LXX) (=MT 2:10–13)	119
2:13 (LXX) (=MT 2:11)	119
2:15 (LXX) (=MT 2:13)	122
2:17 (LXX)	119–20
2:17–18 (LXX) (=MT 2:14–15)	119
2:19 (LXX) (=MT 2:17)	122
2:19–20 (LXX)	120
2:20 (LXX)	120
4:1	58
5:14–6:2	107
10:12	162
11	120
11:1	27, 58, 119
11:2	122
11:6–7	120
11:12	120

Joel

2:18–20	38
2:21–27	38
2:18–3:5	38
2:27	38
2:28–29	67
2:32	67
3	71
3:1 (LXX)	38
3:1–5	38–39
3:5 (LXX)	39
4:1 (LXX)	39
4:1–5 (LXX)	39

Amos

9:11–15	72

Habakkuk

1:1–4	99
1:4	99–100
2	123
2:3	123
2:4	85, 91, 96, 98–100, 123

Zechariah

9	71

Malachi

2:14	118

New Testament

Mark

1:10	71
1:15	123, 133

Acts

2	38

Romans

1–3	122
1:18–32	151
1:29–31	153
2:7	162
2:17–24	153
2:25–29	159
3:20	149
4:12	142
4:13	95, 116, 118
4:17	56
5	108
5:20–21	108
5:21	162
6:22–23	162
7	89, 142, 146
7:5–6	108
7:7–12	90
7:8	142
7:9–11	108
7:11	142

Index of Ancient Sources 191

8	118	2:14	97
8:1–13	108	2:15–21	6, 96, 100, 106, 133, 152, 171
8:2	108		
8:3	100		
8:9–11	159	2:15–4:7	137
8:11	98	2:16	97, 105, 121–122, 137, 140, 149, 152
8:18–25	139		
9:4	118		
10	82–83	2:19	106
10:5	100	2:19–20	87, 100, 109, 159–60, 162, 171
10:16	81, 85		
11	58		
14	152	2:20	136, 140, 145
14–15	173	2:21	136–37
14:17	173	3	7, 9, 79, 82–85, 87, 104–105, 109–11, 129, 134, 137, 148, 163, 165
15:12	77		
15:13	173		
1 Corinthians			
1:7	139	3–4	5, 7, 22, 78, 80, 85, 113, 130–37, 139, 146, 148, 150–51, 154, 165, 167, 171
6:9–10	151, 153		
7–8	152		
9:20–21	124		
10:6	146, 152		
12	173		
12–14	168	3–6	1, 13, 164
15:50–55	140	3:1	85, 114, 129
15:56	108	3:1–5	2, 7, 81–85, 113, 130, 165, 167
2 Corinthians			
3:3	127	3:1–9	109
3:6	98, 106, 108, 166	3:1–14	137
		3:1–4:7	114, 126
5:12	142	3:1–5:5	139
11:12	142	3:2	1, 78–80, 98, 148, 152, 164
		3:2–5	83
Galatians		3:3	133, 137, 140, 142, 146, 162
1–3	82		
1:1	171		
1:4	152	3:5	98, 152
1:6	140	3:6	87
1:6–9	83	3:6–14	2, 87, 98, 100, 109
1:12	83, 85		
1:15	81	3:6–29	114
1:15–16	4, 81	3:6–4:7	79
1:16	83, 85, 140	3:7	137
2:2	83	3:8	83, 87, 137
2:3	89	3:8–9	109
2:4	140	3:9	98–99, 137
2:11–21	89	3:10	13, 86–92, 96–98, 104, 109, 136, 152, 166,
2:12	89		

3:10 (cont'd)	170		126
3:10–12	109	3:28	136
3:10–14	4, 6–7, 13, 80–81, 86–87, 93, 95–96, 100, 106, 110, 112, 114, 124–25, 129, 131, 137, 160, 166, 169–171	3:29	79, 87, 110, 116, 118, 126, 145, 154
		4	79, 82, 113, 121, 127, 162
		4:1	116–23, 126, 154
3:11	96, 99, 123, 137	4:1–2	115–19, 121–123, 125
		4:1–3	117
3:11–12	96–97, 108	4:1–7	7, 81, 114, 115, 117–18, 121–25, 127–129, 131, 166
3:12	90, 100, 104, 137		
3:13	5, 86, 89–90, 96, 105–06, 109, 113–14, 121–22, 124–126, 166, 170	4:1–11	120–21
		4:2	116–17, 119, 123
		4:3	117, 121–22, 124, 160
3:13–14	1, 3, 76, 105–106, 113–14, 124, 126	4:3–6	121
		4:3–7	115-116, 119, 121, 123–24
3:14	79, 105, 109, 113–14, 125, 127, 129, 154, 169	4:4	116, 119, 123, 143, 145, 160, 167
		4:4–5	117–118, 124
3:15	118	4:4–6	1, 113, 128, 149
3:15–18	85		
3:15–29	87	4:4–7	116
3:16	145	4:5	123–26, 129, 151
3:17	87, 115		
3:18	79, 154	4:5–6	125, 143
3:21	6, 79, 87, 90, 96–98, 100, 106, 108, 131, 137, 144, 160, 162, 166, 170	4:6	118, 125–27, 166
		4:6–7	79, 125, 137
		4:7	118, 124–25, 129, 154
3:22	117, 119, 137		
3:22–26	137	4:8	122, 126
3:22–29	117	4:9	119–22, 125, 160
3:23	117, 126, 151		
3:23–24	117, 122	4:10	119
3:23–25	125, 143	4:21	105, 122, 124, 144, 153
3:23–28	114		
3:23–29	115, 117–18, 121, 126	4:21–31	135, 140, 150
		4:21–5:1	82, 85, 130, 151
3:24	137		
3:24–25	119	4:23	140, 143, 154
3:24–26	126	4:27	130
3:25	117, 126	4:29	130, 133, 140, 143, 154
3:26	117–18, 125–		

Index of Ancient Sources 193

4:29–31	1	5:17 (cont'd)	146–147
4:30	154	5:17–18	143, 149
4:31	135	5:18	136, 146–51
5	133, 136, 141–142, 146, 148, 149–50, 154, 156, 160, 162	5:19	153
		5:19–21	141, 144, 151, 153–154, 162, 172
5–6	4, 7, 122, 130–135, 145, 151, 159, 167, 171	5:19–23	157
		5:21	4, 123, 133, 140, 154, 167
5:1	135, 136, 140, 151	5:22	83, 139, 155–158, 167
5:1–4	153	5:22–23	154–56, 158
5:1–5	139	5:22–25	163
5:1–6	136	5:23	158
5:1–12	136	5:24	159
5:2	135–36	5:24–25	159
5:2–3	89, 136	5:24–26	159
5:2–6	134–36, 167	5:25	97, 133, 141, 168, 171
5:2–12	133, 135–36, 139–40, 143	5:25–26	143
5:3	88, 90, 136, 143	5:26	153, 160
		6:1	160
5:4	137	6:1–2	160
5:4–5	136	6:2	90, 145, 161
5:5	1, 137	6:7–8	161
5:5–6	137, 139	6:7–9	134
5:6	89, 136–37, 139–41, 167	6:7–10	135
		6:8	1, 6, 97, 106, 133, 161–63, 167–68, 170–171
5:6–6:16	140		
5:7–10	140		
5:7–12	136		
5:8	140	6:12	152, 167
5:11	136	6:12–13	89, 152–54, 162
5:13	135, 139–40, 141, 143, 146, 161	6:13	88
		6:15	81, 89, 134, 158, 163, 167, 171
5:13 (cont'd)			
5:13–15	143		
5:13–18	152		
5:13–26	134, 140, 143, 167	6:16	4, 6, 22, 83, 138, 142, 160
5:13–6:7	132		
5:13–6:10	136, 139–40	*Ephesians*	
5:14	90, 136, 140, 144–45, 159–161, 167	2:3	153
		2:14	173
		2:17	156
5:15	153	4	128
5:16	146–47	4:4	173
5:16–18	146, 167	4:30	128
5:16–24	143	6:13–17	25
5:16–25	1		
5:17	141–42,		

Philippians
3:6	88	*Hebrews*	
3:16	142	13	128
3:20	139	13:20	128

Old Testament Pseudepigrapha

Jubilees		*1 Enoch*	
1	138	45–57	60
1:4	43–44	47	60–62
1:6	44	47–51	62
1:7–8	44	48	61–62
1:9	44	48:1	61, 139
1:10	44	48:4	61
1:11	45	48:10	61
1:13	45	49	61–63, 139
1:15	45, 138	49:2	61
1:15–16	45–46	49:3	60
1:16	46	50	61
1:19	46	51	60, 61
1:20	46	51:1–2	61–62
1:21	46	51:5	62
1:22–25	126, 129–30	61	62, 64
1:23	46–47	61:3	62
1:24–25	47	61:4–5	62
1:25	138	61:5	63
1:26	44	61:7	63
22:11	95, 116	61:11	63
22:13	95, 116	61:12	62–63
32:19	116, 118	62	63, 139
		62:1	63
Psalms of Solomon		62:2	63
17	57	62:13	64
17:1–20	57	62:15–16	64
17:21	57		
17:21–46	57	*Testament of Judah*	
17:23	58	23	65, 112
17:26	58	23–25	65
17:27	58	23:1	65
17:28	58	23:3	65
17:30	58	23:4	65
17:30–31	58	24	66, 68, 70–73, 112, 158, 169
17:32	58		
17:34	59	24:1	66, 70, 158
17:34–36	59	24:1–3	71
17:37	59, 139	24:1–6	129
17:42	59	24:2	66
17:43	59	24:2–3	66, 70, 112
17:44–45	59	24:3	66–67
		24:4	158

24:4–6	67	18:2	68
24:5–6	73	18:3	68
25	66	18:5	68
25:1	67	18:7	68
25:1–2	109, 112	18:8	68
25:3	67	18:9	68–69
25:4	67	18:10–11	69
25:5	67	18:11	69
		18:14	69

Testament of Levi
18	71–73	*2 Esdras*	
		3:21–22	2

Dead Sea Scrolls

1QpHabakkuk		2.15	53
7.2	123	3.8	53
		3.12–13	53
1QS		5.3–4	53
3.13–15	49	5.6–8	53
3.17–19	49	5.9	53
3.22	49	5.9–12	53–54
4	51	5.11–15	54
4.2–3	49–50	5.15–16	54
4.3–4	50	5.17	55
4.3–6	157	5.18	55
4.6–7	50	6.4	55
4.7	158	6.6–7	55
4.18–19	51	6.13–15	55
4.19	51	frag. 1–2v recto	
4.22	51	3–6	111
4.23	51	11–13	111
4.24	51	15-16	111
4.25	51		
		4Q521	
4Q504		frag. 2	
frags. 1–2		2.1–2	55
2.8–10	52	2.4	55
2.11	52	2.5–7	56
2.13	52–53	2.11	56
2.14	53		

Josephus

Jewish Antiquities		4.165	74
1.27	74	6.222	74
4.108	74	6.223	74
4.118	74	8.295	74
4.119	74	9.10	74

9.168	74	10.239	74

Philo

On Giants
19–21   75
23   74
24–29   74
53-56   75

On Planting
18–20   75
23–25   74

Who Is the Heir?
265   74

On the Life of Moses
1.277   74

On the Special Laws
1.9   162
1.171   75
4.49   74
4.123   75

On the Life of Joseph
116–117   74

On the Decalogue
175   74

On the Creation of the World
134–135   75

Allegorical Interpretation
1.33–42   75

Index of Modern Authors

Numbers in italics indicate citations only in the footnotes.

Bachmann, M. *105*
Balzer, K. *19*, 20, *21*
Barclay, J.M.G. *130*, 132–133, 143–145, 147–148, 152–153, 159, *160*, 161, *162*, 172, *173*
Barton, J. *8*, *14*
Beale, G. K. *4*, *50*, *128*, 155–56, *157*, 158
Becker, J. *70*
Beker, J. C. *139*
Betz, H.-D. *82*, 90, *100*, *105*, 115, *123–124*, *129*, *135–137*, *140*, *144*, *147–149*, *159*
Blenkinsopp, J. *15–18*, 19, *20–23*, *25–27*, *29*, *32*, *34*
Block, D. I. *29*, *32–33*, *35*
Brinsmead, B. H. *144*
Bruce, F. F. *81–82*, *89*, *96*, *110*, 115, *122–123*
Charles, R. H. *138*
Charlesworth, J. H. *57*, *65*, *138*
Chazon, E. G. *52*
Chevallier, M.-A. *5*, *57–59*, 61, *62*, *67*, *72*, *112*
Childs, B. S. *16–23*, *25–27*
Ciampa, R. E. *9*
Clements, R. E. *15–18*
Cole, R. A. *147*
Cosgrove, C. H. 2–3, 79, *80–81*, *90*, *98*, *136*
Crenshaw, J. L. *39*
Davenport, G. L. *57–60*
Davila, J. R. *52–54*, *111*
de Jonge, M. *66*, *67*, 70–71, *72*, 73, *112*
Dibelius, M. *132*
Donaldson, T. L. *113–14*
Dumbrell, W. J. *16*, *28*

Dunn, J. D. G. *82*, *87*, 89, *108*, *115–17*, *122–123*, *127*, *135–137*, *139–140*, 145, *149*, 152, 159, 165
Ebeling, G. *81*
Eco, U. *8–9*
Elliott, M. A. *48*
Esler, P. F. *87*, *92*, *95*,
Evans, C. A. *4*, *15*, *47*, *56*, *88*, *98*, *166*
Falk, D. K. *52*
Fee, G. D. 3–4, *79*, *90*, *117*, *160–61*
Fitzmyer, J. A. *108*
García Martínez, F. *49*, *52*, *56*, *157*
Garlington, D. *106*
Gathercole, S. J. *98*
Gombis, T. G. 91–92
Greenberg, M. *29*, *32–33*
Hafemann, S. J. *116–118*, 119, 121, *123*, *126*
Hanson, P. D. *20–21*, *26*
Harnisch, W. *136*
Harrington, D. J. *43–44*
Hays, R. B. *7*, *82*, *85*, *87*, *92*, *93*, *97–98*, 110–111, *113*, *124*, *133*, *135–137*, 139, 141, *142*, *144*, 145, *149*, *153–154*, *159–161*, 169, 172, *173*
Horn, F. W. *47*, *57*
Hurvitz, A. *102*
Janzen, J. G. *99*
Jewett, R. *135*, *147*
Jobes, K. H. *85*
Johnson, M. D. *99*
Joyce, P. *29*, *31–32*, *35*
Kee, H. C. *65–66*, *73*
Keesmaat, S. C. *9*, *116*, 119, *148*
Knibb, M. A. *15*, *46*, *60*
Koch, D. -A. *93*, *103*
Kugler, R. A. *65*, *73*
Kuck, D. W. *134*, *154*

Kuhn, K. G. *48*
Lambrecht, J. *146*
Levenson, J. D. *31, 79,* 107, *109, 170*
Levison, J. R. *5, 73–74*
Lichtenberger, H. *52*
Lightfoot, J. B. *105, 135–136, 139*
Longenecker, B. W. *88–90, 97, 105, 113, 124*
Longenecker, R. N. *81–82, 88, 100, 115, 121, 123, 125, 129, 135–137, 140, 152, 154, 160*
Lull, D. J. 2, 79, *81, 133*
Lust, J. *35*
Lütgert, W. *133, 151*
Luz, U. *87, 129*
Ma, W. *18*
Marcus, J. *56, 95*
Martyn, J. L. *81,* 91, *92, 99,* 100, *105, 109–110, 115, 122,* 123–124, *127,* 130, *134–137,* 141–142, *145, 149,* 161, *165*
Matera, F. J. *81–82,* 100, *105, 115, 117, 121, 123, 135–137, 139–140, 145, 152, 154, 160*
Mearns, C. L. *60*
Meier, J. P. *10*
Menzies, R. P. *5, 48, 57, 60, 62, 74*
Metzger, B. M. *125*
Meyer, P. W. *142*
Milgrom, J. *101, 103*
Milik, J. T. *60*
Miller, P. D. *94*
Murray, R. *17*
Mussner, F. *132, 135–137*
Nelson, R. D. *36, 37*
Nicholson, E. *102*
Nickelsburg, G. W. E. *43, 57, 61, 69*
Noth, M. *93*
O'Neill, J. C. *116,* 132, *140*
Oswalt, J. N. *19–21, 25–26*
Pao, D. W. *14*
Philip, F. *5, 35, 39*
Pitre, B. *107*
Polk, T. *38*
Polzin, R. *102*
Puech, E. *56*
Räisänen, H. *88*
Ridderbos, H. N. *147*
Roberts, J. J. M. *99*

Robertson, O. P. *99*
Robson, J. *32*
Ropes, J. H. *132, 151*
Russell, W. *133, 139,* 140, *143,* 152–153
Sanders, E. P. 10, *88,* 89, *91,* 100
Schlier, H. *80, 82,* 90, *115, 117, 122–123, 135–136, 139, 147, 149, 154*
Scott, J. M. 4, *9, 48,* 71–72, 88, 92–93, *96, 110,* 115–119, 121, 123–124, *129,* 166, 169–70
Seitz, C. R. *15–18*
Sekki, A. E. *49–50, 54*
Smith, B. D. *47,* 53, *54*
Stanley, C. D. *9,* 90
Stendahl, K. *48, 88*
Strobel, A. *97*
Stuart, D. *38*
Thielman, F. 100–101
Tigay, J. H. *36, 94*
Treves, M. *48*
Ulrichsen, J. H. *65, 73*
Um, S. T. *56*
VanderKam, J. *43–45, 61, 138*
Vos, J. S. *1–2, 47, 82, 110*
Wagner, J. R., Jr. *4, 14–15, 85*
Wakefield, A. H. *97, 100, 106*
Waters, G. *89, 92–93, 105*
Watson, F. *8, 97,* 98
Watts, J. D. W. *15*
Watts, R. E. *14, 97,* 99
Werline, R. A. *43, 46, 52–53, 55*
Wernberg-Møller, P. *48*
Westerholm, S. *144*
Westermann, C. *19–21, 25–27*
Widengren, G. *29, 32*
Wilder, W. N. *148,* 149–150
Williams, S. K. *79, 81–82, 90, 99, 115, 122–123, 135*
Willitts, J. 101–102, *104, 106, 171*
Wilson, T. A. *95, 145, 148*
Wintermute, O. *138*
Wolff, H. W. *38–39*
Wright, N. T. *4, 10, 87, 92–93, 97,* 100–101, *108, 114,* 166, 170
Wright, R. B. *57*
Young, N. H. 113, *114*
Zimmerli, W. *32, 127*

Index of Subjects

Abraham 1, 7, 27, 37, 44, 67, 69, 85, 87–88, 105, 107, 109–12, 114, 116–18, 126, 128–29, 131, 143, 154, 163, 168–70
Adoption 41, 42, 72, 116, 118, 123, 125

Baptism 2, 66, 71, 72, 162
Blessing 1, 9, 22–23, 36, 46, 50–51, 54–55, 57, 66–67, 72, 76–77, 85, 87, 95, 97–98, 103, 105–12, 114, 126–27, 129, 131, 158, 162–63, 166, 168–70

Christ 4, 11, 59, 82–83, 85–87, 89–90, 96, 98, 100, 103, 105–06, 108–10, 112–22, 124–27, 129–30, 133, 136–37, 139–41, 145, 154, 159–62, 165–67, 169–71, 173
Circumcision 47, 80, 89, 124, 134, 136–137, 139–41, 143, 152–53, 159, 162–163, 167
Commandments 31, 33, 36, 38, 45, 47, 54, 66, 76, 90, 92, 94, 97–98, 101–02, 104, 172
Covenant 2, 4, 20, 25, 28, 29, 32–33, 36–39, 44, 51, 53, 55, 58, 80, 86, 93, 95–96, 101–03, 105, 108, 119–20, 138, 143, 166
Creation 6, 14, 16–19, 21, 26–28, 33, 39, 43, 47–49, 51–52, 55–56, 62, 64, 68–69, 74–76, 78, 95, 103, 107, 139, 158
–new creation 2, 3, 6, 13–18, 21, 23, 28, 33, 39, 41, 51, 55–57, 60, 62, 64, 68–69, 76, 78–79, 81, 98, 103, 107, 109, 111, 131, 134, 139, 155, 157–58, 163–64, 167, 171
Cross 2, 11, 17, 85, 92, 105, 109, 136, 137, 159, 163, 167, 170
Curse of the Law 3–5, 9, 79–80, 86–90, 105–06, 108–09, 112–14, 125–26, 129, 131, 135, 137, 162, 168–69, 171

Eschatology 2–3, 5, 10–11, 13–14, 42, 57, 65, 68, 70, 74–75, 78, 80, 97, 123, 127, 133, 150, 157, 164–66, 172
–restoration eschatology 3, 5, 10–11, 13, 15, 29, 38–39, 41–42, 68, 70, 74–75, 78, 80, 127, 150, 157, 164–66
Exile 6, 17–18, 27, 29, 31, 34–35, 43, 45–46, 52, 54–55, 75, 78, 80, 86, 91–93, 95, 101–02, 104, 106–09, 138, 166, 170
Exodus 14, 16–17, 20–23, 26–28, 37–39, 78, 82, 93, 101, 103, 117–20, 124, 128, 148–51, 153
–new exodus 3, 6, 13–15, 17, 20, 23, 41, 78, 81–82, 127, 148, 155, 164

Faith 1, 22, 63, 79, 81–82, 85, 89, 91, 96–98, 100, 113–14, 117, 126, 136–37, 139, 141, 148, 151
Flesh 32, 38, 63, 100, 106, 108, 122, 127, 130, 133–34, 140–43, 146–47, 151–54, 159–63, 167–68, 171, 173

Gentiles 2, 4, 7, 26, 36, 38, 40, 58–60, 65, 69, 72, 76, 86, 88, 90, 92, 105, 109–110, 113–14, 117, 119, 121–22, 124–27, 129–31, 148, 162, 165–66, 170, 172
Gospel 2, 4, 83, 85, 89, 91, 100, 110, 130, 140, 148, 165

Heart 4, 6, 14, 25, 27, 29–32, 35–42, 45–51, 54–56, 61, 65–66, 76, 78, 94, 103, 111, 126–29, 131, 138, 164–66
Heir 115–18, 120, 122–23, 125
Hope 2, 6, 11, 18, 22, 41, 48, 52, 56, 59, 61, 63–64, 67, 89, 100, 109, 112, 134, 137, 139, 155, 164, 167–68

Inheritance 1, 7, 24, 58, 85, 95, 115, 118–119, 123, 128, 154–57, 165

Index of Subjects

Israel 2, 4–11, 13, 14–41, 43, 44–48, 50, 52–55, 57–59, 65–69, 72, 75–76, 78–80, 82–84, 86, 88–89, 91–96, 98, 100–114, 116–130, 137–39, 146, 150–51, 153–55, 157–58, 161–62, 164–66, 168–73
—restoration of 1, 3–4, 6–11, 13, 15, 19–20, 23, 26, 28–29, 31, 33–34, 36, 38–42, 45–46, 48, 52, 55, 57–60, 64–69, 72, 74, 78–80, 86, 109, 151, 155–56, 163, 166–69

Jerusalem 7, 26, 28, 39, 58, 83, 85
Jesus 10–11, 56, 66, 71–73, 79, 82–83, 85, 98, 105, 108, 110, 113–14, 123–25, 128, 131, 139, 141, 151, 166, 169
Justification 1, 81, 100

Kingdom of God 2, 4, 16, 28, 123, 133–134, 140, 154, 167

Land (of Israel) 10–11, 17, 22, 24, 29–30, 33–35, 37–38, 40–41, 44–45, 47, 52–53, 58, 65, 72, 78–79, 86, 94–96, 101–04, 107, 111, 119, 120, 131, 149, 154–55, 166, 170
Law 1, 7, 38, 59, 75, 80, 89–90, 93–97, 104–05, 108, 113, 117, 123, 125–26, 148, 158–59, 167, 172
—fulfillment of the 140, 143–45, 160–161
—works of the 78, 81, 88–90, 96–97, 99, 100, 114, 137, 148, 152, 162–63, 172
Life 2–3, 6, 24, 31, 34, 50, 56, 62–64, 67, 69, 79–80, 84, 86–87, 94–100, 105–09, 112, 130, 131, 133–37, 139, 146, 148, 155, 157–63, 166–68, 170–71
—eschatological life 86, 97–98, 106, 112, 131, 160, 162–63, 166, 171
Life in the Spirit *see Spirit*
Love 31, 36–37, 47, 53, 138–41, 143–45, 156, 159, 161, 167

Messiah 15, 55–58, 60–61, 69, 87

Nations 16–17, 19, 26, 29–30, 32–33, 36, 45–46, 53–54, 58–59, 61, 67–69, 72, 83, 85, 87–88, 102–03, 109, 111–12, 131, 158, 170
New Creation *see Creation*
New Exodus *see Exodus*

Peace 16, 18–19, 23–24, 28, 39, 45, 50–51, 63, 66, 68, 83, 86, 94, 138, 155–56, 158, 160, 164–65
Pneumatology 1, 74, 168, 172

Redemption 4, 5, 10, 22, 27, 28, 40, 55, 79–82, 86, 92, 96, 106–07, 109–12, 114, 118–21, 123–29, 151, 164–66, 169–71
Restoration of Israel *see Israel*
Resurrection 10, 33–34, 39, 62–64, 67, 68–69, 76, 78–79, 86, 103, 107, 109, 112, 131, 140, 159, 162, 164–66, 170–171
Righteousness 16, 18, 20, 24–26, 39, 48–49, 51, 57–64, 66–67, 69–70, 72, 76, 84, 88, 91, 96–98, 100, 106, 108, 120, 133–134, 136–39, 152, 155–56, 158, 164, 166–67

Salvation 1, 10, 22, 25, 39, 64, 67, 83, 89, 111, 114, 124, 150, 158, 165, 170
Slavery 65, 103–04, 117, 119–25, 129, 135, 144, 150–51
Sonship 4, 6, 7, 71, 76, 117, 125, 129
Spirit 1–11, 13–20, 22–29, 31–35, 38–43, 47–50, 52–57, 59–82, 85–86, 90, 92, 97–98, 103, 105–14, 121–23, 125–30, 132–43, 146–72
—fruit of the 35, 154, 156, 158–59, 167
—gift of the 1, 6, 7, 24, 56, 64, 68, 70, 79, 112, 114, 126–27, 130, 134
—holy spirit/Spirit 27, 46–47, 54, 59, 111, 139
—human spirit 13, 32, 47–50
—new spirit 29–32, 39, 41, 43, 46–48, 76, 78, 95, 127, 129, 138, 164
—outpouring of the 1, 4–6, 8–9, 11, 13, 15, 18–20, 22, 26, 38–41, 62, 66, 69–72, 74–75, 80, 86, 98, 109, 112–13, 126–27, 129–31, 134, 138–39, 154–56, 158, 160, 163, 166, 169, 172
—spirit of truth 49–51, 157
—life in the 2, 80, 130–31, 133, 146, 159

Torah 3, 4, 14, 20, 36, 94–95, 98, 100–101, 105, 122, 130, 153–54, 158–59, 162, 167

Wissenschaftliche Untersuchungen zum Neuen Testament
Alphabetical Index of the First and Second Series

Ådna, Jostein: Jesu Stellung zum Tempel. 2000. *Vol. II/119.*
Ådna, Jostein (Ed.): The Formation of the Early Church. 2005. *Vol. 183.*
— and *Kvalbein, Hans* (Ed.): The Mission of the Early Church to Jews and Gentiles. 2000. *Vol. 127.*
Aland, Barbara: Was ist Gnosis? 2009. *Vol. 239.*
Alexeev, Anatoly A., Christos Karakolis and *Ulrich Luz* (Ed.): Einheit der Kirche im Neuen Testament. Dritte europäische orthodox-westliche Exegetenkonferenz in Sankt Petersburg, 24.–31. August 2005. 2008. *Vol. 218.*
Alkier, Stefan: Wunder und Wirklichkeit in den Briefen des Apostels Paulus. 2001. *Vol. 134.*
Allen, David M.: Deuteronomy and Exhortation in Hebrews. 2008. *Vol. II/238.*
Anderson, Paul N.: The Christology of the Fourth Gospel. 1996. *Vol. II/78.*
Appold, Mark L.: The Oneness Motif in the Fourth Gospel. 1976. *Vol. II/1.*
Arnold, Clinton E.: The Colossian Syncretism. 1995. *Vol. II/77.*
Ascough, Richard S.: Paul's Macedonian Associations. 2003. *Vol. II/161.*
Asiedu-Peprah, Martin: Johannine Sabbath Conflicts As Juridical Controversy. 2001. *Vol. II/132.*
Attridge, Harold W.: see *Zangenberg, Jürgen.*
Aune, David E.: Apocalypticism, Prophecy and Magic in Early Christianity. 2006. *Vol. 199.*
Avemarie, Friedrich: Die Tauferzählungen der Apostelgeschichte. 2002. *Vol. 139.*
Avemarie, Friedrich and *Hermann Lichtenberger* (Ed.): Auferstehung – Ressurection. 2001. *Vol. 135.*
— Bund und Tora. 1996. *Vol. 92.*
Baarlink, Heinrich: Verkündigtes Heil. 2004. *Vol. 168.*
Bachmann, Michael: Sünder oder Übertreter. 1992. *Vol. 59.*
Bachmann, Michael (Ed.): Lutherische und Neue Paulusperspektive. 2005. *Vol. 182.*
Back, Frances: Verwandlung durch Offenbarung bei Paulus. 2002. *Vol. II/153.*
Backhaus, Knut: Der sprechende Gott. 2009. *Vol. 240.*

Baker, William R.: Personal Speech-Ethics in the Epistle of James. 1995. *Vol. II/68.*
Bakke, Odd Magne: 'Concord and Peace'. 2001. *Vol. II/143.*
Balch, David L.: Roman Domestic Art and Early House Churches. 2008. *Vol. 228.*
Baldwin, Matthew C.: Whose *Acts of Peter*? 2005. *Vol. II/196.*
Balla, Peter: Challenges to New Testament Theology. 1997. *Vol. II/95.*
— The Child-Parent Relationship in the New Testament and its Environment. 2003. *Vol. 155.*
Bammel, Ernst: Judaica. Vol. I 1986. *Vol. 37.*
— Vol. II 1997. *Vol. 91.*
Barrier, Jeremy W. : The Acts of Paul and Thecla. 2009. *Vol. II/270.*
Barton, Stephen C.: see *Stuckenbruck, Loren T.*
Bash, Anthony: Ambassadors for Christ. 1997. *Vol. II/92.*
Bauckham, Richard: The Jewish World around the New Testament. Collected Essays Volume I. 2008. *Vol. 233.*
Bauernfeind, Otto: Kommentar und Studien zur Apostelgeschichte. 1980. *Vol. 22.*
Baum, Armin Daniel: Pseudepigraphie und literarische Fälschung im frühen Christentum. 2001. *Vol. II/138.*
Bayer, Hans Friedrich: Jesus' Predictions of Vindication and Resurrection. 1986. *Vol. II/20.*
Becker, Eve-Marie: Das Markus-Evangelium im Rahmen antiker Historiographie. 2006. *Vol. 194.*
Becker, Eve-Marie and *Peter Pilhofer* (Ed.): Biographie und Persönlichkeit des Paulus. 2005. *Vol. 187.*
Becker, Michael: Wunder und Wundertäter im frührabbinischen Judentum. 2002. *Vol. II/144.*
Becker, Michael and *Markus Öhler* (Ed.): Apokalyptik als Herausforderung neutestamentlicher Theologie. 2006. *Vol. II/214.*
Bell, Richard H.: Deliver Us from Evil. 2007. *Vol. 216.*
— The Irrevocable Call of God. 2005. *Vol. 184.*
— No One Seeks for God. 1998. *Vol. 106.*
— Provoked to Jealousy. 1994. *Vol. II/63.*

Bennema, Cornelis: The Power of Saving Wisdom. 2002. *Vol. II/148.*
Bergman, Jan: see *Kieffer, René*
Bergmeier, Roland: Das Gesetz im Römerbrief und andere Studien zum Neuen Testament. 2000. *Vol. 121.*
Bernett, Monika: Der Kaiserkult in Judäa unter den Herodiern und Römern. 2007. *Vol. 203.*
Betz, Otto: Jesus, der Messias Israels. 1987. *Vol. 42.*
– Jesus, der Herr der Kirche. 1990. *Vol. 52.*
Beyschlag, Karlmann: Simon Magus und die christliche Gnosis. 1974. *Vol. 16.*
Bieringer, Reimund: see *Koester, Craig.*
Bittner, Wolfgang J.: Jesu Zeichen im Johannesevangelium. 1987. *Vol. II/26.*
Bjerkelund, Carl J.: Tauta Egeneto. 1987. *Vol. 40.*
Blackburn, Barry Lee: Theios Aner and the Markan Miracle Traditions. 1991. *Vol. II/40.*
Blanton IV, Thomas R.: Constructing a New Covenant. 2007. *Vol. II/233.*
Bock, Darrell L.: Blasphemy and Exaltation in Judaism and the Final Examination of Jesus. 1998. *Vol. II/106.*
– and *Robert L. Webb* (Ed.): Key Events in the Life of the Historical Jesus. 2009. *Vol. 247.*
Bockmuehl, Markus N.A.: Revelation and Mystery in Ancient Judaism and Pauline Christianity. 1990. *Vol. II/36.*
Bøe, Sverre: Cross-Bearing in Luke. 2010. *Vol. II/278.*
– Gog and Magog. 2001. *Vol. II/135.*
Böhlig, Alexander: Gnosis und Synkretismus. Vol. 1 1989. *Vol. 47* – Vol. 2 1989. *Vol. 48.*
Böhm, Martina: Samarien und die Samaritai bei Lukas. 1999. *Vol. II/111.*
Börstinghaus, Jens: Sturmfahrt und Schiffbruch. 2010. *Vol. II/274.*
Böttrich, Christfried: Weltweisheit – Menschheitsethik – Urkult. 1992. *Vol. II/50.*
– and *Herzer, Jens* (Ed.): Josephus und das Neue Testament. 2007. *Vol. 209.*
Bolyki, János: Jesu Tischgemeinschaften. 1997. *Vol. II/96.*
Bosman, Philip: Conscience in Philo and Paul. 2003. *Vol. II/166.*
Bovon, François: New Testament and Christian Apocrypha. 2009. *Vol. 237.*
– Studies in Early Christianity. 2003. *Vol. 161.*
Brändl, Martin: Der Agon bei Paulus. 2006. *Vol. II/222.*
Braun, Heike: Geschichte des Gottesvolkes und christliche Identität. 2010. *Vol. II/279.*
Breytenbach, Cilliers: see *Frey, Jörg.*

Brocke, Christoph vom: Thessaloniki – Stadt des Kassander und Gemeinde des Paulus. 2001. *Vol. II/125.*
Brunson, Andrew: Psalm 118 in the Gospel of John. 2003. *Vol. II/158.*
Büchli, Jörg: Der Poimandres – ein paganisiertes Evangelium. 1987. *Vol. II/27.*
Bühner, Jan A.: Der Gesandte und sein Weg im 4. Evangelium. 1977. *Vol. II/2.*
Burchard, Christoph: Untersuchungen zu Joseph und Aseneth. 1965. *Vol. 8.*
– Studien zur Theologie, Sprache und Umwelt des Neuen Testaments. Ed. by D. Sänger. 1998. *Vol. 107.*
Burnett, Richard: Karl Barth's Theological Exegesis. 2001. *Vol. II/145.*
Byron, John: Slavery Metaphors in Early Judaism and Pauline Christianity. 2003. *Vol. II/162.*
Byrskog, Samuel: Story as History – History as Story. 2000. *Vol. 123.*
Cancik, Hubert (Ed.): Markus-Philologie. 1984. *Vol. 33.*
Capes, David B.: Old Testament Yaweh Texts in Paul's Christology. 1992. *Vol. II/47.*
Caragounis, Chrys C.: The Development of Greek and the New Testament. 2004. *Vol. 167.*
– The Son of Man. 1986. *Vol. 38.*
– see *Fridrichsen, Anton.*
Carleton Paget, James: The Epistle of Barnabas. 1994. *Vol. II/64.*
– Jews, Christians and Jewish Christians in Antiquity. 2010. *Vol. 251.*
Carson, D.A., O'Brien, Peter T. and *Mark Seifrid* (Ed.): Justification and Variegated Nomism.
Vol. 1: The Complexities of Second Temple Judaism. 2001. *Vol. II/140.*
Vol. 2: The Paradoxes of Paul. 2004. *Vol. II/181.*
Chae, Young Sam: Jesus as the Eschatological Davidic Shepherd. 2006. *Vol. II/216.*
Chapman, David W.: Ancient Jewish and Christian Perceptions of Crucifixion. 2008. *Vol. II/244.*
Chester, Andrew: Messiah and Exaltation. 2007. *Vol. 207.*
Chibici-Revneanu, Nicole: Die Herrlichkeit des Verherrlichten. 2007. *Vol. II/231.*
Ciampa, Roy E.: The Presence and Function of Scripture in Galatians 1 and 2. 1998. *Vol. II/102.*
Classen, Carl Joachim: Rhetorical Criticsm of the New Testament. 2000. *Vol. 128.*
Colpe, Carsten: Griechen – Byzantiner – Semiten – Muslime. 2008. *Vol. 221.*

- Iranier – Aramäer – Hebräer – Hellenen. 2003. *Vol. 154.*
- Coppins, Wayne: The Interpretation of Freedom in the Letters of Paul. 2009. *Vol. II/261.*
- Crump, David: Jesus the Intercessor. 1992. *Vol. II/49.*
- Dahl, Nils Alstrup: Studies in Ephesians. 2000. *Vol. 131.*
- Daise, Michael A.: Feasts in John. 2007. *Vol. II/229.*
- Deines, Roland: Die Gerechtigkeit der Tora im Reich des Messias. 2004. *Vol. 177.*
- Jüdische Steingefäße und pharisäische Frömmigkeit. 1993. *Vol. II/52.*
- Die Pharisäer. 1997. *Vol. 101.*
- Deines, Roland and Karl-Wilhelm Niebuhr (Ed.): Philo und das Neue Testament. 2004. *Vol. 172.*
- Dennis, John A.: Jesus' Death and the Gathering of True Israel. 2006. *Vol. 217.*
- Dettwiler, Andreas and Jean Zumstein (Ed.): Kreuzestheologie im Neuen Testament. 2002. *Vol. 151.*
- Dickson, John P.: Mission-Commitment in Ancient Judaism and in the Pauline Communities. 2003. *Vol. II/159.*
- Dietzfelbinger, Christian: Der Abschied des Kommenden. 1997. *Vol. 95.*
- Dimitrov, Ivan Z., James D.G. Dunn, Ulrich Luz and Karl-Wilhelm Niebuhr (Ed.): Das Alte Testament als christliche Bibel in orthodoxer und westlicher Sicht. 2004. *Vol. 174.*
- Dobbeler, Axel von: Glaube als Teilhabe. 1987. *Vol. II/22.*
- Docherty, Susan E.: The Use of the Old Testament in Hebrews. 2009. *Vol. II/260.*
- Downs, David J.: The Offering of the Gentiles. 2008. *Vol. II/248.*
- Dryden, J. de Waal: Theology and Ethics in 1 Peter. 2006. *Vol. II/209.*
- Dübbers, Michael: Christologie und Existenz im Kolosserbrief. 2005. *Vol. II/191.*
- Dunn, James D.G.: The New Perspective on Paul. 2005. *Vol. 185.*
- Dunn, James D.G. (Ed.): Jews and Christians. 1992. *Vol. 66.*
- Paul and the Mosaic Law. 1996. *Vol. 89.*
- see Dimitrov, Ivan Z.
- –, Hans Klein, Ulrich Luz, and Vasile Mihoc (Ed.): Auslegung der Bibel in orthodoxer und westlicher Perspektive. 2000. *Vol. 130.*
- Ebel, Eva: Die Attraktivität früher christlicher Gemeinden. 2004. *Vol. II/178.*
- Ebertz, Michael N.: Das Charisma des Gekreuzigten. 1987. *Vol. 45.*
- Eckstein, Hans-Joachim: Der Begriff Syneidesis bei Paulus. 1983. *Vol. II/10.*
- Verheißung und Gesetz. 1996. *Vol. 86.*
- Ego, Beate: Im Himmel wie auf Erden. 1989. *Vol. II/34.*
- Ego, Beate, Armin Lange and Peter Pilhofer (Ed.): Gemeinde ohne Tempel – Community without Temple. 1999. *Vol. 118.*
- and Helmut Merkel (Ed.): Religiöses Lernen in der biblischen, frühjüdischen und frühchristlichen Überlieferung. 2005. *Vol. 180.*
- Eisen, Ute E.: see Paulsen, Henning.
- Elledge, C.D.: Life after Death in Early Judaism. 2006. *Vol. II/208.*
- Ellis, E. Earle: Prophecy and Hermeneutic in Early Christianity. 1978. *Vol. 18.*
- The Old Testament in Early Christianity. 1991. *Vol. 54.*
- Elmer, Ian J.: Paul, Jerusalem and the Judaisers. 2009. *Vol. II/258.*
- Endo, Masanobu: Creation and Christology. 2002. *Vol. 149.*
- Ennulat, Andreas: Die 'Minor Agreements'. 1994. *Vol. II/62.*
- Ensor, Peter W.: Jesus and His 'Works'. 1996. *Vol. II/85.*
- Eskola, Timo: Messiah and the Throne. 2001. *Vol. II/142.*
- Theodicy and Predestination in Pauline Soteriology. 1998. *Vol. II/100.*
- Fatehi, Mehrdad: The Spirit's Relation to the Risen Lord in Paul. 2000. *Vol. II/128.*
- Feldmeier, Reinhard: Die Krisis des Gottessohnes. 1987. *Vol. II/21.*
- Die Christen als Fremde. 1992. *Vol. 64.*
- Feldmeier, Reinhard and Ulrich Heckel (Ed.): Die Heiden. 1994. *Vol. 70.*
- Fletcher-Louis, Crispin H.T.: Luke-Acts: Angels, Christology and Soteriology. 1997. *Vol. II/94.*
- Förster, Niclas: Marcus Magus. 1999. *Vol. 114.*
- Forbes, Christopher Brian: Prophecy and Inspired Speech in Early Christianity and its Hellenistic Environment. 1995. *Vol. II/75.*
- Fornberg, Tord: see Fridrichsen, Anton.
- Fossum, Jarl E.: The Name of God and the Angel of the Lord. 1985. *Vol. 36.*
- Foster, Paul: Community, Law and Mission in Matthew's Gospel. *Vol. II/177.*
- Fotopoulos, John: Food Offered to Idols in Roman Corinth. 2003. *Vol. II/151.*
- Frank, Nicole: Der Kolosserbrief im Kontext des paulinischen Erbes. 2009. *Vol. II/271.*
- Frenschkowski, Marco: Offenbarung und Epiphanie. Vol. 1 1995. *Vol. II/79* – Vol. 2 1997. *Vol. II/80.*
- Frey, Jörg: Eugen Drewermann und die biblische Exegese. 1995. *Vol. II/71.*

- Die johanneische Eschatologie. Vol. I. 1997.
  Vol. 96. – Vol. II. 1998. *Vol. 110.* – Vol. III.
  2000. *Vol. 117.*
Frey, Jörg and *Cilliers Breytenbach* (Ed.): Aufgabe und Durchführung einer Theologie des Neuen Testaments. 2007. *Vol. 205.*
- *Jens Herzer, Martina Janßen* and *Clare K. Rothschild* (Ed.): Pseudepigraphie und Verfasserfiktion in frühchristlichen Briefen. 2009. *Vol. 246.*
- *Stefan Krauter* and *Hermann Lichtenberger* (Ed.): Heil und Geschichte. 2009. *Vol. 248.*
- and *Udo Schnelle (Ed.):* Kontexte des Johannesevangeliums. 2004. *Vol. 175.*
- and *Jens Schröter* (Ed.): Deutungen des Todes Jesu im Neuen Testament. 2005. *Vol. 181.*
- –, *Jan G. van der Watt,* and *Ruben Zimmermann* (Ed.): Imagery in the Gospel of John. 2006. *Vol. 200.*
Freyne, Sean: Galilee and Gospel. 2000. *Vol. 125.*
Fridrichsen, Anton: Exegetical Writings. Edited by C.C. Caragounis and T. Fornberg. 1994. *Vol. 76.*
Gadenz, Pablo T.: Called from the Jews and from the Gentiles. 2009. *Vol. II/267.*
Gäbel, Georg: Die Kulttheologie des Hebräerbriefes. 2006. *Vol. II/212.*
Gäckle, Volker: Die Starken und die Schwachen in Korinth und in Rom. 2005. *Vol. 200.*
Garlington, Don B.: 'The Obedience of Faith'. 1991. *Vol. II/38.*
- Faith, Obedience, and Perseverance. 1994. *Vol. 79.*
Garnet, Paul: Salvation and Atonement in the Qumran Scrolls. 1977. *Vol. II/3.*
Gemünden, Petra von (Ed.): see *Weissenrieder, Annette.*
Gese, Michael: Das Vermächtnis des Apostels. 1997. *Vol. II/99.*
Gheorghita, Radu: The Role of the Septuagint in Hebrews. 2003. *Vol. II/160.*
Gordley, Matthew E.: The Colossian Hymn in Context. 2007. *Vol. II/228.*
Gräbe, Petrus J.: The Power of God in Paul's Letters. 2000, ²2008. *Vol. II/123.*
Gräßer, Erich: Der Alte Bund im Neuen. 1985. *Vol. 35.*
- Forschungen zur Apostelgeschichte. 2001. *Vol. 137.*
Grappe, Christian (Ed.): Le Repas de Dieu / Das Mahl Gottes. 2004. *Vol. 169.*
Gray, Timothy C.: The Temple in the Gospel of Mark. 2008. *Vol. II/242.*
Green, Joel B.: The Death of Jesus. 1988. *Vol. II/33.*

Gregg, Brian Han: The Historical Jesus and the Final Judgment Sayings in Q. 2005. *Vol. II/207.*
Gregory, Andrew: The Reception of Luke and Acts in the Period before Irenaeus. 2003. *Vol. II/169.*
Grindheim, Sigurd: The Crux of Election. 2005. *Vol. II/202.*
Gundry, Robert H.: The Old is Better. 2005. *Vol. 178.*
Gundry Volf, Judith M.: Paul and Perseverance. 1990. *Vol. II/37.*
Häußer, Detlef: Christusbekenntnis und Jesusüberlieferung bei Paulus. 2006. *Vol. 210.*
Hafemann, Scott J.: Suffering and the Spirit. 1986. *Vol. II/19.*
- Paul, Moses, and the History of Israel. 1995. *Vol. 81.*
Hahn, Ferdinand: Studien zum Neuen Testament.
  Vol. I: Grundsatzfragen, Jesusforschung, Evangelien. 2006. *Vol. 191.*
  Vol. II: Bekenntnisbildung und Theologie in urchristlicher Zeit. 2006. *Vol. 192.*
Hahn, Johannes (Ed.): Zerstörungen des Jerusalemer Tempels. 2002. *Vol. 147.*
Hamid-Khani, Saeed: Relevation and Concealment of Christ. 2000. *Vol. II/120.*
Hannah, Darrel D.: Michael and Christ. 1999. *Vol. II/109.*
Hardin, Justin K.: Galatians and the Imperial Cult? 2007. *Vol. II/237.*
Harrison; James R.: Paul's Language of Grace in Its Graeco-Roman Context. 2003. *Vol. II/172.*
Hartman, Lars: Text-Centered New Testament Studies. Ed. von D. Hellholm. 1997. *Vol. 102.*
Hartog, Paul: Polycarp and the New Testament. 2001. *Vol. II/134.*
Hays, Christopher M.: Luke's Wealth Ethics. 2010. *Vol. 275.*
Heckel, Theo K.: Der Innere Mensch. 1993. *Vol. II/53.*
- Vom Evangelium des Markus zum viergestaltigen Evangelium. 1999. *Vol. 120.*
Heckel, Ulrich: Kraft in Schwachheit. 1993. *Vol. II/56.*
- Der Segen im Neuen Testament. 2002. *Vol. 150.*
- see *Feldmeier, Reinhard.*
- see *Hengel, Martin.*
Heemstra, Marius: The Fiscus Judaicus and the Parting of the Ways. 2010. *Vol. II/277.*
Heiligenthal, Roman: Werke als Zeichen. 1983. *Vol. II/9.*

Heliso, Desta: Pistis and the Righteous One. 2007. *Vol. II/235.*
Hellholm, D.: see *Hartman, Lars.*
Hemer, Colin J.: The Book of Acts in the Setting of Hellenistic History. 1989. *Vol. 49.*
Hengel, Martin: Jesus und die Evangelien. Kleine Schriften V. 2007. *Vol. 211.*
- Die johanneische Frage. 1993. *Vol. 67.*
- Judaica et Hellenistica. Kleine Schriften I. 1996. *Vol. 90.*
- Judaica, Hellenistica et Christiana. Kleine Schriften II. 1999. *Vol. 109.*
- Judentum und Hellenismus. 1969, [3]1988. *Vol. 10.*
- Paulus und Jakobus. Kleine Schriften III. 2002. *Vol. 141.*
- Studien zur Christologie. Kleine Schriften IV. 2006. *Vol. 201.*
- Studien zum Urchristentum. Kleine Schriften VI. 2008. *Vol. 234.*
- and *Anna Maria Schwemer:* Paulus zwischen Damaskus und Antiochien. 1998. *Vol. 108.*
- Der messianische Anspruch Jesu und die Anfänge der Christologie. 2001. *Vol. 138.*
- Die vier Evangelien und das eine Evangelium von Jesus Christus. 2008. *Vol. 224.*
Hengel, Martin and *Ulrich Heckel* (Ed.): Paulus und das antike Judentum. 1991. *Vol. 58.*
- and *Hermut Löhr* (Ed.): Schriftauslegung im antiken Judentum und im Urchristentum. 1994. *Vol. 73.*
- and *Anna Maria Schwemer* (Ed.): Königsherrschaft Gottes und himmlischer Kult. 1991. *Vol. 55.*
- Die Septuaginta. 1994. *Vol. 72.*
-, *Siegfried Mittmann* and *Anna Maria Schwemer* (Ed.): La Cité de Dieu / Die Stadt Gottes. 2000. *Vol. 129.*
Hentschel, Anni: Diakonia im Neuen Testament. 2007. *Vol. 226.*
Hernández Jr., Juan: Scribal Habits and Theological Influence in the Apocalypse. 2006. *Vol. II/218.*
Herrenbrück, Fritz: Jesus und die Zöllner. 1990. *Vol. II/41.*
Herzer, Jens: Paulus oder Petrus? 1998. *Vol. 103.*
- see *Böttrich, Christfried.*
- see *Frey, Jörg.*
Hill, Charles E.: From the Lost Teaching of Polycarp. 2005. *Vol. 186.*
Hoegen-Rohls, Christina: Der nachösterliche Johannes. 1996. *Vol. II/84.*
Hoffmann, Matthias Reinhard: The Destroyer and the Lamb. 2005. *Vol. II/203.*
Hofius, Otfried: Katapausis. 1970. *Vol. 11.*
- Der Vorhang vor dem Thron Gottes. 1972. *Vol. 14.*
- Der Christushymnus Philipper 2,6–11. 1976, [2]1991. *Vol. 17.*
- Paulusstudien. 1989, [2]1994. *Vol. 51.*
- Neutestamentliche Studien. 2000. *Vol. 132.*
- Paulusstudien II. 2002. *Vol. 143.*
- Exegetische Studien. 2008. *Vol. 223.*
- and *Hans-Christian Kammler:* Johannesstudien. 1996. *Vol. 88.*
Holloway, Paul A.: Coping with Prejudice. 2009. *Vol. 244.*
Holmberg, Bengt (Ed.): Exploring Early Christian Identity. 2008. *Vol. 226.*
- and *Mikael Winninge* (Ed.): Identity Formation in the New Testament. 2008. *Vol. 227.*
Holtz, Traugott: Geschichte und Theologie des Urchristentums. 1991. *Vol. 57.*
Hommel, Hildebrecht: Sebasmata.
Vol. 1 1983. *Vol. 31.*
Vol. 2 1984. *Vol. 32.*
Horbury, William: Herodian Judaism and New Testament Study. 2006. *Vol. 193.*
Horn, Friedrich Wilhelm and *Ruben Zimmermann* (Ed.): Jenseits von Indikativ und Imperativ. Vol. 1. 2009. *Vol. 238.*
Horst, Pieter W. van der: Jews and Christians in Their Graeco-Roman Context. 2006. *Vol. 196.*
Hultgård, Anders and *Stig Norin* (Ed): Le Jour de Dieu / Der Tag Gottes. 2009. *Vol. 245.*
Hvalvik, Reidar: The Struggle for Scripture and Covenant. 1996. *Vol. II/82.*
Jackson, Ryan: New Creation in Paul's Letters. 2010. *Vol. II/272.*
Janßen, Martina: see *Frey, Jörg.*
Jauhiainen, Marko: The Use of Zechariah in Revelation. 2005. *Vol. II/199.*
Jensen, Morten H.: Herod Antipas in Galilee. 2006. *Vol. II/215.*
Johns, Loren L.: The Lamb Christology of the Apocalypse of John. 2003. *Vol. II/167.*
Jossa, Giorgio: Jews or Christians? 2006. *Vol. 202.*
Joubert, Stephan: Paul as Benefactor. 2000. *Vol. II/124.*
Judge, E. A.: The First Christians in the Roman World. 2008. *Vol. 229.*
Jungbauer, Harry: „Ehre Vater und Mutter". 2002. *Vol. II/146.*
Kähler, Christoph: Jesu Gleichnisse als Poesie und Therapie. 1995. *Vol. 78.*
Kamlah, Ehrhard: Die Form der katalogischen Paränese im Neuen Testament. 1964. *Vol. 7.*
Kammler, Hans-Christian: Christologie und Eschatologie. 2000. *Vol. 126.*
- Kreuz und Weisheit. 2003. *Vol. 159.*

- see *Hofius, Otfried.*
Karakolis, Christos: see *Alexeev, Anatoly A.*
Karrer, Martin und *Wolfgang Kraus* (Ed.): Die Septuaginta – Texte, Kontexte, Lebenswelten. 2008. *Vol. 219.*
- see *Kraus, Wolfgang.*
Kelhoffer, James A.: The Diet of John the Baptist. 2005. *Vol. 176.*
- Miracle and Mission. 1999. *Vol. II/112.*
Kelley, Nicole: Knowledge and Religious Authority in the Pseudo-Clementines. 2006. *Vol. II/213.*
Kennedy, Joel: The Recapitulation of Israel. 2008. *Vol. II/257.*
Kieffer, René and *Jan Bergman* (Ed.): La Main de Dieu / Die Hand Gottes. 1997. *Vol. 94.*
Kierspel, Lars: The Jews and the World in the Fourth Gospel. 2006. *Vol. 220.*
Kim, Seyoon: The Origin of Paul's Gospel. 1981, ²1984. *Vol. II/4.*
- Paul and the New Perspective. 2002. *Vol. 140.*
- "The 'Son of Man'" as the Son of God. 1983. *Vol. 30.*
Klauck, Hans-Josef: Religion und Gesellschaft im frühen Christentum. 2003. *Vol. 152.*
Klein, Hans, Vasile Mihoc und *Karl-Wilhelm Niebuhr* (Ed.): Das Gebet im Neuen Testament. Vierte, europäische orthodox-westliche Exegetenkonferenz in Sambata de Sus, 4. – 8. August 2007. 2009. Vol. 249.
- see Dunn, James D.G.
Kleinknecht, Karl Th.: Der leidende Gerechtfertigte. 1984, ²1988. *Vol. II/13.*
Klinghardt, Matthias: Gesetz und Volk Gottes. 1988. *Vol. II/32.*
Kloppenborg, John S.: The Tenants in the Vineyard. 2006, student edition 2010. *Vol. 195.*
Koch, Michael: Drachenkampf und Sonnenfrau. 2004. *Vol. II/184.*
Koch, Stefan: Rechtliche Regelung von Konflikten im frühen Christentum. 2004. *Vol. II/174.*
Köhler, Wolf-Dietrich: Rezeption des Matthäusevangeliums in der Zeit vor Irenäus. 1987. *Vol. II/24.*
Köhn, Andreas: Der Neutestamentler Ernst Lohmeyer. 2004. *Vol. II/180.*
Koester, Craig and *Reimund Bieringer* (Ed.): The Resurrection of Jesus in the Gospel of John. 2008. *Vol. 222.*
Konradt, Matthias: Israel, Kirche und die Völker im Matthäusevangelium. 2007. *Vol. 215.*
Kooten, George H. van: Cosmic Christology in Paul and the Pauline School. 2003. *Vol. II/171.*
- Paul's Anthropology in Context. 2008. *Vol. 232.*
Korn, Manfred: Die Geschichte Jesu in veränderter Zeit. 1993. *Vol. II/51.*
Koskenniemi, Erkki: Apollonios von Tyana in der neutestamentlichen Exegese. 1994. *Vol. II/61.*
- The Old Testament Miracle-Workers in Early Judaism. 2005. *Vol. II/206.*
Kraus, Thomas J.: Sprache, Stil und historischer Ort des zweiten Petrusbriefes. 2001. *Vol. II/136.*
Kraus, Wolfgang: Das Volk Gottes. 1996. *Vol. 85.*
- see *Karrer, Martin.*
- see *Walter, Nikolaus.*
- and *Martin Karrer* (Hrsg.): Die Septuaginta – Texte, Theologien, Einflüsse. 2010. Bd. 252.
- and *Karl-Wilhelm Niebuhr* (Ed.): Frühjudentum und Neues Testament im Horizont Biblischer Theologie. 2003. *Vol. 162.*
Krauter, Stefan: Studien zu Röm 13,1-7. 2009. *Vol. 243.*
- see *Frey, Jörg.*
Kreplin, Matthias: Das Selbstverständnis Jesu. 2001. *Vol. II/141.*
Kuhn, Karl G.: Achtzehngebet und Vaterunser und der Reim. 1950. *Vol. 1.*
Kvalbein, Hans: see *Ådna, Jostein.*
Kwon, Yon-Gyong: Eschatology in Galatians. 2004. *Vol. II/183.*
Laansma, Jon: I Will Give You Rest. 1997. *Vol. II/98.*
Labahn, Michael: Offenbarung in Zeichen und Wort. 2000. *Vol. II/117.*
Lambers-Petry, Doris: see *Tomson, Peter J.*
Lange, Armin: see *Ego, Beate.*
Lampe, Peter: Die stadtrömischen Christen in den ersten beiden Jahrhunderten. 1987, ²1989. *Vol. II/18.*
Landmesser, Christof: Wahrheit als Grundbegriff neutestamentlicher Wissenschaft. 1999. *Vol. 113.*
- Jüngerberufung und Zuwendung zu Gott. 2000. *Vol. 133.*
Lau, Andrew: Manifest in Flesh. 1996. *Vol. II/86.*
Lawrence, Louise: An Ethnography of the Gospel of Matthew. 2003. *Vol. II/165.*
Lee, Aquila H.I.: From Messiah to Preexistent Son. 2005. *Vol. II/192.*
Lee, Pilchan: The New Jerusalem in the Book of Relevation. 2000. *Vol. II/129.*
Lee, Sang M.: The Cosmic Drama of Salvation. 2010. *Vol. II/276.*

Lee, Simon S.: Jesus' Transfiguration and the Believers' Transformation. 2009. *Vol. II/265.*
Lichtenberger, Hermann: Das Ich Adams und das Ich der Menschheit. 2004. *Vol. 164.*
– see *Avemarie, Friedrich.*
– see *Frey, Jörg.*
Lierman, John: The New Testament Moses. 2004. *Vol. II/173.*
– (Ed.): Challenging Perspectives on the Gospel of John. 2006. *Vol. II/219.*
Lieu, Samuel N.C.: Manichaeism in the Later Roman Empire and Medieval China. ²1992. *Vol. 63.*
Lindemann, Andreas: Die Evangelien und die Apostelgeschichte. 2009. *Vol. 241.*
Lindgård, Fredrik: Paul's Line of Thought in 2 Corinthians 4:16–5:10. 2004. *Vol. II/189.*
Loader, William R.G.: Jesus' Attitude Towards the Law. 1997. *Vol. II/97.*
Löhr, Gebhard: Verherrlichung Gottes durch Philosophie. 1997. *Vol. 97.*
Löhr, Hermut: Studien zum frühchristlichen und frühjüdischen Gebet. 2003. *Vol. 160.*
– see *Hengel, Martin.*
Löhr, Winrich Alfried: Basilides und seine Schule. 1995. *Vol. 83.*
Lorenzen, Stefanie: Das paulinische Eikon-Konzept. 2008. *Vol. II/250.*
Luomanen, Petri: Entering the Kingdom of Heaven. 1998. *Vol. II/101.*
Luz, Ulrich: see *Alexeev, Anatoly A.*
– see *Dunn, James D.G.*
Mackay, Ian D.: John's Raltionship with Mark. 2004. *Vol. II/182.*
Mackie, Scott D.: Eschatology and Exhortation in the Epistle to the Hebrews. 2006. *Vol. II/223.*
Magda, Ksenija: Paul's Territoriality and Mission Strategy. 2009. *Vol. II/266.*
Maier, Gerhard: Mensch und freier Wille. 1971. *Vol. 12.*
– Die Johannesoffenbarung und die Kirche. 1981. *Vol. 25.*
Markschies, Christoph: Valentinus Gnosticus? 1992. *Vol. 65.*
Marshall, Jonathan: Jesus, Patrons, and Benefactors. 2009. *Vol. II/259.*
Marshall, Peter: Enmity in Corinth: Social Conventions in Paul's Relations with the Corinthians. 1987. *Vol. II/23.*
Martin, Dale B.: see *Zangenberg, Jürgen.*
Mayer, Annemarie: Sprache der Einheit im Epheserbrief und in der Ökumene. 2002. *Vol. II/150.*
Mayordomo, Moisés: Argumentiert Paulus logisch? 2005. *Vol. 188.*

McDonough, Sean M.: YHWH at Patmos: Rev. 1:4 in its Hellenistic and Early Jewish Setting. 1999. *Vol. II/107.*
McDowell, Markus: Prayers of Jewish Women. 2006. *Vol. II/211.*
McGlynn, Moyna: Divine Judgement and Divine Benevolence in the Book of Wisdom. 2001. *Vol. II/139.*
Meade, David G.: Pseudonymity and Canon. 1986. *Vol. 39.*
Meadors, Edward P.: Jesus the Messianic Herald of Salvation. 1995. *Vol. II/72.*
Meißner, Stefan: Die Heimholung des Ketzers. 1996. *Vol. II/87.*
Mell, Ulrich: Die „anderen" Winzer. 1994. *Vol. 77.*
– see *Sänger, Dieter.*
Mengel, Berthold: Studien zum Philipperbrief. 1982. *Vol. II/8.*
Merkel, Helmut: Die Widersprüche zwischen den Evangelien. 1971. *Vol. 13.*
– see *Ego, Beate.*
Merklein, Helmut: Studien zu Jesus und Paulus. Vol. 1 1987. *Vol. 43.* – Vol. 2 1998. *Vol. 105.*
Merkt, Andreas: see *Nicklas, Tobias*
Metzdorf, Christina: Die Tempelaktion Jesu. 2003. *Vol. II/168.*
Metzler, Karin: Der griechische Begriff des Verzeihens. 1991. *Vol. II/44.*
Metzner, Rainer: Die Rezeption des Matthäusevangeliums im 1. Petrusbrief. 1995. *Vol. II/74.*
– Das Verständnis der Sünde im Johannesevangelium. 2000. *Vol. 122.*
Mihoc, Vasile: see *Dunn, James D.G.*
– see *Klein, Hans.*
Mineshige, Kiyoshi: Besitzverzicht und Almosen bei Lukas. 2003. *Vol. II/163.*
Mittmann, Siegfried: see *Hengel, Martin.*
Mittmann-Richert, Ulrike: Magnifikat und Benediktus. 1996. *Vol. II/90.*
– Der Sühnetod des Gottesknechts. 2008. *Vol. 220.*
Miura, Yuzuru: David in Luke-Acts. 2007. *Vol. II/232.*
Moll, Sebastian: The Arch-Heretic Marcion. 2010. *Vol. 250.*
Morales, Rodrigo J.: The Spirit and the Restorat. 2010. *Vol. 282.*
Mournet, Terence C.: Oral Tradition and Literary Dependency. 2005. *Vol. II/195.*
Mußner, Franz: Jesus von Nazareth im Umfeld Israels und der Urkirche. Ed. von M. Theobald. 1998. *Vol. 111.*
Mutschler, Bernhard: Das Corpus Johanneum bei Irenäus von Lyon. 2005. *Vol. 189.*

Myers, Susan E.: Spirit Epicleses in the Acts of Thomas. 2010. *Vol. 281.*
Nguyen, V. Henry T.: Christian Identity in Corinth. 2008. *Vol. II/243.*
Nicklas, Tobias, Andreas Merkt und *Joseph Verheyden* (Ed.): Gelitten – Gestorben – Auferstanden. 2010. *Vol. II/273.*
Niebuhr, Karl-Wilhelm: Gesetz and Paränese. 1987. *Vol. II/28.*
– Heidenapostel aus Israel. 1992. *Vol. 62.*
– see *Deines, Roland.*
– see *Dimitrov, Ivan Z.*
– see *Klein, Hans.*
– see *Kraus, Wolfgang.*
Nielsen, Anders E.: "Until it is Fullfilled". 2000. *Vol. II/126.*
Nielsen, Jesper Tang: Die kognitive Dimension des Kreuzes. 2009. *Vol. II/263.*
Nissen, Andreas: Gott und der Nächste im antiken Judentum. 1974. *Vol. 15.*
Noack, Christian: Gottesbewußtsein. 2000. *Vol. II/116.*
Noormann, Rolf: Irenäus als Paulusinterpret. 1994. *Vol. II/66.*
Norin, Stig: see *Hultgård, Anders.*
Novakovic, Lidija: Messiah, the Healer of the Sick. 2003. *Vol. II/170.*
Obermann, Andreas: Die christologische Erfüllung der Schrift im Johannesevangelium. 1996. *Vol. II/83.*
Öhler, Markus: Barnabas. 2003. *Vol. 156.*
– see *Becker, Michael.*
Okure, Teresa: The Johannine Approach to Mission. 1988. *Vol. II/31.*
Onuki, Takashi: Heil und Erlösung. 2004. *Vol. 165.*
Oropeza, B. J.: Paul and Apostasy. 2000. *Vol. II/115.*
Ostmeyer, Karl-Heinrich: Kommunikation mit Gott und Christus. 2006. *Vol. 197.*
– Taufe und Typos. 2000. *Vol. II/118.*
Paulsen, Henning: Studien zur Literatur und Geschichte des frühen Christentums. Ed. von Ute E. Eisen. 1997. *Vol. 99.*
Pao, David W.: Acts and the Isaianic New Exodus. 2000. *Vol. II/130.*
Park, Eung Chun: The Mission Discourse in Matthew's Interpretation. 1995. *Vol. II/81.*
Park, Joseph S.: Conceptions of Afterlife in Jewish Insriptions. 2000. *Vol. II/121.*
Pate, C. Marvin: The Reverse of the Curse. 2000. *Vol. II/114.*
Pearce, Sarah J.K.: The Land of the Body. 2007. *Vol. 208.*
Peres, Imre: Griechische Grabinschriften und neutestamentliche Eschatologie. 2003. *Vol. 157.*

Perry, Peter S.: The Rhetoric of Digressions. 2009. *Vol. II/268.*
Philip, Finny: The Origins of Pauline Pneumatology. 2005. *Vol. II/194.*
Philonenko, Marc (Ed.): Le Trône de Dieu. 1993. *Vol. 69.*
Pilhofer, Peter: Presbyteron Kreitton. 1990. *Vol. II/39.*
– Philippi. Vol. 1 1995. *Vol. 87.* – Vol. 2 ²2009. *Vol. 119.*
– Die frühen Christen und ihre Welt. 2002. *Vol. 145.*
– see *Becker, Eve-Marie.*
– see *Ego, Beate.*
Pitre, Brant: Jesus, the Tribulation, and the End of the Exile. 2005. *Vol. II/204.*
Plümacher, Eckhard: Geschichte und Geschichten. 2004. *Vol. 170.*
Pöhlmann, Wolfgang: Der Verlorene Sohn und das Haus. 1993. *Vol. 68.*
Pokorný, Petr and *Josef B. Souček:* Bibelauslegung als Theologie. 1997. *Vol. 100.*
– and *Jan Roskovec* (Ed.): Philosophical Hermeneutics and Biblical Exegesis. 2002. *Vol. 153.*
Popkes, Enno Edzard: Das Menschenbild des Thomasevangeliums. 2007. *Vol. 206.*
– Die Theologie der Liebe Gottes in den johanneischen Schriften. 2005. *Vol. II/197.*
Porter, Stanley E.: The Paul of Acts. 1999. *Vol. 115.*
Prieur, Alexander: Die Verkündigung der Gottesherrschaft. 1996. *Vol. II/89.*
Probst, Hermann: Paulus und der Brief. 1991. *Vol. II/45.*
Räisänen, Heikki: Paul and the Law. 1983, ²1987. *Vol. 29.*
Rehkopf, Friedrich: Die lukanische Sonderquelle. 1959. *Vol. 5.*
Rein, Matthias: Die Heilung des Blindgeborenen (Joh 9). 1995. *Vol. II/73.*
Reinmuth, Eckart: Pseudo-Philo und Lukas. 1994. *Vol. 74.*
Reiser, Marius: Bibelkritik und Auslegung der Heiligen Schrift. 2007. *Vol. 217.*
– Syntax und Stil des Markusevangeliums. 1984. *Vol. II/11.*
Reynolds, Benjamin E.: The Apocalyptic Son of Man in the Gospel of John. 2008. *Vol. II/249.*
Rhodes, James N.: The Epistle of Barnabas and the Deuteronomic Tradition. 2004. *Vol. II/188.*
Richards, E. Randolph: The Secretary in the Letters of Paul. 1991. *Vol. II/42.*
Riesner, Rainer: Jesus als Lehrer. 1981, ³1988. *Vol. II/7.*

- Die Frühzeit des Apostels Paulus. 1994.
  Vol. 71.
- Rissi, *Mathias:* Die Theologie des Hebräerbriefs. 1987. *Vol. 41.*
- Röcker, *Fritz W.:* Belial und Katechon. 2009. *Vol. II/262.*
- Röhser, *Günter:* Metaphorik und Personifikation der Sünde. 1987. *Vol. II/25.*
- Rose, *Christian:* Theologie als Erzählung im Markusevangelium. 2007. *Vol. II/236.*
- Die Wolke der Zeugen. 1994. *Vol. II/60.*
- Roskovec, *Jan:* see *Pokorný, Petr.*
- Rothschild, *Clare K.:* Baptist Traditions and Q. 2005. *Vol. 190.*
- Hebrews as Pseudepigraphon. 2009. *Vol. 235.*
- Luke Acts and the Rhetoric of History. 2004. *Vol. II/175.*
- see *Frey, Jörg.*
- Rüegger, *Hans-Ulrich:* Verstehen, was Markus erzählt. 2002. *Vol. II/155.*
- Rüger, *Hans Peter:* Die Weisheitsschrift aus der Kairoer Geniza. 1991. *Vol. 53.*
- Sänger, *Dieter:* Antikes Judentum und die Mysterien. 1980. *Vol. II/5.*
- Die Verkündigung des Gekreuzigten und Israel. 1994. *Vol. 75.*
- see *Burchard, Christoph*
- and *Ulrich Mell* (Ed.): Paulus und Johannes. 2006. *Vol. 198.*
- Salier, *Willis Hedley:* The Rhetorical Impact of the Semeia in the Gospel of John. 2004. *Vol. II/186.*
- Salzmann, *Jorg Christian:* Lehren und Ermahnen. 1994. *Vol. II/59.*
- Sandnes, *Karl Olav:* Paul – One of the Prophets? 1991. *Vol. II/43.*
- Sato, *Migaku:* Q und Prophetie. 1988. *Vol. II/29.*
- Schäfer, *Ruth:* Paulus bis zum Apostelkonzil. 2004. *Vol. II/179.*
- Schaper, *Joachim:* Eschatology in the Greek Psalter. 1995. *Vol. II/76.*
- Schimanowski, *Gottfried:* Die himmlische Liturgie in der Apokalypse des Johannes. 2002. *Vol. II/154.*
- Weisheit und Messias. 1985. *Vol. II/17.*
- Schlichting, *Günter:* Ein jüdisches Leben Jesu. 1982. *Vol. 24.*
- Schließer, *Benjamin:* Abraham's Faith in Romans 4. 2007. *Vol. II/224.*
- Schnabel, *Eckhard J.:* Law and Wisdom from Ben Sira to Paul. 1985. *Vol. II/16.*
- Schnelle, *Udo:* see *Frey, Jörg.*
- Schröter, *Jens:* Von Jesus zum Neuen Testament. 2007. *Vol. 204.*
- see *Frey, Jörg.*
- Schutter, *William L.:* Hermeneutic and Composition in I Peter. 1989. *Vol. II/30.*
- Schwartz, *Daniel R.:* Studies in the Jewish Background of Christianity. 1992. *Vol. 60.*
- Schwemer, *Anna Maria:* see *Hengel, Martin*
- Scott, *Ian W.:* Implicit Epistemology in the Letters of Paul. 2005. *Vol. II/205.*
- Scott, *James M.:* Adoption as Sons of God. 1992. *Vol. II/48.*
- Paul and the Nations. 1995. *Vol. 84.*
- Shi, *Wenhua:* Paul's Message of the Cross as Body Language. 2008. *Vol. II/254.*
- Shum, *Shiu-Lun:* Paul's Use of Isaiah in Romans. 2002. *Vol. II/156.*
- Siegert, *Folker:* Drei hellenistisch-jüdische Predigten. Teil I 1980. *Vol. 20* – Teil II 1992. *Vol. 61.*
- Nag-Hammadi-Register. 1982. *Vol. 26.*
- Argumentation bei Paulus. 1985. *Vol. 34.*
- Philon von Alexandrien. 1988. *Vol. 46.*
- Simon, *Marcel:* Le christianisme antique et son contexte religieux I/II. 1981. *Vol. 23.*
- Smit, *Peter-Ben:* Fellowship and Food in the Kingdom. 2008. *Vol. II/234.*
- Snodgrass, *Klyne:* The Parable of the Wicked Tenants. 1983. *Vol. 27.*
- Söding, *Thomas:* Das Wort vom Kreuz. 1997. *Vol. 93.*
- see *Thüsing, Wilhelm.*
- Sommer, *Urs:* Die Passionsgeschichte des Markusevangeliums. 1993. *Vol. II/58.*
- Sorensen, *Eric:* Possession and Exorcism in the New Testament and Early Christianity. 2002. *Vol. II/157.*
- Souček, *Josef B.:* see *Pokorný, Petr.*
- Southall, *David J.:* Rediscovering Righteousness in Romans. 2008. *Vol. 240.*
- Spangenberg, *Volker:* Herrlichkeit des Neuen Bundes. 1993. *Vol. II/55.*
- Spanje, *T.E. van:* Inconsistency in Paul? 1999. *Vol. II/110.*
- Speyer, *Wolfgang:* Frühes Christentum im antiken Strahlungsfeld. Vol. I: 1989. *Vol. 50.*
- Vol. II: 1999. *Vol. 116.*
- Vol. III: 2007. *Vol. 213.*
- Spittler, *Janet E.:* Animals in the Apocryphal Acts of the Apostles. 2008. *Vol. II/247.*
- Sprinkle, *Preston:* Law and Life. 2008. *Vol. II/241.*
- Stadelmann, *Helge:* Ben Sira als Schriftgelehrter. 1980. *Vol. II/6.*
- Stein, *Hans Joachim:* Frühchristliche Mahlfeiern. 2008. *Vol. II/255.*
- Stenschke, *Christoph W.:* Luke's Portrait of Gentiles Prior to Their Coming to Faith. *Vol. II/108.*

Sterck-Degueldre, Jean-Pierre: Eine Frau namens Lydia. 2004. *Vol. II/176.*
Stettler, Christian: Der Kolosserhymnus. 2000. *Vol. II/131.*
Stettler, Hanna: Die Christologie der Pastoralbriefe. 1998. *Vol. II/105.*
Stökl Ben Ezra, Daniel: The Impact of Yom Kippur on Early Christianity. 2003. *Vol. 163.*
Strobel, August: Die Stunde der Wahrheit. 1980. *Vol. 21.*
Stroumsa, Guy G.: Barbarian Philosophy. 1999. *Vol. 112.*
Stuckenbruck, Loren T.: Angel Veneration and Christology. 1995. *Vol. II/70.*
–, *Stephen C. Barton* and *Benjamin G. Wold* (Ed.): Memory in the Bible and Antiquity. 2007. *Vol. 212.*
Stuhlmacher, Peter (Ed.): Das Evangelium und die Evangelien. 1983. *Vol 28.*
– Biblische Theologie und Evangelium. 2002. *Vol. 146.*
Sung, Chong-Hyon: Vergebung der Sünden. 1993. *Vol. II/57.*
Svendsen, Stefan N.: Allegory Transformed. 2009. *Vol. II/269.*
Tajra, Harry W.: The Trial of St. Paul. 1989. *Vol. II/35.*
– The Martyrdom of St. Paul. 1994. *Vol. II/67.*
Tellbe, Mikael: Christ-Believers in Ephesus. 2009. *Vol. 242.*
Theißen, Gerd: Studien zur Soziologie des Urchristentums. 1979, ³1989. *Vol. 19.*
Theobald, Michael: Studien zum Römerbrief. 2001. *Vol. 136.*
Theobald, Michael: see *Mußner, Franz.*
Thornton, Claus-Jürgen: Der Zeuge des Zeugen. 1991. *Vol. 56.*
Thüsing, Wilhelm: Studien zur neutestamentlichen Theologie. Ed. von Thomas Söding. 1995. *Vol. 82.*
Thurén, Lauri: Derhethorizing Paul. 2000. *Vol. 124.*
Thyen, Hartwig: Studien zum Corpus Iohanneum. 2007. *Vol. 214.*
Tibbs, Clint: Religious Experience of the Pneuma. 2007. *Vol. II/230.*
Toit, David S. du: Theios Anthropos. 1997. *Vol. II/91.*
Tolmie, D. Francois: Persuading the Galatians. 2005. *Vol. II/190.*
Tomson, Peter J. and *Doris Lambers-Petry* (Ed.): The Image of the Judaeo-Christians in Ancient Jewish and Christian Literature. 2003. *Vol. 158.*
Toney, Carl N.: Paul's Inclusive Ethic. 2008. *Vol. II/252.*

Trebilco, Paul: The Early Christians in Ephesus from Paul to Ignatius. 2004. *Vol. 166.*
Treloar, Geoffrey R.: Lightfoot the Historian. 1998. *Vol. II/103.*
Troftgruben, Troy M.: A Conclusion Unhindered. 2010. *Vol. II/280.*
Tsuji, Manabu: Glaube zwischen Vollkommenheit und Verweltlichung. 1997. *Vol. II/93.*
Twelftree, Graham H.: Jesus the Exorcist. 1993. *Vol. II/54.*
Ulrichs, Karl Friedrich: Christusglaube. 2007. *Vol. II/227.*
Urban, Christina: Das Menschenbild nach dem Johannesevangelium. 2001. *Vol. II/137.*
Vahrenhorst, Martin: Kultische Sprache in den Paulusbriefen. 2008. *Vol. 230.*
Vegge, Ivar: 2 Corinthians – a Letter about Reconciliation. 2008. *Vol. II/239.*
Verheyden, Josef: see *Nicklas, Tobias*
Visotzky, Burton L.: Fathers of the World. 1995. *Vol. 80.*
Vollenweider, Samuel: Horizonte neutestamentlicher Christologie. 2002. *Vol. 144.*
Vos, Johan S.: Die Kunst der Argumentation bei Paulus. 2002. *Vol. 149.*
Waaler, Erik: The *Shema* and The First Commandment in First Corinthians. 2008. *Vol. II/253.*
Wagener, Ulrike: Die Ordnung des „Hauses Gottes". 1994. *Vol. II/65.*
Wahlen, Clinton: Jesus and the Impurity of Spirits in the Synoptic Gospels. 2004. *Vol. II/185.*
Walker, Donald D.: Paul's Offer of Leniency (2 Cor 10:1). 2002. *Vol. II/152.*
Walter, Nikolaus: Praeparatio Evangelica. Ed. von Wolfgang Kraus und Florian Wilk. 1997. *Vol. 98.*
Wander, Bernd: Gottesfürchtige und Sympathisanten. 1998. *Vol. 104.*
Wasserman, Emma: The Death of the Soul in Romans 7. 2008. *Vol. 256.*
Waters, Guy: The End of Deuteronomy in the Epistles of Paul. 2006. *Vol. 221.*
Watt, Jan G. van der: see *Frey, Jörg*
Watts, Rikki: Isaiah's New Exodus and Mark. 1997. *Vol. II/88.*
Webb, Robert L.: see *Bock, Darrell L.*
Wedderburn, A.J.M.: Baptism and Resurrection. 1987. *Vol. 44.*
Wegner, Uwe: Der Hauptmann von Kafarnaum. 1985. *Vol. II/14.*
Weiß, Hans-Friedrich: Frühes Christentum und Gnosis. 2008. *Vol. 225.*
Weissenrieder, Annette: Images of Illness in the Gospel of Luke. 2003. *Vol. II/164.*

–, *Friederike Wendt* and *Petra von Gemünden* (Ed.): Picturing the New Testament. 2005. *Vol. II/193.*
Welck, Christian: Erzählte ‚Zeichen'. 1994. *Vol. II/69.*
Wendt, Friederike (Ed.): see *Weissenrieder, Annette.*
Wiarda, Timothy: Peter in the Gospels. 2000. *Vol. II/127.*
Wifstrand, Albert: Epochs and Styles. 2005. *Vol. 179.*
Wilk, Florian: see *Walter, Nikolaus.*
Williams, Catrin H.: I am He. 2000. *Vol. II/113.*
Wilson, Todd A.: The Curse of the Law and the Crisis in Galatia. 2007. *Vol. II/225.*
Wilson, Walter T.: Love without Pretense. 1991. *Vol. II/46.*
Winn, Adam: The Purpose of Mark's Gospel. 2008. *Vol. II/245.*
Winninge, Mikael: see *Holmberg, Bengt.*
Wischmeyer, Oda: Von Ben Sira zu Paulus. 2004. *Vol. 173.*
Wisdom, Jeffrey: Blessing for the Nations and the Curse of the Law. 2001. *Vol. II/133.*
Witmer, Stephen E.: Divine Instruction in Early Christianity. 2008. *Vol. II/246.*
Wold, Benjamin G.: Women, Men, and Angels. 2005. *Vol. II/2001.*
Wolter, Michael: Theologie und Ethos im frühen Christentum. 2009. *Vol. 236.*

– see *Stuckenbruck, Loren T.*
Wright, Archie T.: The Origin of Evil Spirits. 2005. *Vol. II/198.*
Wucherpfennig, Ansgar: Heracleon Philologus. 2002. *Vol. 142.*
Yates, John W.: The Spirit and Creation in Paul. 2008. *Vol. II/251.*
Yeung, Maureen: Faith in Jesus and Paul. 2002. *Vol. II/147.*
Zangenberg, Jürgen, Harold W. Attridge and *Dale B. Martin* (Ed.): Religion, Ethnicity and Identity in Ancient Galilee. 2007. *Vol. 210.*
Zimmermann, Alfred E.: Die urchristlichen Lehrer. 1984, ²1988. *Vol. II/12.*
Zimmermann, Johannes: Messianische Texte aus Qumran. 1998. *Vol. II/104.*
Zimmermann, Ruben: Christologie der Bilder im Johannesevangelium. 2004. *Vol. 171.*
– Geschlechtermetaphorik und Gottesverhältnis. 2001. *Vol. II/122.*
– (Ed.): Hermeneutik der Gleichnisse Jesu. 2008. *Vol. 231.*
– see *Frey, Jörg.*
– see *Horn, Friedrich Wilhelm.*
Zugmann, Michael: „Hellenisten" in der Apostelgeschichte. 2009. *Vol. II/264.*
Zumstein, Jean: see *Dettwiler, Andreas*
Zwiep, Arie W.: Judas and the Choice of Matthias. 2004. *Vol. II/187.*

For a complete catalogue please write to the publisher
Mohr Siebeck • P.O. Box 2030 • D–72010 Tübingen/Germany
Up-to-date information on the internet at www.mohr.de